CHANGE IN AGRICULTURE

THE NORTHERN UNITED STATES, 1820-1870

CHANGE IN AGRICULTURE:

THE NORTHERN UNITED STATES,

1820-1870 / *CLARENCE H. DANHOF*

HARVARD UNIVERSITY PRESS

CAMBRIDGE, MASSACHUSETTS 1969

TO RUTH

PREFACE

The highly productive agricultural sector of the modern American economy did not emerge inevitably from the nation's physical resources, nor could it have been forecast by projection from the nation's past. The modern system evolved slowly by an intricate process in which men rather than organizations were the key instruments. As men shook off restraints of convention upon the pursuit of personal advantage, they substituted new points of view, relationships, and techniques for the established ones. Not all such changes survived. But those that in their early, crude stages met the tests applied were slowly improved and perfected. Simultaneously they were imitated by others and thus gradually spread. As a result, by 1870 a system of agricultural production had been firmly established that was vastly different from the system prevailing in 1820. During its development the new agricultural system provided the foundation for equally significant changes in non-agricultural occupations. Indeed, continuing change was one of its outstanding characteristics.

Agricultural development not only supported but paralleled the growth of manufacturing industry. In both, change sprang from the same sources. Men who stood at the forefront of agricultural change possessed qualities comparable to those of leaders in other fields. This similarity has been obscured by the fact that during the period 1820-1870 little change was evident in the externals of the basic unit of agriculture—the family-sized farm. It has also been obscured because traditional points of view and obsolete techniques persisted longer in agriculture than in such rapidly expanding pursuits as transportation, commerce, and industry. Agriculture included among its practitioners a large proportion of men who were unable or unwilling to contribute to, or even participate in, its development. Nevertheless, fundamental changes did occur. The farm unit shifted its orientation from the family to the market, and with that change came many others, as in attitudes toward crops and soil, or toward management and techniques.

Made up as they were, and are, of many small units, the agricultural industries have included comparatively few men who are easily identified as shaping the course of development. Nevertheless, leadership did exist and made itself felt, change of a near revolutionary nature did occur, and vigorous enterprise was common. The effect of such enterprise was to stimulate within the agricultural industries a rate of increase in productivity that contributed an essential ingredient to the expansion of the American economy— the release of labor from food production.

This study is not offered as a history of the technology of agriculture, although technology receives much attention. Nor is it a history of institutions, although the growth of institutions, particularly those that tied agriculture to the rest of the economy, was of great importance. It is far too incomplete to be considered a comprehensive history of agriculture. Rather, it attempts to offer some explanation of the process of agricultural development. In so doing, it examines the reaction of farmers in the northern United States to changing circumstances—to improved transportation, widening markets, more productive plants and animals, new implements and techniques, the availability of virgin lands awaiting conversion into farms, and most significant, the challenge of an expanding urban-industrial society.

Change is viewed as a process of reacting and adjusting to unorthodox insights into the factors involved in productive activity. Farmers were numerous; the conditions under which they worked were highly variable; opportunities to increase the effectiveness of their labor were visualized in many different ways; and reactions ran the gamut from preoccupation with the new and novel to total resistance to infringements upon familiar routines. Although this study is primarily concerned with human reactions, there are no heroes, and there is no attempt to describe and analyze personalities. It is not a series of case studies. It deals with agriculture as a large number of small organizations which classified themselves in various ways to comprise a complex industry. It seeks to define the typical problems of the participants and to describe the variety of reactions that these problems prompted. Emphasis is placed upon problems that presented opportunities for change, and upon solutions that were sufficiently successful to stimulate and eventually force imitation.

The period dealt with is a half-century lifted out of a continuum.

The developments did not begin in 1820, nor did they terminate in 1870. Nevertheless, the period was one of accelerated emergence and firm establishment of a new agricultural economy and technology. Moreover, there is no need to cover again the years before 1820, effectively dealt with by Percy W. Bidwell in Parts I and II of the *History of Agriculture in the Northern United States 1620-1860* (Carnegie Institute of Washington, Pub. No. 358, 1925). The terminal date is less easily rationalized. It was selected partly because the succeeding decades were characterized principally by an extension and continuing absorption of the changes launched earlier. A second and perhaps more persuasive consideration was the fact that in the late 1860's the published literature of agriculture lost much of its informal and personal quality. This change in the nature of source materials, together with the availability after 1869 of much-improved statistical data, suggests an analytical approach different from the one followed here.

The study owes its existence to a suggestion by Arthur H. Cole that entrepreneurship in agriculture be explored. A grant from the Committee (now Council) on Research in Economic History made possible a year's leave of absence from teaching duties, which facilitated the collection of much of the material. Two summer research grants aided that work. A special obligation to the Council on Research in Economic History must be acknowledged, both for finding the manuscript worthy of the Edwin F. Gay Prize, awarded by the Economic History Association, and for providing funds toward its publication.

The manuscript has benefited greatly from the critical comments of Arthur H. Cole, Harold F. Williamson, and William N. Parker, who read and commented on earlier versions. Parts of the manuscript have also been read by Leland Jenks and Thomas C. Cochran, for whose comments I am grateful. My debts to my colleagues at Princeton and Tulane Universities, and to numerous workers in the fields of agricultural and entrepreneurial history, are great. I owe a special debt to the work of Percy W. Bidwell and John I. Falconer, as well as to Paul W. Gates—a debt that is not adequately recognized in the documentation because of space limitations. No one other than myself, however, can be charged with responsibility for the material used or the interpretations presented.

Inasmuch as library holdings of agricultural periodicals and reports are widely scattered, numerous libraries were called on to contribute their resources. Of particular importance were the holdings of the library of the U.S. Department of Agriculture, the Library of Congress, the New York Public Library, and the libraries of the University of Michigan, Princeton, Lehigh, and Rutgers. In addition, the libraries of the Universities of Illinois, Indiana, Wisconsin, and Pennsylvania, the Harvard, Yale, and Tulane libraries, the Free Library of Philadelphia, the American Antiquarian Society, and the New-York Historical Society contributed freely of their resources.

Among the numerous persons who assisted by typing parts of the manuscript in its various stages, special thanks must go to Kathleen Rogow, Peg Trannen, Lise Ford, Sue Bachtel, and Pamela Danhof. Of the countless services contributed to the preparation of the manuscript by my wife, Ruth Ingram Danhof, I acknowledge with particular gratitude her patient understanding of the trials and tribulations of authorship.

C.H.D.

Washington, D.C.
November 1968

CONTENTS

Chapter

1 THE CHANGING ENVIRONMENT   I

The Agricultural Economy About 1820   2
The Market and Its Growth   9
The Rural Response and the Spread of Commercial Farming   13

2 THE GROWTH OF MARKETING INSTITUTIONS   27

The Country Merchant   29
Marketing the Major Products   31
Other Products   38
The Problem of Quality   41
Critique of the Marketing System   44

3 SHARING AND EXPANDING THE FUND OF
  KNOWLEDGE   49

Improving the Technology   52
Books and Pamphlets   54
Agricultural Periodicals   55
State and Local Agricultural Organizations   60
The Federal Government   65
The New Approach   69

4 PREREQUISITES FOR FARMING   73

Acquiring Skills   74
Sources of Capital Funds   75
Renting   87
The Application of Capital   94

5 ACQUIRING TITLE TO A FARM   101

Sources of Virgin Land   105
The Established Eastern Farm   107
Farm-Making: The Forested Frontier   114
Farm-Making: The Prairies   121
The Established Western Farm   126

6 MANAGEMENT OF THE FARM ENTERPRISE   130

The General Consent   132
Application of Method   134
Proportioning the Factors of Production   136
Economizing Time   141
Selection of Products   144
Problems of Choice   147

7 THE MATÉRIEL OF FARM PRODUCTION   155

Plant Varieties   155
Livestock   160

8 REACTIONS TO IMPROVED IMPLEMENTS   181

The Wooden Plow   183
The Cast-Iron Plow   186
The Steel Plow   194
Other Tillage Implements   199
Seeding Machines   206

9 FURTHER REACTIONS TO IMPROVED
IMPLEMENTS   218

The Hay Rake   218
The Thresher   221
The Mechanical Harvester   228
Other Implements   249

10 UTILIZATION OF THE SOIL   251

Escape and Repeat   257
Utilization of the Known Technology   257
Rotations   267

11 CONCLUSION   278

SELECTED BIBLIOGRAPHY   293

INDEX   317

TABLES

1 The agricultural economy, 1820–1870   10
2 Mortgage history, Story County, Iowa, 1854–1870   83

CHANGE IN AGRICULTURE

THE NORTHERN UNITED STATES, 1820-1870

CHAPTER ONE

THE CHANGING ENVIRONMENT

The half-century following 1820 saw the establishment in the northern United States of basic changes in the relationship of agriculture to the larger economy. The foundations of a modern, specialized, highly productive economic organization were laid, based upon an agricultural sector of such productivity as to be able to support a rapidly expanding proportion of the population engaged in nonagricultural activities. Between 1820 and 1870 the total population in the northern states increased by about 4.5 times. The composition of that population changed markedly as its principal classes experienced differing rates of growth. The urban population increased by 14.5 times, the rural by about 3.4, and the farm by approximately 2.9.

The significance of this expansion of population in bringing the nation's land resources into use has been much emphasized in American historiography. The extension to more people over a larger area of the social and economic organization and the productive technology that existed in the East in the early nineteenth century offered little prospect of encouraging the changes that did occur.[1] The rapid growth of the urban population in the face of abundant opportunities to enter agriculture was a critical factor in the nation's economic development. That growth was stimulated by changes in the ability of the agricultural society to exchange increasing volumes of its products for those of urban industries. The

[1] David Potter writes: "An infinitive supply of free land would never, by itself, have raised our standard of living very far, for it would never have freed us from the condition in which more than 70 percent of our labor force was required to produce food for our population." *People of Plenty: Economic Abundance and the American Character* (University of Chicago Press, 1954), p. 162. A similar observation is made in William N. Parker and Judith L. V. Klein, "Productivity Growth in Grain Production in the United States, 1840-1860 and 1900-1910," in *Output, Employment, and Productivity in the United States after 1800*, National Bureau of Economic Research, Studies in Income and Wealth, Vol. 30 (Columbia University Press, 1966), p. 546. William N. Parker, "Sources of Agricultural Productivity in the Nineteenth Century," *Journal of Farm Economics*, XLIX (1967), 1,455-1,468, supplies a theoretical analysis.

portion of farm products not consumed within the rural community but offered for sale on urban markets increased from about 20 percent in 1820 to approximately 40 percent in 1870.[2]

Efforts by many farmers to find more satisfactory opportunities to sell modest quantities of their products, which had been frustrated in the 1820's, developed over the next half-century into a vigorous pursuit of methods that might increase productivity and hence the volume of marketable products and money incomes. These changes within agriculture were both stimulated and supported by changes in the rural-urban distribution of the population, in transportation technology, and in the manufacturing industries as sources of the nonagricultural goods and services in demand in the society. Farmers responded to the new forces by becoming more market-oriented and more highly specialized. The change in motivation stimulated changes in the circumstances under which farming was undertaken as well as in the technology that was applied.

THE AGRICULTURAL ECONOMY ABOUT 1820

The economy of the northern United States in the 1820's differed little from that which had existed for many years. Tocqueville, writing in the early 1830's, pointed out, "the inhabitants of the United States experience all the wants and all the desires which result from an advanced stage of civilization; but as they are not surrounded, as in Europe, by a community skillfully organized, to satisfy them, they are often obliged to procure for themselves the various articles which education and habit have rendered necessaries."[3] The validity of this description varied somewhat across the northern states, depending on the age of settlement and the ac-

---

[2] These and related estimates in this chapter are based on data for population distribution and on farm products consumed and sold shown in Table 1. The estimates should be considered not as precise but as reasonable approximations. The estimates exclude sales of farm products to the rural nonfarm population. For 1820, available evidence suggests that the large nonurban, nonfarm population did not contribute to the supply of marketed agricultural products but produced a substantial portion of their own consumption of food and other farm products. Depending upon their degree of self-sufficiency, purchases by the rural nonfarm populations might increase the portion of farm production sold to 25 percent, or possibly slightly more.

By 1870, rural nonfarm efforts to achieve self-sufficiency in agricultural products were significantly weaker. Allowances for farm sales to the rural nonfarm population might well increase total farm sales to 50 and possibly even 55 percent of total farm products consumed or sold.

[3] Alexis de Tocqueville, *Democracy in America* (Knopf, 1945), I, 442.

cessibility of transportation facilities. Improvements were occurring slowly, but the northern economy had not achieved the specialization of economic effort that characterized the more advanced European societies.

The production organization most typical of the northern United States, involving well over three-quarters of the population, was the single-family farm homestead. The farm homestead utilized its resources so as to supply all the food that the family required, any nonagricultural commodities that it desired and could produce, and whatever food or other products or services that might be bartered or sold. The importance attached to these various objectives, together with the need to make full utilization of the available labor, determined the precise mix of the productive efforts.

Although homesteads were frequently isolated geographically, all of them were part of a rural community centering upon a village or small town. The village and town populations supplied the services supporting agriculture, such as grain milling and the fabrication and repair of iron tools, plows, and wagons; mechanical services requiring special tools and skills, such as shoemaking, carpentry, and masonry; and the professional services of teachers and ministers.[4] Many such communities supplied the needs of travelers by means of inns and livery stables. Villages doubling as county seats also maintained small groups of public officials and lawyers. Many of the men engaged in these occupations did so for only a fraction of their time, frequently owning some land and devoting a part of their time to agriculture.

The village was also characterized by the presence of one or a few merchants, who served as intermediaries with the external economy. The self-sufficiency of the farm unit was never absolute, and the self-containment of the village community should not be exaggerated.[5] Even though the essential goods and services that could not be produced within the family unit were relatively few, they constituted a critical part of the desired consumption mix. No farmstead could be entirely independent of external sources of goods. Items like coffee and tea, tobacco, condiments, salt, molasses,

[4] Percy Bidwell, "Rural Economy of New England at the Beginning of the Nineteenth Century," in Connecticut Academy of Arts and Sciences, *Transactions* (New Haven, 1916), XX, esp. 253-275.

[5] Rodney C. Loehr, "Self-Sufficiency on the Farm," *Agricultural History*, XXVI (1952), 37-41.

gunpowder, firearms, knives, axes, and other metal objects were important if not essential components of the level of living that could not be produced within the homestead or obtained from the village craftsmen. These commodities were obtained from the village store, town merchants, or traveling peddlers. Since merchants could buy or accept in barter only what they in turn could economically transport to market, only those farmers advantageously located with regard to markets or transportation could anticipate with reasonable certainty the sale of any large volume of products, particularly those that were heavy, bulky, or perishable.

In the more recently settled and therefore more remote areas, agriculture frequently came to possess a productive capacity that could not be effectively utilized by the standards applied in long-settled regions. The nonfarm populations in areas being settled usually grew at a rate insufficient to absorb the productive capacity of its agriculture. Many homesteads in such locations selected their products—other than those intended for home use—solely for ease of transportation to a distant market. Under these circumstances, the management of resources closely resembled that applied in earlier frontiers and was inferior to practices that had developed in older regions.[6]

The Transportation Revolution. Fundamental to the changing character of the economy was the development of transportation facilities that permitted the movement of goods between farms and urban centers at a cost encouraging specialization in production for distant markets. A review of the evolution of the various types of transportation media is beyond the scope of this study.[7] It is sufficient to point out that before 1820 steamboats were well established as a practical and economical method of navigating the rivers, bays, and lakes of the northern United States and that they were increasing rapidly in number. Steamboats added to the usefulness of natural waterways, but they did not contribute to solving the

[6] J. A. Nash, evaluating the agriculture of the early part of the nineteenth century by the standards of the late 1850's, held that the cause of agriculture's "decline" to a "lamentable condition" was owing largely to lack of markets and the consequent lack of incentives. Nash, "Positions and Prospects of American Agriculture," in New York State Agricultural Society, *Transactions* (1867), pp. 186-190.

[7] An excellent introduction to the subject and the literature is George R. Taylor, *The Transportation Revolution, 1815-60* (Rinehart, 1951), Ch. IV.

transportation problems of interior locations. In areas distant from navigable water, transportation problems were resolved first by canals and later by railroads. Construction of the nation's first major canal—the Erie—began in 1817. Its success set off a boom in canal building, which by 1850 had resulted in some 3,321 miles of canal.[8] Well before that date, however, interest in canals had waned, and the railroad had established itself as the preferred form of transportation. The 73 miles of railroad existing in the northern states in 1830 increased to 3,328 within a decade and to 34,776 by 1870.[9] Many more miles were projected. Although the technology, organization, and management left much to be desired, the roads connected every major northern city with thousands of towns and villages and provided comparatively low-cost, dependable service to a large proportion of the region's farmers.

Shipments of farm goods were the major source of support for river steamboats, and the struggle to build canals and railroads found advocacy and support from farmers everywhere. Mercantile and financial interests, being the more articulate, assumed leadership, but they received vigorous assistance from farmers as individuals and groups or through local governments. To the farmer, an accessible canal or railroad meant an opportunity to sell what had previously been unsalable, or a far higher return on items that could be marketed only at heavy cost; in either case, it meant a substantial increase in his ability to earn income. The significance of the dramatic reduction in the cost of transportation that occurred with the completion of a canal or particularly a railroad was universally recognized, expressed somewhat exuberantly perhaps in the assertion that, "if the farmers had taxed themselves to build all the railroads in this country, and given them away to any companies who would stock and run them, the . . . increased values of their lands would have well repaid all the outlay."[10] The available

8 On canals, see Carter Goodrich, ed., *Canals and American Economic Development* (Columbia University Press, 1961).

9 Data from Edward C. Kirkland, *A History of American Economic Life* (Appleton-Century-Crofts, 1951), p. 345.

10 *American Agriculturist*, XXVII (1868), 208. Ezra C. Seaman observed, "By reason of the increased facilities furnished by railroads, for the transportation of agricultural products and cattle to the Atlantic cities, they were worth from 50 to 200 per cent more in the Western States in 1860, than they were in 1840; and lands were raised in value in a corresponding manner." Seaman, *Essays on the Progress of Nations* (New York, 1868), p. 571. See also *Rural New Yorker*, IV (1853), 242; *Plough, Loom and Anvil*, X (1857), 157; *Iowa Farmer*, I (1853), 141. Albert Fishlow develops

evidence suggests that an immediate and usually large rise in the value of land everywhere accompanied the appearance of lower-cost transportation facilities.

The enthusiasm for railroads did not extend to roads and highways, which continued to present serious problems. There had been some interest in building improved highways before 1820, either as projects of the federal government or as private toll roads. The interest did not wholly disappear, as evidenced by the boom in plank roads in the 1840's. However, privately built roads did not prove financially successful, and the reluctance of federal and state governments to finance road building left responsibility to local governments. Although local governments were frequently enthusiastic supporters of railroads, they were satisfied to leave the maintenance of roads and highways to the local administration of the traditional road tax, which was frequently paid by a few days of work. While the region did not lack for roads, they were in the opinion of an English authority, "inferior to those of any other civilized country."[11]

The Changing Population and Its Distribution. The Census of 1820 reported 5.7 million people living in the northern states. Of these, 4.8 million were in New England and the Middle Atlantic states. The population of the western states numbered 890,000—two-thirds of them in Ohio. The society was predominantly rural (90 percent) and principally occupied in agriculture (75 percent).

The number of rural residents primarily engaged in nonagricultural occupations exceeded the number residing in the cities. One rural group was engaged in the extractive industries, such as lumbering, mining, and fishing. Still others were occupied in trade, the crafts, or professions. Many of these engaged in agriculture to some degree. Some resided in the villages and small towns that dotted the countryside. Some of these communities in time grew to qualify for the Census definition of urban and thus were added to the urban population. That nonagricultural occupations should be extensively followed in rural areas followed in part from the demand for goods and services by farmers. The restrictions imposed by poor transportation facilities applied to those engaged in nonagricultural oc-

the subject briefly in his *American Railroads and the Transformation of the Ante-Bellum Economy* (Harvard University Press, 1965), pp. 198-200.

[11] W. M. Gillespie, *A Manual of the Principles and Practices of Road Making* (New York and Chicago, 1871), p. 3.

cupations the same as to those in agriculture, with the result that craftsmen pursued their occupations in close proximity to the farmers who were the principal purchasers of their products.

The urban population was small, if "urban" is defined as having 2,500 inhabitants or over. In New England and the Mid-Atlantic states, ten percent of the population was reported to be living in towns and cities. Most of them (7.5 percent of the total population) were found in the eight cities of over 8,000. The largest cities were New York with 124,000, Philadelphia with 113,000, Baltimore with 63,000, and Boston with 43,000.

Population growth over the half-century following 1820 was very rapid. The 5.7 million of 1820 for all the states had increased in 1870 to 26.3 million. New England and the Mid-Atlantic states experienced a growth from 4.8 million to 13.2 million. Rapid as was that growth, it was much exceeded by the population increase in the West, where fewer than 900,000 in 1820 had multiplied to 13 million in 1870.

The growth of the northern population was accompanied by dramatic changes in the relationship between urban and rural dwellers. From 1820 to 1870, the rural population increased by 3.4 times, but the urban by 14.5. The rural population, which constituted 90 percent of the total in 1820, decreased to 68 percent in 1870. If visions of a better living sent men from the hinterlands of the eastern states to the farms of the West, such hopes also sent men to the cities and towns of the Atlantic coast[12] and to the urban communities in the West. The farm resident who preferred trade, transportation, or "tinkering" to the tasks of caring for crops and animals found in the city the opportunity to pursue his interests as a principal occupation and frequently as an enterprise with some employees. The employment opportunities so offered attracted others from the farms and from among foreign immigrants. Urban growth exceeded rural after 1800 in Massachusetts, Rhode Island, Connecticut, Penn-

[12] In Massachusetts, Jesse Chickering points out, most of the land "was taken up by 1790," after which date agriculture remained nearly stationary, with most of the population increase migrating to other states. "This state of things . . . existed until about the year 1820, when a *new* field of industry, promising more agreeable means of support, was opened by manufacturers, which have since detained many at home, and attracted others from abroad into this Commonwealth. Similar processes have commenced in most of the other states in New England, and in some of the other States of the Union." Chickering, *A Statistical View of the Population of Massachusetts from 1765 to 1840* (Boston, 1846), p. 73.

sylvania, and Maryland; after 1820 in New Hampshire, Maine, and New Jersey; after 1830 in New York; and after 1840 in Delaware. As early as 1850 the state of New York had attained an urbanization almost as great as that of Great Britain, while Massachusetts, Connecticut, and Rhode Island were even more heavily urbanized.[13]

Nor were the forces stimulating the growth of urbanization confined to the East. In the West, villages and towns were an intrinsic part of frontier settlement.[14] Once a relatively small rural population had been established, urban growth tended to proceed at a rapid rate.[15] Urban growth rates exceeded the rural in Ohio after 1820; in Missouri after 1840; and in Indiana, Illinois, and Michigan after 1850. By 1870 western cities accounted for 21 percent of the region's population. In 1870 a fourth of the North's urban population was to be found in the West. In 1870 Illinois was as highly urbanized as Massachusetts had been in 1820, and Iowa compared similarly with Pennsylvania.

Before 1820, foreign trade was a basic economic function of most of the cities.[16] Small concentrations of craftsmen and fabricating industries beyond the needs of local markets were appearing. As transportation facilities improved, the advantages of specialization

[13] Cities and towns of over 2,500 population accounted for 52 percent of Great Britain's population in 1851. *The Census of Great Britain in 1851* (London, 1854), pp. 90-106.

[14] Morris Birkbeck noted the stages of growth in western Ohio in 1817: "On any spot where a few settlers cluster together . . . some enterprising proprietor finds in his section what he deems a good site for a town, he has it surveyed, and laid out in lots, which he sells, or offers for sale by auction. The new town then assumes the name of its founder:—a store-keeper builds a little framed store, and sends for a few cases of goods; and then a tavern starts up which becomes the residence of a doctor or lawyer, and the boarding house of the store-keeper, as well as the resort of the weary traveler: soon follow a blacksmith and other handicraftsmen in useful succession: a schoolmaster, who is also the minister of religion becomes an important accession to this rising community. Thus the town proceeds, if it proceeds at all, with accumulating force, until it becomes the metropolis of the neighborhood." Birkbeck, *Notes on a Journey in America, from the Coast of Virginia to the Territory of Illinois* (Philadelphia, 1818), pp. 98-99. On the rapidity of development of villages in Iowa, see Mildred Thorne, "Southern Iowa Agriculture, 1833-1890: The Progress from Subsistence to Commercial Corn-Belt Farming," *Agricultural History*, XXIII (1949), 125-127.

[15] On the earlier period, see Richard Wade, *The Urban Frontier: The Rise of Western Cities, 1790-1820* (Harvard University Press, 1959). For later years, see Lewis Atherton, *Main Street on the Middle Border* (Indiana University Press, 1954).

[16] George R. Taylor, "American Urban Growth Preceding the Railway Age," *Journal of Economic History*, XXVII (1967), 309-339; David T. Gilchrist, ed., *The Growth of the Seaport Cities, 1790-1825,* (University Press of Virginia, 1967), esp. Julius Rubin, "Urban Growth and Regional Development," pp. 2-21.

and the increasingly diverse resources of the cities encouraged the growth of manufacturing.[17] Many of the towns and villages that had developed fabricating specialities experienced sufficient growth to classify as cities.[18] The increasing concentration of population in the urban centers was highly significant in providing markets for farm products, in supplying sources of fabricated products for farm needs, and in strengthening farmer interest and motivation. The metal, textile, woodworking, and other industries in the cities and towns supplied their products in variety and at prices that could not be matched by either the jack-of-all-trades farmer or the village craftsman. The money incomes attainable in urban pursuits became increasingly attractive and established standards against which farming incomes and prospects were measured. The educational and recreational facilities available to urban populations were superior to those accessible to most rural families. It was in the cities that changes in desired levels of consumption had their origin, and there also that a way of life emerged which was competitive with the traditional farm homestead and slowly drew agriculture into its orbit.

THE MARKET AND ITS GROWTH

About 1820, the data shown in Table 1 indicate that approximately 80 percent of the food products of northern farms were consumed by the rural population. Of the portion that moved to markets outside the northern rural community, about three-quarters was consumed by the northern urban population, a small quantity was consumed in the South, and the remainder (about 4 percent of

[17] Allen Pred, *The Spatial Dynamics of U. S. Urban-Industrial Growth, 1800-1914* (M.I.T. Press, 1966). Brief discussions of the advantageous external economies offered by urban centers appear in Samuel B. Warner, Jr., "Innovation and Industrialization in Philadelphia," and Higeto Tsuru, "The Economic Significance of Cities," in Oscar Handlin and John Burchard, eds., *The Historian and the City* (M.I.T. and Harvard University Press, 1963), pp. 45, 64.

[18] External economies as well as economies of scale apparently also operated with regard to the villages and small towns. A New York State correspondent observed: "While the country was being settled and cleared up, small villages were wanted, where the post office, two or three stores, as many taverns, blacksmith shops, etc., supplied the wants of the immediate vicinity. As the roads improved, and the canals furnished facilities for reaching distant markets, these villages began to dwindle; many enterprising merchants removed to more important places, and gradually business centered at a few favored points." New York State Agricultural Society, *Transactions* (1859), p. 320.

9

Table 1. The agricultural economy, 1820-1870.

	United States		Northern States[a]	
	1820	1870	1820	1870
1. Population (thousands)				
Total	9,638	39,905	5,732	26,318
Urban	697	9,902	589	8,580
Farm	7,700	22,400	4,081	11,696
Other rural	1,241	7,603	1,062	6,042
2. Gainfully employed workers (thousands)				
Total	2,881	12,925	1,315	8,489
Agriculture	2,069	6,850	997	3,145
Other	812	6,075	318	5,344
3. Labor force (thousands)				
Total	3,135	12,930	1,661	8,663
Agriculture	2,470	6,790	1,284	3,205
Other	665	6,140	377	5,458
4. Number of farms (thousands)	609	2,660	320	1,761
5. Farm gross product, including improvements & home manufacture (millions of dollars)	323	2,631	172	1,683
Value of farm products consumed or sold: Current prices	308	2,553	163	1,613
Constant prices (1910-1914)	555	2,436	294	1,559
6. Value of farm exports (millions of dollars, current prices)				
Raw materials	31	214	—	—
Foods	12	93	—	—

Sources: 1. Population. Total and urban (defined as 2,500 or more): Bureau of the Census, *16th Census of Population* (Washington, D. C., 1942), I, 1-7. Farm population: Martin R. Cooper, Glenn T. Barton, and Albert P. Brodell, *Progress of Farm Mechanization,* Department of Agriculture, Misc. Pub. 630 (Washington, D. C., 1947), pp. 5-7. Farm population, northern states, estimated. Rural nonfarm population is a residual.

2. Gainfully employed workers: *16th Census of Population: Comparative Occupation Statistics of the United States, 1870-1940* (Washington, D. C., 1942), pp. 93, 100, 142. Refinements of the census data, such as that of Solomon Fabricant, are not available for regions and states and in any case are not large for the dates shown. See Solomon Fabricant, "The Changing Industrial Distribution of Gainful Workers: Some Comments on the American Decennial Statistics for 1820-1940," *Studies in Income and Wealth,* vol. 11 (National Bureau of Economic Research: New York, 1949), pp. 3-45.

3. Labor force. Estimates for the United States from Stanley Lebergott, *Manpower and Economic Growth* (McGraw-Hill, 1964), pp. 510-511. Estimates for the northern states based on Lebergott's estimate of the regional distribution of the labor force in Seymour E. Harris, *American Economic History* (McGraw-Hill, 1961), p. 289.

Although the labor force is conceptually clearly superior, the data used in this analysis are of the gainfully employed. The labor force estimates for 1820 and to a large degree for 1870 involve forcing the dual- and multi-occupations characteristic of

the total product) was exported.[19] By 1870 the portion of farm production consumed within the rural community had fallen to about 60 percent. The northern urban populations now absorbed approximately 80 percent of farm products offered for sale, or about 35 percent of total production. The volume of exports had increased substantially but remained at about 4 percent of total production.

Over the half-century the growth of the urban population, supported by foreign immigration, was the central and most dynamic factor in providing northern farmers with opportunities to sell their products. The urban consuming population and the capacity of farmers to place their products on the market grew in such close relationship as to relegate overseas markets to a buffer role. The North possessed no agricultural staples for which there existed a

[19] This estimate is reasonably consistent with the observation of Secretary of the Treasury Albert Gallatin in his 1810 Report on Manufacturers, with regard to the situation a decade earlier: "It is not improbable that the raw material used, and the provisions and other articles consumed by the manufacturers create a home market for agricultural products not very inferior to that which arises from foreign markets." Cited in Stuart Bruchey, *The Roots of American Economic Growth, 1607-1861* (Harper & Row, 1965), p. 87. By 1820 exports were much less significant than in 1810. George R. Taylor points out that the decade 1810-1820 constituted the great "turnabout" in American economic history, marked by a high point in American dependence on foreign trade followed by a decline in the importance of that trade and an increasing concentration on domestic trade. Taylor, "American Urban Growth Preceding the Railway Age," p. 328.

(*Table 1 cont.*) the period into single categories—a procedure that obscures more than it reveals. See Stanley Lebergott, "Labor Force and Employment, 1800-1960," in *Output, Employment and Productivity in the United States after 1800*, National Bureau of Economic Research, Studies in Income and Wealth, vol. 30 (Columbia University Press, 1966), p. 140. References in the text to the rural community are made without attempting to distinguish occupations of the rural, nonagricultural sector.

4. Number of farms. 1870: U. S. Census. 1820: U. S. estimated by Marvin W. Towne and Wayne E. Rasmussen, "Farm Gross Product and Gross Investment During the Nineteenth Century," in *Trends in the American Economy in the Nineteenth Century*, National Bureau of Economic Research, Studies in Income and Wealth, vol. 24 (Princeton, 1960), p. 269. 1820: northern states estimated from 1850 ratio of farms and farm population.

5. Farm gross product. U. S. estimated by Towne and Rasmussen, "Farm Gross Product," pp. 265-269. Northern states estimated from extrapolation of regional income distribution data for 1840, 1860, and 1880 in Richard A. Easterlin, "Regional Income Trends, 1840-1950," in Harris, *American Economic History*, p. 535. Such extrapolation may introduce substantial errors, as may the conversion of current into constant dollars.

6. Value of farm exports. Bureau of the Census, *Historical Statistics of the United States from Colonial Times* (Washington, D. C., 1960), p. 545. Exports of crude and processed foodstuffs for 1866-1870 averaged $70 million. For 1820-1824, $11.4 million. Douglas North, *The Economic Growth of the United States, 1760-1860* (Prentice-Hall, 1961), p. 284.

a. Including Delaware, Maryland, all states north of the Potomac and Ohio rivers, Missouri, and states to its north.

consistent, substantial, expanding, and profitable foreign demand, such as the South enjoyed in cotton and tobacco. All the products of northern farmers that could be offered on foreign markets, ranging from apples to wheat, were also products of European farms. Wheat in the form of grain or flour was the most important export, followed by pork products, such as salt pork and lard. Limited and essentially static markets existed in the West Indies for some of these products. Until the 1860's, European markets took only a limited and erratic interest in them, principally when wars or crop failures temporarily affected normal sources of supply. In the late 1850's British buyers did display a heightened willingness to buy northern foodstuffs, principally wheat and flour.[20] This expansion of the overseas market was to prove permanent and without doubt supported the continuing expansion of western wheat production. European markets, however, cannot be viewed as the source stimulating the basic changes that had occurred.

Over the period of 1820-1870 the growth of urban markets—in the increasingly food-deficient East as well as the cities of the West —provided the stimulus for market farming. The products of the farms of the more northerly sections of such states as Ohio, Indiana, and Illinois from their earliest settlement moved eastward via the Great Lakes; after the opening of the Erie Canal they could travel by water as far as New York City. The question of the significance of the southern markets for foodstuffs produced in the western areas tributary to the Ohio and Mississippi rivers has been long debated. That the trade was substantial by 1820 and grew to large proportions has been emphasized by many historians.[21]

[20] The upsurge in western wheat production in the late 1850's and early 1860's might have resulted in discouragingly low prices. Fortunately, as Paul W. Gates points out, "Poor crops in Great Britain and France saved the day for the American wheat farmer." Gates, *Agriculture and the Civil War* (Knopf, 1965), p. 224.

[21] The view that the South was a food-deficit area and therefore a consumer of western products is held by Louis B. Schmidt, "Internal Commerce and the Development of the National Economy Before 1860," *Journal of Political Economy*, XLVII (1939), 798-822; Douglass C. North, *The Economic Growth of the United States, 1790-1860* (Prentice-Hall, 1961), Ch. IX; John G. Clark, *The Grain Trade of the Old Northwest* (University of Illinois Press, 1966). A contrary view is held by Isaac Lippincott, "Internal Trade of the United States, 1765-1860," *Washington University Studies*, IV, Pt. II, No. 1 (1916), 63-150. Other scholars who conclude that the South was almost if not wholly self-sufficient include Donald L. Kemmerer, "The Pre-Civil War South's Leading Crop, Corn," *Agricultural History*, XXIII (1949), 236-239; Richard Easterlin, book review in *Journal of Economic History*, XXII (1962), 125; Gates, *Agriculture and the Civil War*, p. 9.

The goods transported down the Mississippi might move into overseas exports or into intercoastal trade destined for the Northeast or for southern ports, and hence to consumers in New Orleans and the smaller towns and plantations along the river system. It is clear that the Mississippi served the Midwest primarily as a route to northern and overseas destinations. Albert Fishlow estimates that between 1839 and 1860 southern consumption of western foodstuffs ranged from 12 to 18 percent of the region's total exports.[22] Although the quantities involved were significant, southern consumption of western foodstuffs was hardly critical to the development of western agriculture.

THE RURAL RESPONSE AND THE SPREAD OF COMMERCIAL FARMING

Fertile soil capable of yielding average or better-than-average crops and located so that urban markets were economically accessible was the physical requisite to the spread of market-oriented agriculture. The shift from subsistence to commercial farming first occurred among those farmers possessing the most fertile lands within a few miles of eastern urban centers or near waterways that permitted cheap shipment to such markets. In the 1820's farms so operated were to be found along the Connecticut, Hudson, Delaware, Susquehanna, and Potomac rivers, as well as on many lesser streams. These farms might sell as much as 40 to 50 percent of their products, although 20 to 25 percent was more typical, and many sold a smaller proportion.[23]

Circumstances were unfavorable, however, to the development of market-oriented agriculture. In the East, the productive capacity of lands well located to transportation facilities was near full realization, given the technology in use. To a limited degree, more intensive cultivation was being undertaken as a result of the subdivision of farms in well-located areas, particularly near the major cities. However, large areas were showing serious signs of depleted

22 Albert Fishlow, *American Railroads*, pp. 275-288.

23 James T. Lemon, "Household Consumption in Eighteenth-Century America and Its Relationship to Production and Trade: The Situation Among Farmers in Southeastern Pennsylvania," *Agricultural History*, XLI (1967), pp. 59-70. Scattered and fragmentary evidence suggests that these estimates for the late eighteenth century apply also to the 1820-1840 period.

soil fertility and hence were declining in productivity.[24] Moreover, the principal areas of new farm settlement were increasingly distant from the eastern cities and from water transportation. Population pressure had for some time forced settlement into the hilly and mountainous interiors of New Hampshire, Vermont, New York, Pennsylvania, and Maine, as well as west of the Appalachians. Farmers settling in such areas accepted the immediate necessity of a higher degree of self-sufficiency and independence of market contacts than was the case in the older areas. The hope and expectation of many that the growth of local nonagricultural populations would provide markets were frequently disappointed. The opportunities to sell that had existed during the settlement period of these areas had disappeared. Furthermore, the mountain soils were thin, and many areas experienced declines in productivity after a decade or two of cultivation. The technology applied in farming tended to remain more primitive than that applied in areas closer to markets.

The trans-Appalachian West was to offer much greater opportunities in the long run. In the 1820's, however, settlers in the West also accepted the lower productivity inherent in the nonspecialized character of the activities pursued within the isolated homestead. For some time both before and after 1820, the growth of farm population and the expansion of cultivated acreage did not contribute proportionately to marketable food supplies and added correspondingly little to the demand for urban products and services.

The appearance of better transportation facilities—as in the case of the Erie Canal—stimulated a quick but initially superficial response. The surpluses of the semisubsistence homestead were now more readily sold, and urban products purchased. The second step was to increase specialization, as by shifting resources from home

[24] The economic history of Pawlett town in Vermont is relevant. The settlers were described as motivated by a desire to grow wheat both for home use and for raising money to pay for their land. "Brought up on the brown bread of old Connecticut, they hoped by coming here to indulge in the wheaten loaf. But their high expectations were not fully realized. Most of the newly cleared fields produced wheat in rich luxuriance and some fields held out for a long series of years. But to speak generally, wheat growing was a failure . . . By degrees our people had to fall back on the brown bread of their fathers. The coarser grains yielded abundant harvests. But they were of small account for distant markets. Hence distilleries were introduced to absorb our surplus grain which was about as valuable for feed after the alcohol was extracted as before . . . But in a few years, say from 1810 to 1830, these crops diminished sensibly. A new impetus was given to emigration." Hiel Hollister, *Pawlett for One Hundred Years* (Montpelier, 1867), pp. 54-56.

manufactures to marketable food products. This step was more drastic but still simply accomplished. Realizing the potential of newly enlarged markets to a locality required experimentation to determine profitable products and methods of marketing. Such experimentation was sometimes undertaken by farmers, but frequently it awaited the appearance of men who would exercise the specialized functions of buying and shipping and who, through their offers to purchase, would guide production efforts. Moreover, the effect of new transportation facilities in creating a broad regional market was to bring farmers into competition with each other over widening areas.[25] The farms of New England and the Mid-Atlantic states were most immediately and clearly affected by such competition, but the pressures were eventually felt by all.

It also became clear over time that the orientation of farm operations to the opportunities and constraints of a widening market was not effectively accomplished by the productive techniques that had been utilized for semisubsistence objectives. The re-examination of those techniques and the values upon which they were based presented difficult problems, dealt with only over a prolonged period of time. A few undertook the tasks involved and accepted the uncertainties inherent in experimentation with new methods. Most found it difficult to question customary attitudes and deeply rooted procedures.

The tremendous effort directed to the clearing of land, the establishment of farms, and all the other activities that went into the subjugation of the forests of the northern United States are ample evidence that its farming population was not lacking in the desire for self-improvement, nor wanting in the energy required for its attainment. In the process of building a society on the new land, the settlers carried over from the society as a whole its established concepts of acceptable ambitions, of a desirable standard of living, and of channels through which these might be attained.

The rural sector shared with the larger American society the belief that any man could and should constantly seek to improve his position.[26] Within the semisubsistence society this general atti-

25 For an argument against railroads because they lowered prices for farm products in a local market, see *Prairie Farmer*, IV (1844), 268.

26 The point is made by many contemporary observers. Tocqueville, for example, observes, "Almost all the farmers of the United States combine some trade with

tude had been structured into specific objectives and acceptable courses of action, the whole supported by informal social sanctions, particularly local public opinion. The roles that farmers were expected to play were defined. While economic gain was central, the manner and means by which it was to be achieved differed significantly from the methods that characterized the newly emerging society at large. The result was a prolonged conflict over values and social relationships, between ideologies and practice.

The first obligation of a farmer with a family was to supply, in generous quantity, the necessary food, clothing, and shelter. The standard of living allowed for the purchase of some "store" commodities, such as molasses and cottons, although insofar as possible these were obtained by bartering farm products or services rather than by money transactions. Money expenditures were held to a minimum, partly because opportunities to sell produce for cash were usually limited and thus money was difficult to come by, but also because money was valued most highly as liquid capital and hence as the means to self-improvement. Since self-improvement was defined as accumulating lands, a man was judged by his ability to apply such money as he had acquired to the purchase of land. Correspondingly, a high degree of approval was attached to the skill with which the purchase of consumer goods was avoided. As an acute observer in the 1850's wrote with reference to conditions a generation earlier: "The great effort then was for every farmer to produce anything he required within the circle of his own family; and he was esteemed the best farmer, to use a phrase of the day, 'who did everything within himself.' "[27] Necessity was converted into a virtue, as reflected in the system of social sanctions.

The ultimate economic goal was the ownership of one or more farms of desirable quality. Except for inheritance, title to a farm, or land to be made into a farm, was obtainable only by money purchase. Ownership was attained by the accumulation of liquid funds which, when sufficient, were applied to the purchase of an equity in a farm. As debts so acquired were paid, the more successful and strongly motivated farmers moved on to secure ownership of as many more farms as possible: "no farmer is considered forehanded,

---

agriculture; most of them make agriculture itself a trade," which implies a basic contrast with the peasant agriculture of Europe. *Democracy in America*, II, 166.

[27] New York State Agricultural Society, *Transactions* (1852), p. 29.

or I should say, considers himself so, unless he owns an adjoining farm which generally takes the name of the 'Other Place.' "[28] A father's ability to provide a farm for each of his children represented a high degree of success. Farms differed, of course, and rank based on the desirability of each farm was an inherent part of the value structure. The owner of even a nondescript farm, however, commanded a respect from the rural society that was not accorded to the man who owned none.

These established objectives and attitudes and their corresponding patterns of ambition and action, while appropriate to an earlier time, presented obstacles to the adoption of points of view and methods required by an agriculture in the process of becoming closely integrated with the national market. The test of family need in determining production did not readily give way to the view that a farm was a source of net money income, with all activities subject to scrutiny from the point of view of money income maximization. The latter kind of farming required that full utilization be made of any advantageous factors in determining production plans, and that a rationalized approach to their execution be adopted, including alertness in the appraisal and application of new methods and equipment. The appearance of opportunities did not always and immediately elicit a sensitivity to market considerations or the application of a cost-profit calculus. Acceptance of such determinants of farm operation conflicted with deeply rooted points of view, standards of performance, and routines of activity. The disapproval that had long attached to the purchase of anything that could be produced persisted for some time, operating to restrict the amount of specialization that was acquired. Certainly in the earlier years many felt a sharp conflict between the traditional motives and patterns of self-sufficiency and the new criteria emphasizing costs and prices.

As long as family needs were the immediate and direct objective of production, the small quantities of grain or livestock produced beyond such needs were referred to as "surpluses." This word appears again and again in the literature of the earlier part of the period and lingers on as the market economy slowly established dominance over much of agriculture. It was these surpluses that

[28] *New England Farmer*, VII (1857), 419.

constituted a farmer's salable products. The ratio of surplus to total product measured a man's relationship with the market.

As some farmers accepted the advantages of relying more and more heavily upon markets for some of their needs, and as the goods available on the market increased in variety, farm requirements for exchangeable products increased correspondingly. The surplus—once a secondary objective, considered as merely a security factor, or perhaps only a fortuitous result—achieved an importance equal to the products raised for family use. As the market came to be more widely accepted as the objective, the production of salable commodities became the primary purpose of an increasing number of farm operations. The goal of the farmer became more highly focused on money income, obtainable through the sale of products raised for that purpose. The concept of surplus slowly lost its significance, replaced by considerations of marketability, cost, and profit. Family need as a determinant of the application of productive effort became subject to a cost-price calculus. The homestead gradually surrendered many of the functions that had given it a subsistence character and became increasingly specialized in its activities. The farm became an integrated and dependent unit in the market economy.

At the same time, values changed, and although the farmer's reputation for frugality persisted, few failed to attempt to participate in the rising level of consumption represented by goods of urban origin.[29] Very many, in fact, made strenuous efforts to raise their consumption level. To a small extent, a rise in the standard of living was accomplished within the subsistence framework, as in a shift to wheat bread from rye and corn, or to butter from lard, and in an increase in the consumption of meat, particularly beef, and of vegetables and fruits. The increased use of salt, condiments, molasses, and sugar, however, was supplied by the market. More important were the efforts to obtain a wider variety of nonfood items, objects that the household manufacturer could not supply economically if at all. Over the half-century, a desirable level of

[29] Tocqueville did not exclude farmers when he wrote, "In America the passion for physical well-being is not always exclusive, but it is general; and if all do not feel it in the same manner, yet it is felt by all. The effort to satisfy even the least wants of the body and to provide the little conveniences of life is uppermost in every mind." *Democracy in America*, II, 136.

living came to include an increasing variety and volume of products that were obtainable more economically and sometimes exclusively by money purchase. Of great significance was the displacement of homespun linens and woolens by factory-woven cottons and woolens. Factory-made shoes and hats displaced those of local fabrication. Log cabins and rough plank homes were abandoned for buildings constructed of brick, stone, or mill-sawn lumber, requiring the purchase of millwork, nails, and similar materials as well as the services of skilled craftsmen. Iron stoves and ranges supplemented or displaced the open fireplace. Rough, homemade furniture was supplemented and displaced by the work of urban cabinet makers. Urban industries added rugs and carpets, curtains, household linens, musical instruments, books, newspapers, and magazines, as well as clocks and watches. Wooden trenchers were displaced by a variety of china, earthen, glass, and metal table and kitchenware, as the cast iron kettle was supplemented by tinware.[30] Factory-made candles and oil burning lamps displaced homemade products. The productive equipment of farming came increasingly from specialized urban sources. The rough wagon formerly made by the local wheelwright, with only the axles purchased, became a factory product, as did carriages and horse harnesses, churns and corn shellers.[31]

The farm population, because it represented such a large proportion of the total population and because of its ability to produce goods for sale or exchange, was the largest market for the products of consumer-goods manufacturing industries, such as textiles, and

[30] An account by a Hanover, New Hampshire, farmer in 1859 describes the marked rise in the standard of living despite the problems encountered. Although farming in that state was "severe toil" because the "climate is so cold that it requires the labor of a large part of the year to provide fuel for our fires and fodder for our cattle. . . . Within twenty-five years, the style of living in this state has been greatly improved. Men have better furniture, richer apparel, and take more newspapers. Within my own recollection, it was rare to see a farmer's house painted—if it was colored at all, it was daubed red. Now it is almost as rare to find a thrifty farmer living in an unpainted house, and the color is usually white, set off by Venetian blinds. Thirty years ago, a carpet in a farmer's house, or a piano, was everywhere spoken against as a sign of insufferable pride. Now both the carpet and the piano adorn many a parlor among the hills and valleys of this comparatively sterile country." VIII (1950), 362. For a more general analysis of the changing level of living, see Edgar W. Martin, *The Standard of Living in 1860: American Consumption Levels on the Eve of the Civil War* (University of Chicago Press, 1942).

[31] For an analysis of the forces encouraging change in terms of the attractiveness of the prices of manufactured articles, see Dorothy Brady, "Relative Prices in the Nineteenth Century," *Journal of Economic History*, XXIV (1964), 172-185.

of such industries as iron and steel.[32] Farm demands for quality products placed heavy pressures upon the engineering ingenuity of these industries, even as farmer interest in new products had provided the stimulus of a large prospective market.

Typically, the first major step toward commercial farming was the abandonment of home manufactures and the application of the resources thus released to products that might be sold. Efforts to manufacture for family use were given up before 1820 in the more densely settled parts of New England; soon afterward, in other areas settled before 1820. In the West, home manufactures were never as important as in the East, and such activities were not undertaken on a large scale.[33] In the 1820's and particularly in the following decades, many eastern farmers also took the significant step of abandoning efforts to produce for themselves any food needs that could be purchased more cheaply, such as wheat.[34] Subsistence farming persisted, however, sometimes from preference, though more frequently out of necessity, as in the more remote interior parts of all the eastern states.

West of the Alleghanies, production for market, at least on a small scale, developed quickly after settlement, lagging only slightly behind the expansion of commercial farming in the East. Settlement in Ohio and Indiana was strongly influenced by the accessibility of markets via the Ohio River and its tributaries, and to a lesser degree by the fact that animals could be driven over the mountains to the eastern urban centers. As early as 1821, southeastern Michigan was

[32] On the importance of the agricultural markets for iron and steel products, see Stanley Lebergott, "Labor Force and Employment, 1800-1960," p. 128-129.

[33] Rolla M. Tryon, *Household Manufactures in the United States, 1640-1860* (University of Chicago Press, 1917), Chs. VII-VIII; Arthur H. Cole, *The American Wool Manufacture* (Harvard University Press, 1926), I, 282-284.

[34] "Massachusetts [in the 1850's] does but little towards supplying the wants of her own citizens. The same is true of Connecticut and Rhode Island. The three northern states produce perhaps enough for their own consumption or what is equivalent to it. Yet there are few families who do not depend upon the West or Canada for flour, and all the large towns are indebted to Ohio or Maryland for corn.

"Not only flour, but corn, rye, beef, pork and mutton, butter and cheese, are now brought in quantities from the West. Even in the Connecticut Valley, formerly regarded as the Egypt of New England, where the sons of Jacob from the hill countries might always find grain, corn is now imported for consumption by the farmers themselves. New Hampshire is emphatically a grazing state. Her granite sides furnish but few arable acres. Formerly she did much towards supplying the Boston market with meats and butter and cheese. Now most of her stores are supplied not only with Western flour, but with Ohio pork and New York butter and cheese." *Plough, Loom and Anvil*, VIII (1858), 538.

being recommended as a desirable area for settlement by reason of its water connection with markets.[35] Thereafter, appraisals of market opportunities were standard. Canal and railroad facilities appeared early in the settlement of the West, which, together with the superior productivity of western soil, served to prevent the dominance of subsistence agriculture beyond the earliest farm-making period. The rapidity with which population flowed into the West in itself partially assured this result, since new settlers represented a body of consumers of considerable significance.

The change to commercially oriented farming took place slowly, was not without protest, and suffered from the instability of the market structure. The financial difficulties of 1837-1838, for example, stimulated some reconsideration.[36] Nevertheless, by the 1850's, market-oriented agriculture was firmly established as the dominant type, clearly distinguishable from the semisubsistence approach. About that time, Horatio Seymour, a president of the New York State Agricultural Society, could look back to reminisce about the "old" and rationalize the "new":

At an early period "production for self consumption" was the leading purpose; now no farmer would find it profitable "to do everything within himself." He now sells for money, and it is his interest to buy for money, every article that he cannot produce cheaper than he can buy. He cannot afford to make at home his clothing, the furniture or his farming utensils; he buys many articles for consumption for his table. He produces that which he can raise and sell to the best advantage, and he is in a situation to buy all that he can purchase, cheaper than he can produce. Time and labor have become cash articles, and he neither lends nor barters them. His farm does not merely afford him a subsistence; it produces capital, and therefore demands the expenditure of capital for its improvement.

An extended cash market also enables him to simplify his processes. He can now take advantage of the principle which lies at the foundation of success in commercial and manufacturing pursuits, of "doing one thing; doing it extensively and well." It is true that the necessity for rotation of crops and improvement of his soil sometimes prevents him from carrying this principle out to its fullest extent, but as he approximates to it, he in-

[35] *Plough Boy,* III (1821), 148. It became increasingly common for farmers to favor the development of manufacturing or to urge more rapid industrial growth as the way to expand the home market for agricultural products. See *Genesee Farmer,* II (1832), 379; *New England Farmer,* XIV (1835), 177-178.

[36] The depression of 1837 led some, like Henry Colman, to speculate on the possible necessity of a return to the system of household manufactures. Such views were not uncommon in the 1837-1840 period but then disappeared from the literature. See *New England Farmer,* XVII (1839), 289-90; Sidney L. Jackson, *America's Struggle for Free Schools* (American Council on Public Affairs, 1941).

creases his profit, as it enables him to methodize his business and to acquire a thorough knowledge of everything relating to the article he procures. He who has a large amount of any one thing to sell, can dispose of it with less loss of time to himself and the buyers, with a more perfect understanding of the market than the man who has an equal amount in value but made up of a diversity of articles.[37]

The point of view here expressed represented an acceptance of agriculture as market-focused, profit-motivated, and characterized by a rational approach to technology; that is, of agriculture as business. This attitude, though to be found before 1820, had spread only slowly. As the dominant approach to farming, it was a development of the generation reading Seymour's observations. The activities that followed from this point of view determined the nation's economic development.

It must, nevertheless, be recognized that the concept of agriculture as a market-focused, profit-making business was by no means universally accepted even in 1850. Almost at the same time that Seymour made the remarks quoted above, a correspondent of the Patent Office found himself impelled to defend his motivations by writing: "Some may sneer at the idea of money-making as a part of good farming, but with all due deference, I submit that it is, in our country at least, the main point in farming, mechanics, and the sciences in church and state."[38]

Farming with the purpose of producing whatever was to be consumed with a minimal resort to the market continued to be very common.[39] Many of those who attempted to produce for market did so with significant reservations. A New England farmer, discuss-

[37] Horatio Seymour in New York State Agricultural Society, *Transactions* (1852), pp. 26, 29-30. In the late 1860's the *Prairie Farmer* reminded its readers: "The old rule that a farmer should produce all that he required, and that the surplus represented his gains, is part of the past. Agriculture, like all other business, is better for its subdivisions, each one growing that which is best suited to his soil, skill, climate and market, and with its proceeds purchase his other needs." *Prairie Farmer*, XXI (1868), 17. See also, *Homestead*, III (1857), 156.

[38] William Buckminister, an outstanding spokesman for New England agriculture, argued for self-sufficiency in wheat production: "Though we cannot afford to raise grain to be carried to market, neither can we afford to resort to our seaports to buy it. It may cost us an eighth to purchase and bring it home. By raising our own grain, we avoid both these charges—these two-eighths or one-fourth its value . . . Hence the maxim that farmers should live principally on their own production." *Genesee Farmer*, VIII (1838), 358. See also, *Maine Farmer*, I (1833), 4-5. For arguments advanced in support of the wheat bounties offered by several New England states, see *Genesee Farmer*, VIII (1838), 58; *Farmer and Gardener*, IV (1838), 340-341.

[39] *Plough, Loom and Anvil*, VIII (1858), 438.

ing the problems involved in selecting crops in the light of market conditions, held that: "As a general rule, however, it is better that the farmer should produce what he needs for home consumption . . . He may obtain more money from tobacco, hops or broom corn, than from breadstuffs but taking all things into consideration, will he be better off?"[40]

While there were few men who completely rejected profits as a proper motive, there were many farm owner-operators throughout this half-century who, because of conflicting values or otherwise, were incapable of rationally applying profits as a guide to their activities. This was most clearly apparent in the indifference or hostility that was frequently, almost normally, shown to new ideas and techniques. In 1822 Asher Robbins complained of the farmer "who turns a deaf or incredulous ear to all instruction; who condemns new things because they are new; who dislikes to see them attempted, and likes to see them fail; who derides the innovation, as a project, and the innovator as a projector; who keeps himself aloof, and warns others, from the specious and dangerous novelty."[41] Similar complaints were voiced many times in a variety of ways. In 1852 the "old" type of farmer, of which there were still many, was described as one who "knows how to conduct a farm only by imitation, and looks to the past for his models, without knowing or understanding the results of his own or their operations. To him there is no such thing as progress, and failure or success are words without meaning. Twenty bushels of corn to the acre is quite satisfactory so long as he departs from no established usage, and is not outdone by his neighbors."[42]

What distinguished the new from the old was an interest in and a more or less prompt acceptance of more effective ways of conducting production operations and a readiness to adopt those that promised to increase money income. Profitable participation in the market called for a recurring re-examination of techniques, and replacement of one technique by another as suggestion and experience indicated that advantage might be obtained. It called for an analysis of market opportunities, an ability to carry out a cost-

40 U. S. Patent Office, *Report* (1852), p. 246.

41 *Address to the Rhode Island Society for the Encouragement of Domestic Industry* (1822), pp. 10-11. Cf. Thomas Moore, *The Great Error of American Agriculture Exposed* (1801), pp. 6-7; *Farmer's Monthly Visitor*, (1848), 187-188.

42 *Plough, Loom and Anvil*, IV (1852), 686. Cf. Mitchell, *My Farm of Edgewood* (New York, 1863), pp. 248-249.

value-profit calculus, and a responsiveness to conclusions reached, so that productivity might be enhanced to the profit of the enterprise. These considerations were foreign to subsistence agriculture and were accepted by many only slowly and with difficulty.

These changes also evoked protests of a more fundamental nature. It is abundantly clear that urban life and opportunities held attractions that were felt by many farmers as competitive with, and therefore threatening to, the established pattern of motivations and values.[43] The conflict originated well before 1820, highlighted in the differences between the philosophies and programs of such men as Alexander Hamilton and Thomas Jefferson.[44] As urbanism slowly developed, it provoked a variety of reactions from agriculturists. A substantial portion of the agricultural press and of the speeches made at agricultural fairs was devoted to a defense of agriculture as the most fundamental of occupations, and to a laudation of its values, such as independence, security, and the opportunity of enjoying close communion with nature—all, it was held, lacking in the city.[45] It was further widely argued that, though farming was

[43] A Connecticut farmer in the 1860's expressed what others had been saying for several decades, when he wrote that farmers "are surrounded by those who are most successfully engaged in mechanical and manufacturing pursuits, and who seem to be making fortunes in less time and with less labor than the farmer requires. This draws from the farm a great many of the most enterprising of the young men, who are not content to follow so slow a business. Some of them succeed in making a fortune beyond the expectation of a small farmer, and this makes farming in view of many a second or third-rate business, and it loses its respectable standing, and of course, is less inviting to those who are more ambitious to occupy the best places. And the same cause also affects the price of labor and makes suitable farm laborers very difficult to be obtained. The skillful hands are better paid in the shops and factories and shipyards or they go on the water . . . It is plain that their farming with all the other disadvantages cannot pay such prices for labor." *Cultivator,* XIII (1865), 307.

[44] During this period, the authority of George Washington was cited most frequently in defense of agriculture or when some action favorable to agriculture was sought from state or federal government. The popular ideology, constantly reiterated, held agriculture to be the most fundamental, virtuous, and rewarding of occupations. Jefferson's efforts to relate that ideology to responsible, democratic government articulated the common farm point of view. See Paul H. Johnstone, "In Praise of Husbandry," *Agricultural History,* XI (1937), 80-95, and "Turnips and Romanticism," *Agricultural History,* XII (1938), 224-255; Erwin Graue, "Agriculture versus Urban Enterprise," *Journal of Farm Economics,* XI (1929), 609-622; Gilbert C. Fite, "The Historical Development of Agricultural Fundamentalism in the Nineteenth Century," *Journal of Farm Economics,* 44 (1962), 1,203-1,211. The standard critique is Joseph Davis, "Agricultural Fundamentalism," in O. B. Jesness, ed., *Readings on Agricultural Policy* (Blakiston, 1949), pp. 1-7.

[45] See *Genesee Farmer,* XXIII (1862), 103. Jackson, *America's Struggle for Free Schools,* is useful on the subject.

a slow way, it was also a safe and certain way toward the achievement of economic competence, and that it possessed an immunity to financial crises that was of particularly significant advantage.[46] Such apologia were especially numerous and urgent in the 1850's when farmers, both East and West, became conscious of the fact that many of their most enterprising young sons and daughters were deserting agriculture for urban occupations.[47] Their defense of the long-established ideology was at the same time one part of the social process of establishing the new structure of values, motivations, and methods supporting the emerging society.

A changing society is a complex of individual reactions and interactions within an environment, which may possess the capacity to both facilitate and retard growth. In the following pages the reaction of northern farmers to the changing circumstances within which they operated is described and analyzed. Chapters Two and Three deal with the institutional environment of transportation and communication facilities that linked agriculture with the broader society.

The circumstances that control entry into farming strongly influence the character of the farmer and the farm enterprise, as well as reflecting the nature of the larger economy. Chapter Four describes the resources required by farm enterprises and the methods by which control over such resources could be obtained. Chapter Five deals with the general considerations that were relevant in selecting specific farm locations.

The analysis then turns to the management and operation of

---

[46] *Cultivator*, IV (1847), 205-207; Connecticut State Agricultural Society, *Transactions* (1855), pp. 299-300; *Country Gentleman*, XVIII (1861), 354.

[47] The loss of the most enterprising members of the farm population aroused particular concern. "Business has gone down from the hills and farming villages to the waterfalls, where our New England rivers and brooks leap down over a staircase of stone dams to the far-off sea. And it is exceedingly to be feared that with the business, the enterprise has gone there too. For within the hum of a single cotton mill there is more machinery, more close calculation in saving waste materials, more skill and science applied to practical art and labor, than in a township of farms." Connecticut State Agricultural Society, *Transactions* (1855), pp. 299-300. Another observer stated: "there are multitudes of villages in the older Eastern states which have been almost stripped of their young men by these migrations. Compare for a moment those who go with those who stay. It is self-evident that the dash, the pluck, and ambition of such a village, as a general rule, goes away, while the timid, the weak and unenterprising stay at home." *Rural New Yorker*, XII (1861), 21. See also *New England Farmer*, V (1853), 119; *Cultivator*, XIII (1865), 307.

farm enterprises as they faced changing opportunities and problems over the half-century. Chapter Six summarizes contemporary views of farm management in broad, abstract terms, reflecting the conflicts of interest as well as the primitive level of managerial concepts. The process of change is more specifically dealt with in the next four chapters, covering the selection of plant and animal materials, reactions to new implements and machines, and changing attitudes toward soil use. To develop an appreciation of the nature of the processes of change, these chapters describe in detail the diverse reactions of farmers when alternatives to conventional modes of operation became available.

Generalizations regarding the principal characteristics of the process of change in northern farming are presented in Chapter Eleven. Although these generalizations are based on a unique pattern of events within a unique environment, the process described may perhaps be anticipated whenever large populations face the task of moving from traditional to more rational technologies and forms of economic and social organization.

CHAPTER TWO

THE GROWTH OF MARKETING INSTITUTIONS

 The circumstances under which a farmer could seek a buyer for his produce differed with his distance from the ultimate consumer and with the nature of his product, particularly if further processing were necessary, as was usually the case. Farmers who could make a round trip to a town or city market within a day enjoyed an advantage not only in lower costs of transportation but also in easy contacts with consumers and buyers. Public market places at which farmers could expose their products for sale were maintained in virtually all cities and towns. In the larger cities these markets were numerous, some of them devoted to specific products such as vegetables and fruits, hay, meats, livestock, and cordwood.[1] Farmers might also negotiate the sale of their produce to storekeepers, urban millers, livery stable operators, butchers, or general produce dealers. An overnight trip of perhaps twelve to fifteen miles represented roughly the distance within which frequent contacts with such markets could be maintained. Four or five miles was about the maximum distance for daily deliveries of fluid milk.

Sales directly to consumers were also important on the routes of travel and near the frontier settlements. In most farm-making frontiers the sale of produce to more recent settlers constituted an important source of income to the early comers. The earliest of settlers of Vermont, for example, found an excellent market for their products with those who came somewhat later, and the same relationship prevailed as the farm-making frontier moved West.[2] It was common

---

[1] Fred Jones, *Middlemen in the Domestic Trade of the United States, 1800-1860* (University of Illinois Press, 1937), pp. 59-61. For detailed descriptions of the large city markets, see Thomas F. de Voe, *The Market Book* (New York, 1862), vol. I. On Philadelphia, see Stevenson W. Fletcher, *Pennsylvania Agriculture and Country Life, 1640-1840* (Pennsylvania Historical and Museum Commission, 1950), p. 275. On Boston, see Abram E. Brown, *Faneuil Hall and Faneuil Hall Market* (Boston, 1900). A general, critical survey is "The Market Systems of the Country, Their Usages and Abuses," in U.S. Commissioner of Agriculture, *Report* (1870), pp. 241-254.

[2] Lewis D. Stilwell, *Migration from Vermont* (Montpelier, 1937), p. 103.

for farm produce to move westward from the older and more densely settled frontier areas to the newer areas of settlement. Detroit in 1817, and for some years thereafter, was an importer of agricultural products from the East, some of its flour coming from northern Pennsylvania.[3] Chicago was likewise dependent upon eastern food-stuffs until about 1839, as was Minneapolis until the middle of the 1850's.[4]

The problem of disposing of produce was most difficult for the farmers located in settled areas but distant from a consuming center. Although many farmers held to the belief that direct dealing with the ultimate consumer was the most desirable and remunerative method of disposing of their products, few could act upon that preference. Most, of necessity, saw the market in terms of the nearest merchants. In time these became more specialized and numerous, forming a complex institutional structure. The omnipresent country merchants and millers were supplemented by peddlers willing to barter, drovers, traveling agents purchasing for urban wholesaling and processing firms, and in more densely settled areas, general produce firms.[5] Forwarding firms became important in handling the movement of goods, and commission firms came to play an increasingly important role in disposing of farm produce on central markets. Both dealt primarily with country merchants and country produce dealers, but sometimes were used by farmers. Teamsters, the operators of rafts, canal barges, and steamships, and the forwarding firms associated with them usually limited their activities to moving goods on consignment to firms or buyers in the major markets, but occasionally they purchased produce for their own account.[6] All buyers were transport oriented, locating on the navigable streams, canals, and railroads. Most of the labor of hauling produce from farm to water and rail siding continued to be done by farmers.

[3] *Hazard's Commercial Register,* I (1839), 2; VI (1842), 177; Fletcher, *Pennsylvania Agriculture,* p. 289; James F. W. Johnston, *Notes on North America: Agricultural, Economical, and Social* (Boston, 1852), I, 222.

[4] William V. Pooley, *Settlement of Illinois, 1830-1850* (University of Wisconsin, 1908), p. 289; Charles B. Kuhlman, *The Development of the Flour-Milling Industry in the United States* (Houghton Mifflin, 1929), pp. 104-107.

[5] R. Malcolm Keir, "The Tin Peddler," *Journal of Political Economy,* XXI (1913), 255-258; Jones, *Middlemen,* pp. 61-62.

[6] Louis C. Hunter, *Steamboats on the Western Rivers* (Harvard University Press, 1949), pp. 354-355.

Railroads and canals did not eliminate road-hauls; almost all produce and animals moved some distance over dirt roads. As canals and railroads penetrated the country, the value of products rose within a belt of up to fifty miles or so on each side.[7] Railroads and canals made central markets economically accessible and increased the value of products on the farm, insofar as costs of road haulage were reduced.

THE COUNTRY MERCHANT

For the majority of farmers the country merchant was, before 1820, the principal and sometimes the sole contact with markets. In New England before 1820 there were one or two country merchants in every town, and much the same was true throughout the older settled areas.[8] Merchants appeared in the West as members of the earliest wave of settlement.[9] The 1840 census reported 58,000 retail dry goods, grocery, and other stores in the United States, representing an average of one store for each three hundred of the population.[10] While the merchants were somewhat concentrated in the cities, they served the settled rural areas as well.

The merchant played many roles. In addition to his retail store, he frequently owned the local grist mill, the sawmill, perhaps the inn, and a livery stable. In sparsely populated areas the merchant might also function as a banker, since the transfer of funds, which was a major problem, was most readily solved by the contact of the rural or village merchant with urban business firms.[11] Merchants of limited financial resources were primarily interested in the retail sale of the needs of farm families for such merchandise as cloth, metal objects, tea, coffee, and molasses. Such sales were typically made by barter, and the merchant assumed the task of assembling

[7] *American Agriculturist,* XXVII (1868), 208; *Plough, Loom and Anvil,* X (1857), 157; *Iowa Farmer,* I (1853), 141.

[8] Percy W. Bidwell, *Rural Economy in New England at the Beginning of the Nineteenth Century,* in Connecticut Academy of Arts and Sciences, *Transactions,* XX (New Haven, 1916), 258.

[9] Henry Bradshaw Fearon, *Sketches of America: A Narrative of a Journey of 5,000 Miles Through the Eastern and Western States* (London, 1818), p. 199. See also Rebecca Burland, *A True Picture of Emigration* (Lakeside Press, 1936); George E. Parker, *Iowa Pioneer Foundations* (University of Iowa Press, 1940), pp. 328-336.

[10] Jones, *Middlemen,* p. 56.

[11] Lewis E. Atherton, *The Pioneer Merchant in Mid-America* (University of Missouri Studies, 1939), XIV, 11.

many small lots of produce and forwarding them to consuming points.[12] Although small amounts might be disposed of locally, most could be sold only by shipping to a central market, where they were consigned to a commission merchant or to the merchant's wholesale supplier. The merchant enjoyed the advantage of possessing contacts with transportation and forwarding agents, whose services he utilized in securing his stock of merchandise and in shipping out produce, as well as with the wholesalers and commission firms on the central markets, to whom he could forward his produce with confidence in securing fair and honest treatment.[13]

As the volume of produce intended for sale in any given locality increased beyond that needed to cover purchases at the store, the role of the country merchant as purchaser and forwarder of farm products declined. Many merchants limited their acceptance of produce to amounts covering purchases of store goods; there was a widespread reluctance or inability on their part to involve their limited capital in large quantities of produce of uncertain value. The major staples, including the cereals, as well as animals were therefore not disposable through country merchants. To some degree, particularly in the earlier part of the period, farmers turned their products over to a dealer or drover for payment at the market price upon his return from the central market. More appealing to the farmers were local buyers who offered cash. Before 1820 in those parts of the East enjoying good transportation facilities, and by the 1830's in many areas in the West, the principal purchasers of farm products offered for sale, even in the small towns, were produce buyers and forwarders, sometimes handling all types of products, sometimes specializing, as in wheat or cattle or hogs.[14] The country merchant continued his role as purchaser of butter, eggs, cheese, and a wide variety of minor products but increasingly shared this function with specialized buyers. By the 1850's, the

---

[12] Jones, *Middlemen*, pp. 45-46; *Hunt's Merchant Magazine*, XXXII (1855), 776. For general descriptions of the country merchant, see Gerald Carson, *The Old Country Store* (Oxford, 1954); R. E. Gould, *Yankee Storekeeper* (Whittlesey, 1946). See also J. M. D. Burrows, *Fifty Years in Iowa* (Davenport, 1888); R. P. Beaver, "Joseph Hough, an Early Miami Merchant," *Ohio Historical Quarterly*, XLV (1936), 27-45.

[13] Atherton, *Pioneer Merchant*, pp. 90-102.

[14] For example, the following advertisement of a firm in Jackson, Michigan, appeared in 1844: "Farmers Look at This! Farmers are requested to call at Hayden & Co's Produce Ware-House . . . where they can sell at the highest price in cash any quantity of wheat, grass seed, flax seed, cranberries, hides and skins, pork, lard, etc." *Michigan Farmer*, II (1845), 175.

country merchant dealt with the same produce merchants in the cities with whom other local produce dealers traded, and with whom the farmer might also have direct contacts.

MARKETING THE MAJOR PRODUCTS

Wheat. Grist mills existed everywhere in settled areas. Milling was among the first of the specialized occupations to appear on the frontier. The miller's absence meant for the farm family a diet centered about home-pounded cornbread; his presence made possible white wheat bread and also furnished a market for flour. Small mills were scattered throughout the country, wherever there was water power; lacking water, horsepower as well as windmills were used in some areas.[15] These mills were established for the purpose of doing custom work for the farmer, grinding whatever might be offered, with the miller securing an income by selling the flour ground from the grain he had collected as his customary fee.

Before the 1820's in the East, and later elsewhere, three types of mill operations developed, as the density of population and the importance of wheat growing permitted. Earliest to appear and most numerous was the small country mill that engaged primarily in custom work, though it might also buy wheat on a small scale when opportunities to sell flour were attractive. In areas where wheat production achieved particular importance and which possessed adequate transportation facilities, a second type appeared: the country merchant mill, generally larger than the custom mill, which might do some custom grinding but was more concerned with purchasing grain and marketing the flour. The Cincinnati trade in flour originated in such mills. The third type was the city merchant mill, which developed in the larger centers that enjoyed water power resources. Such mills purchased wheat through traveling agents or in the central market.

In the earlier years, and as long as transportation was difficult, wheat was carried by the farmer to the miller in bags and then went on to market as barrelled flour. The growth of canal and railroad transportation facilities and the development of methods by which

[15] A probably incomplete survey counted 199 flour and grist mills in thirty counties in Iowa in 1859. Iowa State Agricultural Society, *Transactions* (1859) pp. 170 ff. The New York State Census of 1855 reported 1,419 such mills in the state's sixty counties.

grain might be handled in loose bulk rather than bagged, made wheat transportation much cheaper and less risky than flour. The corresponding development of city mills and of an export market for wheat meant that a large-scale market existed for the grain as well as for the ground product. Most of the ports of the Great Lakes —Chicago, Detroit, Toledo, Milwaukee, Cleveland—exported wheat in much larger quantities than flour.

By the 1840's the handling and warehousing of grain had become a specialized business. The country merchant mill was generally dependent upon the wheat supplies of the restricted area within which it might be the principal purchaser. Dealers specializing in wheat were operating in Rochester, Oswego, and St. Louis in the 1830's and in Chicago before 1840,[16] as well as elsewhere. Sometimes these dealers were exclusively concerned with grain, though in smaller centers they were more likely to be dealers in general agricultural products. In the larger centers, the problems of storage encouraged the development of grain warehousing firms, which functioned not only as storage operators but as buyers and sellers as well. In Chicago, warehouse receipts for stored grain became a medium of purchase and sale of wheat, facilitating the financing and handling of the increasing quantities.[17]

While these institutional developments constituted the national wheat market, the market as the farmer saw it was much simpler. Since wheat could not be hauled profitably any great distance by wagon, only well-located farmers enjoyed the advantages of being able to negotiate with more than one buyer. For many, the nearest country merchant mill continued for long periods to be the sole market. As an area developed, farmers might find buyers in general produce merchants, in the traveling agents of city mills, or in the

16 "Chicago generally presents a highly interesting and animated spectacle during the fall and a portion of the winter. Wheat, the great staple of Northern Illinois, is brought into the city in wagons, not infrequently from a distance of two hundred and fifty miles. Long trains, reminding one of the caravans of the East, are seen crossing the prairies, and approaching the city, heralded by clouds of dust in all directions. The busiest streets are rendered almost impassable, by the number of wheat wagons and the fine strings of oxen attached to them. Those employed in the warehouses are constantly and actively engaged in the reception of this grain; runners are eagerly and noisily competing with each other in the purchase of it; you run against a load of wheat or a wheat buyer at every turn." *The National Magazine and Industrial Record,* I (1845), 462.

17 Guy A. Lee, "The Historical Significance of the Chicago Grain Elevator System," *Agricultural History,* XI (1937), 19-27.

wheat warehouse merchants found in most towns in the wheat-producing areas, who typically offered to purchase whatever was delivered at their establishment.[18] With the development of a railroad network in the wheat-producing areas, it became possible for a farmer to load his wheat in a railroad car at the nearest station, consign it to a warehouse or elevator, and either sell immediately or take a receipt and sell at some later time. Although local prices were determined by regional quotations, the grade allowed by the local purchaser and the terms offered at purchase were very important factors.

Cattle. From the farmer's point of view, the major market for animals was on the hoof, and most livestock were disposed of in that way. In the smaller towns and villages, farm-slaughtered meats, both fresh and packed, continued to be sold by farmers to country merchants for local sale, or in the case of packed meat, for shipment to central markets. Cattle were usually slaughtered at the consuming market, although a minor beef-packing industry developed in Buffalo in the 1830's and later in Cleveland, Chicago, and Milwaukee.[19]

The major markets for beef lay in the urban centers of the East, and while cattle were raised everywhere, the largest producing areas were in the West, at considerable distances from the consuming areas.[20] Locally raised and fattened cattle were the source of most eastern supplies until the 1820's, after which date western cattle became increasingly important, particularly in supplying New York and Pennsylvania. The Brighton market that served Boston continued to draw largely from New England sources until railroad facilities linked that city with Albany and the West.[21]

[18] In Winona, Minnesota, for example, in 1860 there were 32 grain dealers and 30 grain warehouses with capacities ranging from 5,000 to 100,000 bushels. Hastings, second largest wheat market in the state, had 18 wheat dealers. *Minnesota Farmer and Gardener,* I (1860), 119; II (1861), 69. See also Henrietta M. Larson, *The Wheat Market and the Farmer in Minnesota* (Columbia University Press, 1926).

[19] Charles T. Leavitt, "Transportation and the Livestock Industry of the Middle West to 1860," *Agricultural History,* VIII (1934), 20-33.

[20] Silas J. Loomis, "Distribution and Movement of Meat Cattle," in U. S. Commissioner of Agriculture, *Report* (1863), pp. 248-264. In 1853 the population of New York City was estimated to consume an average of one-half pound of meat per day; roughly one-half beef and one-quarter each pork and mutton. New York State Agricultural Society, *Transactions* (1853), p. 565.

[21] For descriptions of Brighton market, see Henry Coleman, *Agriculture of Massa-*

From the beginning of the century, cattle were driven across the Alleghenies to eastern markets.[22] At first these animals were three-year-olds, which were sold to eastern farmers for fattening. The fattening of western cattle had become an important industry, particularly in southeastern Pennsylvania and Delaware.[23] After 1805, four- and five-year-old cattle, fattened in Ohio, were also being driven eastward, and they came to constitute the bulk of the trade.[24] Cattle raising was an industry of the prairie frontier, and it moved westward as lands were brought into cultivation. The cattle-fattening industry followed, utilizing much of the corn produced. After 1820, some Western-fattened cattle were being driven to the Philadelphia and New York markets.[25] As the eastward movement increased in volume, farmers turned westward for feeder stock. In the forties, Missouri and Iowa cattle, and in the fifties cattle from Texas, were moving east. The cattle of northern New York and Ohio moved on foot or by lake and canal through New York state to Albany. Albany had become in the fifties one of the nation's most important cattle markets, the animals being shipped both to New York City and into New England.[26] Chicago, from which many of the animals destined for Albany were shipped, had become an im-

---

chusetts: *Fourth Report* (1841), p. 297; *Boston Cultivator* (June 20, 1840); *Country Gentleman*, XVI (1860), 100. On the Cambridge market, see *New England Farmer*, II (1850), 366. The cattle markets of New York City are described in *Plough, Loom and Anvil*, I (1848), 38.

22 Julia P. Cutler, *Life and Times of Ephrain Cutler* (Cincinnati, 1890), pp. 89-103, 229-238. See also R. C. Downes, "Trade in Frontier Ohio," *Mississippi Valley Historical Review*, XVI (1930), 493.

23 One observer noted of the area between Philadelphia and Wilmington, "every roadside inn is a cattle-market." Most of the cattle were purchased from drovers. Western sheep were also fattened in this area: in New Castle County, Delaware, "not less than 15,000 have been purchased by our farmers this season from the West." *American Agriculturist*, IX (1850), 138; U. S. Patent Office, *Report* (1855), pp. 27 ff; (1853), p. 39.

24 *Ohio Cultivator*, IX (1853), 34-35; Paul C. Henlein, "Cattle Driving from the Ohio Country, 1800-1850," *Agricultural History*, XXVIII (1954), 83-95, and "Early Cattle Ranges of the Ohio Valley," *Agricultural History*, XXXV (1961), 150-154; Isaac K. Felton, "Coming and Going of Ohio Droving," *Ohio State Archaeological and Historical Quarterly*, XVII (1908), 247-253.

25 Charles T. Leavitt, "Transportation and the Livestock Industry of the Middle West to 1860," *Agricultural History*, VIII (1934), 20-33; Robert Leslie Jones, "The Beef Cattle Industry of Ohio Prior to the Civil War," *Ohio Historical Quarterly*, LXIV (1955), 168-194, 287-319; Paul C. Henlein, "Shifting Range-Feeder Patterns in the Ohio Valley Before 1860," *Agricultural History*, XXXI (1957), 1-12.

26 Johnston, *Notes on North America*, I, 239-40; *Country Gentleman*, XXXV (1870), 440-441.

portant market for drovers and a center for beef packing by the middle forties.[27]

Cattle were raised in some number by most northern farmers, both large and small. In the East, single farmers or groups of them might drive small herds to nearby markets, usually sharing in the proceeds after the sale was made. More likely, they would sell their animals to a drover, who might be a local dealer, or to a buyer from one of the urban markets.[28] Wherever long distances were involved, economy required that drives be large, from several hundred to a thousand head. In both the East and the West, the key figure in the movement of large numbers of cattle from raiser to feeder and from feeder to markets was the drover. He arranged for financing, assembled the drove by purchasing the animals from perhaps scores of farms, and supervised the time-consuming drive.[29] The drover assumed the risks of lost animals and loss of weight, as well as the uncertainties of the condition of the final market.[30] In the West the cattle-raising industry included many farmers with substantial resources, some of whom were able to finance and conduct their own drives to markets.[31] While some of these farmers engaged in

[27] New York State Agricultural Society, *Transactions* (1843), p. 447; Rudolph A. Clemen, *American Livestock and Meat Industry* (Ronald Press, 1923), p. 106.

[28] *Yankee Farmer,* VI (1841), 147.

[29] The drover was also the key figure in supplying horses for the major cities as well as the western frontier. Horses were raised in small numbers by many widely scattered farmers. In the 1850's Cincinnati claimed to be the largest horse market in the United States. Some horses were brought in by farmers, but most by "dealers who make regular excursions through" the western states. The city had three horse auction establishments and four principal drover and sale stables. Sales were made to buyers from New York City and to drovers who operated throughout the East and the South. Estimated total sales in 1852 were 19,000 animals. Estimated sales in New York were placed at 15,000. *Iowa Farmer,* I (1853), 12; II (1854), 37; R. L. Jones, "The Horse and Mule Industry in Ohio to 1865," *Mississippi Valley Historical Review,* XXXIII (1946-1947), 61-88.

[30] W. G. Edmundson estimated that in 1851 it cost $10 to $12 per head to drive cattle from Ohio's Scioto Valley to the New York market, "without including the loss of flesh sustained by driving, which may safely be calculated at $10 per head, reckoning beef at $7 per hundred pounds, which is much below the New York price. The cattle driven were 4 to 5 year old steers, weighing 700 to 800 pounds and valued at $50 to $60." For accounts of the financing of cattle drives in Ohio, see *Maine Farmer* (August 23, 1849); *Prairie Farmer,* VIII (1861), 407; *Monthly Journal of Agriculture,* I (1840), 584.

[31] In 1859 a New York observer noted that the business of raising beef in the West was "mainly carried on by extensive graziers owning large tracts of prairie or other pasture . . . Some of these graziers are also drovers, bringing in their own cattle and occasionally selling them. Others raise the animals and sell to cattle dealers, or drovers, or bring in and sell to the butchers, or more frequently consign them to commission men who make a business of selling for $2 and $2.50 a head, and

driving on a large scale, even the large farm-operators tended to look upon it as a specialized business and many preferred to sell their cattle at their doors.

Cattle driven into Ohio from further West for fattening were sold by the drovers to farmers at market fairs at stated intervals. The fairs held in Madison County, Ohio, were particularly important.[32] Cattle driven to the East were sold in a variety of ways—at roadside inns, which became informal meeting places, at the yards adjacent to slaughter houses in all the major cities, to smaller butchers, or to agents who intercepted the droves en route.

The growing volume of animals, both hogs and cattle, shipped to market and the spread of railroad transportation facilities stimulated the development of a different marketing structure. The opportunity to ship animals by carload reduced the marketing unit from the large number of animals included in drives to a carlot—which in the case of cattle was twelve to eighteen animals. In Chicago the trade in livestock grew with great rapidity, and the organization of the marketing structure developed correspondingly. The first true commission merchant dealing only in livestock appeared on the Chicago market in 1857.[33] The need of handling large numbers of animals in a competitive market led to the consolidation of a number of livestock yards and the establishment of the Union Stockyards in 1865.[34] While the operators of large farms could and did deal directly with central market commission men such as these, farmers by and large continued to sell to the former drover, now primarily a country dealer in livestock.

Hogs. The methods by which hogs were marketed developed somewhat differently because of the nature of the pork-packing industry. In the 1830's the demand for fresh pork in the growing eastern urban centers was supplied by hogs driven across the mountains or shipped by lake steamer and canal barge.[35] That trade continued important in northern Ohio, but the growth of the packing industry

---

guaranteeing the sales." *American Agriculturist,* XVIII (1961). In 1835, fifty-eight Ohio graziers had 11,802 cattle. *Cultivator,* III (1836-1837), 32.

[32] U. S. Commissioner of Agriculture, *Report* (1869), pp. 371-377.

[33] There were twenty-eight commission firms operating in the city as early as 1845. *Hunt's Merchants' Magazine,* XVIII (1848), 171.

[34] Clemen, *American Livestock,* pp. 83-87.

[35] The "Sandusky and Buffalo steamship line carries little else in the fall." *Working Farmer,* III (1856), 256.

on the Ohio River reduced its significance elsewhere in the state and further west. The trans-Allegheny driving of hogs remained important chiefly in reaching southeastern markets.[36] The major market for western hogs was in the form of salt pork, which was in demand in the South and for export. Salt pork had achieved considerable importance early in the agricultural development of the East, and it became one of the major products as settlement increased in the Ohio Valley.[37]

In the early development of the industry, hogs were slaughtered and packed on the farm, the barreled product then being hauled to a river town and sold to merchants. Although this farm-packed pork did not disappear, it declined substantially as packing firms in the river towns and cities gained advantages from standardization of cutting and packing practices in conformance with the preferences of their ultimate markets. These packing firms sometimes bought hog carcasses from farmers, but it was generally more economical to drive hogs to local markets. The buyers were urban packing firms, the industry being sufficiently specialized to support firms that slaughtered for the by-products. As early as 1826, three-fourths of the Cincinnati pork packed represented purchases of live hogs by the packers; by 1843, the percentage had risen to ninety.[38] Cincinnati dominated this industry, although every town on the Ohio River was a packing center. Alton and St. Louis were leading packing points on the Mississippi. Chicago achieved prominence in the industry in the fifties, and by 1861 surpassed Cincinnati in the amount packed.[39]

The physical distance between the farmer and the pork packer market was much less than in the case of the cattle market, while the amount of capital represented in a hog drove was likewise much smaller. For these reasons, farmers had greater opportunity to undertake the driving function themselves, and many drovers were farmers who entered the business seasonally, handling only one or

[36] The pork industry in the late 1840's is described in *Wisconsin and Iowa Farmer and Northwest Cultivator*, II (1850), 89. See also William T. Utter, *The History of the State of Ohio* (Columbus, 1942), II, 156.

[37] Clemen, *American Livestock*, pp. 91 ff; *Cultivator*, X (1843), 85; *Ohio Cultivator*, X (1854), 33.

[38] Clemen, *American Livestock*, p. 58.

[39] For contemporary descriptions of the pork packing industry, see *American Agriculturist*, I (1842), 299; XV (1856), 11.

a few herds.[40] Whether a professional or a part-time operator, the drover was the key figure in this trade, as in cattle selling, and the typical farmer's sales were made at his barn door.[41] A northern Ohio farmer described the business as it related to the sale of hogs for the eastern market: "A shrewd Yankee from the Berkshire hills comes this way with money in pocket, travels around among the Buckeyes ready for a bargain, and soon picks up a drove of several hundred hogs at from 1 cent to 1½ cents per pound. He buys a few sleek horses, and then with a hired hand or two starts his grunters for down east. He drives them at the rate of 12 to 15 miles per day, feeds them well, and, in about 50 days, reaches Albany where the swine are shipped on the cars for Brighton and, increased in weight by the journey, they there bring from 5 to 6 cents per pound, alive and squalling, and are scattered among the farmers in the region round about to be fattened for customers and a market."[42] To some extent, competition among drovers and between drovers and packing firms led to the practice of offering contracts to farmers during the summer for their hogs for winter delivery at a price agreed upon at the time of the sale.[43]

OTHER PRODUCTS

A variety of marketing patterns developed for other products, supplementing and, to a considerable degree, displacing the role of the country merchant as purchaser. Although country merchants continued to be important agencies for the handling of very small

---

[40] *National Magazine and Industrial Record,* I (1845), 462.

[41] See, for example, the country reports on selling practices with regard to both hogs and cattle in Iowa Agricultural Society, *Report* (1859), pp. 166 ff.

[42] *American Agriculturist,* VIII (1849), 160. The financial statement of an Iowa hog dealer illustrates the magnitude of the operations carried on by some drovers. The account was published with the following comment by the shipper, "I want the farmers to know how fast we easy working dealers are getting rich." The sales were presumably in Chicago, except for one lot sold in New York.

Costs		Receipts	
3,000 hogs @ $10 per head	$30,000	Six droves sold in West	$31,500
10,000 bushels corn @ 18¢	1,800	One drove sold in N. Y.	2,900
Six droves at $200	1,200	Corn and pork on hand	300
Freight, 300 hogs to N. Y.	900		
Other labor and commissions	600		
	34,500		34,700

Iowa Farmer, IV (1856), 52.

[43] Indiana State Agricultural Society, *Report,* IV (1854-1855), 109.

lots from numerous farmers, the development of a large volume of production as a speciality in an area was followed by the appearance of special marketing institutions and practices. In the case of both wool and tobacco, manufacturers early established the practice of purchasing either directly from farmers who brought their product to the mill or warehouse, or through agents sent into the country.[44] Specialized dealers in wool were operating in Boston before 1820, and both they and the mills maintained traveling purchasing agents. Difficulties in agreeing on grades stimulated a number of efforts to establish "wool depots" where farmers might send their wool for unprejudiced grading and for sale through competitive bids by buyers.[45] With the development of railroads, it became possible for buyers to send their wool on consignment to eastern commission houses, and this method seems to have acquired some importance in disposing of western fleeces.[46] Wool was also at times sold on contract before the sheep were sheared.[47]

Tobacco in Connecticut was likewise sold to men generally called "speculators"; i.e., agents of manufacturers as well as wholesalers. However, in 1856 a Tobacco Grower's Convention resulted in the establishment of a warehouse in Hartford where tobacco was sold on a competitive basis.[48] Wisconsin tobacco, which was becoming a significant crop in the late fifties, was sold to traveling agents.[49]

Butter, cheese, and eggs were almost everywhere considered acceptable items at the country store. In the case of eggs, growing

[44] Connecticut State Agricultural Society, *Transactions* (1855), p. 165; *Maine Farmer,* I (1833), 211; *New England Farmer,* XIII (1834), 53; Arthur H. Cole, *The American Wool Manufacture* (Harvard University Press, 1926), I, 83-85; New York State Agricultural Society, *Transactions* (1842), p. 216; *Plough, Loom and Anvil,* V (1852), 20-21.

[45] One "wool depot" was established at Kinderhook, N. Y., in 1845. *Cultivator,* n. s. II (1845), 200. An earlier effort by Maine farmers apparently failed. *Maine Farmer,* I (1833), 178; II (1834), 162; *New York Farmer,* VII (1834), 301. The most ambitious effort of this nature was made by T. C. Peters, who established a wool warehouse in Buffalo in 1851 and gave it considerable publicity in the periodical he edited, the *Wool Grower and Stock Register.* A movement to establish such warehouses also appeared in Ohio about the same time. *Ohio Cultivator,* VIII (1852), 54, citing Theo Faber, *Circular to the Wool-Growers of Ohio.*

[46] Illinois State Agricultural Society, *Transactions* (1865-1866), pp. 162-163.

[47] *Homestead,* I (1856), 247; II (1857), 98; III (1858), 278, 280.

[48] Connecticut State Agricultural Society, *Transactions* (1856), p. 439. Cf. Elizabeth Ramsey, *The History of Tobacco Production in the Connecticut Valley,* Smith College Studies in History, XV (Northampton, 1930), pp. 139-146; *American Agriculturist* XXIV (1863), 71.

[49] *Rural New Yorker,* IV (1853), 170.

urban demands and better transportation stimulated the development of wholesale egg dealers, who provided the country merchants with better markets and the urban centers with larger supplies.[50]

Butter typically moved to market through the country store, where it was collected in small quantities and indiscriminately mixed, the accumulations being sent to market a few times a year as quantities and opportunities permitted. Some farmers located close to central markets, however, had long found it profitable to furnish superior qualities of fresh butter. As the railroad network extended outward from the major cities, it became possible for larger numbers of farmers to specialize in the production of superior butter, sending it to market at short intervals. Such butter was frequently shipped via the express companies operating on the railroads, to be sold on commission.[51] In the neighborhood of New York City, "the system of marketing which prevails . . . is for the producer, to send his produce once or twice a week to market, by a man called a captain, from the fact that formerly this service was all performed by captains of North River barges. The captain, whether of a barge or freight car, soon attracts to himself a regular line of customers who know just when to expect him, and what class of goods he has to sell them. His interest lies in getting all he can for the goods, as he sells on commission and is anxious to please his patrons, lest they withdraw their patronage and give it to somebody else."[52] Country produce dealers also handled increasing quantities.

Prior to 1850, cheese was produced on the farm and sold through the country store or, in a few eastern localities, on contract to country produce dealers. Thereafter in some areas, particularly in New

[50] "The country merchants in western towns take in eggs and 'pay in goods.' These they pack and send direct to a commission merchant here, or more frequently sell them out to migratory dealers at the nominal cost price, depending upon the profits of their 'goods' for their remuneration. The traveling dealers frequently have on hand half a million or more of eggs, and sales of 50 to 150 barrels (containing 75 to 80 dozen each) to a single egg merchant are very common transactions." *American Agriculturist*, XV (1855), 78.

[51] *Connecticut Valley Farmer and Mechanic*, I (1853), 58.

[52] Vermont Dairyman's Association, *Transactions* (1869-1870), p. 117. In Vermont, butter was "often sold to country dealers who buy for wholesale houses, who in turn sell to retailers and these again to the consumer." The criticism was made that this "common practice by which our butter is permitted to pass through the hands of so many middle men before it reaches the consumer is decidedly injurious to the interests of the producer." Vermont Dairyman's Association, *Transactions* (1870-1871), p. 46. See also Ohio Board of Agriculture, *Report* (1851), p. 402; Indiana State Board of Agriculture, *Report*, II (1852), 156.

York, production tended to be concentrated in cheese factories, to which the participating farmers made daily shipments of their milk and curds.[53] The result was large-scale production of a higher quality product. It was sold both on contract and spot sale to wholesale produce firms or by consignment to commission houses.[54] Dissatisfaction with these methods existed, but little progress was made in securing more satisfactory relations with the market.[55] However, a weekly cheese market-fair operated very successfully in the sixties in Little Falls, New York.

The availability of railroad transportation made possible a vastly expanded market for poultry. Local dealers as well as traveling agents of city dealers in these products appeared wherever supplies might be shipped by rail, some of them sending large quantities of dressed poultry as well as eggs to market.[56] Commission merchants likewise invited direct shipments from farmers, some utilizing the agents of the express companies to purchase such items for their accounts.[57]

THE PROBLEM OF QUALITY

An important factor in agricultural change in this half-century, affecting both farming opportunities and the marketing mechanism, was the development of quality standards for farm products higher than those acceptable for on-the-farm consumption. A few quality standards had earlier come into existence. The necessity of identifying products by grades as a basis for export trade had been recognized in the colonial period and had led to the establishment of

[53] New York State Agricultural Society, *Transactions* (1847), 263; (1864), p. 226; Vermont Dairyman's Association, *Transactions* (1872), p. 13. In the 1860's factory-made cheese enjoyed a premium of a cent or two per pound over cheese made in small dairies. *Rural New Yorker*, XIV (1863), 398; X. A. Willard in Wisconsin State Agricultural Society, *Transactions* (1861), p. 442. For an analysis of the speculative aspects of wholesale cheese dealing, see *Country Gentleman*, XXVI (1860), 111.

[54] *Homestead*, I (1855), 138; *Ohio Cultivator*, V (1849), 198; VI (1850), 297.

[55] For a description and appraisal of the cheese market, see *Country Gentleman*, XXXV (1870), 377.

[56] A New York City produce firm suggested in its advertisements that farmers apply to their local express agent, quoting prices on butter, poultry, and eggs. "Likely we will put him in funds to buy of you if we can agree upon prices. We are in want of half a ton of turkeys, chickens, and geese every week, at our Express Produce Store." *American Agriculturist*, XV (1857), 191.

[57] New York State Agricultural Society, *Transactions* (1860), p. 547. Eggs from Wisconsin and Minnesota were moving to the New York market in 1863. *American Agriculturist*, XX (1867), 331.

government inspection and grading requirements in seaport cities for such products as flour and tobacco.

With the growth of urban populations came an increase in demand for higher quality products—wheat that would produce better and whiter bread, beef of superior tenderness, pork cut and cured to market requirements, fresh butter, superior cheeses, and higher quality fruit, among others. In addition, as the agricultural products of the northern states began to seek entry in larger quantity and variety into European markets, and more particularly into British ones, they encountered well-established quality grades. American exporters experienced difficulties in selling American products which, as in the case of salt pork, differed in cut and packing from British customs and standards.[58] In other cases the low quality of American products brought disappointing returns. The editor of the *American Agriculturist* pointed out: "The negligence of American farmers in putting up provisions for market whether at home or abroad, has for a long period, been proverbial. They may do much better to feed American mouths, which have become accustomed to these preparations; and the producer has the further advantage that we must take them as furnished or starve; while the proximity to our domestic markets, prevents that excessive deterioration, before reaching the consumer, which they experience when sent abroad. We are so much accustomed to soft, rancid butter; hard, strong cheese; lean, stringy beef; and gristly, flabby pork, that it would seem to have become a vested right in our producers to furnish them to the extent of the demand . . . But when we send our commodities to Europe, they have to be tried by other tastes and customs. The predilections of Victoria's subjects will not permit cramming with stale, rancid, and offensive provisions, and the result is that we receive, but one half, and sometimes not one third, the price we might have received for good articles."[59]

On the whole, the quality of the products supplied by the smaller, semisubsistence farms was low. Wheat, improperly cleaned, possibly of mixed red and white varieties, and including small amounts of rye or oats, was acceptable as a source of flour for the farm family, but it could be sold only at a discount that cut heavily into farm

---

[58] *Ohio Cultivator*, I (1845), 15; U. S. Patent Office, *Report* (1843), pp. 213-215, 218-231; (1845), p. 307.
[59] *American Agriculturist*, IX (1850), 55.

revenues. It made no difference to a farm family if its potatoes were an assortment of white and red varieties, but such mixtures suffered significant discounts when offered for sale.[60] Butter improperly salted or stored, or cheese with too high a moisture content, likewise brought unsatisfactory returns when sold upon a competitive market.[61] Pork prepared to supply the family's needs and adequate for that purpose might bring only a low price when offered for sale if cuts or preparation were not as desired by urban consumers. Low quality resulted also from the operation of the marketing system. The country storekeeper or miller received a fairly large number of small lots of any given type of product. These were usually lumped together and shipped with no effort to differentiate between grades of quality. In the case of perishables, such as butter and eggs, and also of flour, further deterioration occurred over the period of accumulation and during the overland transportation to the central market. As a result, the label "western country" was synonymous with low quality.[62]

Farmers in long settled areas responded to market demands, and products of consistently high quality soon came to be known by the region of their origin, such as Genesee flour, Orange County or Goshen butter, Herkimer and Hamburg cheese. These and similar designations served in some degree as guarantees of quality, and were generally accepted by the wholesalers as designations of grade. As products of superior quality appeared elsewhere, they were frequently sold under the well-known name. Michigan flour in the 1820's, for example, was sold under the Genesee label.[63] By the 1850's, the term Goshen was applied to butter coming from the southern tier of New York counties west of Orange. Much northern Pennsylvania and northeastern Ohio butter was similarly labeled, and some years later the better quality butter of Illinois and other western states was so designated. Westerners, long accustomed to

---

[60] *Wisconsin Farmer,* XVI (1864), 59.

[61] "In England, American butter is a poor article, generally . . . and does not find purchasers for table use, but is used to grease machinery in the manufacturing districts." U. S. Patent Office, *Report* (1847), p. 207. Complaints about the quality of American butter were made as early as 1820. *Agricultural Intelligencer,* I (1820), 157. Solon Robinson estimated that not one-tenth of the butter in the New York market was "first rate." *Facts for Farmers* (New York, 1864), p. 441.

[62] *American Agriculturist,* XXII (1863), 330.

[63] Later Wisconsin flour was also sold under the Michigan label. *Farmer's Companion,* IV (1854), 224.

buying eastern cheese if they wished a quality product, were offered the higher quality western grades under the Hamburg name.[64]

Industrial buyers of such products as wool and tobacco paid premiums for superior goods, as did buyers of such commodities as wheat, butter, and cheese for urban and export markets. The razorback hog gave way to improved breeds in the West because, though easy to raise and able to stand long drives, he could be sold only at a heavy discount, if at all, for pork-packing purposes. Awareness of the premium market for quality products was a channel through which the more aggressive farmers could secure returns well above their more traditional fellows. The application of grades to products was, however, a persistent source of conflict between farmers and merchants.[65]

CRITIQUE OF THE MARKETING SYSTEM

By the 1860's the nation's marketing system, though still immature, comprised the basic elements that have characterized it since. The system was the product of a high degree of enterprise, ingenuity, and risk assumption on the part of a relatively small group of men, who sought to capitalize on the opportunities presented by expanding agricultural production, growing markets, and new transportation facilities.[66] Although farmers incessantly discussed their need for markets and marketing institutions, and supported both public and private efforts to expand transportation facilities, they became increasingly specialized as farmers. Lewis F. Allen, a careful contemporary observer of agricultural matters, pointed out in 1863: "In these actively commercial times, there is a class of middle-men, or speculators, if you please, who range all through the country, purchasing grain, butter, cheese, fruit, pigs, sheep,—in short, all that a farmer has to sell, and the competition

[64] *American Agriculturist,* XVIII (1859), 186; *Rural New Yorker,* XIV (1863), 93; XIV (1863), 382.

[65] For example, grain grading in Chicago caused controversy. See *Prairie Farmer,* XXIV (1861), 40; XXV (1862), 216, 280. For the case of a commission merchant criticizing farmers for a propensity to cheat, see *Rural New Yorker,* XX (1869), 326. The grading of wool was also a source of conflict. *New England Farmer,* XVI (1838), 380-381; *Rural New Yorker,* XI (1860), 285; XII (1861); XVI (1865), 13, 53, 406; *Wool Grower,* IV (1852), 10.

[66] For an evaluation of the merchant's role in the West, see Nathan H. Parker, *Iowa As It Is in 1856* (Chicago, 1856), pp. 331-336.

among them is such that they frequently pay more for articles than they can get for them in the large markets, after paying charges, losses on perishable articles, interest on money, and various risks and charges, always incident to speculation. When the farmer sells his produce and he gets his pay for it, as he should always be sure to do, his risks are at an end."[67]

On the whole, the initial effect of the expansion of the canal and railroad networks was to provide such an increase in profit opportunities that farmers had very little inclination to criticize transportation rates or service or the marketing system that had developed. But profit experiences were capitalized into higher land values, while the continuing expansion of the railroad network brought the products of ever-expanding areas into competition on the national market. Judging by the lack of attention given to the subject of marketing in the agricultural press, the mass of farmers were reasonably well satisfied with their marketing opportunities at least until the late 1850's. Criticism increased during the 1850's and after the Civil War assumed a vigorous form.

Dissatisfaction with the system arose from the fact that, as the functions of distributing products over an ever-widening market were taken over by others, farmers became acutely aware of the wide margin between the prices they received for their products and the prices[68] prevailing upon the central markets or paid by the ultimate consumer. Middlemen, always suspected of being unproductive parasites and price manipulators, became a target for increasingly vigorous criticism and resentment.[69] Dissatisfaction was accentuated by the fact that many farmers had only a few potential buyers with whom to negotiate the sale of their products, so that when they arrived upon the market with a load of produce, they rarely had any alternative to accepting the prices offered. In their negotiations, the advantage of detailed knowledge of market trends all lay with the buyer. The common advice farmers exchanged with each other—to watch the markets, determine their costs, and refuse to sell for less—was not very helpful.[70] Discussions of marketing

[67] *Rural New Yorker*, XIV (1863), 278, 293.
[68] *Rural New Yorker*, XX (1869), 441; *Northwestern Prairie Farmer*, I (1858), 93; *Plough, Loom and Anvil*, VII (1855), 525-529; *Prairie Farmer*, XXI (1860), 312; *New England Farmer*, XII (1860), 541-542.
[69] *Rural New Yorker*, XII (1862), 317.
[70] *Prairie Farmer*, XXI (1860), 328. See also *Rural New Yorker*, XXI (1870), 320.

rarely went much beyond the question of "when to sell" and were not very conclusive.[71] Withholding products from market was a retaliatory weapon that involved great risks. "Next to selling too soon, the greatest trouble is found in holding too long."[72] Although consignment of products to city commission merchants was possible in many cases, perhaps on the basis of preliminary negotiations based upon samples, some unsatisfactory experiences and general suspicion of such middlemen limited the use of that method of sale.[73] Moreover, in a day when railroad freight rates were a subject of individual bargaining, the small shipper was at a great disadvantage.[74] Resentment against the level of railroad rates, against discriminatory rates, and against the monopolistic arrangements that existed between some railroads and central market warehouses was being vigorously expressed before the Civil War.[75]

Horace Greeley, no doubt, summed up the sentiments of many farmers the nation over, and for most of the half-century, when he said, "The machinery whereby the farmer of our day converts into cash or other values that portion of his products which is not consumed in his house or on his farm, seems to me lamentably imperfect."[76] Apparently what the farmer desired most was competitive bidding for his products and in his presence.[77] Market fairs at

[71] *American Agriculturist*, XXII (1863), 2.

[72] *Country Gentleman*, XXV (1863), 313. Farmers tended to sell quicker when prices were low than when high. *American Agriculturist*, XXXI (1868), 148, 221.

[73] *American Agriculturist*, XVI (1860), 162.

[74] In 1859, for example, rates from central Illinois to New York for cattle ranged from $3 to $10 per head. *American Agriculturist*, XVIII (1859), 196. In 1860, "the charge for freight at present from Chicago or other large shipping points at the West appears to be just what may be agreed upon, and often stock shipped by different owners upon the same train pay different rates of freight." *Prairie Farmer*, XXI (1860), 328, 297.

[75] Some of the earliest protests were made in Ohio. M. L. Sullivant, one of the largest landowners in the state and president of the State Board of Agriculture, vigorously attacked railroad rate-making practices. Ohio State Board of Agriculture, *Report* (1851), pp. 21, 32, 342. For other protests, see Wisconsin State Agricultural Society, *Transactions* (1861-1868), pp. 99-100; *Prairie Farmer*, XVIII (1858), 85; XXV (1862), 121; XXII (1860); 73; *Wisconsin Farmer*, XVII (1865), 384; American Institute, *Transactions* (1865-1866), p. 308; *Country Gentleman*, XXIV (1869), 178; XXXV (1870), 277; *Illinois Farmer*, VII (1862), 226-227.

[76] Horace Greeley, *What I Know of Farming* (New York, 1871), pp. 297-301.

[77] "The farmer wants free trade and an open market in order to protect himself. In this country, an agent from the city slips round before harvest, and bargains privately for all the wheat, or wool, or apples, for all the butter, cheese, poultry and everything else at the farmer's door, and monopolizing the article adds a frightful commission and giving the farmer the lowest prices, compels the consumer in the city to pay the highest prices. Thus both producer and consumer are being kept apart, supporting

which buyers and sellers gathered at stated intervals to buy and
sell were one solution to the problem. A very few such fairs were
in existence in the 1820's in New England. Henry Colman, in his
survey of European agriculture in the forties, was much impressed
with the European market fairs that he had seen in operation and
urged the establishment of a similar system of marketing produce
and livestock in the United States.[78] Little attention was given to
his and similar proposals until the sixties, although in many towns
and villages Saturday was "by common consent, market day when
purchasers might be expected to be present."[79] Discussion of the
desirability of market fairs reappears at that time.[80] A few were
established in New York and Ohio.[81] These proved most successful
when the market centered about some important specialty—such as
cattle or cheese—and it was recognized by some at least that such
a specialty was essential if an adequate number of buyers were to
be attracted to the market.[82] These market fairs were too few to
make much of an impression on the nation's marketing machinery.
Efforts were made in a number of localities—Chicago, Battle Creek,
Fort Wayne, and others—to establish farmer-controlled union
stores and warehouses.[83] The record of such attempts prior to 1870
was one of underestimating the difficulties involved, overestimating
the possible gains, mismanagement, and in some cases dishonesty.[84]

Despite widespread criticism of the marketing facilities as they
operated, and minor efforts to overcome some of their deficiencies,
the system seems to have served its purposes well. Over the period,
most farmers acquired alternative methods of disposing of their
products and could expect to gain from the care with which they
approached the problem. From such information as is available, it
would appear that the typical farmer wished to sell his produce

---

a large class of middlemen who wax fat at their expense." *New England Farmer,* XII
(1860), 541-542.

[78] Henry Colman, *European Agriculture and Rural Economy* (Boston, 1844), I, 297-
299.

[79] *Rural New Yorker,* XXI (1870), 320.

[80] Discussion of market fairs appeared particularly in the *Rural New Yorker* and the
Country Gentleman.

[81] See *Country Gentleman,* XXXV (1870), 377, 457; XVII (1866), 17; *Rural New
Yorker,* XXL (1870), 320.

[82] *Country Gentleman,* XXV (1870), 377.

[83] *Prairie Farmer,* XX (1859), 200; XXII (1860), 360; XXIV (1861), 294.

[84] *Rural New Yorker,* XIV (1869), 278, 293, 310, 317; *Country Gentleman,* XXXIII
(1869), 198, 332.

with as little effort and attention as possible. His ideal was to sell at his barn door, and certainly at a distance no greater than the nearest county seat. By the sixties, the great majority of farmers enjoyed such a situation.

CHAPTER THREE

SHARING AND EXPANDING THE FUND OF KNOWLEDGE

Both the methods and the kinds of materials utilized in husbandry in America about 1820 derived from three principal sources. Most of the plant and animal materials and the techniques for their use had originally been brought from Europe, chiefly from Great Britain, but also from the Low Countries, France, Sweden, and Germany, frequently by way of Britain.[1] From the coastal Indian tribes the early settlers had acquired maize and a number of other plants, together with the techniques that the aborigine had employed in their culture. The third source was domestic, comprising the numerous modifications and adaptations that American farmers had made in the borrowed techniques.

The technology and institutions of American agriculture were thus a unique amalgam. They developed slowly in the course of finding solutions to the problems faced in settling a new country. To make a farm on the forested frontier required the development and application of techniques unknown or little used elsewhere. Each generation devoted much of its effort to clearing land, with the consequence that the techniques of land use associated with the availability of virgin acreage were imbedded in the technology. In the process of settlement, much of the European methodology was discarded, while European plants and animals underwent selective adjustment to American conditions.

The small acreages available for cultivation in the early years of a farm-making effort allowed most farmers no option but to plant the cleared land to the same crops year after year. The fertility of the land when newly cleared suggested that the labor of fertilizing it was better applied to other objectives, principally clearing. In any case, since livestock were few, there was little accumulation of fertilizing materials. As a farm-making project developed into an

[1] See Lyman Carrier, *The Beginnings of Agriculture in America* (McGraw Hill, 1923); A. H. Hirsh, "French Influence on American Agriculture in the Colonial Period," *Agricultural History*, IV (1930), 1-9.

49

established farm with cleared acreage sufficient to occupy the labor force, the necessity that had led to the adoption of exploitative practices disappeared, but the methods employed tended to continue unchanged. With land abundant, American farmers saw their best interest in spreading their labor and capital over very large areas. Throughout this period, "to compel the earth to produce the largest return with the least possible outlay of time and labor constitutes the chief study of the mass of farmers. Hence to secure large farms, and lay them under the severest contributions is the effort of most of them. And when their land is exhausted they abandon it for virgin fields, apparently exulting in the thought that there is a best area yet intact in the far West."[2]

This approach to soil use was paralleled by similar attitudes toward plants and animals. In animals, hardiness—the ability to survive under conditions of poor shelter and food during winter—possessed a higher value than did rapid and economical growth. The strong propensity to apply available resources toward the acquisition of more land—either in clearing what was already owned or in purchasing additional acreage—meant that farm buildings were held to a minimum. Native grasses did not for any long period provide adequate fodder for cattle, but rarely did farmers invest the cost and effort required to establish domesticated grasses for meadows and pastures. Tools and implements were few, and here, too, economy of capital was sought, in that implements were of a multipurpose character whenever possible. The English observer, Patrick Shirreff, was more understanding than many of his countrymen when he wrote, "The agriculture of a country is affected by local circumstances and farming in Britain and in the remote parts of America may be considered the extreme of the art. In the one country the farmer aims to assist and in the other to rob nature. When the results of capital and labour are low, compared with the hire of them, they are sparingly applied to the cultivation of the soil, in which case nature is oppressed and neglected if I may be allowed to use such terms; and when they are high compared with their hire, she is aided and caressed. Both systems are proper in the respective countries; and by assuming a fixed result for nature, they admit of arithmetical demonstration."[3]

2 John Lorain, *Nature and Reason Harmonized in the Practice of Husbandry* (Philadelphia, 1819), pp. 358, 362.
3 Patrick Shirreff, *Tour Through North America* (Edinburgh, 1835), p. 341.

The availability of land waiting to be cleared on the farmstead or on the frontier determined the motives and methods that in 1820 were firmly established as the traditional agriculture. This body of techniques persisted long after the conditions that had called them into being had disappeared. American farm management tended to become static at a level which, when compared with that of the English, was primitive in its materials and techniques. The vast majority of farmers applied the traditional body of knowledge and the readily available plants and animals to their operations in routine, unquestioning fashion. Such "random practices" and "complicated absurdities," as one contemporary called them, were "sufficient to produce a tolerable but at the same time a precarious supply of the fruits of the earth."[4]

As long as distance from markets necessitated subsistence farming, or as long as such farming was continued merely by force of habit, the yields obtained from the traditional technology were acceptable. But as farming became increasingly influenced by market considerations, and as the growth of urban population induced comparisons between the returns from farming and incomes obtainable from other occupations, interest in improving techniques attracted greater attention. Dissatisfaction with the traditional technology tended to be most strongly felt by farmers in older settled areas whose operations were adjusted to markets that they now found increasingly supplied with the products of the newer soils of the West, offered at prices that could not be met by the yields obtained from conventional practices. Such farmers found themselves in precarious and often intolerable positions. In addition to these competitive pressures, the fertility of long cultivated soils was declining, and the ravages of plant and animal diseases and insect pests were becoming more severe. Returns from animals were low, since the "native" strains of hogs and cattle continued to be widely raised even in the well-settled eastern areas, although the conditions justifying them had disappeared. Despite the expanding marketing opportunities that followed from increasing urban populations, agriculture in New England and the Middle States in the 1820's and 1830's was viewed as unprofitable by many, though by no means by all. Location was becoming an increasingly important factor in determining the returns from farming.

[4] John Lorain, *Nature and Reason*, p. 11.

IMPROVING THE TECHNOLOGY

Although the majority of farmers clung unquestioningly to their time-tested technology, the inadequacies of its methods and materials were clear to some. Throughout this half-century there was among American farmers a small but active group, by no means limited to so-called gentlemen farmers, who were ready to view their dissatisfactions as problems susceptible to solution. Taken as a whole, this group looked upon almost every phase of agriculture as posing challenges to analysis, experimentations, and ingenuity. They were open-minded toward the new and novel, and aggressively interested in the materials and methods employed by their like-minded fellows at home as well as abroad. They were irritated into closer self-examination and more critical rationalization of their methods by the derogatory comments freely made by Europeans traveling in the United States. In the 1820's, as earlier, some of these men felt the need for exchanging information on new plants, animals, and implements, or on the results of experiments that held promise of contributing to a greater certainty and profitability of agriculture. It was this group that was the source of change.

Many of these farmers found stimulus and inspiration in the developments in Great Britain. After the American colonies had been well established, extremely significant changes had occurred in England in agricultural knowledge, techniques, and materials. In the latter half of the eighteenth century such men as Jethro Tull, Viscount Townshend, and Robert Bakewell were laying the basis of what has since been called an agricultural revolution. Knowledge of the achievements of these and other men came to the colonies and the young republic not only in the form of books and periodicals but also as firsthand knowledge from at least a few immigrants and travelers.[5]

Attention centered particularly on the development in Europe of improved varieties of animals, first the Spanish Merino and later English cattle and hogs. There was also a continuing interest in European plant materials, both in superior strains of commonly cultivated plants and in plants little known or not cultivated at all

[5] See Rodney C. Loehr, "Influence of English Agriculture on American Agriculture, 1775-1825," *Agricultural History*, XI (1937), 3-15.

in the United States. In the matter of techniques, as in tillage and rotation practices, Europe provided invaluable stimulus. Experience early taught American observers, however, that developments in Europe could not be successfully borrowed *in toto*. Thomas Moore, observing as early as 1801 that Americans had not derived from European improvements and discoveries the advantages that might have been expected, commented: "Many of them having been implicitly adopted here without the necessary variation for the difference in soil and climate have failed. These unsuccessful experiments have tended to confirm the people of America in their former prejudices and to induce them to treat with contempt every appearance of innovation in theory or in practice."[6]

While alert to developments in Europe, farmers centered their search for new insights and understandings at home. Throughout the half-century the most important method involved observing, recording, and evaluating differences in materials and techniques found in various localities, including an analysis of the differences between the average and superior farmers in a given locality. Reports on farming practices observed on tours, which frequently had been made specifically for that purpose, were common in the United States, paralleling similar activities in England, particularly those of Arthur Young. Accounts of such travels appeared sometimes in books, but periodicals were the most important vehicle of dissemination. Agricultural editors produced many of the most useful accounts of this type, although voluntary correspondents made numerous contributions.

A second source of new knowledge was the planned experiments carried on in sporadic fashion by small numbers of widely scattered farmers. Although typically amateurish, frequently lacking the controls fundamental to a truly scientific approach, and therefore inconclusive, such activities attracted considerable attention in the press. The earliest agricultural organizations were formed to encourage this kind of experimentation, hear reports, observe results, and exchange critical comments. The promotion of such experimentation was one of the functions undertaken by agricultural societies, particularly after 1840.

[6] Thomas Moore, *The Great Error of American Agriculture Exposed* (Baltimore, 1801), p.6.

BOOKS AND PAMPHLETS

Prior to 1820, the farmer who sought printed information on an agricultural subject turned to one of the numerous agricultural almanacs and possibly to his local newspaper. Aside from providing a convenient working calendar, particularly for those who guided their activities by the phases of the moon, the almanacs contained little of value.[7] Nevertheless, for many they represented the sole printed source of information employed in farm operations.

The farmer seeking more detailed or authoritative information on an agricultural problem had a choice of about fifty books on agricultural subjects published in the United States, together with a variety of English works. A few of them were encyclopedic surveys; others were monographic studies of such subjects as Merinos, hemp, and Hessian fly. Most, particularly the encyclopedic guides, were merely reviews of the well-known folklore and hence offered little, if anything, that was new to an experienced farmer. Although some reported on experiments or presented observations on American conditions, few were as scientific in their point of view as Humphry Davy's *Elements of Agricultural Chemistry,* which was published for American readers in 1815.

After 1820, American writing on agricultural subjects became increasingly voluminous. In the next fifty years, at least four hundred books dealing with American agricultural problems were published.[8] Among the most important authors were Jesse Buel, Thomas Fessenden, Edmund Ruffin, Henry Colman, Solon Robinson, John Pitkin, Saul Dean, Henry Randall, the Allen brothers, Samuel W. Cole, and J. B. Miner. The publication in 1841 of the American edition of Justus Liebig's *Chemistry in Its Application to Agriculture and Physiology* was noteworthy for the interest it aroused and the influence it exerted. The publication in the same decade of Henry Colman's thick volumes describing European agriculture marked a high point in works of that type.[9] Among the growing

---

[7] For an analysis of the *Farmer's Almanac,* one of the more popular almanacs, see George Lyman Kittredge, *The Old Farmer and His Almanac* (Boston, 1904).

[8] U. S. Patent Office, *Report* (1861), pp. 596-607.

[9] Henry Colman, *European Agriculture and Rural Economy from Personal Observation* (Boston, 1844), 2 vols.; *Agriculture and Rural Economy in France, Belgium, Holland, and Switzerland* (New York, 1851); and *European Life and Manners in Familiar Letters to Friends* (Boston, 1849), 2 vols. See Clarence H. Danhof, "Ameri-

number of guidebooks offered as works of reference for the average farmer, Solon Robinson's *Facts for Farmers,* published in 1865, deserves mention. The product of a keen and observant mind, it bore few traces of the English influence characteristic of the other books of this type.

The establishment in New York in 1847 of the publishing firm of C. M. Saxton & Co., devoted exclusively to agricultural subjects, was an event of considerable significance.[10] Although there had previously been no lack of publication opportunities—Harper & Brothers, for example, published numerous agricultural works— C. M. Saxton carried on aggressive advertising of an extensive list of agricultural titles, including many original works as well as reprints of older American and English authors. The success of the firm is evidence of the increasing attention that a large number of farmers were giving to acquiring the best available information on matters affecting their operations. The *Valley Farmer* in 1856 paid C. M. Saxton & Co. the compliment of calling them the "most enterprising Agricultural book Publishers in the world," who were "yearly doing more for the cause of agriculture than any other men or class of men in the country."[11]

AGRICULTURAL PERIODICALS

The major vehicle by which agricultural information was circulated and expanded during the half-century from 1820 to 1870 was not by books but by the agricultural periodical press.[12] In 1810 *The*

---

can Evaluations of European Agriculture," *Journal of Economic History,* Supplement, IX (1949), 66-68.

[10] *American Agriculturist,* VI (1847), 72; XXV (1866), 200; *Working Farmer,* XII (1860), 192.

[11] *Valley Farmer,* VIII (1856), 34. The occasion for the tribute was the announcement that C. M. Saxton & Co. was opening a "Farmer's Reading Room" in its New York offices, where "all the agricultural periodicals published in Europe and America can be found upon their tables." Such reading rooms were maintained by the leading agricultural periodicals and by some agricultural supply firms.

[12] An excellent source of information on agricultural periodicals is Albert L. Demaree, *The American Agricultural Press, 1819-1860* (Albany, N. Y., 1941). This volume is also valuable for its biographical sketches of the editors of some of the more important journals. See also George F. Lemmer and Norman J. Lemmer, *Colman and Colman's Rural World: A Study in Agricultural Leadership* (University of Missouri Press, 1953) ; George F. Lemmer, "Early Agricultural Editors and Their Farm Philosophies," *Agricultural History,* XXXI (1957), 3-22. See also Stephen Conrad Stuntz, *List of the Agricultural Periodicals of the United States and Canada Published during the Century July, 1810, to July, 1910,* U. S. Department of Agriculture, Misc. Pub. No. 398 (1941).

Agricultural Museum appeared for a short time laying claim to the title of first American agricultural magazine.[13] With the appearance in 1819 of the *Plough Boy* in Albany and the *American Farmer* in Baltimore, an agricultural press was firmly established. The *Plough Boy* was shortlived, expiring in 1823. Under the able leadership of John Stuart Skinner, the *American Farmer* was much longer-lived and far more valuable in its editorial content.[14] During the 1820's it was the most important single source of agricultural information available.

Over the next half-century there was a surfeit rather than a scarcity of publication efforts. Scores of weekly, monthly, and quarterly publications appeared to seek public support. From the 1830's there were usually at least thirty and at times upwards of fifty periodicals in circulation at any given moment. Of this large number, only a small group succeeded in acquiring a sufficient number of paying subscribers to assure their continuance over a significant period of time.

The Readers. The audience reached by the agricultural journals, which was very small in the 1820's, grew rapidly. Jesse Buel estimated, perhaps optimistically, that the thirty journals in existence in 1838 reached 100,000 readers among the 500,000 farm families in the country.[15] By 1860 national circulation had risen to an estimated 350,000, and it continued to increase during the Civil War decade.[16] The largest number of readers was in the East, where the

13 See Claribel R. Barnett, "*The Agricultural Museum;* an Early American Periodical," *Agricultural History,* II (1928), 99-102.

14 See Demaree, *The American Agricultural Press,* Ch. II; Harold T. Pinkett, "*The American Farmer,* A Pioneer Agricultural Journal, 1819-1834," *Agricultural History,* XXIV (1950), 146-151.

15 *Cultivator,* V (1838-1839), 29; VI (1839-1840), 67; IX (1839), 130. The *Cultivator* achieved a circulation of 15,000 in its first year, and in 1839 it was credited with 20,000, while the *Genesee Farmer* claimed 10,000. *Cultivator,* I (1834), 67; *Genesee Farmer,* VIII (1838), 233; *Farmer's Monthly Visitor,* I (1839), 7.

16 Only scattered data are available on circulation, and at best they are rough estimates. The *Farmer's Monthly Visitor* in 1846 had 2,400, half the number it had two years earlier. The *New England Farmer* claimed 16,000 in 1854. Subscribers to the *Northern Farmer* ranged from 4,000 to 8,000, though it claimed 16,000 in 1854. *The Homestead* achieved a circulation of 3,000 copies in 1855, its first year. The *Prairie Farmer* in 1855, its sixteenth year, had 8,900. The *Iowa Farmer* had 1,000 subscribers in 1855 at the end of its second year and 2,000 its third year. The *Ohio Cultivator* claimed 10,000 in the late forties; 12,000 in 1859. The *Indiana Farmer* reported in 1853, its third year, that it was increasing its printing from 3,000 to 5,000. The *Maine Farmer* had 200 its first year (1833) and 2,200 in 1845. The *Working Farmer* claimed 30,000 subscribers in 1861. *Farmer's Monthly Visitor,* VIII (1846), 184: *New*

greatest number of journals was also published. New York, Albany, and Boston were the major publication centers. Such journals as the *Cultivator, Country Gentleman,* and *American Agriculturist,* and to a lesser degree the *Genesee Farmer* and *Rural New Yorker,* had subcribers throughout the country as well.[17] In New England in the 1850's the three agricultural periodicals published in Boston had 35,000 subscribers, while the numerous other journals published in the area may have accounted for a similar number.[18] At about the same time in Michigan, where there were some 34,000 farmers, the editor of the *Michigan Farmer* estimated that there were probably "about eight thousand subscribers to agricultural papers in the state; viz., six thousand to the *Michigan Farmer,* say one thousand to the *Genesee Farmer,* five hundred to the *Albany Cultivator,* and five hundred to all others."[19] This audience, though only a fraction of the nation's farmers, was nevertheless by the 1840's the largest farm readership in the world. Nowhere else did there exist such an outpouring of printed matter dealing with agricultural affairs. Nor could any other city boast such a concentration of agricultural publishing as existed in New York City.[20]

Prior to the establishment of the agricultural periodicals, news-

England Farmer, II (1853), 130; I (1852), 65; *Northern Farmer,* II (1854), 427; IV (1857), 97; *Homestead,* I (1855), 385; *Prairie Farmer,* XV (1855), 380; *Iowa Farmer,* III (1856), 162; *Ohio Cultivator,* II (1846), 9; XV (1859), 112; *Indiana Farmer,* II (1853), 373; *Maine Farmer,* VIII (Jan. 11, 1840), 1; XIII (Dec. 25, 1845), 205; *Working Farmer,* XIII (1861), 141.

[17] Largest circulation was that of the *American Agriculturist,* which claimed 80,000 in 1859, 100,000 in 1864, and 150,000 in 1867. *American Agriculturist,* XVIII (1859), 349; XXIII (1864), 334; XXVIII (1868), 440; U. S. Commissioner of Agriculture, *Report* (1867), p. 405.

[18] In the fifties the *New England Farmer* was credited with 4,000 subscribers; the *Ploughman* with 10,000, and the Boston *Cultivator* with 21,000. *The Journal of Horticulture* had 1,000. *Cultivator,* Jan. 19, 1850; April 6, 1850. Cf. *New England Farmer,* V (1853), 51. In 1839, the Boston *Cultivator* had 3,000 to 4,000 subscribers. *Cultivator,* Oct. 12, 1839.

[19] *Michigan Farmer,* XI (1853), 49. The editor noted that five years earlier the journal had 1,000 subscribers.

[20] *Wisconsin Farmer,* VIII (1856), 370. In 1859 the *Genesee Farmer* asserted, "English farmers as a class do not read as much as American farmers. The aggregate circulation of all the English agricultural papers is not greater than that of the *Genesee Farmer* alone." And the *Rural Register,* commenting on English agricultural literature, noted there were "no agricultural journals in that country except such as teach the higher branches of science, and even those are few in number. They have nothing in England like the *Rural Register, The Country Gentleman, The Maine Farmer,* the *Southern Field and Fireside,* the *Rural New Yorker,* and that host of weekly, semi-monthly, and monthly journals which disseminate knowledge over our country." *Genesee Farmer,* XX (1859), 74; *Rural Register,* II (1860), 49; see also U. S. Patent Office, *Report* (1852), p. 16.

papers frequently carried important information on agricultural matters.[21] Although the editors of the agricultural periodicals did not altogether approve,[22] numerous newspapers in the late 1840's gave increased attention to farming matters, frequently by presenting an agricultural column. Few of these columns offered original material. Many of them borrowed generously from the periodicals, though items of local interest were common, such as unusual crops, plant specimens, and animals, novel implements and machinery, or the proceedings of local agricultural societies and fairs. There were a few important exceptions. In the sixties the *New York Tribune*, with Solon Robinson as its agricultural editor, and the *New York Times*, under Luther Tucker, published considerable original material, which was freely borrowed by the periodicals. Also of significance were the agricultural columns carried by such newspapers as the *Germantown* (Pennsylvania) *Telegraph*, the *Louisville Journal*, and the *Chicago Republican*. In addition, many newspapers devoted space to the prices prevailing in local markets for agricultural products, and these reports were a principal source of information on market conditions.

Functions of the Journals. The agricultural journals were the clearing house of agricultural facts, opinions, and problems. The editors served as diligent observers of the current scene and constituted the most competent group of critics and appraisers of the industry. It was to them that operating farmers looked for information and evaluations of new plants, animals, and implements and for suggestions on management problems. The most influential editors traveled widely, reporting on the superior farms visited, on the fairs attended, and on the proceedings and discussions at meetings of agricultural societies and farmers' clubs. They kept the farmer in touch with developments abroad by excerpting from European journals

[21] Demaree, *American Agricultural Press*, p. 11; Richard Bardolph, *Agricultural Literature and the Early Illinois Farmer*, Illinois Studies in Social Science, XXIX (University of Illinois Press, 1948), pp. 46-92; Carl R. Woodward, *The Development of Agriculture in New Jersey, 1640-1880* (Rutgers University Press, 1927), p. 80.

[22] "It has of late become the fashion for daily papers to have agricultural columns, and for these they have 'agricultural editors.' These are a variable lot; some of them holding their places for the sake of the perquisites, and eke out their scanty pay by announcing themselves as purchasing agents. Others are well-meaning men, who can write as well on one subject as another, and then again, we find one who knows just what he is talking about." *American Agriculturist*, XXVII (1868), 211.

and book reviews, as well as by printing the observations of travelers. Economic matters received far less attention than did problems of techniques, although prices current in one or more markets generally appeared in their pages,[23] as did occasional articles on market conditions with regard to Europe, particularly after 1840.

The contents of the agricultural periodicals were furnished by the editor and voluntary, unpaid correspondents, augmented by transcriptions of speeches at agricultural fairs and excerpts from other published material. Some of the more important journals developed departments handled by special writers. In the 1850's a few achieved enough financial support to maintain substantial staffs. Outstanding in this respect was the *American Agriculturist,* which for many years employed Solon Robinson as a roving correspondent and a general promoter of all things agricultural, including the magazine.[24] By the 1860's the voluntary correspondent had been mostly displaced on that journal and on others, such as the *Country Gentleman.* Increasingly the contents of these magazines were prepared by staff writers, who also conducted question departments and handled what was sometimes a voluminous correspondence.[25] Although some journals were initiated by agricultural organizations and others enjoyed their support, no journal was operated solely from altruistic motives.[26] The periodicals were expected to pay their way and to return editor and publisher an adequate income.

[23] The *Genesee Farmer* in the late fifties carried the prices prevailing for the major agricultural staples in New York, Rochester, Philadelphia, Chicago, Buffalo, Toronto, London, Liverpool, and the Brighton cattle market.

[24] Robinson was a prolific author until his death in 1880. His writings for the period 1845-1851 have been edited by Herbert A. Kellar, *Solon Robinson, Pioneer and Agriculturist,* Indiana Historical Collections, XXI-XXII (Indiana Historical Bureau, 1936), 2 vols.

[25] In 1863 the *American Agriculturist* reported a correspondence totaling 75,000 to 100,000 letters a year. *American Agriculturist,* XXII (1863), 22.

[26] For example, the *Cultivator* was initiated by the New York State Agricultural Society, under the editorship of Jesse Buel, who later purchased it. The *New York Farmer* was inaugurated by the New York Horticultural Society; the *Union Agriculturist* was founded by the Union Agricultural Society of Chicago; and a close relationship existed between the *Farmer's Cabinet* and the Philadelphia Agricultural Society. The Rhode Island Society for the Encouragement of Domestic Industry regularly made partial payments on subscriptions to the *New England Farmer,* which permitted its members to obtain the journal at very low rates. It was common practice to use subscriptions to the journals as premiums at fairs. At Keene, New Hampshire, an association of farmers took the *Cheshire Farmer* under their patronage, although such support did not save the paper from early oblivion. *Farmer's Monthly Visitor,* I (1839), p. 7.

STATE AND LOCAL AGRICULTURAL ORGANIZATIONS

Farmers who were conscious of problems that could not be over-come unaided characteristically sought assistance through agricultural organizations or through government. Agricultural societies served as a major channel for improving agricultural technology as well as diffusing knowledge. State governments were early induced to support agricultural societies and to give financial aid to a variety of specific projects. Individual officials of the federal government used their positions to aid agriculture, a practice that led to more formalized assistance in the 1840's. The efforts of aggressive farmers to expand the services available to them culminated in the sixties in the establishment of the Department of Agriculture. During the same period the new agricultural colleges produced a group of professional agriculturists, whose needs for scientific information led to the formation of true experiment stations.

Agricultural organizations did not attain widespread importance until the 1840's. Before that time, however, two general types of organization had come into existence. Before 1800, small groups of men in Philadelphia, New York, and a few other places formed societies for the purpose of discussing agricultural experiments.[27] These earliest societies included among their membership not only outstanding farmers but also men noted for accomplishments in other activities, who held strong interests in agriculture—as did almost everyone in an agrarian society—either for personal reasons, in the name of science, or out of regard for the national welfare. These organizations chiefly attracted the wealthy. Their activities were confined to meetings at which papers were read.

A different type of organization appeared early in the nineteenth century when Elkanah Watson, wool manufacturer and farmer, successfully promoted a series of livestock shows in western Massachusetts.[28] His original purpose, to stimulate interest in superior

[27] The Philadelphia Society for Promoting Agriculture, 1785; the Kennebec, Maine, Agricultural Society, 1787; the New York Society for the Promotion of Agriculture, Arts and Manufactures, 1791; the Massachusetts Society for Promoting Agriculture, 1792; and the Western Society of Middlesex Husbandmen, Middlesex County, Massachusetts, 1794. Alfred Charles True, *History of Agricultural Education, 1785-1925*, U. S. Department of Agriculture, Misc. Pub. No. 36, pp. 7-10; U. S. Patent Office, *Report* (1859), p. 139.

[28] Elkanah Watson, *History of Agricultural Societies on the Modern Berkshire System* (Albany, 1820); Wayne Caldwell Neely, *The Agricultural Fair* (Columbia University Press, 1935), pp. 51-71.

animals, broadened into a concern for the general improvement of agriculture. As a result of Watson's zeal, particularly his success in persuading state legislators to make funds available, hundreds of societies came into existence throughout New York, Pennsylvania, and New England. Their chief function was the promotion of animal fairs, which featured competitive exhibits of animals and homestead products.

During the twenties the societies established under Watson's leadership lost both public interest and the financial support of state legislatures. While the large majority of local societies disappeared, the movement survived.[29] Local agricultural societies were also organized early in the settlement of the West—in Ohio in 1828, Michigan in 1830, and Iowa by 1848.[30] These organizations, in contrast with Watson's, were firmly rooted in the desire of farmers to secure the benefits of group consideration for their problems and to stimulate competitive exhibitions.

State financial support for agricultural societies was viewed as essential by many of their promoters. State aid had typically been made available to the societies through state-wide agricultural organizations, but only two of them—the Massachusetts Society for Promoting Agriculture and the Rhode Island Society for the Encouragement of Domestic Industry—had survived the decline of Watson's movement. As a result of pressure brought upon legislatures, Maine in 1832 resumed a program of state aid to agricultural societies, and Ohio adopted such a program in 1833.[31] In New York the campaign for resumption of state aid was carried on with particular vigor under the leadership of Jesse Buel. Although the legislature responded to petitions for aid with indictments of farm management, Buel's work was crowned with success in 1841 when a substantial appropriation was granted and the State Agricultural Society reorganized. Others followed, so that by 1860 every northern state

[29] About forty county and local societies that had been organized before 1841 were active in 1867. Neely, *Agricultural Fair,* p. 87. The New York Farmers Club, organized in 1843 as part of the American Institute of the City of New York, claimed in 1859 to be the oldest agricultural association. *American Agriculturist,* I (1842), 129-131; American Institute, *Reports* (1849), p. 8; (1859), p. 137.

[30] U. S. Patent Office, *Report* (1858), pp. 92 ff; U. S. Commissioner of Agriculture, *Report* (1875), p. 450; Illinois Agricultural Society, *Transactions* (1869-1870), p. 207.

[31] William Bacon, "History of the Agricultural Association of New York from 1791 to 1862," in New York Agricultural Society, *Transactions,* XXIII (1862), 143-168.

excepting Vermont, New Hampshire, New Jersey, Maryland, and Delaware possessed a state-wide organization. State societies were usually voluntary membership organizations; the state boards differed in that they were composed of representatives delegated to serve by the county societies. In either case, the chief function of these organizations was to disburse legislative funds to the local societies and to sponsor a state-wide fair.

The opportunity to secure a state grant stimulated the growth of county and local agricultural societies, particularly in the 1850's and even in the next decade despite the disruptive influence of the war.[32] The societies were most numerous relative to population in the Middle West, particularly in Ohio, though they were also strong in Massachusetts and New York. In no state did memberships exceed a small percentage of the farmers of the area.

The objective of the leaders and active members of these societies was the improvement of agricultural techniques. Among the local societies the exchange of information and experiences at meetings was sometimes the most important function.[33] In the case of the state societies the task of gathering and disseminating information was primarily discharged through the publication of the proceedings of the county societies, to which were usually added reports of the secretary as well as area surveys and essays on special topics.

The most characteristic function of all the societies was, however, the sponsorship of a fair, usually held annually. The central feature of the fair was the premium list indicating the exhibits for which prizes would be awarded and their amounts.[34] The list of competitive classes, relatively short in the earlier years, increased so that the larger state fairs were in the fifties offering premiums in hundreds of classes. Animals and crops were the most important categories, but the list also included implements, items of domestic

[32] Neely, *Agricultural Fair,* pp. 85-87; U. S. Commissioner of Agriculture, *Report* (1867), pp. 371-403.

[33] See descriptions of the societies' activities in U. S. Patent Office, *Report* (1858), pp. 122 ff; also in the state reports, such as the Ohio Board of Agriculture, *Report* (1861), pp. 99 ff.

[34] Between 1841 and 1850 the New York State Agricultural Society distributed in premiums "upwards of $40,000," as well as medals, copies of the *Transactions,* and other printed matter. United States Agricultural Society, *Journal,* I (1853), 31. For a description of these fairs, see Neely, *Agricultural Fair,* pp. 155-264.

manufacture, skills such as plowing, and essays on specified subjects, such as farm management, or on experiments that had been made.

Many of the exhibitions and trials conducted by the local fairs, and even some of those held by the state organizations, were managed in haphazard fashion. Awards were sometimes made by acclamation. More often, awards were made as a result of casual inspection by committees whose members had no particular qualifications, who were sometimes charged with prejudice, and who were occasionally suspected of unethical relations with exhibitors. As a result, the usefulness of such affairs suffered. Some manufacturers of agricultural implements adopted the policies of refusing to submit their products for competitive exhibition.[35]

These organizations also engaged in numerous other activities. The Massachusetts Society for Promoting Agriculture imported and bred fine British cattle in 1819 and continued the program for many years. The state societies were active promoters of geological surveys. The New York society administered the legislative-sponsored survey of the state's agricultural resources. The Massachusetts Society in the 1850's offered a prize of $10,000 for a "sure remedy for the potato rot." A few societies retained the services of an agricultural chemist, chiefly for the purpose of preparing analyses of commercial fertilizers. The New York State society employed the first agricultural entomologist, and in 1863 it sent a commissioner to the western states to gather information on the popular sorghum culture, to determine the desirability of its introduction in New York.[36] Finally, it was through the local agricultural societies that the federal Patent Office was able to do its most effective work, both in distributing its seeds and publications as well as in gathering information.

Numerous special interest groups appeared, although their memberships were usually small and they tended to be short-lived. Most numerous were those interested in tree fruits, their cultivation and

---

[35] See J. S. Wright's protest in *Farmer's Companion*, III (1853), 94-95. For a justification, see *Prairie Farmer*, XIV (1854), 261; *Rural New Yorker*, XII (1861), 342. For a criticism of the management of fairs, see *Rural New Yorker*, XI (1860), 269, 341; Neely, *Agricultural Fair*, pp. 170-172.

[36] New York State Agricultural Society, *Transactions* (1866), p. 156.

diseases, and the chaos among named varieties. Among others, wool growers formed many organizations in the earlier part of the period and again in the 1850's.[37] Cheese manufacturers had a number of organizations in the East and held a cheese manufacturers' convention in 1864.[38] There were organizations to promote silk-culture, while the hen fever and the sorghum boom likewise produced organizations and conventions. Almost all of the many booms in one or another commodity in the period 1820-1870 resulted in organizations intended to serve the special interests involved.[39]

While the membership of the state organizations was made up of outstanding farmers in each area, leadership came from a much smaller group, frequently including men whose interests ranged far beyond the operation of a farm. The tasks of carrying out the objectives of the organization were in most cases delegated to a salaried official, usually designated as the secretary. After the 1840's, the small group of secretaries developed great influence, some of them being among the outstanding agriculturists of their time.

The society and board secretaries together with the editors of the agricultural journals were vigorous specialists in the advancement of rationalized agricultural techniques. They were in constant search for answers to problems plaguing farmers and were free with advice to any farmer who cared to ask. They thus constituted a professionalized group in the service of farmers. They were not themselves farmers, though a few of them owned farms to which they gave general managerial direction. They came to their work from a variety of nonagricultural backgrounds: training in law, medicine, and the ministry were common, and a few had backgrounds in chemistry and engineering. A number of editors came to journalism after apprenticeships in printing. As a group, they were characterized by educational experience far above that which the typical farmer had enjoyed. To this they added a deep concern with the promotion of the interests of farmers. There were few aggressive farmers who were not directly indebted to one or more of these men, and all felt their influence.

[37] For example, the Wool Grower's Association of Western New York. New York State Agricultural Society, *Transactions* (1855), p. 675; *Wool Grower,* IX (1865), 165; *Cultivator,* XII (1864), 292.

[38] *Cultivator,* XII (1864), 48.

[39] For example, the Silk Convention (1843), the New England Society for the Improvement of Domestic Poultry (1850), and the various state sorghum associations.

THE FEDERAL GOVERNMENT

To men intent upon expanding the fund of agricultural information, enlistment of the resources of the federal government offered attractive possibilities. In the government's consular offices and Navy, it possessed numerous overseas contacts as well as transportation facilities, which might be utilized to procure whatever materials in foreign countries might improve American agriculture. In a day of expensive postal communications, the franking privilege enjoyed by government officials was likewise extremely important. Moreover, if the battle to secure public expenditures for the advancement of agriculture through experimentation and education could not be won at the state level, the resources of Congress were even greater. Beginning with George Washington, numerous Presidents and members of Congress had asserted the general principle that the government should promote the welfare of its largest, most important, and most fundamental economic group. President Washington in his last message had recommended "the establishment of boards composed of proper characters charged with collecting and diffusing information, and enabled by premiums and small pecuniary aids to encourage and assist a spirit of discovery and improvement."[40] The proposal was debated until Jefferson's opposition, based upon a narrow view of federal powers, put a temporary end to it. A similar proposal by Elkanah Watson found President Madison likewise opposed on constitutional grounds.[41]

Nevertheless, the facilities of the consular offices and the Navy were used informally by a number of individuals and groups before 1820. Elkanah Watson in 1817 circularized most of the American consuls in Europe, requesting samples of seeds of important varieties of local plant materials. He received outstanding cooperation from an American consul in Spain; as a consequence, Watson introduced two strains of wheat which within a few years became standard in important sections of the northern wheat-growing areas.[42] Others followed a similar procedure, with officials of the American

[40] Cited by W. D. Bishop, "Historical Sketch of the United States Agricultural Society," in U. S. Patent Office, *Report* (1859), pp. 22-30.

[41] A. C. True, *History of Agricultural Experimentation and Research in the United States,* U. S. Department of Agriculture, Misc. Pub. No. 251 (1937).

[42] Hugh M. Flick, "Elkanah Watson's Activities in Behalf of Agriculture," *Agricultural History,* XXI (1947), 197.

Navy rendering important services.[43] In addition, government officials abroad occasionally returned to the United States with choice plants and animals.[44]

Executive approval and stimulus to this process were given in 1819 when Secretary of the Treasury William H. Crawford instructed all consuls in a circular letter to procure useful seeds and plants to be distributed in the United States by the collectors of the ports. Similar instructions were issued again in 1827.[45] Little is known of the results of these orders but they seem to have made little impact.

When Henry L. Ellsworth became Commissioner of Patents in 1836, he brought to his office the view that it should be a clearing house of information, not only for industry but also for all phases of agriculture. In Ellsworth's judgment, the efforts to utilize the consular system to secure new plant materials had failed because of the absence of an effective center in the United States to receive and distribute the materials.[46] Ellsworth proposed that the Patent Office become the distribution center, and in 1837 he undertook this work on his own initiative, without congressional authorization.[47] His action aroused congressional criticism, but in 1839 Congress appropriated $1,000 for the collection of information on agriculture and the distribution of seeds and plants.[48] This was the first federal appropriation made specifically in aid of agriculture.[49] Beginning in 1842 annual appropriations were made, these becoming substantial in the fifties. Seed distribution was considerably expanded in

[43] *American Farmer,* IV (1822), 313. See Nelson Klose, *America's Crop Heritage* (Iowa State College Press, 1950), p. 27.

[44] For example, William Jarvis, consul at Lisbon, brought in several thousand Spanish Merinos and established them on a large sheep run in Vermont. *Genesee Farmer,* XVIII (1848), 266.

[45] Klose, *America's Crop Heritage,* p. 26; True, *Agricultural Experimentation,* p. 22; Knowles A. Ryerson, "History and Significance of the Foreign Plant Introduction Work of the United States Department of Agriculture," *Agricultural History,* VII (1933), 113.

[46] U. S. Patent Office, *Report* (1838), p. 57.

[47] Various agricultural groups and journal editors had strongly urged that the surplus revenue embarrassing the federal government be used to promote agricultural interests, such as supporting pattern farms, agricultural schools, and state and county societies. Efforts were made to secure the dedication of the Smithsonian fund to similar purposes. *Farmer and Gardener,* III (1837), 289-290, 296-297.

[48] Ellsworth had suggested the appropriation in 1837 and campaigned actively for it. Zadock Pratt is given credit for passage of the 1838 appropriation. *Genesee Farmer,* X (1849), 14.

[49] True, *Agricultural Experimentation,* p. 25.

volume and variety in the succeeding years.[50] As consular collecting activities proved inadequate, heavy reliance came to be placed upon the purchase of seed from commercial seed firms in Europe.[51] In addition, collectors were sent throughout the world. A steady flow of materials moved through the Patent Office to individuals throughout the United States. By the mid-fifties, the resources of the agricultural division of the Patent Office were absorbed by seed distribution activities, which was hardly justified in terms of the successful introduction of new varieties.[52] The greatest impression was undoubtedly made by several varieties of African and Asiatic sorghums, which enjoyed considerable popularity in the West.

Ellsworth envisaged a second function for his office—the collection and dissemination of agricultural information. He shared the thought of his time that substantial progress could be achieved through an exchange of experiences of practicing farmers. Under Ellsworth and his successors the annual reports of the Patent Office became vehicles for dissemination of a vast body of agricultural information. The reports were widely circulated through free distribution by members of Congress as well as through other channels. Fifteen thousand copies of the 1843 report were printed. Circulation reached 270,000 for the 1855 and 1856 reports, and it was maintained at from 200,000 to 275,000 copies up to 1869.[53]

In content, these volumes were essentially similar to the agricultural periodicals, though the articles tended to be longer, and the material covered by correspondents was more complete and systematic. The reports also evidenced much the same evolution in content that characterized the better periodicals. Until the late 1850's, reliance was placed on contributions of voluntary correspondents and on replies received to questionnaires that had been extensively circulated.[54] Reprints of materials published elsewhere filled their

---

[50] The number of packages of seed distributed were: 30,000 in 1840, 60,000 in 1847, 474,000 in 1861, and 312,000 in 1869. True, *Agricultural Experimentation*, pp. 25, 27, 34; U. S. Department of Agriculture, *Report* (1869), p. 17.

[51] U. S. Patent Office, *Report* (1855), 111.

[52] Protests against the demands upon the Patent Office for seeds of well-known plants appear in its reports in the 1850's. Commissioner William D. Bishop in 1859 recommended abandonment of the distribution of seeds of domestic growth, but Congress expanded the practice instead. U. S. Patent Office, *Report* (1855), p. VI; (1859), p. V.

[53] U. S. Patent Office, *Report* (1857), p. 25; U. S. Commissioner of Agriculture, *Report* (1875), p. 17.

[54] In 1859 the Advisory Board of Agriculture to the Patent Office approved a revised questionnaire including 1,710 questions.

pages. Articles by staff members or by professional experts retained for specific topics,[55] at first relatively few, became increasingly important, particularly after 1856 when Congress broadened the function of the Patent Office to include "the collection of agricultural statistics, investigations for promoting agriculture and rural economy, and the procurement and distribution of cuttings and seeds." The appropriation for carrying out these functions was $75,000, of which about half was for seeds and cuttings.[56] In 1860 the staff of the Agricultural Division of the Patent Office consisted of the superintendent, four clerks, a curator, and assistants.[57] In 1862, years of agitation came to fruition when Congress established the Department of Agriculture, charged with the duties of acquiring and diffusing "among the people of the United States useful information on subjects connected with agriculture in the most general and comprehensive sense of that word, and to procure, propagate and distribute among the people new and valuable seeds and plants." The first Commissioner was Isaac Newton, who had also been superintendent of the former Agricultural Division of the Patent Office. Under his direction the federal government slowly expanded the range of its scientific investigations in agriculture. In 1862 a chemist was added to the staff; in 1863 an entomologist and a statistician were added, and a cooperative agreement on meteorology was reached with the Smithsonian Institution. In 1869 a botanist was added, as well as a veterinarian to work on animal diseases.[58] In 1868 the Department announced that from thenceforth its reports would include only "the reports of the Commissioner and of division officers and special agents of the Department."[59] By 1870 the principle of utilizing

[55] In 1848 the U. S. Patent Office employed Lewis C. Beck of Rutgers College to make a chemical analysis of wheat and wheat flour. True, *Agricultural Experimentation*, p. 31.

[56] U. S. Patent Office, *Report* (1856), p. 11.

[57] True, *Agricultural Experimentation*, p. 33.

[58] True, *Agricultural Experimentation*, pp. 43ff. The appropriation in 1869 was $177,000. U. S. Commissioner of Agriculture, *Report* (1869), p. 18.

[59] J. R. Dodge, editor of the 1868 *Report*, wrote: "The abandonment of the long-continued usage of admitting voluminous and desultory essays into the annual report of the Department which was contemplated and in part accomplished in the volume for 1867, is made complete in the present issue. It was difficult to recognize the propriety of competing with private publishers in the presentation of exhaustive treatises upon special topics, written by private individuals, and in no sense official, however valuable or complete the information presented.

"While the domain of book-making and newspaper enterprise was invaded, the matter was not always of the kind contemplated by the organic act requiring reports upon agricultural progress and investigation. The essay was the work of a single

federal funds to support a staff of scientists working on agricultural problems had been firmly established.

THE NEW APPROACH

When John Lorain wrote in 1825 of the need "for harmonizing agriculture with nature," he was pointing dimly, as had others, to the need for acquiring scientific information upon which could be based a rational technology, to be substituted for the current diverse, empirical practices.[60] During the next two generations a relatively small group of men began to assume the functions of a profession serving agriculture in the exchange of experiences and knowledge.[61] The editors of the agricultural periodicals; the commissioners, secretaries, and occasional scientists who served the agricultural societies; and the small staff of the Agricultural Division of the Patent Office principally comprised this group. In addition, a few scattered individuals devoted private resources to experimentation and rationalized observation. Throughout this period reliance was placed upon the work of individuals, on the theory that through a sharing of experiences, the best practices could be determined and agricultural technology advanced. From an early date men were aware that such a program was inadequate, with the result that pattern farms, on which experiments could be carried out, were widely and persistently, if unsuccessfully, advocated.

By the 1850's the fund of common experience had been exhausted, and the bankruptcy of the program was becoming increasingly clear. Thus, Daniel Lee could write in 1852: "Until it is decided either for

mind, covering a limited field of observation, and prepared with the aid of private resources only. It was not a statement of results of Department labor and investigation. It was not legitimately an official report." U. S. Commissioner of Agriculture, *Report* (1868), p. 190. See also Earle D. Ross, "The United States Department of Agriculture during the Commissionership," *Agricultural History*, XX (1946), 129-143.

[60] John Lorain urged the application of "mathematical precision" as necessary to improved husbandry. "We know," he wrote, "but little of the proper depth for planting and sowing the different seeds or of the space which should be allowed for different plants. There can be no doubt, however, that the proper depth and space exists in nature." Lorain, *Nature and Reason*, pp. 359-360.

[61] A few "consulting agriculturists" also appeared in the 1850's. This activity was inaugurated in 1852 by J. J. Mapes, editor of the *Working Farmer*, and was expanded by several of his students and associates, particularly George E. Waring and Henry C. Vail. A number of others were not associated with Mapes, such as R. T. Pell. Woodward, *Development of Agriculture*, pp. 132-149; *Genesee Farmer*, XVI (1855), 197.

or against a systematic effort to increase our professional knowledge, advancement in rural sciences, except by accident, is impracticable. Hence, in the fifty new volumes of agriculture yearly furnished by State and County agricultural societies, agricultural journals, Patent Office reports, horticultural reviews, and book publishers in cities and villages, one searches in vain for enough that is new to fill six hundred pages octavo. Important original researches are nowhere prosecuted, so that the discovery of new truths is neither respected nor made. Under such a state of things, how is it possible to enrich our rural literature by additions to our present stock of professional knowledge? We may all repeat what little we really know a million times each, and leave the sum total of knowledge just as we found it. Progress implies an advancement from things known to things unknown—an addition to the aggregate wisdom of the world. Of the true principles of tillage and husbandry the world is profoundly ignorant, and the evils resulting from this ignorance are increasing in this country faster than the population increases. We suggest not merely the manufacture of fewer works on agriculture, but the expenditure of more time and money to develop new and useful facts to be printed in these works for the instruction of their readers."[62] And a few years later James S. Gould, president of the New York State Agricultural Society, summarized the frustrations: "We have had theories of agriculture without end, propounded for our consideration; innumerable guesses have been hazarded upon every conceivable topic; inconclusive experiments which no man can number have been made, and yet to our shame be it spoken, there is scarcely a single question which has been mooted in American agriculture that can be said to be settled on the sure basis of reliable experiments."[63]

John Nicholson had advised in 1820, "there is no way for making improvements in farming, but by experiments. If the farmer is

[62] "American Agricultural Literature," U. S. Patent Office, *Report* (1852), p. 21. The statement was made to support Lee's argument for agricultural colleges, which, he asserted, were "really the only literary agricultural question before the public."

[63] New York State Agricultural Society, *Annual Report* (1866), p. 158; Horace Greeley had observed a few years earlier, "Every question of the science and practice of Agriculture, such as plowing, draining, drilling, quantity of seed per acre, time of harvesting, cutting hay, feeding, manuring, and so on through every labor of the farm to sowing the seed again, is in doubt and uncertainty, and on almost any of these various questions two parties could be arrayed nearly equal in numbers." Ohio State Board of Agriculture, *Report* (1860), p. 455.

informed of, or has conceived, a different and better method of culture or management in any branch of farming, he is to test the goodness of that method by experiments; and if these prove successful he may congratulate himself on having performed an act which is serviceable to this country and honourable to himself." He went on to make a suggestion that was by no means new, but which was to be repeated many times over in the next half-century: "Perhaps it would be well, if some institution were devised, and supported at the expense of the State, which would be so organized as would tend most effectually to produce a due degree of emulation among Farmers, by rewards and honorary distinctions conferred on those who, by their successful experimental efforts and improvements, should render themselves duly entitled to them. It might also be advisable to have two or three experimental farms, in different parts of the state, under the direction of suitable Superintendents, who should have the profits of the farms to themselves, and who should be excited to a degree of emulation, by a reward given yearly to that Superintendent, which should be found the best entitled to his superior culture, and by the success of his experiments."[64]

This mixture of objectives—the advancement of agricultural knowledge and the education of farmers under the stimulus of example and appeals to pride—was characteristic of the progressive thinking of the entire period. In face of the repeated refusals of state legislatures to establish the kind of pattern farms that Nicholson and others had in mind, the aggressive and experimentally minded turned to more formal avenues to accomplish their objectives. A number of private schools offering courses in agriculture had been established, some requiring manual labor on farms. The objective of providing institutions of higher education in agriculture was furthered by enlisting the resources of government. Michigan led the way with the establishment of a state university in 1837, specifying that agriculture was to be an integral part of the curriculum. Little was accomplished, however, and that little was not to the satisfaction of the farmers, with the result that in 1855 the state authorized a new college to be devoted to agriculture and to be independent of the university. New York had in 1853 provided for an agricultural college, Maryland acted similarly in 1856, and the following year the legislature of Pennsylvania appropriated a match-

[64] *Farmer's Assistant* (Lancaster, 1820), p. 92.

ing fund to establish a college of agriculture. The agitation for even greater efforts in agriculture instruction continued. Federal support came in 1862 with the passage of the Morrill Act, providing federal assistance to any state supporting an agricultural college.

For more than fifty years leading American farmers had sought to improve their operations through organized exchanges of information on experiences and experiments. The enterprising farmer was of necessity a book farmer. Although that means of exchanging information had accomplished much, by mid-century it had exhausted its effectiveness. The establishment of programs in agricultural education emphasized the limitations of existing knowledge. The need was for organized scientific research on a substantial scale, but this concept was novel and suspect. Beginning in 1847, Yale University provided the chemist John Pitkin Norton an opportunity to apply ideas on agricultural research acquired in Scotland. His successor, Samuel W. Johnson, carried on Norton's agitation for organized agricultural research centers, inspired in part by his observations of such institutions in Saxony.[65] The work of these and other professionals, as well as of farmers who shared the ideas of men like Nicholson, the demonstrated limitations of the state agricultural organizations in dealing with problems that required new knowledge, and the needs of the faculties of the new agricultural colleges to develop material for their courses—all provided support for new efforts to organize professional research activities. The critical role was played by the federal government in the establishment and development of the Department of Agriculture. The staff of the Department not only undertook a variety of research efforts but also served as a major influence in securing the acceptance of research as a proper function of the agricultural college. This new approach to the technological problems of farmers, however, evolved slowly and had no significant impact prior to 1870.

[65] H. C. Knoblauch, E. M. Law, and W. P. Meyer, *State Agricultural Experiment Stations: A History of Research Policy and Procedure,* U. S. Department of Agriculture, Misc. Pub. No. 904 (Washington, 1964), pp. 9-17.

CHAPTER FOUR

PREREQUISITES FOR FARMING

The possibility of entering farming as an occupation and the further hope of one day acquiring ownership of a farm was part of the thinking of the vast majority of young men throughout the period 1820-1870. In earlier years there had been few alternatives, since wage-employment or apprentice training in a nonfarm occupation was possible for only a few. Even during this half-century, when the range of choice expanded as nonagricultural opportunities increased substantially in number and attractiveness, agriculture continued to be a major occupation. Thousands of young men each year chose to embark on careers having as goal the ownership of a farm.

Although an agricultural enterprise was relatively easy to establish, important requirements had to be met, particularly if more than a minimum subsistence return was hoped for. To operate his own farm, a young man had to possess appropriate mechanical skills and managerial capacities. He also had to possess some capital and the credit that would command what he needed but did not own.

Employment opportunities in American agriculture were generally abundant, but the terms of such employment were rarely sufficiently attractive to induce long-continued work for wages. Except at harvest time, wages were low compared with other occupations. There was little prospect for significant increases in income as a result of acquiring experience, for over and above the possession of certain simple skills, the employing farmer was interested only in strength, endurance, and reliability. Moreover, agricultural labor was seasonal, and while there was usually a demand for all available wage-labor during its season of seven or eight months, employment opportunities were scarce during the winter. The relatively few farmers who hired help for the entire year limited such employment to a fraction of the labor they required during the season.[1]

If there was little to attract an ambitious young man into agriculture as a permanent wage-earner, farm operation, preferably as an owner, offered stronger attractions. Many individuals entered farming, of course, as the only occupation or form of enterprise with which they were familiar. The independence of farming in contrast with other occupations was no doubt a factor encouraging the decision to enter it. The abundance of opportunities to secure a farm was another important factor. Some men must have been generally persuaded that farming offered the possibility of an income comparing favorably with what might be obtained elsewhere. Some no doubt also gave thought to the possibilities of substantial long-term gains from increases in the value of the land.

ACQUIRING SKILLS

In a society such as that of the United States about 1820, no sharp line existed between urban and rural pursuits, and almost every man acquired some familiarity with farming operations. The sons of farmers were assigned to farm chores as soon as they were physically able to perform them, and they reached independence with a thorough knowledge of agriculture as conducted by their fathers. It was a common practice throughout this period for men, engaged primarily in trade or industry, to operate farms on which their sons, together with hired hands, supplied the labor. Similarly, farmers frequently employed boys other than their sons, perhaps children of town and village families, for short periods, and sometimes under longer apprentice-type arrangements. Men primarily engaged in nonagricultural wage work were drawn to farm labor at harvest time by the attractive wages offered.[2] While urban occu-

---

[1] The practice of employing by the season rather than the year seems to have increased over this period. In the 1850's there were protests that seasonal employment created serious problems, causing uncertainty as to the supply of labor for the employer while constituting an obstacle to saving and advancement for the employee. See Charles W. Dickerman, *How to Make the Farm Pay* (Philadelphia, 1869), pp. 679-681; New York State Agricultural Society, *Transactions* (1850), pp. 557-558; *Ohio Cultivator*, X (1854), 218-219.

[2] For example, loggers of New York's Alleghany County harvested wheat in the Genesee country. Neil A. McNall, *An Agricultural History of the Genesee Valley* (University of Pennsylvania Press, 1952), p. 112.

pations became increasingly important over the half-century, it remained true that close acquaintanceship with farming operations was a part of the early work experience of most young men.

The knowledge acquired, however, was limited to the heavier and simpler tasks. The increasing commercialization of agriculture called attention to the need for more careful analysis of resources and opportunities and particularly for employing the best techniques known. The development of an urban population from which individuals occasionally entered farming,[3] together with the flow of European immigrants desiring to operate farms but lacking familiarity with American methods, emphasized the fact that the knowledge necessary for profitable agriculture was not an unconscious cultural heritage but was rather the product of conscious experience and purposeful observation. After about 1840, editors of the agricultural journals habitually urged the importance of securing a sound foundation of practical experience before undertaking independent farming. Such training might best be obtained by working as a laborer under a superior farmer, the knowledge so acquired to be supplemented by reading in the available literature so as to become aware of alternative and possibly superior techniques and opportunities.[4]

SOURCES OF CAPITAL FUNDS

In order to embark upon his own enterprise, a farmer had to possess certain properties, or the means to secure them. Provisions for support and shelter for himself and his family during the period from seedtime to harvest were essential, as were the seed, tools, implements, vehicles, draft animals, and livestock for his operations. If he preferred to own rather than to rent the necessary land, substantial additional funds were necessary.

Acquiring Personal Capital. The necessary funds—in the form of real goods or in a liquid form—were sometimes obtained by inheritance or by gift. In most cases, however, such resources were obtained as savings from income. Although credit might be relied

[3] See Carter Goodrich and Sol Davison, "The Wage-Earner in the Westward Movement," *Political Science Quarterly*, L (1935), 161-185; LI (1936), 61-116.
[4] *Country Gentleman*, XIX (1862), 74.

upon to secure many things necessary in carrying out a farming plan, the ability to command credit depended upon the possession of at least some personal capital. Entry into farming thus rested upon the possession of a significant amount of appropriate personal property. A writer in 1861 urged, "it cannot be too strongly impressed in the minds of all young men that the starting point in their fortune is to lay up the first $500 or $1,000. Not only for the help that amount will be in gaining more money, but in firmly fixing in their minds the principles of industry, economy, and self-denial, which are to be the foundations of their future success."[5]

The most common method by which men acquired capital was by employment as a farm laborer, supplemented by off-season work in such occupations as land clearing, logging, teaming, or driving stock to market. Given employment throughout the year and rigid economy, the farm laborer could save a large proportion of his cash wages. He might continue at such labor until the sum accumulated was sufficiently large to permit operating a farm on shares, or until it constituted the minimum sum that a seller would accept as downpayment for a farm. Many who had accumulated adequate funds to purchase land or a small farm apparently continued to engage primarily in wage labor while developing their property. Others supplemented their income by such employment.[6]

Money wages were higher in urban occupations than in agricultural, even for common labor, and were much higher in skilled occupations. Higher costs of living and possibly higher consumption levels in urban living make it difficult to generalize about savings potentials. Undoubtedly men in urban occupations put money into farms, either through mortgages or by outright purchase, as a sound investment or as the first step in making farming their principal occupation. In a rapidly growing society, however, there were innumerable investment opportunities outside agriculture which in many cases were more tempting to those who possessed funds available for investment than the purchase of farms.

[5] *Country Gentleman,* XVIII (1861), 288.
[6] The large numbers of men who were classified by the federal censuses as "laborers" apparently included a substantial number who had progressed toward the status of farmers to the extent of owning some land, although still dependent chiefly upon wage-employment. Paul W. Gates, "Frontier Estate Builders and Farm Laborers" in Walker D. Wyman and Clifton B. Kroeber, eds., *The Frontier in Perspective* (University of Wisconsin Press, 1957), p. 452; Merle Curti, *The Making of an American Community* (Stanford University Press, 1959), pp. 149-156.

Since farm work offered training in the skills involved as well as an opportunity to accumulate funds, it served as the almost universal route to farm ownership. The wages paid for farm labor therefore require analysis from the point of view of the opportunities they provided to accumulate capital. Earnings from wage labor in agriculture varied not only over the year but also between regions and according to the terms of employment. The highest wages went to labor hired by the day during the short harvest period. Most labor was hired for the season, varying from eight to ten months, and was paid a higher rate per month than labor employed around the year. Hence, a full year of work yielded money earnings only five to ten percent higher than those obtained for a season's work. Rates varied also as to whether the terms of employment called for board and lodging, board only, or for the worker's "finding himself."[7]

Broadly generalized, in the 1820's the earnings of farm labor employed by the month for the season, with board and room, ranged from $7 to as much as $16 or $17 per month, and averaged about $9. Wages were somewhat higher in the thirties and forties, ranging from $8 to $15 and averaging about $11. In the fifties the average moved to about $13, rising in the next decade to about $20 in the East and somewhat less in the West.

Although farm labor was not highly paid, living expenses were usually small, needs were few, and opportunities for accumulating savings were substantial, particularly if farm employment could be supplemented by other types of work during the winter.[8] The farm laborer who worked by the month for a cash wage plus room and board received ample food of standard quality, adequate shelter, and a money income equal to two or three times the cost of sub-

[7] The available data on wages paid to farm labor is very unsatisfactory, consisting for the most part of casual and unrelated observations of commonly paid rates expressed sometimes as "averages," sometimes as ranges. An important exception is the series of Vermont wages computed from contemporary account books by T. M. Adams, *Prices Paid by Vermont Farmers for Goods and Services and Received by Them for Farm Products, 1790-1840; Wages of Vermont Farm Labor, 1780-1940*, Vermont Agricultural Experiment Station, Bulletin No. 507 (1944). For surveys of the available data, see Stanley Lebergott, *Manpower in Economic Growth* (McGraw-Hill, 1964), pp. 257-264; and his "Wage Trends, 1800-1900" in *Trends in the American Economy in the Nineteenth Century*, Studies in Income and Wealth, XXIV, National Bureau of Economic Research (Princeton University Press, 1960), pp. 449-498.

[8] Unemployment was, however, a factor of some significance. See Lebergott, *Manpower in Economic Growth*, p. 169.

sistence. Unmarried laborers could, if so motivated, save a large fraction of their money wages. Whereas married men were generally believed to be able to save less, the wife might occasionally be employed as a domestic servant or dairymaid, in which case the possible rate of savings was little less than the unmarried laborer's and perhaps even somewhat higher.

Contemporary accounts bear out these statements. We are told, for example, of a young man in New England who in the early fifties at twenty-one years of age began work at $125 per year, continuing for two more years at $150. "By stringent economy he spent only $125 over these three years. With his savings of $300 he then went to Michigan where he purchased 160 acres for $200."[9] In two other instances, young men beginning farm wage work at twenty-one were able to save $840 and $850, respectively, by age twenty-eight, when both bought farms.[10] Such figures are consistent with Horace Greeley's assertion, misleading though its implications were, that the price of an eighty-acre homestead could be saved "out of the proceeds of a year's faithful industry."[11]

Under very favorable wage conditions and continuous employment, as little as five years of careful saving and investment could produce a capital accumulation of $500. Under average conditions during the period from 1820 to 1850, about ten years were necessary. Thereafter, higher wages permitted a more rapid accumulation of funds at a rate of perhaps $500 per five to seven years, with opportunities rising somewhat in the decade of the sixties.[12]

Credit. There can be no doubt that most men entering farming had very inadequate resources for the operations they sought to undertake, and that their hopes of establishing a remunerative farm were dependent upon their ability to secure temporary use of the property of others. Agriculture, like all other sectors of the economy, generally rested upon the extensive use of credit. Credit was frequently a condition of a purchase—received by the farmer when he bought and extended by the farmer when he sold. It was almost universal for the farm family to secure its needs on credit from a

[9] *American Agriculturist*, XII (1854), 232.
[10] Massachusetts Board of Agriculture, *Report* (1858), 113; *Country Gentleman*, XIX (1862), 59; U. S. Patent Office, *Report* (1851), pp. 185-186.
[11] *New York Weekly Tribune*, December 13, 1845.
[12] *Country Gentleman*, XVIII (1861), 288; XIX (1862), 74, 346-347.

village or crossroads store. Resources were also acquired by the simple process of delaying payment on such items as blacksmith bills, animal purchases, and the wages of hired help until crops were sold. Credits of this type were supplemented by personal advances of cash or goods, with or without the formality of a signed note. Bankers were a source of funds, sometimes by making advances at the beginning of a crop season, or by discounting notes to allow a purchase, as of feeder cattle or hogs. Bankers also supplied bills of exchange to finance the shipment of goods and produce to a distant market. Farms were purchased with the aid of mortgages, which frequently represented large percentages of their market value.

In the early 1830's, New England was described as a community "free, flourishing, and prosperous, beyond example; there never was a country in which all men from the highest to the lowest; from the richest to the poorest, could be more independent. And yet . . . if . . . we were to inquire into the state of property, and the degree of real independence and comfort that prevail, we would be astonished at the appalling amount and distressing burden of pecuniary obligation. We should find an almost incredible proportion of the community laboring under this load and pressure. Debt, universal debt, would meet us wherever we turned our eyes. The farmer owes the trader, the mechanic owes for the raw material, the trader owes the importer. In many districts the country traders will testify that a considerable proportion of the debts contracted for what are considered the necessaries of life, lie unpaid for two or three years— yes, and they lie, in the shape of mortgages upon real estate."[13]

Although the credit system was well established and its use widespread, it was attacked, as were many other aspects of the changing nature of farming, as conflicting with the ideal of the independent, self-sufficient homestead. A Jacksonian fear of debt, although clearly ignored in practice, counseled its avoidance under all circumstances.[14] In the earlier part of the period it was customary to view debt with alarm and to decry it as arising from extravagance or speculation. "Money is generally borrowed," wrote Samuel Fleet, editor of the *New York Farmer,* "from one of two motives—with a view to speculate—or to relieve from present embarrassments."

[13] *New York Farmer,* IV (1831), 181.
[14] Bray Hammond, *Banks and Politics in America, from the Revolution to the Civil War* (Princeton University Press, 1950), pp. 540, 607, 623.

His disapproval of acquiring debt in either instance was consistent with an agriculture that was homestead-centered, which did not differentiate between capital and consumable income, and which possessed little ability to repay. Samuel Fleet continued his analysis by admonishing the farmer not to consider borrowing before he had reduced his living expenses "according to that of the circle of his neighbors in which he has moved." He concluded, "When farmers get in arrears, they are too much in the practice of raising money by mortgaging their farms, instead of selling off a portion, and reducing their expenses. They who have farms of two or three hundred acres, will generally prefer mortgaging them one half their value rather than sell half and pay off the debt. But the policy is most miserable; and he who does it, is sure to lead a life of anxiety, and very probably to have at death his property entirely consumed to satisfy the claims of the mortgage."[15]

Quite different attitudes were nevertheless expressed. At about the same time a writer in the *New England Farmer* expressed the view that hiring money to work a farm was wise if the borrower "is possessed of much resolution and discretion, as to be in no danger of ever appropriating money so raised to any other use." He added, "Before a mortgage can press heavily upon his farm, the money can be repaid, and at the worst he has only to return to his former method of farming by the halves, and without either satisfaction or profit."[16] As farmers became more market conscious, this point of view became more common. Men found it advantageous to borrow capital to exploit opportunities that promised to return not only the capital borrowed but also a profit. Only a decade after Samuel Fleet had expressed the views quoted, the editor of the *New England Farmer* explained mortgage debt as arising from two very different types of situation: "When the father of a family dies, one of the sons often buys out the other heirs; a young man works at farming by the month until he accumulates twelve or fifteen hundred dollars and then buys a small place for twenty or twenty-five hundred dollars and gives a mortgage . . . These are common cases, and in very many cases these young men pursue a wise course. 'Honest industry' with sound economy in expenditures and good judgement in buying and selling will ordinarily relieve such men

[15] *New York Farmer*, IV (1821), 154-155; *Genesee Farmer*, II (1832), 207, 219.
[16] *New England Farmer*, XI (1833), 346.

from their obligations in a few years—it is desirable that every farmer should be striving to take up the mortgage upon his place; but the cases are numerous in which there is a want of discretion in giving up the mortgage."[17]

By the 1860's the attitude that borrowing capital should be avoided was no longer widely held. The accepted view was that borrowing was not only legitimate but even desirable. A contemporary reported, "among farmers the remark is often heard, 'that the best way to make money by farming is to buy and run in debt for land, and then go to work and pay for it.' " Purchasing a farm by means of a mortgage was held to possess the advantage that it would induce the farmer "to work harder and manage better than he has ever done before, rather than fail in it."[18]

One observer expressed the opinion that it was safe to buy a farm when the purchaser could pay half down and "had a modest allowance of farm stock suitable to the system of farming he intends to pursue, together with suitable teams, tools, etc., to begin with," urging further that repayment be arranged by small payments over a ten-year period.[19] The caution was expressed, however, that a prospective farmer should never begin "by making a heavy debt on his land, and another large one for his teams, stock, etc." Many violated such advice, and lack of discretion in giving up a mortgage was common, with consequent heavy burdens and risks. Farmers suffered severely in the violent financial crises that plagued the nation's economy. This was particularly true in the West, where farmers employed credit not only to establish farms but also to speculate in land. Debt-free farmers would have remained relatively unscathed by the periodic collapse of prices.[20]

---

[17] *New England Farmer,* XX (1841), 113-114; (1853), 119.

[18] *Country Gentleman,* XXI (1863), 203. "A mortgage is, after all, the great conservative power in American society and about the only thing that can make 'Young America' old-fogeyish and keep it steady." Getting out of debt was the first step toward improved and more profitable farming. *Rural New Yorker,* XI (1860), 29.

[19] *Country Gentleman,* IX (1862), 221.

[20] Accounts of financial distress associated with the major financial crises are numerous. According to a report from Barrington, Illinois, in 1858, "The farmers here are almost universally in debt, and they expected to pay with the incoming crops, but they are doomed to disappointment. Many have run into debt with storekeepers and the merchants tell them they must pay. 'We are owing,' say they, 'large debts in New York and you know these New York folks wait neither for time nor tide—they must be paid, or we shall be ruined. If you can't do any better, you must mortgage your farms—we must have our pay.' Alas, too many mortgaged their farms

Mortgages. A British observer of the American scene in the 1850's reported, "A great help to parties with small capital is the facilities given for the purchasing of land. In very few cases, indeed, is the purchase money at all demanded. The general way of doing business is paying by yearly or half-yearly installments. Where the purchase-money amounts to four or five thousand dollars, the time may extend over a period of six or seven years."[21] Such financial arrangements involved a mortgage.

The frequent and casual references to mortgages in the literature suggest that financing the purchase or operation of a farm by means of credit thus secured was a common and long-standing procedure. Contemporary observers asserted that in the 1830's half the farms of New England, three-fifths of those in Maine, and large numbers in New York were mortgaged.[22] Modern historians increasingly recognize that this source of financing played a fundamental role in the settlement of the West.[23]

The rough estimates cited find support in the limited statistical data available. In Ohio in 1858, for example, there were 52,709 conveyances of real estate involving 22,451 recorded mortgages. Ninety percent of these mortgages involved farms. The average life of a recorded mortgage was estimated at about two years, a figure that reflects the rapid turnover of land in Ohio in this period, with

---

in prosperous times in order to buy more land, and are now paying heavy interest for money that lies deep in the soil." *Rural New Yorker,* IX (1858), 294. The collapse of land prices about Taylorville, Iowa, "left almost every man here in debt." *Prairie Farmer,* III (1859), 1. And in 1869 the farmers of Sangemon County, Illinois, were facing "certain bankruptcy" with hundreds of farms mortgaged. Illinois State Agricultural Society, *Transactions* (1869-1870), p. 256; cf. *Rural New Yorker,* XI (1860), 262, 350.

21 *Working Farmer,* II (1850), 269, from the *British Journal of Agriculture.*

22 *Plough Boy,* I (1820), 355; *Northern Farmer,* I (1833), 123; *New England Farmer,* X (1831), 64; XX (1841), 112; *Farmer's Gazette,* I (1840), 181; *American Farmer,* VIII (1827), 383. Judge Jacob Collamer of Vermont, speaking at a fair of the New Hampshire Agricultural Society in 1859, cited as one evidence of progress the fact that farmers were generally free of debt. "Thirty years ago a large part of the farmers (of New England) were embarrassed with debts, and many of the farms were mortgaged. The best farms seemed most subject to the disease, as creditors much preferred such owners for debtors or sureties." New Hampshire State Agricultural Society, *Transactions* (1859), p. 82.

23 See Allan G. Bogue, *Money at Interest: The Farm Mortgage on the Middle Border* (Cornell University Press, 1955); Margaret Beattie Bogue, *Patterns from the Sod: Land Use and Tenure in the Grand Prairie, 1850-1900,* Collections of the Illinois State Historical Library, XXXIV Land Series, Vol. I (Springfield, Illinois Historical Library, 1959); Curti, *Making of an American Community,* pp. 156-157.

sales averaging about 10 percent of the acreage in the state each year.[24]

The important role of the mortgage on the farm-making frontier may be illustrated by the considerable data available for Story County, Iowa (Table 2). The county's government was organized

Table 2. Mortgage history, Story County, Iowa, 1854-1870.

Farm numbers, acreages, and mortgages	1854-1860	1860	1861-1870	1870
Number of farms	—	471	—	434
Number of land purchase transactions	3,455	—	4,758	—
Number of mortgages recorded	415	—	1,526	—
Total amount of mortgages recorded[a]	$185,582	—	$780,709	—
Number of mortgages released	203	—	906	—
Amount of mortgages released	$99,607	—	$394,706	—
Number of mortgages outstanding[b]	—	212	—	832
Amount of mortgages outstanding	—	$85,976	—	$471,979
Acreage mortgaged	—	22,434	—	79,204
Acreage in farms	—	73,385	—	76,498
Acreage improved	—	24,711	—	44,474

Sources: William G. Murray, *An Economic Analysis of Farm Mortgages in Story County, Iowa, 1854-1931,* Research Bulletin No. 156, Agricultural Experiment Station, Iowa State College (Ames, Iowa, 1933). Data on number and acreage of farms from U. S. Census Office, *Agriculture of the United States in 1860* (Washington, D.C., 1864); *Ninth Census of the United States, 1870: Agriculture* (Washington, D.C., 1872).

a. Includes first and junior mortgages. Junior liens were not a large portion of the total.
b. Excludes renewals.

in 1853, and the first mortgage was recorded on January 1, 1854. Mortgages played an ever larger part in the active land market as virgin, second-hand, and improved lands changed hands. Almost a third of the transactions in land in the 1860-1870 period involved recorded mortgages. Although much virgin land remained available

[24] Commissioner of Statistics, *Annual Reports to the Governor of the State of Ohio* (1858), p. 37; (1859), p. 48.

in the county during this period—farm land constituted little more than a fifth of the county's area in 1870, and the number of farms even declined slightly—a doubling of the "improved" acreage between 1860 and 1870 was accompanied by an increase in mortgage indebtedness equivalent to about a third of the increase in the reported cash value of farms. The outstanding mortgage debt in 1869 was equal to 24 percent of the cash value of farms as reported by the census.

Such data suggest that while raw land was sometimes acceptable as security for a mortgage, mortgages were more frequently generated in a transaction involving at least partially improved farms, with the seller accepting a mortgage as part payment, and the buyer anticipating that operation of the property would yield a return adequate to meet payments of the principal as well as the interest. Mortgages might also originate in the settlement of debts to shopkeepers and similar suppliers.

In the earlier years, particularly in the earlier stages of settlement, the bulk of mortgage financing was between individuals. In Story County most mortgages were accepted by sellers of the property or purchased by private investors. However, in that area mortgage brokers had gained some importance by 1870. The county school funds were in the early years a significant source of mortgage funds. In the East, institutional lending on farm mortgage loans, as by life insurance firms, seems to have begun in the 1830's, when farm lands were added to the well-established practice of lending on urban properties.[25]

Short-Term Credit. Most farmers needed to supplement their own resources to conduct effective operations or found it profitable to extend their activities by means of credit. The principal types of short-term credit available were mercantile credit, personal loans, and bank discounts. Although no estimate of the volume of such credits is possible in the present state of our knowledge, no reader of contemporary farmers' analyses of their financial problems nor browser in the account books of merchants or small bankers can escape the impression that the amounts involved were large.

Loans from individuals might be cash advances, but probably

---

[25] Allan Bogue, *Money at Interest,* p. 264.

more frequently they took the form of delayed payment for purchases of livestock or other farming needs. Such transactions were frequently documented by a note and occasionally supported by a recorded chattel mortgage. The purchase on credit of items from the country store, though much denounced, was virtually universal by 1820.[26] It was standard practice to acquire the tools, lumber, and other supplies needed to carry out farm operations on credit, with payment made at harvest time. Family requirements for store goods were similarly obtained on credit, thereby releasing available funds for farm operations. Such debts were paid in part as produce acceptable to the store became available, with full payment expected at the end of the crop year. Final settlement might be made in kind, but the country store much preferred and frequently required cash payment. Payments in cash became more possible as wheat buyers and dealers in livestock expanded their activities.

A significant form of mercantile credit was that granted by the manufacturers and selling agents of the new agricultural implements that appeared during the half-century. Small cash down payments supplemented by notes of indebtedness constituted the usual method of payment. In the case of the reaper and harvester, manufacturers granted credits in such volume as to provide the major source of financing. This type of credit allowed the purchaser of the implement to figure that payment would be made in part from the increased productivity contributed by the new implement.[27]

The banking system was the source of much of the capital used by merchants. It was made available sometimes through loans to merchants by local banks, but also less directly through credits extended by eastern wholesalers—based on bank loans—to local merchants.[28] Banks were also a direct source of funds to farmers. In the 1840's in the West, for instance, farmers borrowed heavily from banks to buy feeder cattle and hogs, to work growing crops, and to finance shipments of produce and droves of animals. These loans were normally for short periods of sixty to ninety days, though occasionally for the entire growing season. They frequently involved

---

[26] *Plough Boy,* I (1820), 356.

[27] William T. Hutchinson, *Cyrus Hall McCormick: Seed-Time* (Appleton, Century, Crofts, 1930), pp. 362, 368.

[28] A contemporary estimate places the aggregate debt of merchants in 1857 at $2,282,000,000. "Business Failures in the Panic of 1857," *Business History Review,* XXXVII (1963), 437.

bills of exchange, so that the sale of the pledged crop or animals was the source of payment. In contrast to credits, which represented postponement of payment for purchases, bank loans brought the farmer up against the competition of merchants and manufacturers, who could more readily meet the security and repayment preferences of bankers than could the farmer. In the thirties there were complaints that loans from banks were not readily obtainable and that the sixty- to ninety-day maturities which bankers preferred were ill-adapted to farm needs.[29] Horace Capron, in discussing the capital requirements of farmers, asked: "Why is it that capital, wherever it comes into existence, maketh itself wings and flieth away into the towns? Even country banks, created in the promise of assistance to farmers in the way of advancements on their crops, soon fall under the influence of this centripetal tendency, and, applied to for a loan, take special care to make the farmer understand that he is first to give them an "acceptance" in the Metropolitan City at 60 days and to consider it a great favor to get it at that."[30] Agencies specifically adapted to supplying agriculture's needs for seed-to-harvest credits were being advocated in the forties and fifties.[31]

Credit was costly because of the vigorous demand for a relatively limited supply of funds. Interest rates quoted in the press were usually in the 6 to 7 percent range, but the terms of a loan frequently concealed a real cost substantially higher than the nominal rate. In the case of mercantile credits, a dual price system—one price for cash and another for credit—was common. Farmers felt that an additional cost lay in the fact that repayment was expected at harvest time when produce prices tended to be low. The necessity for an immediate sale of crops to meet the terms of loans and mercantile indebtedness was considered an unfair burden, since other farmers frequently held their produce in the hope of rising prices. A contemporary defense of the more common practice of selling

[29] Bray Hammond, "Banking in the Early West: Monopoly, Prohibition, and Laissez-Faire," *Journal of Economic History,* XIV (1948), 16.

[30] *Plough, Loom, and Anvil,* II (1849), 47.

[31] *Valley Farmer,* II (1850), 38; Iowa State Agricultural Society, *Transactions* (1860), pp. 5-6. A writer in the *Monthly Journal of Agriculture,* I (1840), 406, concluded an analysis of credit resources available to farmers with a demand for a "bank that would pay bills drawn on it expressly for lime and plaster and clover seed and the necessary implements and buildings." See *Homestead,* II (1857), 268-269, 394-395; III (1858), 394-395; *Country Gentleman,* XXV (1866), 420.

produce immediately after harvest reveals the role that credit played in western agriculture:

The being obliged to sell crops as soon as harvested is an evil, it is true. But the statement that half or more goes to pay store bills is a little uncharitable. Our state is new, our land was cheap and reasonable, but the farming population, in the main, are men of limited means. Many have bought lands, in the purchase of which all their resources have been exhausted. Horses, barns and fences are needed; teams, tools, sheep and cows must be purchased, all of which must be paid for from the proceeds of yet unimproved farms. The newcomer, a single handed man, with an empty purse, yet with unflinching nerves, and indomitable will, sets to work to improve, beautify, and pay for a home. Small sums of money are hired of loan sharks, (there's nothing made in vain) at enormous rates of interest. Credit is obtained on lumber, tools, etc., all in good faith for prompt payment after harvest. And this prompt selling of crops to pay honest debts, instead of putting off creditors in the hope of getting better prices is to be set down to the credit of our farmers. . . I admit that many have miscalculated and got into inextricable debt, and multitudes in avoiding debt have been obliged to slight everything on their farms not yielding immediate and direct returns; but failure of crops, a tight money market, depreciation of breadstuffs, and other drawbacks incumbent to a new country should have much weight in excusing defects in farming, and delinquencies in liquidation of debts.[32]

Credits played a critically important role in all farming motivated by production for market. Effective use of the available labor supply on the abundant acreage was possible only if the farmer could apply the animals, tools, implements, and numerous other materials that were necessary. Failure to use such articles as might be secured on credit meant a less productive enterprise and lower income. The credit system was attacked because it tempted many into assuming obligations that were beyond reasonable prospects of repayment, but such optimism was characteristic of much agricultural enterprise. Distress from debts following miscalculations was inevitable. The economic crises that produced more widespread difficulties resulted, in part at least, from the conflict over the objectives of the society that prevented the establishment of a sounder banking system.

RENTING

The man who had accumulated $500 or more and who could anticipate securing some of his needs on credit was ready to invest

[32] *American Agriculturist,* XVIII (1859), p. 38.

in a farm. He was well-advised to take a small and fertile farm rather than a larger one of dubious productivity and undesirable location. He could also go West, to take up such acreage as his resources could command. There were abundant warnings against this second course, however. Opinion generally favored that a person continue working until he had accumulated perhaps $1000, which together with his credit would purchase a farm offering the possibility of much higher levels of productivity. Even more attractive to many was the renting of land. Five hundred dollars was sufficient capital to undertake such an arrangement, which offered the prospect of substantially higher income than continued wage labor.

Renting a farm was an important step toward ownership throughout this period. There has existed in American economic historiography an assumption that farm tenancy in the northern United States was uncommon or virtually nonexistent because the cheapness of land and the tradition of independence made tenancy unattractive. The acceptance of tenancy conflicted with the freeholder ideal as expressed by Thomas Jefferson and other founders of the nation's dominant political philosophy—an ideal supported by the federal government's land alienation policies.[33] The question was asked in 1844, for instance, why "should a man in our free country where land, as rich as the sun ever shone upon, can be had for $1.25 per acre, be willing to live in servile dependency on others all his days?"[34] Or as the British traveler Lyell commented in the same period, "To be a lessee, indeed, of a farm where acres may be bought so cheap, is a rare exception to the general rule throughout the United States."[35]

The fact was, however, as many other observers pointed out, that while very few lived in "servile dependency," the renting of farms was common throughout the area and period of this study, certainly after 1840. Most of the demand for rented farms came from younger men who had not yet been able to obtain the neces-

[33] Fear of tenancy underlay much of the debate over federal land policies. See, e.g., Thomas Hart Benton, *Thirty Years' View: A History of American Government for Thirty Years, from 1820 to 1850* (New York, 1854), I, 103-107.

[34] *Cultivator,* I (1844), 15.

[35] Charles Lyell, *Travels in North America in the Years 1841-1842* (New York, 1855), I, 58.

sary funds to purchase a farm of their own.[36] That an appreciable number of farms were available for rent can be readily understood from the popularity of investment in land beyond the owner's ability to utilize it, as well as from the accumulation of farm properties in the hands of the older generation, who by reason of incapacity or widowhood sought income through rentals. Moreover, both the migration to the West and the movement to the cities left idle many farms held as an investment.

That the practice of leasing farms was common cannot be demonstrated statistically but may be inferred from the numerous contemporary discussions of the problems associated with renting. Comment on the problems of declining soil fertility and of worn-out farms frequently pointed to rented farms as offering the worst examples. The need to provide for soil protection in the terms of leasing arrangements was occasionally discussed, although the long-term leases advocated for that purpose did not become popular with tenants.[37]

Tenancy was particularly important in some sections of New England, such as New London County, Connecticut.[38] Solon Robinson, in reporting considerable tenancy in the area about Camden, New Jersey, and southward to Wilmington, commented, "In other parts of the Union, the fee simple forever of far better land can be had for less money, which will produce more, without manure, and yet is not worth cultivating for the very simple reason that the cultivator has no market for his surplus products."[39] It was reported

36 The place of tenancy in the "agricultural ladder" was clearly recognized in the 1830's, though formalization of the concept did not occur until the twentieth century. See Henry C. Taylor and Anne D. Taylor, *The Story of Agricultural Economics in the United States, 1840-1932* (Iowa College Press, 1952), pp. 820-826; LaWanda F. Cox, "Tenancy in the United States, 1865-1900: A Consideration of the Validity of the Agricultural Ladder Hypothesis," *Agricultural History*, XVIII (1944), 97.

37 *New York Farmer*, IV (1831), 289; *Working Farmer*, VIII (1856), 36; *Western Agriculturist*, II (1852), 57.

38 *Homestead*, III (1858), 825-826. Cf., *Homestead*, I (1856), 546; II (1857), 186; *American Agriculturist*, XV (1856), 297.

39 *American Agriculturist*, IX (1850), 108. Robinson noted of the region between Philadelphia and Wilmington that "the road passes over a very valuable agricultural district, much of which being owned in England, is but poorly improved by the tenantry." *American Agriculturist*, X (1851), 91. Cf. *New Jersey Farmer*, II (1856), 70. There was also much tenancy on the eastern shore of Maryland. See Lewis C. Gray, *History of Agriculture in the Southern United States to 1860* (Carnegie Institution of Washington, 1933), I, 646.

that half the land in Kent County, Delaware, was worked by tenants.[40]

In eastern New York, along the Hudson River, tenancy possessing certain feudal characteristics persisted into the sixties. In western New York tenancy was of considerable importance in the Genesee area. There the Wadsworth family in particular gave close supervision to their large land-holdings, including careful consideration of the terms of their leases.[41] Tenants in the Genesee Valley were reported not usually to "possess more than one pound an acre of capital," and tenancy was described as "an opportunity for persons to begin life who do not possess money enough of their own to begin farming, at least in the neighborhood." Such tenants customarily remained from four to eight years.[42] In Herkimer County, "it is a common way of renting dairy farms for tenants to pay landlords from $13 to $15 per cow for as many cows as the premises will keep well throughout the year—landlords furnishing all cows, fixtures, etc., except losses on stock that may occur from carelessness and neglect. When such lands are let on shares, the tenants have half of all the product by paying landlords interest on one-half of the value of the cows, paying taxes and bearing half the loss in stock; or has two fifths of the dairy product and half of all other products—the landlord furnishing all the stock and fixtures and his relative proportion of contingent expenses of what is bought and sold again and not produced from the premises."[43]

In the West, numerous very large land-holdings came into private ownership, and it was even more common for men to hold two or more farms or own acreages of wild land that, though measured in the hundreds rather than thousands of acres, exceeded their ability to utilize them. Lacking buyers at desired prices, many owners found themselves under pressure to secure immediate returns from their land so as to meet taxes and other costs. Such land came onto the rental market, where at times the supply exceeded the demand. Rents in kind, ranging from one- to two-thirds of the crop, were

[40] U. S. Patent Office, *Report* (1852-1853), p. 114; *Genesee Farmer*, XVI (1855), 44.

[41] Paul W. Gates, *The Farmer's Age: Agriculture, 1815-1860* (Holt, Rinehart and Winston, New York, 1960), pp. 39-40; McNall, *Agricultural History of the Genesee Valley*, pp. 13 ff.

[42] James F. W. Johnston, *Notes on North America* (Boston, 1852), I, 164, 207.

[43] New York State Agricultural Society, *Transactions* (1851), p. 518.

common, but terms varied considerably. Occasionally the holder of virgin lands offered to transfer title in return for the first crop, an arrangement that required considerable capital on the part of the renter.[44] Others offered the use of wild land for a period of a few years in return for its breaking and fencing. The crops thus acquired might provide the renter the opportunity to accumulate sufficient funds to buy a farm of his own.[45]

Although some large holdings were operated by hired labor, most were exploited by a tenant system. In Ohio about 1835, "a majority of the farms" in the northern part of the state were in the hands of tenants, while "the system of renting prevails in many districts," involving "sometimes whole townships," as in the valleys of the Muskingum and Scioto rivers.[46] Contemporary opinion held that tenant operation of large acreages was common in Indiana, Illinois, and southern Wisconsin.[47] The renting of land was a significant practice in Iowa from the earliest settlement and increased over time.[48]

If there were good reasons that farms should be available for rent in significant numbers, there were equally good reasons that the demand should be substantial. For almost any young would-be farmer with the requisite capital, the rental of a farm represented an opportunity to utilize his funds, his skills, and possibly the labor of his family to maximum advantage, with the prospect of accumulating money at a rate perhaps double that possible by wage work. There were other factors, too. As it was pointed out: "Taking a

[44] *Western Agriculturist,* I (1851), 12; J. Richard Beste, *The Wabash* (London, 1856), I, 190.

[45] *Illinois Farmer,* V (1860), 177. Tocqueville reports a conversation with a farmer-landowner in Michigan on the general subject of "pioneering without money." The farmer observed, "One can put the income from an acre of cultivated soil at twenty dollars and very often more. Buying the land is nothing; the real expense is getting it ready on account of the cost of labor. "This is how one must set about making a profit, when one does not cultivate the soil oneself (a very infrequent case). I get a man to clear twenty acres. I give him five dollars per acre, and I provide cart and oxen for the work. Besides I give him the seed, and then we share between us the first year's harvest. If the harvest is good, the half that goes to me more than pays the outlay of the five dollars. The subsequent harvests all belong to me." *Journey to America* (Faber & Faber, 1960), p. 210.

[46] Ohio Board of Agriculture, *Report,* XXVI (1858); cf. *Cultivator,* I (1844), 115, 151; VII (1850), 358; Percy W. Bidwell and John I. Falconer, *History of Agriculture in the Northern United States* (Carnegie Institution of Washington, 1925), p. 449.

[47] Gates, *Farmer's Age,* pp. 66-67.

[48] Allan G. Bogue, *From Prairie to Corn Belt* (University of Chicago Press, 1963), pp. 56-66.

farm to work on shares seems to be considered the next best thing to owning one. Hiring out by the day, month, or year, is accounted comparatively vulgar, and with native Americans, is fast becoming obsolete. Judging from the frequency and urgency of inquiry one hears made for chances to work land on shares, it is to be supposed that applicants believe they see a decided advantage to themselves in applying their labor to land for a portion of the products over what they would enjoy by working as hired laborers. The gain of the former method is counted in two ways; greater personal independence and increased pecuniary profit."[49]

The attractiveness of renting depended more upon the quality of the land available than upon the terms. Cash rentals existed and could be attractive to the man who had the capital required and was willing to take the greater risks for the greater possible gains. Such cash rentals varied considerably with the prices of products and with the supply and demand for such contracts.[50] Much more common was a sharing arrangement that obviated any agreement on dollar rentals. Both East and West, the customary terms in the forties and thereafter were as follows: "The land alone draws one-third, the renter furnishing his own team, tools, house, etc. Where the owner finds team, tools, house-rent, fire-wood, etc. . . . and half the seed, he receives one-half in the half bushel . . . This gives the man who has no capital as good a chance as he can ask. One man with a good team can cultivate from forty to fifty acres. True, he cannot do it in the thorough manner required in the worn-out lands of the Eastern states, but he can do it so as to obtain, in a common season, an average of from 16 to 20 bushels of wheat per acre; from 40 to 70 of corn, and from 40 to 60 of oats. Surely such a prospect offers strong inducements to a poor man; for if he is industrious and economical, in a short time he can purchase a farm of his own."[51]

A minimum capital of $500 in animals, equipment, and cash was

---

[49] *Rural New Yorker*, XII (1861), 78.

[50] Cash rents varied from 75¢ to $3.00 and occasionally up to $6.00 per acre. *Prairie Farmer*, VII (1847), 120; *Farmer's Library*, II (1846-1847), 585-587; Fred Gerhard, *Illinois As It Is in 1855* (Chicago, 1857), p. 404; Howe Parker, *Iowa As It Is in 1855* (Chicago, 1855), p. 67; *Country Gentleman*, XIX (1862), 59, 74, 315, 346.

[51] Correspondent in *Rural New Yorker*, VI (1856), 294, in reply to a query about the possibility of leasing farms. See also *Farmer and Mechanic*, V (1851), 46; *New England Farmer*, XII (1852), 258; *Working Farmer*, II (1850), 270; *Michigan Farmer*, XV (1857), 105.

necessary if the renter was to obtain a two-thirds division of the product in the typical rental arrangement. With $250 or $300 in capital a half-and-half division was more likely.[52] Obviously the larger fund was highly desirable. Even with a fund of $500, heavy use of credit was usually necessary. If the farm was fertile and a market offering attractive prices was accessible, the potential gains were very attractive. There were also hazards, such as crop failures and low prices, which might absorb some of the renter's small capital. The circumstances of an Indiana renter in 1856 provide a typical example:

A man with a team, plow, and wagon goes to work the first of April, and puts in five acres of oats, and thirty of corn, which he and two boys manage right well. With good luck, this gets worth three hundred dollars. The owner takes one-third, leaving two hundred. This will not support a common family. Horses must be fed one year out of this, as well as some hogs for meat, and every article of clothing to buy, boots, shoes, flour, mechanical work, etc. It will take five months to mature this crop. Wood must now be hauled, or ought to be, while the roads are good. This is got at a distance varying from four to fifteen miles, one load a day being the average, at a cost of from twenty to fifty cents per load. Now comes corn cutting, for everyone has one cow or more, some three, and fodder being the cheapest and best. This done, next is husking; this takes until December. But there is some time to be put in for other men for pay between these jobs of work; for the balance of expenses must be made up, somehow, and in doing it, he must often leave his own out until winter, and also the wood hauling is put off until winter, for he can get no employment through the winter from others.

But I got ahead of some facts. This man has not the necessaries of life about him at all times. The first of April he is sure to be needy, so he goes in debt for some things he can't see how to do without. The corn merchant sees this, and invites him in to buy on "tick" being careful to fix the time to pay at Christmas, when corn is at a low price. I have seen many drawing corn fifteen miles to pay the store debt, and I know of many who are deeply in debt. The credit system has been mainly shut down in this region for the last summer. Our crops were almost a total failure on the Prairie last year; we have some broken merchants, as well as broken renters. Land monopoly and Banks only, are greater curses than the credit system. You are ready to say this is a gloomy picture. It is, but there is another side to it in part. Those renters most in debt, owe part of it for another team, which is worked by their boys or a hired hand. Some feel the galling chain of poverty more sensibly than

---

[52] The sum of $277 was suggested as the amount necessary to undertake farming on a half-and-half basis on 40 acres of forested land in Michigan. *Michigan Farmer,* VIII (1850), 265.

others,—deprive themselves of some things they really need, and finally get a piece of land. But all such have more energy, or judgement, or both, than the commonalty of them.[53]

Tenancy existed because individuals lacking capital to undertake the purchase and operation of a farm, but possessing funds sufficient to finance a year's farming operations, acted upon the prospect of securing an income and accumulating capital at a faster rate than was possible by continuing as a laborer. Contemporary advice on the desirability of renting was conflicting.[54] The risks were significant, and care was required in determining that the soil of the farm selected was reasonably productive.[55] Nevertheless, it seems clear that renting was frequently judged to be a better use of labor and capital than purchasing a small, cheap farm of low productivity.[56] With an abundant supply of farms available for rent, failure usually meant a renewed effort elsewhere, with the ever present hope that a few good years would yield the funds necessary for the downpayment on a farm purchase. Those who suffered disappointment—and there must have been many—left few records. Successive failures frustrated the objective of securing ownership of a commercially profitable farm, but there is no evidence that a significant group remained renters throughout their careers. The less successful usually managed to secure ownership of a small farm on which they could eke out a livelihood.

THE APPLICATION OF CAPITAL

Having acquired some capital and assurances of credit, a farmer had to make decisions as to the manner in which to use the capital. Successful farming required an effective distribution of funds among three categories: permanent investment in land and the improvements on it; livestock, tools, and implements; and items essential to carry on each season's operations, including wages for hired help,

[53] *Ohio Cultivator*, XIII (1857), 164-166.

[54] See discussion in *Country Gentleman*, XVIII (1861), 288; XIX (1862), 59 ff; XXI (1863), 203.

[55] "As for taking land to the shares, I am of the opinion that could good land be got in this way, something might be made, but nine-tenths of the farms thus obtained are so poor and exhausted that the owners cannot live to the wholes." *Country Gentleman*, XVII (1861), 411.

[56] *Country Gentleman*, XX (1862), 78.

seed, livestock feed, and the support of the farmer's own family. Ownership of a piece of land was only one step, and not necessarily the critical step, in the process of acquiring a remunerative farm. Informed opinion of the period emphasized the absolute necessity not only of adequate capital but also of proper use of the available funds, if profits were to be gained from the operation of the farm. Farmers and farm-makers were extensively criticized for their general tendency to put too large a proportion of their funds in land, leaving themselves unable to operate their holdings efficiently. "No error," wrote one, "is more universal than for Tyros in farming operations to suppose that the business of farming may be pursued without means and that first crops may be obtained from the soil without additions."[57] The editor of the *American Agriculturist* noted similarly that farmers "almost invariably purchase or hire too much land, and thereby exhaust their resources at once, leaving nothing but their manual labor and a precarious credit to turn the use of this land to good account."[58] By adequate capital was meant a fund of property sufficiently large so that when distributed among land and improvements, stock and implements, and a working fund of cash, the available labor could be fully and efficiently utilized. An adequate fund well distributed permitted the farmer to act as his judgment dictated and not as he might be forced by circumstances.

Working Capital. The production cycle in agriculture is long—ranging from four to six months in the case of corn and some of the small grains, to three or four years for cattle or horses, and even longer periods for such crops as tree fruits. The investment of labor and supplies in plowing and seeding is returned only after an appreciable interval, during which further applications must usually be made. No farmer could operate without having available at the beginning of a working year the requisite capital, whether in the form of ownership of a stock of seed, animals, tools, and consumable goods, or of cash and credit with which to obtain these productive needs.

[57] *New England Farmer,* I (1852), 201.
[58] *American Agriculturist,* XV (1856), 127. Earlier comments of a similar nature are in *Genesee Farmer,* II (1832), 51; *Cultivator,* VI (1839), 197; *Western Farmer,* II (1841), 74-76; *Connecticut Valley Farmer,* II (1850), 98; *Pennsylvania Farm Journal,* IV (1854), 180.

An analysis of capital requirements in 1855 by the editors of the *Country Gentleman* is particularly complete and detailed.[59] It begins:

The leading error of most of the young farmers of our country is in not "counting the cost." The first thing they do is to expend not only all their capital in buying as large a farm as possible, but most usually they run largely into debt. Their desire for large possessions leaves them nothing to stock and improve the farm, and hence for many years while loaded with a discouraging debt, their farms remain poorly provided with animals, with good implements, and with a good supply of manure. They are therefore compelled to perform all their operations to a great disadvantage; their small crops afford no net profits, and they become discouraged and lose the energy and enterprise essential to success. These causes are the most fruitful source of poor and slip-shod farming in America. It is not very difficult in traversing the country to point out among the various occupants of the land, from the appearance of the premises, such as are burdened with heavy debt, from those who have a good supply of spare capital...

One great reason why young (and often old) farmers are so poorly supplied with surplus capital after buying land, is that they have never estimated how much they will want. An estimate of this sort would prevent many heavy purchases of farms and the entire consumption of means— it would induce smaller outlays in and larger expenditures in the means for making heavy net profits. We therefore propose by way of affording some assistance in this respect to point out what a moderate farmer actually and indispensably requires besides a farm and good buildings.

The capital required for the profitable operation of a hundred-acre farm was estimated at roughly two thousand dollars. This sum included the following:

Livestock: This will vary much with the character and quality of the land, its connection with the market, etc., but the following is a fair average for fertile land.

3 horses at $100	$300
1 yoke of oxen	100
8 milch cows at $25	200
10 steers, heifers, calves	100
20 pigs at $5	100
100 sheep at $2	200
poultry, etc.	10
	$1010

[59] *Country Gentleman,* V (1855), 213-214.

Implements: To farm economically, these must be of the best sort, especially those that are daily used. A plow, for instance, that saves only one-eighth of a team's strength, will save an hour a day, or more than twelve days (worth $24) in a hundred, an amount annually, that would be well worth paying for freely in the best plot. . .

2 plows fitted for work and 1 small	$25.00
1 cultivator	7.00
1 harrow	10.00
1 roller	10.00
1 seed planter	15.00
1 fanning mill, 1 straw cutter	40.00
1 root slicer	28.00
1 farm wagon, 1 ox-cart, one-horse cart, hayracks	180.00
Harness of three horses	50.00
1 horse rake	8.00
1 shovel, 1 spade, 2 manure forks, 3 hay forks, 1 pointed shovel, 1 grain shovel, 1 pick, 1 hammer, 1 wood saw, 1 turnip hook, 2 ladders, 2 sheep shearers, 2 steelyards (large and small), 1 half bushel measure. Each $1	20.00
2 grain cradles, 2 scythes	12.00
1 wheelbarrow	5.00
1 maul and wedges, 2 axes	6.50
1 hay-knife, 1 ox chain	6.00
1 tape line, for measuring fields and crops	2.00
1 grindstone	3.00
1 crowbar	2.00
1 sled and fixtures	30.00
Hand hoes, hand rakes, basket, stable lanterns, curry comb and brush, grain bags, etc.	15.00
	$474.50

The addition of a subsoil plow, sowing machine, mower and reaper, thrashing machines, horse power for sawing wood, cutting straw, etc., would more than double the amount but young farmers may hire most of these during the earlier periods of their practice. A set of the simpler carpenters tools, for repairing implements in rainy weather, would more than repay their cost.

Besides the preceding, the seeds for the various farm crops would cost not less than $75; hired labor for one year, to do the work well, would probably be as much as $350; and food for maintaining all the domestic animals from the opening of spring until grass, and grain for horses 'til harvest, would not be less in value than $100; $525 in all.

For domestic animals	$1010.00
for implements	474.50
for seeds, food, and labor	525.00

This analysis suggests that approximately $2,000 was needed to cultivate 100 acres effectively. The writer did not exaggerate when he wrote in concluding, "this sum will no doubt seem frightfully large to some who have never made a similar estimate." He challenged his readers to make similar computations: "We would therefore request such to set down and see how much they can reduce the amount, for vigorous and energetic farming," and predicted that "They will probably be surprised to find how few of the items they can spare without inconvenience or loss."

Other estimates confirm Tucker's analysis. Freedley, for example, suggested $1,832 "as the amount of capital needed for the first year, in stocking and conducting satisfactorily the operations of one hundred acres of improved land."[60] His estimate, like Tucker's, includes no heavy implements such as drills, threshing machines, reapers, or mowers, while the amount provided for livestock was the minimum required by an operation focused on grains rather than the more profitable specialization in livestock.

Horace Capron in 1849 recommended $20.00 per arable acre as the minimum required for "floating capital."[61] The editor of the *American Agriculturist* suggested that a cash working capital of $3.00 to $7.00 per acre was desirable "to take advantage of circumstances and markets, after paying for stocking his farm, and furnishing it with agricultural implements, seed, and manure."[62] A farmer held that "to farm within a hundred miles of New York requires that on the first day of spring, the farmer should have at his command at least three thousand dollars, and this will enable him to carry out his operations for cash, and therefore more cheaply than when performed on credit."[63] Other suggestions called for a liquid capital equal to half the value of the land, though one noted that "the necessity of such a sum has not yet been considered by the great body of American farmers."[64]

At an earlier date the estimates for tools and implements might have been somewhat smaller, not because they were undesirable but

[60] Edwin T. Freedley, *A Practical Treatise on Business* (Philadelphia, 1852), pp. 67-71. See also *Genesee Farmer*, XIX (1858), 213; *Scientific American*, XII (1857), 292; U. S. Patent Office, *Report* (1851), p. 443.

[61] *Plough, Loom and Anvil*, II (1849), 47.

[62] *American Agriculturist*, XV (1856), 127.

[63] *Working Farmer*, XI (1859), 148-149.

[64] *New England Farmer*, IX (1831), 148; *Country Gentleman*, XIX (1862), 168.

because they were unavailable or too expensive. Oxen might have been substituted for horses, but again on the grounds of expense. In the 1820's the cost of providing animals for profitable operation and the amounts of working capital necessary for effective utilization of the land were roughly as estimated for 1855. From the 1830's comes the observation that "a farmer cannot with a capital of $10,000 purchase a productive farm, stock it with the necessary cattle and implements of husbandry, pay his laborers and mechanics, maintain his family, and run the hazards of the season, with a less expenditure of $3000 per annum; and if his farm is unpaid for, or he has buildings to erect, it is with extreme difficulty he can ever attain an independent rank in society."[65]

Another New England farmer calculated in 1833 that a farm with an annual product of $1,000 required $570 "loose capital" if the farmer were to carry on his affairs "without being pinched or obliged to slight his work." The $570 was for carrying on operations and paying for wages and subsistence only. The calculation was based on the proposition that to produce $1,000 in products, $770 had to be expended before returns were received, "and if the farmer himself supplies the work of one good hired hand equal to about $200," the sum of $570 remained. This working capital was necessary for a number of reasons:

> Farmers who live so far from market as to find it impossible, or inconvenient to get the produce of their farms to market before winter (and these constitute a very large majority) it will be seen at once, must incur the entire expense of working their farms and providing for their families for the year, before they realize anything worth naming from the produce of their farms. Their hired hands must be paid in autumn, if not sooner, and if they expect to get store goods and mechanics work at reasonable rate, they must pay as they go along. A farmer sells his pork, butter, cheese, grain, etc., from January to April. The cost of producing all these was paid for (or ought to have been) the summer and autumn before. His sheep are sheared in May, and should he be able to convert their fleeces immediately into money, (which he cannot always do) still the whole expense of producing this wool, excepting about two months young pasturing, was paid the year before, a considerable portion of it the August before.[66]

All the factors discussed here were matters of concern to the farmer seeking to establish and operate his own enterprise. Land

[65] *Genesee Farmer,* VIII (1838), 68.
[66] *New England Farmer,* XI (1833), 346.

was so abundant that the problems it presented were of a wide range of alternatives as to location, crops, and the type of culture to be pursued. Capital requirements set stringent limits to the ability to take advantage of opportunities, although important differences existed in the manner in which such opportunities were visualized. The analyses quoted are concerned with establishing the ratios between land and the other inputs of an agricultural enterprise that would result in maximizing the total product and hence the profitability of the enterprise. The task of the new entrant into farming was to utilize available capital and credit resources so as to maximize his productivity. Virtually all sought to increase their capital by accepting low consumption levels and by saving as rapidly as possible. Heavy reliance on credit was expensive and introduced an element of precariousness. At the same time, the returns possible on borrowed funds were high and were frequently the critical component in the success of an enterprise. Because the variety of specific reactions was great, generalization is difficult.

CHAPTER FIVE

ACQUIRING TITLE TO A FARM

 Given a knowledge of the standard agricultural techniques, the common crops, and livestock, possessing some capital and the prospect of credit, and determined to undertake farming for his own account, the prospective farmer next faced the problem of acquiring a farm in the general area of his preference. The basic choice lay between the purchase of an operating farm in a well-settled area, a partially developed farm closer to the frontier of settlement, or a totally undeveloped farm on virgin land. Throughout this half-century the range of possibilities was great. Farms with improvements varying from slight to extensive, which had been operated for a year or two up to a century or more, were offered for sale in large numbers. One traveler observed in the late 1840's that "speaking generally, every farm from Eastport in Maine to Buffalo on Lake Erie is for sale. The owner has already fixed a price in his mind for which he would be willing, and even hopes to sell."[1] This willingness to sell reflected a common desire to realize whatever capital gains might have accrued. The purchase of lands farther west so as to continue farming was the principal method of reinvesting such earnings.

In the East, well-established farms of proven productivity, advantageously located near the larger cities, were sometimes valued at more than $100 per acre, but $30 to $40 were more common

---

[1] James F. W. Johnston, *Notes on North America: Agricultural, Economical, and Social* (Boston, 1851), pp. 162-163. Tocqueville observed, "It seldom happens that an American farmer settles for good upon the land which he occupies; especially in the districts of the Far West he brings land into tillage in order to sell it again, and not to farm it." Alexis de Tocqueville, *Democracy in America* (Knopf, 1945), II, 166. In 1855, Ohio farmers were described as being "tenants at will—that is, at the will of someone to buy them out." Ohio Board of Agriculture, *Report* (1855), p. 138. The Commissioner of Statistics of Ohio observed in 1859 that land sales in the state were occurring at an annual rate of two million acres, or one-twelfth of the state's area, noting also, "notwithstanding there are many farms which continue in the same family for many years, there are many more which are transferred repeatedly in twelve years." Ohio Commissioner of Statistics, *Report* (1859), p. 48.

values for superior farms. Farms of average productivity without the advantage of nearby markets tended to bring substantially lower prices. Poorly located farms with unproductive or worn-out soils were occasionally sold for as little as $3 or $4 per acre. As the West developed, prices for established farms displayed a similarly wide range.

If the choice was to create a farm on virgin land rather than to buy one already in production, there were numerous sellers and a wide diversity in the possible terms of payment. Virgin land inviting conversion into farms was available by the millions of acres west of the Alleghenies. Such land was also to be found in Maine, as well as in the large areas bypassed by earlier waves of settlement, such as northwestern Pennsylvania, southern New Jersey, and Long Island.[2]

The decisions relating to the location of settlement reflected a wide variety of considerations. For some, the necessity of securing a livelihood with limited knowledge and means meant securing land wherever it could be had most cheaply. Yet limitations of capital and credit, while significant in determining the magnitude of a man's venture, were not necessarily the most important determinants in his choice. A man's concept of the objectives of farming, his own knowledge, and his estimates of the long-range prospects for a given area and for a specific farm were more important factors.

Furthermore, some individuals attached importance to residence in a well-settled area, with its advantages for social intercourse, educational facilities, and established religious institutions. Others were guided in their choice by participation in religious or ethnic

[2] Although the *Genesee Farmer,* VIII (1838), 33, declared as early as 1838 that the idea of the "barrenness of Long Island's lands is done away with," the debate on their profitability was long continued, and their settlement slow. See *American Agriculturist,* VII (1848), 109-110; XIX (1860), 135; *Boston Cultivator,* XII (Oct. 12, 1850); XIII (Jan. 25, 1851); American Institute, *Proceedings* (1855), p. 331; *New England Farmer,* XII (1862), 243-244; *Working Farmer,* XII (1860), 29, 63; *Rural New Yorker,* XII (1860), 54; *Genesee Farmer,* XIX (1858), 238-239. The sandy areas of New Jersey remained largely unoccupied until the growth of New York and Philadelphia, the development of fruit and vegetable markets, and the perfection of fertilization techniques. *Maine Farmer,* Aug. 19, 1858; *American Agriculturist,* XXIII (1863), 104; XXIV (1865), 153, 262; *Practical Farmer,* V (1868), 131; VI (1869), 117; *New Hampshire Journal of Agriculture,* May 19, 1859; *Rural New Yorker,* XVI (1865), 89. Other unoccupied eastern areas that were attracting settlers included the northern tier of counties in Pennsylvania and the Aroostook country of Maine. *Farm Journal and Progressive Farmer,* VI (1856), 159; Maine Board of Agriculture, *Report* (1861), p. 386.

groups. Romantic considerations also played a part. The young man's impulse to repeat the farm-making experience of his father and therefore to accept the challenge and opportunity of the frontier was an unquestionably important factor, even though it escapes specific evaluation.[3]

Income possibilities were necessarily visualized by the would-be farmer in the light of techniques with which he was familiar and in view of the funds at his command. While raw land at the frontier was inexpensive, the capital required to convert it into an operating farm was substantial. However, some of the capital necessary to develop a productive farm could be supplied by the labor of the farm family applying familiar techniques. Also of basic importance in any decision was the fact that the forested frontier offered the opportunity to continue to apply the older, well-known technology for some years after the farm-making period had passed; in long-settled areas of increasingly dense population there came, sooner or later, a time when it was unprofitable to continue employing the methods appropriate when the farm had been established. Unwillingness or inability to change, uncertainty or imperfect knowledge about alternative methods, and doubts about the profitability of such changes—particularly those required to restore soil fertility—were weighty influences on decisions. It seems likely that the decision to seek a farm at or near the frontier was frequently reached because the knowledge of agricultural techniques was limited to those practiced on the parental farm.

While some farmers seemed to be solely concerned with short-range income prospects, others were highly sensitive to the capitalized value of the income-producing capacity of their own farms and the farms of others. Men differed, therefore, in their approach to the acquisition of a farm. Some sought assured income-producing ability based on the record and condition of a farm. Others directed their attention to farms that provided less assurance of immediate income but a better opportunity for growth of income valued for its own sake, as well as for the increase in capital value that would follow from success in exploiting such possibilities.

Increases in capital value were sought by a variety of methods. A farm's productivity might be improved by rotation techniques that

[3] See Maine Board of Agriculture, *Report* (1857), pp. 39-40.

enhanced the soil's fertility, by open or under-drainage of the land, or by such external developments as the appearance of new transportation facilities. The route to capital gains that attracted the most attention, however, was the purchase of land to be held for a rise in prices. Speculation of this nature was nearly universal. It was common in the vicinity of the larger cities and particularly in the development of the towns and cities of the West. Speculative land purchases in excess of the acreage that could or was intended to be cultivated were characteristic of the farm-making frontier, where increases in value of some multiple of the cost of the land were possible within a relatively short period of time.[4] If large capital gains were by no means assured, the risks of loss were relatively small.[5] Such purchases were attractive because of the high probability that farm populations would increase and that better methods of transportation would appear.[6] A contributing factor was the failure of the federal government to make any successful effort to differentiate the sale price of land as to its fertility or location, except in the case of the alternate sections of railroad grants. The federal system of auctioning its lands failed to operate to this end.[7] Instead, superior and average lands sold at virtually the same prices, with large acreages of the poorest land tending to remain unsold for considerable periods. No social opprobrium was attached to such speculative activities except when very large acreages were held out of use, and then principally because the resulting slow rate of settlement was felt to be a disadvantage by other landholders in the area.[8]

[4] In 1840 Henry Clay charged that of the 67 officials of the land office, 64 were defrauders. "Hardly an officer had refrained from using the public funds in his possession to buy land which was rising in value each day. They would sell out, repay the government and retain fortunes for themselves." Cited in Fish, *The Rise of the Common Man* (Macmillan, 1937), pp. 157-158.

[5] Allan G. Bogue and Margaret Beattie Bogue, "Profits and the Frontier Land Speculator," *Journal of Economic History,* XVII (1957), 1-24; Roy Allen Billington, "The Origin of the Land Speculator as a Frontier Type," *Agricultural History,* XIX (1945), 211; Paul W. Gates, "Role of the Land Speculator in Western Development," *Pennsylvania Magazine of History and Biography,* LXVI (1942), 314-333. See also Paul W. Gates, *The Farmer's Age: Agriculture, 1815-1860* (Holt, Rinehart and Winston, 1960), pp. 57-62, 70-84.

[6] Thomas LeDuc points out that the real motive of many squatters was to secure and protect the speculative equity in lands selected in advance of sale proclamation. LeDuc "Public Policy, Private Investment, and Land Use in American Agriculture, 1825-1875," *Agricultural History,* XXXVII (1964), 3.

[7] Benjamin H. Hibbard, *A History of Public Land Policies* (Peter Smith, 1939), pp. 105-108.

[8] Gates, *The Farmer's Age,* pp. 85-89.

SOURCES OF VIRGIN LAND

The importance of farm-making on virgin land throughout this period necessitates a brief review of the conditions by which virgin land could be obtained. With the exception of the lands held by the original states within their borders, and the lands reserved in Ohio by Connecticut and Virginia, all lands west of Pennsylvania were under the jurisdiction of the federal government, which arranged to eliminate such Indian titles as it had recognized, provided for mapping and surveying, and established policies to permit utilization. The objectives of the alienation policies of the federal Congress are subject to various interpretations, but their effect was to maintain on the market a supply of land available for transfer to private ownership substantially in excess of the demand from farm-makers.

Throughout this half-century the virgin lands open to settlement were marked not by a line but by a belt of considerable depth advancing westward. The eastern side of the belt included established farms and lands being converted into farms, virgin lands in private ownership, and virgin lands held by the federal or state governments. As property moved from public to private ownership, those lands judged least desirable for cultivation remained in the hands of the federal government. At the western boundary were the lands recently opened to purchase, with the most desirable acreage moving quickly into private hands. Farms in various stages of cultivation were scattered about, though clustering near avenues of transportation. At the far western fringe of the belt were lands not yet opened for sale by the federal government but having scattered occupants or squatters.

The buyer in search of virgin lands about 1820 found the sources to include not only the land offices of the federal government but also agencies of state governments, land companies that held large blocks in Ohio, and private holders. Early in 1820, federal lands were offered in minimum lots of 80 acres at $2.00 per acre, one-fourth payable immediately with the balance due over a period of four years.[9] Later in that year Congress adopted a sales policy that was maintained until 1862. The minimum auction price was reduced

[9] This brief discussion is based on Hibbard, *A History of Public Land Policies;* Roy W. Robbins, *Our Land Heritage: The Public Domain, 1776-1936* (Princeton University Press, 1942); and the numerous works of Paul W. Gates cited in the bibliography.

to $1.25 per acre, payable in cash, the minimum sale being retained at 80 acres. As a result of this legislation, private sources assumed the functions of extending credit to buyers. Prices for lands held by private groups or individuals were usually, though not always, higher than the federal government's $1.25 minimum, with credit usually extended.

Over the following years the land disposal policies of the federal government operated to make the sources of virgin land for purchase much more numerous. To the land grants given the states in support of education were added grants for internal improvements, such as roads, canals, river improvements, and railroads, as well as gifts of land classified as swamp. Large acreages were also awarded to private individuals in recognition of military service. Veterans of the War of 1812 received warrants for 160 acres, intended for use in land settlement and unassignable. After 1847, warrants were issued to veterans of the Mexican War that were transferrable into script with a face value of $100 when exchanged for land at the federal land offices. By act of 1852 all warrants were made assignable, and by an act of 1855 the federal government gave an assignable bounty of 160 acres to every man or his heirs who had served in any war, including the Revolution. An active market existed in such script and warrants, with prices quoted at substantial discounts from the government's $1.25 minimum. The absence of restrictions on the acreage that might be purchased with such claims and the low prices at which they were available made them particularly attractive to purchasers of large acreages, usually for speculative purposes.

There were other modifications of the basic sale policy. In the Pre-emption Act of 1841, settlers on federal lands not yet opened for sale were relieved of the threat of competitive bidders by being allowed the purchase of 160 acres for the minimum $1.25 per acre. In 1854 the Graduation Act reduced the price of land that had long remained unsold. Prices were graduated according to the number of years the land had been on the market, the low being 12½¢ per acre for land available thirty years or more. Quite different in nature were the grants in aid for the construction of western railroads. After 1854 such railroads received large acreages, which they typically offered at prices substantially higher than the federal minimum. In the case of such grants the government reserved alternate sections, which it offered for sale at double the standard minimum.

In 1862, incessant demands that federal lands be made available to actual settlers finally achieved their objective when Congress instituted another program of land grants to veterans of military service. The lands made available by the Homestead Act were almost entirely located west of the Missouri river, were less desirable than the railroad lands in the same region, and played an insignificant role in agricultural development prior to 1870.

The man in search of land to be converted into a farm in the 1820's had a wide choice as to location and terms of purchase. Over time the choices became more numerous, the terms of acquisition more variable, and the probability greater that he would purchase not from a federal land office but from a second-hand owner. It is probably true that location and quality of land as well as availability of credit were more important considerations than the differences in quoted price, wide as the range of those prices might be. In any case, the cost of land was normally a fraction of the investment necessary to convert it into a remunerative farm, while its location and the fertility of its soil were critical to the long-run success of the enterprise.

THE ESTABLISHED EASTERN FARM

A young man could acquire a farm by the inheritance or gift of a family farm, by purchase of an established operation, or by making his own farm out of virgin land. As a result of the large families of the period, only a few aspirants could anticipate an outright gift or legacy. Young men were sometimes established in farming by the break-up of a large operation into portions for each of the children. There is little evidence that the practice was common in the East during this period, although some land purchases made in the West were clearly motivated to provide adequate farms for the purchaser's sons.[10] In the older New England and Middle Atlantic states, the decline in average acreage per farm that occurred can be accounted for by the increase in the number of very small, typically part-time farm operations near the cities and towns. There is, in fact, some evidence that in the East, farms were being consolidated into large, more economic units as one response of the eastern farm-

[10] *Cultivator*, XIII (1865), 307; *Genesee Farmer*, XI (1862), 123.

ers to the increasing commercialization of agriculture and the impact of western competition.

About 1820, the man whose objective was farm production for market faced the fact that desirable farms in advantageous locations were, in terms of prevailing wage rates, very high in price. The opening of the Erie Canal, the establishment of profitable hog and cattle drives across the Alleghenies, and the growth of steamboating on the Ohio and Mississippi rivers changed prospects drastically. These changes were extended and accentuated by the development of the railroad, which acquired significance in the decade of the forties. As these agencies increased the attractiveness of the trans-Allegheny area, they decreased the returns of farming in the older regions. The Erie Canal destroyed the profitability of grain culture in much of the East and narrowed the opportunities in hog and cattle production. In the early 1850's a New Haven, Connecticut, farmer wrote: "As much of the land in this county has been cultivated for about two centuries, and as most of the farms are not large, as compared with those in some other States; as the primitive soil was not remarkably rich; as fertilizers are not very abundant; and as labor commands a high price, you will readily see the circumstances in which the products of agriculture are produced."[11]

Under such conditions, efforts to compete with western New York wheat, butter, and cheese, or Ohio beef and pork, led many an eastern farmer to agree with the editor of the *Union Agriculturist* who wrote from Chicago in 1842: "There is no mistake about it; thousands and thousands of your Eastern farmers have got to come West or give up farming. You have just begun to feel the effects of what has been going on here for the last twenty years. Heretofore, our farmers have scarcely been able to supply newcomers with bread and meat; and butter, cheese, fruit, etc., have been brought from New York. But hereafter we will pour upon you a perfect deluge of all the great staples such as you have had the last year in pork. Even the supplying of the Eastern country will be too small a business; a foreign market must be opened or our farmers will be put to their wits ends to know what to raise to make a living out of."[12]

[11] U. S. Patent Office, *Report* (1851), p. 179.
[12] *Union Agriculturist,* II (1842), 49.

Even for farmers applying the best of the known techniques to lands of better than average quality, the year-to-year rewards were considered modest, while there was little hope of significant increases in the capital values of their properties. Some farms in the New England and Middle Atlantic areas that had been valued on the basis of returns before the rise in importance of the Erie Canal were overvalued thereafter. The productivity of such farms could not support the values that had been established, particularly since the growing industries of the urban centers served to increase the wages of hired labor as well as to place pressure upon the standards of acceptable incomes for the farmers themselves. Complaints about the high costs of labor, the burden of taxation, and the inability to earn more than 2 or 3 percent on capital values were very common.[13]

Prospective entrants were frequently assured that opportunities in the East were substantial if a farm was purchased that was well located, low in price but reduced in fertility, and offering the possibility of restoration by skillful handling. To acquire such a farm was better than to go West, "where half of the profits of the crops are absorbed in the expense of transportation to market."[14] It was claimed that eastern lands might be had at no greater cost than in the West. "A farm of one to three hundred acres, in many localities in Vermont, with good buildings and stone fences, surrounded with permanent roads and bridges, churches, school-houses, and the like can be bought at a price—that counting all these improvements and advantages to the farmer—will hardly leave the soil at $1.25 per acre."[15]

It was important to avoid acquiring one of the many New England farms that combined small acreage with intrinsically infertile soil. Such farms had been established in large numbers as semi-self-sufficient homesteads, but were unsuitable to the larger-scale, lower-cost production essential to participation in a competitive market. The low prices at which many such farms were offered frequently represented the preliminary step toward sale for consolidation or even complete abandonment.[16] Even though one or more such farms

---

[13] See *New England Farmer*, XXIV (1846), 242; II (1850), 190; VIX (1855), 454; *Genesee Farmer*, IX (1839), 391; VII (1837), 121; II (1841), 61; *Rural New Yorker*, XII (1861), 317; XVI (1865), 85, 317.

[14] *American Agriculturist*, XIV (1854), 355.

[15] *Plough, Loom and Anvil*, VIII (1856), 662.

[16] On abandonment of New England farms in the 1820's and after, see *New England*

might be found at favorable prices, the renovating process was slow, with a prospect of five to ten years of low returns. Examples of successful renovation projects existed in sufficient numbers to demonstrate the technical feasibility of the approach.[17] But, as one New Hampshire farmer wrote: "To do it in a reasonable time, so that the generation that operates may realize the benefit—there is the rub . . . It is said in trade that a 'nimble sixpence is better than a slow shilling,' so say I, in culture. My impression is, when lands have been so misused, or badly managed that they cease to be productive, pull up stakes and be off."[18] Many agreed, though there were also many who made the effort to find some profitable way to utilize the older eastern lands.

The problems that confronted the man intent upon taking over an established eastern farm can be illustrated by a few contemporary accounts. A generalized but unusually complete analysis of the problems and prospects of purchasing a farm in Connecticut in the 1850's begins by pointing out that:

Most of our farmers begin with small means. The ancestral farm if subdivided would be too small to meet their views. To purchase one, a debt is incurred and though this is soon cancelled by diligence and economy, yet that liberal expenditure in improvement which would render farming in the highest degree pleasant and profitable is prevented. The education of children and their establishment employs the surplus funds. Thus great wealth is rarely obtained but a comfortable support is secured.

How is this done on a farm of one hundred and fifty acres, which is a fair average for this section? A good farm well located with tolerable buildings will cost about forty dollars per acre. One third may be in wood of different ages and will furnish fuel, fencing, and building timber, and a surplus for sale. The remaining hundred acres will furnish a few small fields for the plow, and keep about thirty head of cattle. These may be fifteen cows, one pair of oxen, a horse, and about a dozen head of young cattle. Thirty acres in meadow with cornstalks will winter them. The produce of each cow will be about two hundred fifty pounds of cheese, at ten cents, fifty pounds of butter at twenty cents, and a calf worth five dollars, making forty dollars as the income from each cow. As prices and seasons vary we will take thirty-five as the average, though many entire dairies rise much above the estimate. The growth of the young

---

Farmer, VIII (1856), 445-446; Maine Board of Agriculture, *Report, Abstracts* (1858), p. 62; *Country Gentleman,* XXXIII (1869), 312.

[17] *American Agriculturist,* IV (1845), 266; XVII (1857), 133; *Plough, Loom and Anvil,* V, pt. 2 (1853), 361; X (1857), 327-329; *Working Farmer,* XII (1860), 42.

[18] *New Hampshire Journal of Agriculture,* Jan. 29, 1859; see also April 14, 1859; *Northern Farmer,* I (1852), 466; *Cultivator,* I (1844), 176.

cattle will cover all losses on stock from age, accident, or disease and furnish a pair of oxen or steers annually for sale, worth at least $130, besides beef for the family and some surplus which we will estimate at fifty dollars. Another hundred may be added as the amount of poultry, fruit, potatoes, or turnips sold as these items are very variable and there are but few farms where some of them are not made available. Small fields of a few acres each will be devoted to corn, oats, rye, and buckwheat, and variable amounts will be disposed of, which we will also put at one hundred dollars. Grass and clover seed, if raised, hay sold, wood and timber, will add perhaps fifty dollars. Work done off the farm will pay the shoemaker, tailor, and blacksmith, and purchase new tools as needed.

Now for the expenses. We would set apart two hundred dollars to pay the store bills of a moderate sized family, also to furnish salt for the dairy, plaster and grass seed when purchased. A hired man for eight months will cost one hundred and twenty dollars and a boy for the year, his clothes, perhaps twenty-five more. And a girl for the year, (though her help is too often dispensed with,) sixty dollars. Taxes and society expenses fifty dollars. Interest on $7000 investment is $420. The account will then stand thus:

Credit		Debit	
Dairy	$525	Store bills	$200
Oxen and beef	180	Hired help	205
Pork	100	Taxes	50
Grain	100	Interest	420
Wood, etc.	50		875
	1055		
Debit	875		
Surplus	180		

Extra expenses such as new buildings or repairs, traveling expenses and education of children, unless other means exist to meet these, will deduct from these profits. Permanent improvements, such as drains and heavy walls, must stand on the credit side. Also the farmer gets his rent, fuel, and almost entire provision for his family from his farm. By our schedule he receives full interest on his capital, the support of his family, and one hundred and eighty dollars. If he has interest to pay, unless his family is such that he can dispense with some of the hired labor, he may find it difficult to make both ends meet. But the fact that many hard working men do run in debt for farms and pay for them, and in middle life find themselves in possession of good homesteads prepared to educate and establish their children, is proof that farming is reasonably profitable. A more pleasant position would surely be one free from debt with a surplus fund from which to draw for extra expenses; and we should advise to buy less land and cultivate more highly. We consider our farmer as an improving one and, blessed with health, his surplus receipts will not lie idle. Judiciously invested in improvements they will pay more than six per cent, and add rapidly to the net income of the family. The fact that many with no extra advantages in a market, but in the common routine of farming do much better than we have estimated is settled. Others by supplying the demand for some kind of fancy stock, or meeting a very favorable market for their produce, acquire sudden gains and feel some of the excitements of those engaged in trade, but simply legitimate farming supports well those who practice it well.[19]

It need scarcely be pointed out that there is in this analysis no promise of any rapid accumulation of funds. Over and above the support of the family, the enterprise produces an income of $600, if debt free, and very much less if interest must be paid on a mortgage and the principal reduced. There is here only a narrow margin of profit to compensate for the inevitable years of poor crops or unremunerative prices. Other accounts run along similar veins.

From Massachusetts we have an account of a farm comprising eighty-five run-down acres, purchased in 1843 for $4,337. The farmer wrote: "in order to pay for it, I mortgaged it for $4,100, paying only $237, all that I had, after buying my stock." Nine years later he reported having made extensive improvements in drains and stone walls and developed an orchard, earned $300 off the farm, and paid wages on the farm of $156. Progress was slow, however. In his words:

These things, with my limited means have been the work of time. I have not done as I would, but have been obliged to do as I could. With a young family dependent upon me, unable to earn their living, but, thank God, almost always able to eat their share; with my interest money ($250 a year) to make out, and my farm to improve, I have so far weathered the storm, with a head wind, and am a little nearer the harbor than I was when I commenced the voyage. I have paid up about $600 on the mortgage, and laid out nearly $2000 in permanent improvements on my buildings and farm.[20]

From Vermont comes a similar story of a long, laborious struggle to acquire ownership:

I commenced working out at the age of one-and-twenty, for ten dollars per month in summer, and eight in winter. Worked until I laid up about

---

[19] The writer adds: "True, close economy is aimed at everything, and the utmost care taken that no loss shall accrue—except in one department. There is a neglect of the manure heap which has been truly called the 'farmer's mine,' and because it's most subtle and valuable elements are invisible they are often allowed to escape." *Homestead*, I (1855), 642; also in *Genesee Farmer*, XVII (1856), 241.

[20] Agricultural Society of Massachusetts, *Transactions* (1852), pp. 93-94.

$550, purchased a farm for $1,550, paid $550, mortgaged the farm to secure the remainder, paid between $400 and $500 interest, laid out about $500 in improvements, have paid up the whole, owe no man anything but good will, and have money to pay my expenses as I go along, all without receiving by gift or heirship, what would be equivalent to $100 at the age of one-and-twenty.[21]

There is a strong element of pride of achievement in the account of a Vermont farmer who followed a somewhat different route to attain control over a farm operation:

I would say a word to those that think farming is a hard and a slow way to make money. It is so, but it is a safe way. I will tell you how I began. I was bound out at the age of 14 years until I was 21 for $100, and learn to read, write, and cypher as far as the single rule of three, and learn the trade of a farmer. At 23 I married. At that time I had added $200 more to the $100. I moved home with my father-in-law, on to a farm of 100 acres, somewhat out of repair. I then purchased a pasture, for which I paid $800, which brought me in debt $500. I carried on said farm eight years, at the halves, giving him one-half of the income of my pasture for the income of one-half of his stock. At the expiration of eight years he died. From that to the present time, I have had three-fourths of the income, paying my mother-in-law one-fourth. During that time, I have improved the farm, kept the buildings in repair, attended meeting regular, always paid the printer in advance and purchased a farm of 120 acres, for which I paid $1400. I am now out of debt, and have some money to let—besides having $400 stock in the Central Railroad, as a permanent fund.[22]

These few instances illustrate the circumstances of entry in the older farming areas. The amounts of capital required to make a beginning were little different from those necessary for the establishment of a farm in the newer regions, as will be shown in the following pages. The possession of capital was scarcely the determining factor in the choice between East and West. More important were the modest returns that seemed to be in prospect, as illustrated by the above four accounts. Although there were significant numbers of eastern farms that paid their operators handsome returns, the more general situation was expressed by the following: "Farmers in New England do not average one hundred dollars yearly, each, by ordinary farming, as the result of their own earnings; (that is, amount of inheritance deducted). Stick a pin here, and set this

21 *New England Farmer*, V (1853), 568.
22 *New England Farmer*, XIII (1861), 422-423. See also *New England Farmer*, XII (1860), 387.

down as truth; all that is said about the money making business of farming, the contrary not withstanding. Mark this, I say, not as a discouragement, but because the truth is better than delusion."[23] Either farming in the West or an eastern urban occupation offered far more attractive prospects.

FARM-MAKING: THE FORESTED FRONTIER

The more aggressive turned to the frontier, either to secure virgin lands to be converted into productive fields, to purchase land on which some work had been accomplished, or to purchase a fully developed farm. Many were lured into the task of carving a homestead for themselves on some small part of the vast acreage of heavily forested land that lay to the West.

In 1821 a New York farmer offered a plan for a "small pattern farm" so "arranged and made perfect as with the least labour and expense to produce the largest crop and yield the greatest net profits, yearly, keeping neatness and regularity constantly in view."[24] The farm was to be made from 50 acres of woodland, of which 30 were to be cleared and cultivated. Five acres were to be occupied by the house, barn, stables, shed, a garden, orchard, and hog and calf pastures. Pasture and meadowland occupied 5 acres each. The 15 acres in crops were to include 2½ acres each of wheat, corn, rye-barley, and oats-millet, and 1½ acres each in potatoes, turnips, lucerne, and flax-hops-madder-woad.

The investment, not including the cost of 50 acres of woodland, was estimated at $1,000, itemized as follows:

Clearing 30 acres at $10	$300
Fencing 700 rods	70
Log house and frame barn	200
Out houses, well, and orchard	150
1 yoke oxen	50
1 horse	50
2 cows, good	40
2 hogs, grass-fed	10
10 sheep, best kind	50
Utensils and harness	50

The 50 acres of land were obtainable at anywhere from $1.00 to $5.00 or $6.00 an acre. In addition, a sum of about $50 or $100

[23] *Homestead*, III (1857), 80-81. See also *Genesee Farmer*, XX (1839), 255.
[24] *Plough Boy*, III (1821), 20.

should be added to the account to cover seed and the needs of the farmer and his family for the first season of the operation.

No doubt this estimate does not reflect the original investments actually made by most farm-makers of the time. The first four items listed, accounting for $700, usually were the product of the farm-maker's own labor. Cash payments, and perhaps costs also, were thereby reduced, although to carry on such work the farm-maker required funds to secure family provisions for a longer period, at least two years. At the end of that time, the farm-maker might hope to have his land in such a condition as to obtain his necessities from his own crops, though the quantity of salable products would be extremely small. While a yoke of oxen was very useful in clearing timber, other animals were not essential and were a problem to feed before the development of crops, so that their acquisition was frequently postponed.

Though many doubtless attempted farm-making with less capital,[25] about $500 was the necessary minimum, exclusive of land, even at this early date, and that sum would finance the establishment of only a modest operation. Farm-makers strove to achieve that amount of capital over a period of time by practicing great frugality and sometimes accepting considerable privation. If for some that capital was a point of departure, for others it was a goal to be achieved only with arduous labor.

Contemporary accounts illustrate the objectives, the resources, and the accomplishments of new farmers on the forested frontier. The following analysis, written of northern Pennsylvania in the early 1850's, was applicable to almost any wooded area in the period:

A healthy man, with or without family, and no other property than an axe and hoe, might thus get possession of one hundred acres; the first year he might erect a cabin, and clear and sow with wheat ten acres, besides earning sufficient in the vicinity for his subsistence; the second year he would have a crop to dispose of that would be sufficient to enable him to buy a cow, a yoke of oxen, twenty sheep, some hogs, a plough, and a

[25] For example, John Lorain wrote of the Pennsylvania backwoodsmen: "They seldom have more money than will pay their expenses on the road; and often do not bring more than a horse and cow with them, therefore are commonly much better stocked with young, helpless children than they are with cattle; consequently they are compelled to exercise those talents which nature distributes without partiality or starve." Lorain, *Nature and Reason Harmonized in the Practice of Husbandry* (Philadelphia, 1819), p. 186.

harrow, besides increasing his household furniture and supporting his family; the third year he could clear fifteen acres more, and every subsequent year continue to clear and cultivate and on third-rate land could keep the increase of his flock, until in ten years, his one hundred acres would be cleared and fenced, and he might have ten cows, two yoke of oxen, ten hogs, and two hundred sheep. After which, suppose the profit of each cow to be annually twenty dollars; that of each sheep, including the lambs, to be one dollar and fifty cents; there would be two hundred dollars for the cows and three hundred dollars for the sheep—making five hundred dollars; the other proceeds would doubtless, support his family.[26]

This is an account of modest achievement, slowly attained, though sufficiently attractive to lure many who saw no future for themselves in the East. But even the most skeptical would find irresistible the news and rumors of far greater profits that flowed from West to East. One such is the following summary of a farming career in Ohio:

Mr. Elias Simpson was married in 1842—the only heritage possessed by himself and wife were strong hands and willing hearts. Mr. Simpson had no advantages from education, but he has a good mind and sound judgment. When married, he took a lease which he worked for three years. When this expired, he rented ground for three years, and had now gained sufficient property to take, in 1848, a lease upon one hundred acres of Scioto bottom. This he cleared, fenced, and farmed, making more or less money each year, until, on the expiration of his lease in 1854, he bought the farm he had improved. This was soon paid for, and another hundred acres of improved Scioto bottom was added to his farm.

The history of each succeeding year would be a rehearsal of the above. His farm last year (1863) consisted of about 650 acres, well improved good fertile land, embracing corn and wheat lands, meadow and pastures.

This spring Mr. Simpson had purchased, adjoining him, 200 acres of bottom and 100 acres of upland at a cost of $28,000, on which he paid down $14,000, this being less than his profits for 1863.

Thus he married in 1842 without a dollar, and the spring of 1864 finds him worth at least $100,000. In this there has been no speculation, but it is all the result of hard labor and good management.[27]

The selection of a farm in new territory—particularly the selection of raw land and its conversion into an operating farm—required a high degree of enterprise combined with good judgment. The location chosen was of great importance, from the point of view not only of soil fertility and transportation facilities, but also of

---

[26] U. S. Patent Office, *Report* (1852), p. 234.
[27] *Cultivator,* XII (1864), 143. See also *New England Farmer,* II (1850), 391.

healthfulness and social amenities. Many a farmer spent considerable time reconnoitering the general area that attracted him, and frequently he purchased only after spending much time and money in making comparisons.[28] Thereafter skill and judgment in the investment of funds and labor in every phase of the operation determined success.

The essential elements in the task of carving a farm out of the forest were building a shelter for the farm-maker and his family; providing an adequate water supply; laying out the fields, clearing immediately as much land as possible, and at least enough to permit the seeding of crops to provide minimum food requirements; and fencing the fields to protect crops from the farmer's own animals as well as others'.

The first and for some time the chief task was to clear away the brush and trees. The most common procedure was to begin that work in the early summer. As much timber as possible was then cut, so that a burning might be held in late August. Thereupon the cleared land was sown to wheat. Cutting continued throughout the autumn and winter to provide further clearings for the spring planting. Ten to fifteen acres might be roughly cleared in the first year in this manner. Thereafter crops received priority in the application of labor, the clearing being continued as time permitted.

Important differences existed in the character of the clearing operation.[29] Some farmers sought to remove all vestiges of the original forest in one operation, a procedure which yielded "old fields" in the shortest time but which was slow, laborious, and expensive. Most left those stumps to rot that could not be removed by a plow. Others removed the brush and smaller trees, girdled the larger timber, and left them to blow down or to be removed at some later date. These methods were expeditious and less expensive, al-

---

[28] For example, in 1836 William Fitch of Rensselaer County, New York, spent a month and $150 on a trip to Licking County, Ohio, which resulted in the purchase of a farm for $3,000. Robert Price, "Travel in the 1830's," *Ohio State Archaeological and Historical Quarterly*, LIV (1945), 40-45. Accounts of such exploratory trips are numerous and provide much of our knowledge of agricultural conditions. See *Ohio Cultivator*, X (1845), 185; *Michigan Farmer*, X (1853), 7; Rodney Loehr, "Moving Back from the Atlantic Seaboard," *Agricultural History*, XVII (1943), 91-92; Solon J. Buck, "Making a Farm on the Frontier, Extracts from the Diaries of Mitchell Young Jackson," *Agricultural History*, IV (1930), 92.

[29] *Cultivator*, VII (1841), 162; *Central New York Farmer*, III (1841), 125; *Michigan Farmer*, VIII (1850), 275; XIII (1855), 365-366; XIV (1856), 202-203; *Ohio Cultivator*, XV (1859), 2-3, 36, 119; *Western Farmer*, I (1840), 320-322.

though the fields were not clear of obstacles for ten years or more.

Fencing was an integral and essential part of the forest clearing operation. Though fencing material existed in superabundance, the labor involved in preparing poles or the more usual split rails was heavy. Generally logs of desirable size of straight-grained species were cut to standard lengths and set aside for the winter task of splitting. The zig-zag or Virginia rail fence was built almost universally since, though it required a great deal of timber, no digging of post holes was necessary.[30] Even so, the labor cost of such fencing was substantial, estimates ranging from 50¢ to $1.00 per rod. Costs of fencing per acre were particularly high for the smaller fields enclosed in the earlier phases of farm-making. Excessively small fields with exhorbitant fencing costs were a common criticism of American, and particularly of eastern, farming.

Because of these differences in the character of the work and because clearing was usually performed along with other tasks, performances varied, and it is difficult to estimate the rates at which lands were made available for cropping. Fifteen acres per year may be considered the largest possible under favorable conditions, the larger stumps being permitted to remain. Since many farm-makers found it necessary to give attention to such pursuits as lumbering, cordwood cutting, ash collecting, or teaming, as well as crop cultivation, the rate of clearing was more likely to be in the vicinity of five to ten acres per year.[31]

By the late forties and early fifties, the growth of markets made profitable the investment of capital in hired labor for clearing forested land, much as labor was frequently hired to break prairie. Estimates of the money costs of clearing forested land depended on the nature of the work and ranged from $3 to $25 per acre, the latter figure including the building of rail fences.[32] The most com-

---

[30] *Genesee Farmer,* XVI (1855), 242-243.

[31] On fencing, see Clarence H. Danhof, "The Fencing Problem in the Eighteen-Fifties," *Agricultural History,* XIX (1944), 168-186; Earl W. Hayter, "Livestock-Fencing Conflicts in Rural America," *Agricultural History,* XXXVII (1963), 10-20.

[32] For estimates by farmers of the cost of clearing timbered land, see *New England Farmer,* XVII (Sept. 5, 1838); *American Agriculturist,* III (1841), 174, 354; *Cultivator,* IV (1847), 300; *Michigan Farmer,* VIII (1850), 374; IX (1851), 71; XII (1854), 297; *Ohio Cultivator,* IX (1853), 338-339; *New Jersey Farmer,* III (1858), 216; *Maine Farmer,* Aug. 3, 1854; Wisconsin State Agricultural Society, *Transactions* (1851), pp. 243-246. A statistical analysis is in Martin L. Primach, "Land Clearing Under Nineteenth Century Techniques: Some Preliminary Calculations," *Journal of Economic History,* XXII (1962), 484-497.

mon figures quoted in the 1840's and 1850's were $10 to 12, which suggest that approximately one man's labor for one month was required for the task.

In some locations the sale of lumber and cordwood aided in financing the farm-making task. In the East, the growth of towns and cities had lagged too far behind agricultural settlement to have played an important role in this respect, although it is doubtless true that much of the later clearing of land in areas within transportation distance of the larger towns and villages was undertaken because the cleared land was obtained without cost in the process of shipping lumber and cordwood to market. Anthracite coal ousted cordwood in the major cities of the East after 1831 and had become the common fuel by 1860. In the West, however, urban markets and farm-making tended to develop contemporaneously, and farmers found the selling of cordwood a remunerative activity. This seems to have been the case, for example, around Buffalo, while farmers in western Michigan found a market for cordwood in Chicago, easily reached by steamboat.[33] In addition to the urban markets, steamboats and railroads were large consumers of cordwood. Everywhere along navigable streams, cordwood could be sold for steamboat use or for shipment to urban centers. With the spread of the railroad, the sale of cordwood became an even more important factor, enabling farmers conveniently situated to continue clearing their land at little or no cost, with an immediate return for their labor.

In areas of coniferous forests, lumbering and the cutting of hemlock for bark provided both wage employment and, for farmers working their own lands, money income and clearings. The cleared land that was a byproduct of these industries was important in western New York, northern Pennsylvania, and Maine in the 1830's, and thereafter the pine forests of Michigan, Wisconsin, and Minnesota were successively drawn upon for lumber supplies.[34] East of the Ohio in the pine and hemlock areas, lumbering and farming were often combined, although lumbering tended to be the domi-

[33] New York State Agricultural Society, *Transactions* (1843), p. 175. In the late 1850's, Chicago buyers were going as far north as Michigan's Grand Traverse Bay for cordwood. In that area a settler could "chop out a home for himself . . . and his cordwood will purchase provisions." *Michigan Farmer,* XIII (1855), 169; XIV (1856), 100.
[34] *Farm Journal and Progressive Farmer,* VI (1856), 285; *Maine Farmer,* Jan. 27, 1853.

nant occupation because it offered an immediate cash return. In Maine, Michigan, Wisconsin, and Minnesota, such farming as developed in the lumbering areas remained small scale and largely of a subsistence character until the timber was gone.[35] In those states, lumbering operations were more frequently carried on by large companies operating on their own lands and with wage employees. In the East, lumbering was typically a small-scale enterprise, conducted by the men who owned the land from which they cut and sold the logs. On the whole, the initial clearing of farms in the hardwood forest was made without significant revenue from timber.[36]

Land newly cleared of timber and fenced was sown to crops, chiefly corn and potatoes but also the small grains and whatever else the family might wish to attempt. Such land was rarely plowed for the first five or six years.

The possession of livestock was not essential to the tasks to be performed, although a pair of oxen was useful for disposing of large logs, for drawing the harrow over a field seeded to wheat, and for transportation. Hogs, which fed unattended in the woods, were desirable as an inexpensive source of food. Sheep, though they required protection, were useful not only as a source of wool for the women's weaving but also as an aid in killing tree and brush sprouts on the new clearings. The presence of any large number of animals, however, presented feeding problems. Until an adequate area of grass in pasture and meadow had been established, the problem of providing winter supplies severely restricted the number of cattle and sheep.

After seven to ten years, the farmer would have cleared and fenced about as much land as he could care for in crops, and the

---

[35] In Maine, "Farmers . . . make as much calculation to provide themselves with employment for the winter as they do for their work in the summer. Most of those who reside in the back part of the State, engage in lumbering of some form. Some hire by the month to go into the woods; others get what they term *small lumber,* such as staves, shingles, clapboards, hoops, etc., etc. Many have trades at which they work in the winter. Those who live near the railroads or canals get out wood for market, or to be used by the locomotives, so that all find employment during the long winter at which they 'can earn a penny,' so that by industry and perseverance, they are, as a class, what is termed in 'easy circumstances.' " *Country Gentleman,* I (1853), 54. In the pine areas of the West, agriculture alone was considered a precarious business, although the farmer with adequate grasslands found the lumber camps a good market for hay, corn, and grasses. *Boston Cultivator,* Oct. 25, 1851; Maine Board of Agriculture, *Report* (1858), p. 19. See also *American Agriculturist,* XII (1854), 322; *Rural New Yorker,* IV (1853), 294.

[36] Cf. *Cultivator,* IV (1847), 300.

farm-making phase was ended. If the soil had proved productive, and if it had been possible to increase the number of livestock, the farm-maker possessed a farm of average productivity. The field first brought into cultivation was now clear of all but the largest stumps, but it was also probably showing the effects of continuous cropping in its reduced yields. This matter was not serious since it could be put to use as pasture and was, in fact, needed for the increasing number of animals. Clearing of the forest was continued so that the acreage tilled might be maintained, the net effect being an increase in pasturage. The eventual conversion of all the reasonably level wooded acreage into fields represented not so much a triumph as a crisis, requiring a change in the technique of farming adapted to the effective use of "old fields." Many a farmer sought new land instead, and spent a lifetime chopping in winter, clearing in spring, and cropping in summer.

FARM-MAKING: THE PRAIRIES

As settlement pushed beyond the forests and onto the grasslands of Illinois, there flowed eastward numerous accounts of the fertility of the prairies, the ease with which they might be cultivated, and the speed with which a substantial farm might be acquired. The prairies of Illinois and Iowa were the subject of one of the greatest spontaneous promotional campaigns of history.

Englishmen were told that the annual rental of an English acre would buy 20 or 30 acres of wild but fertile soil. Eastern farmers operating fully capitalized farms, enjoying no increase in the values of their land but suffering from shrinking prices, higher costs, and declining fertility, were urged to note that the $2,000 or $3,000 for which their farm might be sold would buy ten to twenty times its acreage in the West, and that far richer land. "It is here, with the labor of his own hands, and the trifling outlay for a 'a quarter section' or an 'eighty' and a few head of cattle, the emigrant of one or two hundred dollars finds himself in the short space of six or eight years, possessor of a cultivated farm upon which he has erected tenements commensurate with the comforts of a family and the already numerous herds which have imperceptibly grown from his little beginning."[37] So wrote the editor of the *Union Agriculturist*

---

[37] *Union Agriculturist*, I (1844), 60.

from Chicago in 1841. Or from Iowa in 1843: "It is surprising how soon your industrious settler makes himself a home and farm here. He plants himself down, say on a lot of 160 acres, a half of a quarter of which is in timber, and the rest prairie. If he hires the work done, he can get his fence, nine rails with stake and rider made for $1 or 75¢ a rod. His prairie he can get broken up for $1 or $1.25 per acre, and thus for little more than a hundred dollars he may have fifty acres in cultivation, two months after settlement."[38] Other reports claimed that the cost of establishing a farm was repaid from the first crop.[39] The man without capital was assured of abundant employment opportunities and the powerful incentive of acquiring his own farm within a very short time: "Many a poor Eastern boy who has gone West with but a small balance of funds in his pocket, has been hired out to work the first year on the farm. The proceeds of this enables him to work on a farm on shares the second and third years, and by the end of the fourth year would enable him to purchase a farm of his own."[40] Such stories could not fail to impress easterners.[41] There were also other accounts, however, which were less extravagant and which warned that the opportunities on the prairie lands were not to be achieved without substantial expenditures of capital and labor, that failures occurred, and that hardships and difficulties must be faced.

The elements of the farm-making task were everywhere essentially the same: there was the land to clear of its natural growth, to fence, and to seed; shelter to be built; a water supply to be provided; and provisions to be assured. The fact that western soils were covered with grasses rather than trees however, presented significant differences both technologically and economically.

Unbroken, the grass was an important asset for the farmer possessing or able to build up a herd of cattle. In forested areas, herds of animals were built up only slowly, as continued land-clearing increased the acreages in pasture and animal grains. On the prairies, in contrast, cattle could be maintained throughout the year on the native grasses. Although these grasses did not usually long persist

---

38 *American Agriculturist,* II (1843), 210; *Rural New Yorker,* VI (1855), 14.

39 *Northern Farmer,* I (1854), 290-291.

40 *Rural American,* I (1854), 130. Cf. *Rural New Yorker,* V (1854), 234; *Minnesota Farmer,* I (1860), 282.

41 *Northern Farmer,* V (1858), 76; *Ohio Farmer,* VIII (1859), 201.

under heavy grazing, domesticated pastures were relatively easy and quick to establish. Much of the land, moreover, was far more productive of income when planted in corn or grains than in grass, while the grass-bred cattle required corn-fattening for some time before they were marketable.

The preparation of virgin grasslands for tilled crops required far less labor and time than that involved in removing timber, though tilling the newly turned grassland was more difficult than cultivating soils newly cleared of timber. The virgin sod was tough, and prairie breaking required three to eight yoke of oxen, a specially heavy plow, and skill applied in the right season, sometime between May and August.[42] It was common practice to hire the work out to specialists at a cost of from $2.00 to $5.00 per acre, the land being broken at the rate of about two acres per day.[43] Although a crop might be had from newly broken land, yields were usually small, and a fair return was not expected until the following season.[44] The cost of breaking, therefore, "had to be advanced about fifteen months before any returns can be obtained from the land."[45]

The absence of timber was also a disadvantage, rendering subsistence farming much less practicable than was the case in wooded areas. Wood was needed for buildings, fencing, and fuel. Early set-

[42] "Strangers cannot know and many residents have not observed how much better the conditions and production of prairie ground will be (for years) if broken shallow and after the spring rains; say from the first of June until August." *Union Agriculturist*, II (1842), 26, 34, 42-43, 67. Elsewhere May and June were suggested as the most desirable months. *American Agriculturist*, XXIII (1864), 74; XXIV (1865), 363; *Cultivator*, VIII (1851), 277-278; *Genesee Farmer*, XVIII (1857), 84, 141, 179, 302; *Prairie Farmer*, III (1843), 90; IV (1844), 118; VI (1846), 138-139; III (1859), 339; *Northwestern Farmer and Horticultural Journal*, V (1860), 352-353; *Rural American*, I (1856), 130; *Rural New Yorker*, III (1852), 358; VI (1855), 358; Wisconsin State Agricultural Society, *Transactions* (1851), pp. 243-246.

[43] *Cultivator*, IX (1852), 67; *American Agriculturist*, XVI (1857), 252; *Genesee Farmer*, XVIII (1856), 84-85; *Northwestern Farmer*, I (1856), 128; Frederick Gerhard, *Illinois As It Is* (Chicago, 1857), p. 311.

[44] In Iowa, "The sod is sometimes turned over in the spring and immediately planted to corn, which sometimes produces fifteen or twenty bushels per acre, but frequently fails to produce anything." *Genesee Farmer*, XVIII (1857), 141. In Iowa a farmer "raised partial crops of 'sod corn' on my earliest breaking—costing nothing but the seed in planting—but, of course, only partial crops." *Rural New Yorker*, VI (1855), 358. See also *Cultivator*, VI (1850), 277-278; *New England Farmer*, XI (1860), 250-251; *American Agriculturist*, XII (1850), 128; *DeBow's Commercial Review*, XXI (1856), 96-97; *Genesee Farmer*, XVII (1856), 84-85; *Plough, Loom and Anvil*, VI (1854), 519-520.

[45] *Wisconsin Farmer and Northwestern Cultivator*, IX (1857), 122.

tlers sought location on the edge of the prairie with an adequate supply of wood readily on hand. Those who came later sometimes found it possible to purchase a stand of timber within a reasonable distance, from which wood could be obtained. The alternative was to purchase the needed lumber and to haul it from the nearest forested area, navigable stream, or railroad. An Illinois farmer commented on the problem: "Fencing in many places costs far more than the land and not only is this true, but fencing must be paid for in cash while the land can be bought on such terms that the money for the payments of both principal and interest can be realized from the land."[46] However obtained and financed, there was wide agreement with a contemporary observation that "fences are to a prairie farm, one-third its value."[47]

Most farm-makers, requiring immediate returns, planted corn, potatoes, buckwheat, and similar crops on the broken sod. Such plantings might yield enough for the needs of the family, but failures were common.[48] The majority of newcomers did not raise enough food to supply themselves in their first year of cropping, and older settlers considered the more recent arrivals a profitable market for their products. After the first or second year, production was generally sufficient to support the family, but its labor continued for some years to be heavily devoted to developing the future productivity of the enterprise. Although land could be broken with comparative rapidity, a period of years elapsed before the products of even a well-financed and well-managed farm reached proportions that permitted substantial sales. With regard to Illinois, one contemporary observed, "every experienced farmer will confirm the statement that it required four or five years before new settlers, even upon our easily managed prairie soils, can furnish a large surplus for market; and I think, will agree, that the effect of the extraordinary emigration to this State between 1852 and 1856 was not apparent in the surplus products until the harvest of 1860."[49]

[46] *Rural New Yorker*, VIII (1857), 269. See also *Valley Farmer*, II (1850), 74; *Northern Farmer*, I (1854), 117.

[47] *American Agriculturist*, XVI (1857), 278. See also *Wisconsin Farmer and Northwestern Cultivator*, IX (1857), 116-118.

[48] *Genesee Farmer*, XVIII (1857), 141; *Cultivator*, VII (1850), 277; *Rural New Yorker*, VI (1855), 358; X (1859), 204; *Country Gentleman*, XII (1858), 316.

[49] Illinois State Agricultural Society, *Quarterly Journal*, II, no. 1 (1863), 6.

Capital and credit were therefore more important factors in farm-making on the western grasslands than in the East, and the approach to farm-making varied widely with the amount of capital available. This diversity is reflected in the numerous contemporary estimates of the cost of establishing a farm.

Given sufficient capital and careful timing, it was possible to establish a farm enterprise on virgin prairie that would provide some support for the family by the end of the first year, full support by the end of the second year, and some marketable products by the end of the third year. A modest enterprise in the 1830's would have been an 80-acre farm equipped with a minimum shelter at a cost of about $150. The supplies needed to break, fence, seed, and harvest 30 acres in wheat and 30 acres in corn, including subsistence for the farmer and his family, amounted to about $600. To this must be added the cost of the land and $200 to $400 for the essential draft animals and the hogs and cattle that were highly desirable to make profitable use of the grass and corn.[50] As eighty acres was generally considered too small for a farm, more acreage was usually purchased at small additional cost. Excluding moving costs, resources in cash, credit, and equipment totaling about $1,000 were necessary in the 1850's in order to establish an enterprise of some 160 acres with the object of having in tillage within a three- or four-year period all the acreage that the labor could handle. In terms of capital needs per acre, estimates ranged from $14 to $21 per acre. A foothold on farm ownership might be obtained with less than $1,000, but it would be a tenuous one, placing the farm-maker under the necessity of working at wage labor whenever possible while his own enterprise was slowly developing. At the same time, the recommended figure was not of itself a guarantee of success or of avoidance of difficulties and even privation.[51]

[50] The estimate applies to Illinois in 1830. Patrick Shirreff, *Tour Through North America* (Philadelphia, 1835) pp. 446-449. For similar estimates of the 1830's, see American Institute, *Journal*, II (1837), 293; Robert Baird, *View of the Valley of the Mississippi, or the Emigrant's and Traveler's Guide to the West* (Philadelphia, 1835), pp. 215-216; *Western Farmer*, I (1840), 121. For estimates of the 1850's, see Clarence H. Danhof, "Farm-Making Costs and the Safety Valve: 1850-1860," *Journal of Political Economy*, XLIX (1941), 327-328. Estimates reflecting the somewhat higher costs of the 1860's are in Iowa State Agricultural Society, *Report* (1864), pp. 113-114; *Country Gentleman*, XXVII (1866), 26.

[51] On the economic hazards, see American Institute, *Transactions* (1865-1866), p. 388; *Rural Register*, II (1861), 356.

THE ESTABLISHED WESTERN FARM

The purchase of a farm at least partially developed and previously operated for a period of time was an important alternative to making a farm from virgin land. Although the characteristics of such farms varied greatly, they included, at a minimum, some acreage cleared or broken, fenced and in cultivation, as well as housing and usually other buildings. Near the frontier of settlement, farms on which some housing and crop land were available attracted many as a means of avoiding certain difficulties of the early period in the farm-making process. In more densely settled areas, it was easier to ascertain the fertility of the soil and the desirability of the location with reference to markets. Other noneconomic considerations, such as proven healthfulness or the presence of desirable social institutions, especially schools and churches, were important. In any case, farms of all degrees of development were available in all sections in large numbers. One contemporary observed of the prairie frontier that "of the whole number of farms thus commenced, the owners of about *one-half* remain . . . as permanent residents. The other half consists of a nomad class, that is wandering but never satisfied in any one place."[52]

The supply of such farms on the market resulted from a number of factors. On the frontier, narrowly defined, there was the well-recognized type, the epitome of the pioneer, who preferred isolation, crude farming, and hunting opportunities, to neighbors, "sound husbandry," and society.[53] Many of these sold readily, satisfied with relatively small gains in the value of their holdings. Others remained longer, pursuing the exploitative agriculture characteristic

---

[52] *American Agriculturist,* XVI (1857), 277. See also *American Agriculturist,* XV (1856), 222; *American Farmer's Magazine,* VIII (1858), 212; *Indiana Farmer,* IV (1854-1855), 146; *Plough, Loom and Anvil,* VI (1854), 594; *Prairie Farmer,* XII (1852), 378; *Rural New Yorker,* II (1856), 122.

[53] The sequence of hunter-farmer, exploitative farmer, and permanent settler was well recognized in forest settlement. See, e.g., Sidney Smith, *The Settler's New Home* (London 1850), p. 142. See also sources cited in Percy W. Bidwell and John I. Falconer, *History of Agriculture in the Northern United States, 1620-1860* (Carnegie Institution of Washington, 1925), p. 166. The successive steps of settlement were thus approached by a form of specialization that overcame the lack of adaptability of many farmers. Though some experience with an area was lost as a result of this mobility (as Allan G. Bogue points out in "Farming in the Prairie Peninsula," *Journal of Economic History,* XXIII (1963), 5), on the whole the mobility of specialists served to accelerate development of the agricultural economy.

of the farm-making period.[54] Eventually they found that their farms had increased in value but also showed signs of declining fertility. Dwindling crops created pressure to give up the familiar activities of exploitative agriculture and to assume those necessary to farm remuneratively under more exacting conditions. Many such farmers—half, according to one estimate—preferred to sell out and move westward with the proceeds, there to repeat the sequence.[55]

Still others remained only until the development of local population and transportation had increased the value of their farms to a point beyond which they could see no further, early advance.[56] Or a farmer sold out so that he might move farther West to provide his sons with more adequate acreages of cheaper land.[57] Certain farms on the market represented defeat: Some men found the tasks too difficult; many more faced financial stringencies resulting from inadequate capitals, which induced them to sell or, after a year or two of poor crops, face foreclosure.[58] Failure of markets to materialize or the realization that the soil of a location was below expectations were other factors that doubtless operated, though for obvious reasons they did not find their way into print.

A going farm represented important advantages over farm-making on wild land. A second-hand farm was immediately productive of returns. A. D. Jones urged the purchase of farms on which some "improvements" had been made, arguing that the two years necessary to secure any product from wild land would be saved, "and the crops from the improved farm will often pay its whole cost in

---

[54] For an example from Illinois in 1831, see Rebecca Burlend, *A True Picture of Emigration* (Lakeside Press, 1936), pp. 53-57.

[55] *Rural New Yorker*, V (1854), 317; VII (1856), 46.

[56] It is obviously difficult to establish when this point was reached for any given area, because a variety of forces were involved. On the frontier, where wild land remained available at the government's prices, a rise of from $7 to $10 seems to have stimulated sales. Yet in Ohio in the 1850's an observer wrote: "For the last ten years there has been a vast migration to Illinois, Iowa, Minnesota, and Nebraska. This has uniformly been the case with all the states where lands come to $30 or $50 per acre, and is caused by the fact that it then becomes a speculation for farmers to sell out and commence new farms at government prices." *Journal of Commerce*, Feb. 11, 1857. A correspondent from the Grand River Valley of Michigan wrote in the *Michigan Farmer*, XII (1854), 141: "Old improved farms are now valued at a rate that would make it profitable for those wishing to sell out, and wild land is rising very fast. Land that can now be had for $3 or $4 per acre will soon be worth $6 or $8." See also *Rural New Yorker*, VII (1856), 58.

[57] Robert Baird, *West Indies and North America* (Philadelphia, 1850), p. 144.

[58] *Prairie Farmer*, XIV (1854), 346.

one year, generally in two or three at farthest."[59] The transition
from the farming methods and objectives of one area to those of
another was rendered considerably less difficult. Such farms could
sometimes be purchased for less than the cost of development.[60]
The deprivations and hardships of the frontier might be avoided,
while the economic and social advantages of a settled community
were enjoyed. European immigrants, in particular, were advised
that making farms on the frontier presented serious problems and
called for skills unknown to them. These difficulties might be avoided
by the purchase of a farm at least partially developed.[61] But they
were also warned that locations must be carefully considered and
that a farm seriously depleted by poor culture should be avoided.[62]
The price of any given farm as compared with the cost of improving wild land was the essential determinant. The price asked would
of course have to be balanced against the prospects for yielding an
increase in income.

Judgment of the alternatives was critical, though the uncertainties as to the potential of any given farm were great. The amount
of available capital determined whether the would-be farmer concerned himself principally with farm-making or farming. For the
man with little capital, the alternatives were farm-making, with its
emphasis on capital formation, or a low-cost farm, offering limited
prospects of more than a subsistence yield. The man with moderate

[59] A. D. Jones, *Illinois and the West* (Boston, 1838), p. 159. See also *American
Agriculturist*, XV (1856), 224; Cuthbert W. Johnson, *Farmer's Encyclopedia* (Philadelphia, 1839), p. 453.

[60] "As a man has but one lease on life, if he can command a few hundred dollars,
he had better pay $5 an acre for his farm where it is already settled, than $1.25 for
that where it is a desolate wilderness." *Northern Farmer*, III (1856), 395. "You can
buy an improved farm cheaper than you can buy wild land and improve it." *Iowa
Farmer*, I (1853), 192-193. See also William and Robert Chambers, *The Emigrant's
Manual* (1851), p. 121.

[61] Baird wrote: "I found it to be the generally expressed opinion of intelligent
Americans, that the emigrant from Europe would find it more to his advantage to
secure lands in some of the older states, even though he should do so by the payment
of a considerably enhanced price . . . the price of the land in the older settlements
is not very much higher than it is in the new—at least if favorable opportunities of
purchase be watched and taken advantage of." Baird, *West Indies and North America*,
pp. 144-145, 336. See also William Cobbett, *The Emigrant's Guide in Ten Letters*
(London, 1829), p. 98; John Regan, *The Emigrant's Guide to the Western States of
America* (1852), pp. 353, 356.

[62] For advice opposing the purchase of "improved" farms, see Thomas Mooney,
Nine Years in America (Dublin, 1850), p. 21; John Gregory, *Industrial Resources of
Wisconsin* (Milwaukee, 1855), p. 310; *Illinois Farmer*, I (1856), 26; *New England
Farmer*, VII (1855), 554; *Northwestern Review*, I (1857), 4-5.

capital had a similar choice, but he could more readily hope immediately to combine higher income with appreciation in the value of his farm. His route to these objectives was by careful selection of a farm for its natural productivity and favorable market location and by the application of superior technology.

CHAPTER SIX

MANAGEMENT OF THE FARM ENTERPRISE

 "In every neighborhood," wrote an observer in the 1850's "a striking difference in the productiveness of farms may be noted and this variation, when acre is matched against acre, cannot, in most cases, justly be attributed to the diversity of the soil, but rather to the effect of the methods by which the farming is conducted. It is the difference of character in the farmers, and of the objects they aim at, which are illustrated in their labor and its products."[1] That there existed a very wide range in the effectiveness with which farming operations were conducted, and consequently in results, was generally acknowledged. Such differences sprang from many sources. Fundamental were the changes in objectives and methods that characterized the period.

The transition from farming for own use to farming for sale involved far-reaching adjustments in the nature and conduct of the farm enterprise. In both situations, similar questions regarding the use of resources faced the enterpriser: What, among known possibilities, should be produced? How much? What variety? By what methods? Under subsistence conditions these queries were readily and simply answered because the determinations were guided wholly, or virtually so, by family needs and desires. Since the products to be secured and the quantities of each were selected as needed within the household, little serious consideration of relative costs was necessary; the importance attached by the family to the commodity determined the effort to be given to it. The varieties of crops and animals raised were common to the area, as were the techniques applied.

Under market conditions, the answers to the questions "what," "how much," "what variety," "which methods," were more difficult.

---

[1] Charles W. Dickerman, *How to Make the Farm Pay* (Philadelphia, 1869), pp. 668-669.

Decisions were made with less assurance because they were dependent upon the farmer's interpretations of a variety of factors relating to the market and of alternative techniques of which he characteristically had only imperfect knowledge. The decisions made also required more or less continuous review, since conditions changed. The farmer's problems were further complicated by a set of questions having little significance to the subsistence homestead: How, when, and on what terms would the products be sold?

Decisions about the choice of products were reached by evaluating the productive capacities of the enterprise as it changed with shifts in the technology, in the light of the readiness with which products might be sold and the prices that might be offered on the market. While it was obviously desirable to maximize the product obtained with a given amount of labor, concentration of available labor and other resources upon a few products in an effort to maximize net money income greatly increased the importance of selecting the most desirable varieties of crops and animals. The same was true of the methods followed in production. Even if the techniques employed in subsistence farming were reasonably adequate to that purpose, methods used in securing the product of four acres of wheat, corn, or hay were not necessarily those that would satisfactorily or effectively derive marketable products from thirty or forty acres. As farming became more closely integrated with the market, the application of subsistence methods to the changing objectives was increasingly viewed by the more enterprising as clearly inadequate. New objectives invited the development and use of new techniques to take advantage of opportunities that had been nonexistent or unimportant under earlier circumstances.

As an entrepeneur determining the use to which resources were to be put, the farmer's task was to relate the market prospects as he saw them to the nature and capacity of his operations. The resulting plan of operations involved:

1. Selection of the commodities to be produced for home use and for market. Such decisions required knowledge of the characteristics and capacities of all types of resources available. They also rested upon familiarity with the prices that each commodity had commanded in the recent past, knowledge of the costs of producing each crop, and some rough estimates of the prices that might prevail in the comming year.

2. The specific varieties of plants and animals to be raised.

3. The methods to be employed for each type of product.

4. A calender of operations so designed that the available labor force was adequate to meet all requirements and fully utilized at all possible times.

5. A general long-range plan of operations, particularly including soil utilization, with which the plan for any given year would be generally consistent. Effective plans were necessarily based upon a record of past experience, including financial accounts.

Prices quoted or received for products in the preceding year or two were the basic guides in determining the objectives of a farming program. Since an analysis of alternative courses of action based on price experience required a knowledge of costs as well, in the 1840's there developed a considerable public discussion of the costs of producing various crops and of undertaking the various operations involved. The available literature reveals little regarding the ways in which farmers utilized such information. In many situations there was slight possibility of prompt reaction although long-range shifts frequently took place. However, cost data were a standard consideration in choosing between alternative production methods—as in analyzing the merits of a new implement. In their consideration of the problems of resource use, farmers reacted only slowly to market conditions, directing their attention to areas in which their actions had greater impact.

THE GENERAL CONSENT

The question of what to produce and how was of critical importance to every farmer. Factors were involved that made the problem unique to each enterprise—such as the nature of the soil and the capital available. Yet leadership in searching out satisfactory and effective answers was concentrated in the hands of a few. The majority of farmers gave such questions little serious investigation or even much thought. The "course of farming," wrote one, "is determined by 'general consent' and in accordance with first principles. It soon becomes known what crops are suited to a particular section."[2] That this was a rough but accurate description of the manner in which resource use was determined in most instances is

2 *Rural New Yorker,* XIV (1863), 269; cf. p. 385.

scarcely open to doubt. A common fund of experience with products and methods—their failures and successes—not only formed the basis upon which most farmers approached the task of determining objectives, but also provided ready-made a plan of operations. The specific objectives, material, and methods that had proven satisfactory in any locality in the past constituted the accepted routine.[3] Adherence to such a routine was the rule, its results acceptable according to the standards of the immediate, face-to-face group. "Farmers," wrote one, "do not generally inform themselves as they ought. They do not think and plan, but strive to make up the deficiency by working like brutes. Many are, voluntarily, perfect hacks."[4] Even worse was their active prejudice against change— prejudices that were not merely passive but applied actual pressures upon those who did seek to improve their operations.[5] "The great difficulty with the body of our farmers," wrote one, "is that they cannot and will not think of a new channel for their industry; neither will they let a neighbor think in peace. If it is proposed to go into the culture of . . . anything new, the horrors of shipwreck are held up to him, and if language of this kind is not used, that which is more effective is, a low species of ridicule. A man sometimes hardly feels a free agent, and rather than encounter the laugh of a neighbor, or forfeit his good standing with them for prudence and judgment, he pursues the old way."[6]

William West, one of the agricultural leaders of southeastern

---

[3] "The fact is that our farmers get into a certain routine and the round of work already on hand takes their whole time and means." Iowa State Agricultural Society, *Transactions* (1861-1862), p. 90.

[4] *Rural New Yorker*, XVI (1865), 317.

[5] Donald G. Mitchell criticized New England farmers: "It is hard to make intelligible to a third party, his apparent inaccessibility to new ideas, his satisfied quietude, his invincible *inertium*, his stolid, and yet shrewd capacity to resist novelties, his self-assurance, his scrutinizing contempt for outsideness of whatever sort—his supreme and ineradicable faith in his own peculiar doctrine, whether of politics, religion, ethnology, ham-curing, manuring, or farming generally.

"It is not alone, that men of this class cling to a particular method of culture, because their neighborhood has followed the same for years, and the results are fair; but it is their pure contempt for being taught; their undervaluation of what they do not know, as not worth knowing; their conviction that their schooling, their faith, their principles, and their understanding are among God's best works; and that other people's schooling, faith, principles, and views of truth—whether human or divine—are inferior and unimportant." Mitchell, *My Farm of Edgewood* (New York, 1862), p. 248. See also Asher Robbins, *Address to the Rhode Island Society for the Encouragement of Domestic Industry* (Pawtuxet, 1822), p. 10; *Farmer's Monthly Visitor*, X (1848), 187-188.

[6] *Quarterly Journal of Agriculture*, III (1846), 110.

Pennsylvania in the early decades of the century, felt this pressure to conformity when he sought to build up the fertility of his soil by manuring his meadows and pastures. He reported that this "alternation of the farming system . . . from the random plans of the country, did not fail to be noticed by his neighbors, and in some of them to excite animadversions; and as in every instance of deviation from prevalent customs or practices, predictions of failure were with great confidence generally made."[7] The large majority made no independent decisions: they followed well-trodden paths and made no serious examination of alternatives. Deviations from the established way by a member of almost any community were looked upon as foolhardy, a courting of failure, and hence a waste of effort, if not worse.[8] Although such pressures were probably somewhat heavier in 1820 than half a century later, they continued to operate as powerful deterrents to change.

APPLICATION OF METHOD

Although unquestioning conformance with the "general consent" constituted the major approach to farming, substantial exceptions existed. "Farming," wrote a Massachusetts observer of the 1850's "may be so conducted as to be made profitable, or merely to afford a living or to run out the farm. Taking the land as it averages in the state, this depends more on the farmer than on the soil." In explanation he suggested, "The man who makes no provision for raising of his crops cannot reasonably expect any. Agriculture like all other business to be made profitable, must be conducted with some method as well as energy."[9]

The effective use of energy thus required method, that is, a carefully developed but flexible plan of operations carried out with good day-to-day management. Such management involved not only the execution of the plan but also a sensitivity to the countless minor problems which arose from day to day and which called for the exercise of judgment in reaching decisions and taking action. Although matters of this nature were ignored by many farmers, su-

[7] *Agricultural Intelligencer*, I (1820), 51.

[8] Charles W. Dickerman, *How to Make the Farm Pay* (Philadelphia, 1869), pp. 668-669.

[9] Josiah Newhall, "How to Make Farming Profitable," in Massachusetts Agricultural Society, *Transactions* (1849), pp. 191-192.

perior returns came from constant attention to them and the development of reasonably correct answers for them. Problems that others ignored were viewed by some as opportunities awaiting solution, and an anxiety to secure information leading toward remunerative answers was a characteristic of the good manager.

A lengthy discussion of the problems of farm management written in the 1860's concludes:

after reading all the best books, after obtaining the best tools and farm implements, and after consulting the best authorities for carrying on farm operations, success will depend on a man's *general management*. It is the *management*—management first, management last, as well as the best of management, intermediately and collaterally—that crowns a farmer's labors with success. This will involve *everything* when taken in one harmonious combination—the management of the soil and the management of stock . . . the management of crops and the management of manures; the management in the field and the management within doors . . .

If a farmer does not possess the faculty of being a good manager in every department of his business it will be the height of folly to cherish the idea that he is going to be successful as a farmer. In order to be able to manage a farm as it should be a farmer needs more drilling in his business than a general does in military tactics to be able to manage an army of soldiers.[10]

Farmers throughout the country were accused of slovenliness. The carelessness with which they carried out their activities was compared unfavorably with the precise manner in which manufacturing was conducted.[11] They were advised that, "Like other men, the farmer may expect success proportionate to the skill, care, judgment, and perseverance with which his operations are conducted."[12] Another held that "The whole secret of the successful farmer often

---

[10] Sereno E. Todd, *The Young Farmer's Manual* (New York, 1868), II, 76. Note also: "The business or management of a farm . . . is a practice that demands constant care and attention, as well as much activity and judgment, to conduct it in a proper and advantageous manner. It requires an intimate and practical knowledge of all the arts of cultivation and management, as well as of the nature and value of every kind of live-stock; and still further, a perfect acquaintance with the various modes of buying and selling, and the constant state of different markets and fairs." Cuthbert W. Johnson, *Farmer's Encyclopedia and Dictionary of Rural Affairs* (Philadelphia, 1839), p. 453.

[11] "For within the hum of a single cotton mill there is more machinery, more close calculation in saving waste materials, more skill and science applied to practical art and labor, than in a township of farms." Connecticut State Agricultural Society, *Transactions* (1855), p. 300. Cf. Massachusetts Agricultural Society, *Abstracts* (1850), pp. 309-310; *Dollar Farmer*, IV (1845), 50.

[12] Maine Board of Agriculture, *Report* (1850), p. 57. *Iowa Farmer*, I (1853), 2.

lies in his having a fixed plan of operations. Multitudes have no plan but to meet their immediate necessities and make money by the easiest and seemingly shortest methods."[13]

In the judgment of an Iowa farmer in 1857, "there is not in this country a farmer who is *thoroughly master* of his business, one who applies his labor to the best advantage, who uses all means to secure the best ends. As a class, farmers care too little for the deductions of science and rely too much upon the practical, as they have been accustomed to see it wrought out."[14] Such criticism was by no means limited to frontier areas. "It would have been difficult," wrote one farmer, with reference to New England, "in any county to have found ten farmers who looked forward to the blending of the operations of two or three years together, or who had any system of farming or of agricultural economy."[15]

For most farmers, almanacs served as calenders of operations, and Benjamin Franklin's maxims served as principles of management. Superior management required a plan of operations sensitively adjusted to circumstances, a willingness to consider change, appraise new alternatives, and vary plans and actions according to the conclusions reached. Leadership in the agricultural industries belonged to those who more or less continuously re-examined the specific objectives of their farming activities and the routine of their operations in the light of shifting circumstances, who operated according to a plan developed for their purposes but were willing to abandon one crop for another, change techniques, or shift from one farm to another when conditions suggested its profitability. Such men not only accepted the necessity of securing the largest possible "salable production" but also distinguished between gross and net returns and hence appraised alternatives in terms of costs and profits.[16]

PROPORTIONING THE FACTORS OF PRODUCTION

One critical problem faced by every owner of a farm enterprise was to develop an efficient relationship between the amounts of traditional factors employed in the operation: land, labor, and capital.

[13] *American Agriculturist*, XVII (1868), 405.
[14] Iowa Agricultural Society, *Report* (1857), p. 244; (1865), p. 518.
[15] *New England Farmer*, VIII (1855), 459.
[16] Wisconsin Agricultural Society, *Transactions* (1851), p. 36.

The acreage in crops that one man could care for was dependent upon the technology applied, each crop presenting some task that limited production. For instance, the operations involved in harvesting small grains and hay set limits on the acreages in those crops that the available labor force could care for, while in the case of corn the capacity to cultivate the crop properly was the limiting factor. These principles were well understood. One farmer wrote: "In the adjustment of farm labor, the great art is to divide it as equally as possible throughout the year. Thus, it would not answer in any situation to sow exclusively autumn crops, as wheat or rye; nor only spring crops, as oats or barley, for by so doing all the labor of seed time would come at once, and the same of harvest work, while the rest of the year there would be little to do on the farm. But by sowing a portion of each of these and other crops, the labour both of seed-time and harvest is divided, and rendered easier, and is more likely to be done well and in season."[17] Given such considerations, the farmer's success depended in large part on the skill with which he arrived at a combination of crops that would maximize the use of his labor force in the most remunerative operations throughout the year, with the possibility of hiring harvest labor providing some flexibility, although uncertainties too, particularly as to costs.

Before the adoption of the reaper, twenty acres in tilled crops and mown grass were about the maximum that one man could handle in the East. Many cultivated less. On the more level soils of the West, thirty acres per man was a common ratio, although some farms employed their labor with such skill as to cultivate forty.[18] The typical farm devoted some acreage to pasturage and a woodlot, bringing the land requirements per man up to a maximum of perhaps sixty acres in the East, and as much as eighty acres in the West. Given such data, the amount of labor available determined the acreage required by the enterprise; conversely, the amount of land determined the amount of labor to be applied as well as the amount of capital (animals, implements, and working funds) necessary.

17 *Complete Practical Farmer* (New York, 1839), p. 71.

18 These estimates were arrived at by examining several hundred detailed accounts of farm enterprises. For contemporary generalizations, see Maine Board of Agriculture, *Report, Abstracts* (1858), p. 29; Wisconsin State Agricultural Society, *Transactions*, I (1851), 161; *Prairie Farmer*, XV (1855), 204-205; U. S. Patent Office, *Report* (1850), p. 463; Robert Russell, *North America: Its Agriculture and Climate* (Edinburgh, 1857), p. 123.

The amount of land that could be efficiently utilized per man was roughly the amount which one man could harvest when planted in a sequence of crops, unless harvest labor was available for hire, in which case the capacity to plow and plant was the limiting factor.

No criticism of farming during this period was more frequently reiterated than that farmers owned too much land.[19] Whereas a significant portion of the land held within farms was of little or no value for agricultural purposes, there was also a large portion of suitable land that lay idle. Such land was frequently considered as a reserve, to be exploited at some future time, but the costs in interest on the invested capital and in taxes were heavy. One agricultural editor argued, "The ownership of this very unimproved land will be sure to prevent them (the owners) from ever having the means to improve it. They don't reflect that the interest upon the value of this unimproved land and the taxes upon it, would buy the land twice over at the end of ten years."[20]

Aside from such lands, there was "an almost universal disposition to attempt to cultivate more than could be advantageously handled."[21] Contemporary observers lacked the tools whereby they might have defined precisely what they meant by "advantageously handled," except in the broadest terms. One, however, pointed out that "many farmers diminish the net profit to augment the gross." He argued that farmers disregarded the fact that "the best husbandry is that which yields most clear profit to the cultivator for the capital and labor employed." Implied in his analysis is the suggestion that land was frequently cultivated in such extent that returns to labor and capital were reduced below what lesser acreage would have provided; he attributed "the low state of husbandry principally to the inconceivable misapprehension of this subject."[22] However, those who, citing English and Dutch practice, urged the

[19] Henry Colman, *Agriculture of the United States* (New York, 1841), p. 12; *Cultivator,* VI (1839), 197; *Genesee Farmer,* II (1832), 51; *Plough, Loom and Anvil,* IV (1851), 723; *Journal of Agriculture,* II (1846), 361; *Connecticut Valley Farmer and Mechanic,* I (1853), 7; *Boston Cultivator,* August 17, 1839; *Farmer's Companion,* I (1852), 21; *Western Agriculturist,* I (1851), 55; U. S. Patent Office, *Report* (1852), p. 134; John L. Blake, *The Modern Farmer* (1854), pp. 347-349; *Northern Farmer,* I (1832), 67.
[20] *Iowa Farmer,* I (1853), 3; cf. *Michigan Farmer,* VIII (1851), 372-373; Massachusetts Board of Agriculture, *Report,* IX (1861), 107; *Wisconsin Farmer,* XVI (1864), 64-65; *Prairie Farmer,* XI (1851), 164.
[21] E. G. Wakefield, *England and America* (London, 1833), pp. 11, 51.
[22] *Farmer's Register,* I (1833), 232.

profitability of "little farms well tilled" took too extreme a position to find much support.[23]

Since adequate capital would make possible the employment of the labor and equipment necessary for a given acreage, the problem was also viewed, and more accurately, as one of attempting too much with too little capital. Governor George S. Boutwell of Massachusetts, in speaking before an audience of farmers of his state, reminded them that "capital, active capital, is as necessary in farming as in commerce of manufactures," adding that "the majority have very little."[24] Others complained that the greatest deficiency in agriculture was the irrational manner in which farmers invested their capital. Whether true or not that "more than half of the property of most of our farmers is in the shape of unproductive capital," there was agreement that farmers invested too large a proportion of their funds in land, resulting in an inability to stock their farms properly or otherwise make profitable utilization of the lands.[25] As a consequence, labor was less productive than it might have been, and much land remained unremunerative, wasting the capital invested in it.[26]

Even reasonably successful farmers failed to retain adequate funds to finance their normal operations but relied on credit, while investing their profits, not in improvements on their own land, but in the purchase of more land, mortages, or nonagricultural securities. One agricultural editor asked:

How many farmers do we find whose fear of subjecting themselves to a slight loss of interest, invest all their means on mortgage, purchasing

[23] See Maine Board of Agriculture, *Report, Abstracts* (1858), pp. 29-30.

[24] *Hunt's Merchant Magazine,* XXXI (1854), 695.

[25] *Connecticut Valley Farmer,* II (1850), 98.

[26] The editor of the *Homestead* claimed that agriculture was the worst industry for wasting capital. *Homestead,* I (1855), 753, 786. He also observed: "Dead capital, we may say is the besetting sin of our calling. We think three-fourths of all the land in the state does not pay three per cent on its reputed value. Nothing is more common than to find a man with two or three hundred acres, and yet not improving fifty of it, so as to get six per cent for it. He has a portion in swamp from which he gets nothing, another portion in poor pasture, paying one per cent, another in poor mowing paying three per cent, and the balance about half cultivated. After putting nearly or quite all of his capital into this unproductive state, he has nothing left to work his land with, without incurring debt, and he has no such faith in the lucrativeness of his business, as to lead him to hire money to carry it on. His fault is not in having too much land, but in his not having capital enough to work it with. A farmer wants full one half of his capital in available funds, to stock his farm with and to procure the necessary labor for draining, manuring, and improving it. This would make his whole capital productive." *Homestead,* IV (1859), 138. Cf. *American Agriculturist,* XV (1856), 127.

everything on credit, paying indirectly more interest than they receive, by such practice, putting off their settling until the days when they receive their interest from others, and thus, imagining that they are benefitting by the delay? To avoid the purchase of a one-horse cart a wheelbarrow is often substituted, until the extra cost is greater than that of a cart; besides occupying the time of a man in doing that which might be performed by the horse at much cheaper rates. Small tools are used where larger ones would be more profitable. Potatoes are often dug by hand to save the purchase of a potato digger. A hoe is made to answer the purpose of a horse tool, and at a cost greater per month, than the value of the absent horse tool. Farmers having money at interest are short of barn room and their crops are injured for want of it, to a much greater extent than the interest on the value of the barn, including its wear and tear, etc. Many of our wealthiest farmers, indeed, nine-tenths of them, are operating on farms not under-drained, simply because they have more confidence in their neighbor's bond than they have in the laws of God, commonly known as natural laws.[27]

In view of the fact that land holdings were usually in excess of those that one man could handle profitably, the ability to make effective use of hired labor was an important element in successful enterprise, as it was also a test of managerial capacity. Successful farmers tended to employ hired labor on a larger scale than was typical, confirming the comment that "farming cannot be successfully and profitably carried on even on a small scale by one man alone and that a good farmer must and will hire—for nearly one half of farming work can only be performed at the greatest disadvantage by one man."[28] Some farmers complained about the quality of the labor available for hire. In the East the principal supply of labor came increasingly to be foreign-born immigrants, who lacked the skills of native, farm-born men. In the West, the more desirable labor was primarily interested in temporary employment incidental to the goal of securing a farm. In either case, good supervision was required to employ profitably labor of "divided allegiance" or lacking in skills.[29] Many avoided the test by relying on the unpaid labor

[27] *Working Farmer,* XI (1859), 148-149. See also New York State Agricultural Society, *Transactions* (1867), p. 26; *Valley Farmer,* II (1850), 254; *Northern Farmer,* II (1855), 266.

[28] *Prairie Farmer,* XIII (1853), 463; see also p. 303.

[29] Donald G. Mitchell pointed out: "Upon the old system of growing all that a man might need within his own grounds, a proper farm education embraced a considerable knowledge of a score of different crops and avocations. The tendency is now, however, to centralize attention upon that line of cropping which is best suited to the land; this limits the range of labor, while the improved mechanical appliances

of their sons. Despite the relatively low wages paid agricultural labor, among those who did hire were many who complained that wage payments absorbed most or all of their profits and frequently most of the money income of their enterprise.[30] They were a marginal group, most numerous in the East, particularly after 1850. It is clear that there were also many farmers with adequate land and capital who, with good management, found hired help very profitable.

ECONOMIZING TIME

It was also characteristic of the aggressive, commercially minded farmer that he attached a high value to time; that is, he was willing to make an appreciable financial investment in order to reduce the time required to perform those activities which determined his marketable production. This was the fundamental consideration in the adoption of new implements. It also figured in the choice of draft animals.

Oxen were the typical work animals of precommercial farming. These animals were easily raised from stock found on almost every farm. They reached useful maturity quickly and lost little value, if any, with age, for when no longer useful for work, they were fattened for market or slaughtered for food. They were hardy, required relatively little care, were easily trained, and were well adapted to the principal tasks requiring animal power: pulling heavy inefficient plows and drawing heavy loads over poor roads. While they thus provided low-cost animal labor, they were also very slow.

---

fill a thousand wants, which were once only to be met by a dexterous handicraft at home . . . It is noticeable in this connection, that the implements in the use of which the native workers were most unmatchable are precisely the ones which in practical farming are growing less and less important every year; to wit, the axe and scythe, the first being now confined mostly to clearings of timber, and the second is fast becoming merely a garden implement for the dressing of lawns." Mitchell, *My Farm of Edgewood*, pp. 77-78.

30 In discussing the profitability of farming at a western New York farmer's club, someone said that he "had often heard it remarked that farmers could not afford to hire; as it often took the produce of the hired hand and of the employer to pay the help, and even farm labor is generally cheap as compared with that paid other classes. We must come to one of the two conclusions: Either farming does not pay, or else the majority do not understand their business. Merchants, mechanics, manufacturers, miners, lumbermen, and boatmen, all can and do hire and at liberal wages, while with farmers, it is a constant theme that they cannot afford to hire." *Rural New Yorker*, XVI (1865), 317.

The more rapid movement characteristic of the horse was obtained only at appreciably higher costs, both directly and indirectly. The animals were more expensive to purchase or to raise. They were slower to reach maturity, subject to more disabling hazards, required more care and greater expense to maintain, and were of no value when their working life was over. In the early fifties, three-year-old horses of average quality were worth from $100 to $150, with better animals worth much more—"it is but a common nag that is worth only $150."[31] Prices were highest in the eastern cities, considerably lower in the West. At the same time, oxen were valued in New England at from $75 to $100 per yoke, though the range of prices was wide.[32]

The choice between the two animals was determined by the importance of speed in accomplishing necessary tasks as contrasted with the costs involved. In subsistence agriculture there were few if any operations where speed was of critical importance. The needs of the typical subsistence farmer for a wide variety of self-produced goods required that a minimum of effort be given to any single item among the variety of products desired. Maximum economy was achieved by the production of items of multiple use, even at substantial sacrifice of quality or convenience, since capital was thereby conserved. This was as true of draft animals as of implements and crops.

In commercial agriculture, however, the conservation of time was an important consideration since the human effort that could be applied set upper limits on the value of the products of the enterprise. The speed with which the critical bottleneck operations could be performed was a determinant of total income. The rate at which a plowing task was accomplished was of no great consequence if only three or four acres were involved but became critically important if thirty or forty acres were to be prepared for seeding. Similarly, the farmer who took only one or two loads of produce to market had relatively little interest in speed, as compared with the individual who had numerous loads to transport. Speed was obtained at a substantial cost, which could be justified only in terms of ad-

[31] *Hunt's Merchant Magazine,* XXXVI (1857), 756. For extensive information on values and costs, see U. S. Patent Office, *Report* (1851), pp. 143 ff; (1852), pp. 103 ff; (1853), pp. 28-36; (1854), pp. 22-26; (1855), pp. 38-43.

[32] See data in U. S. Patent Office, *Report* (1850), pp. 180 ff; (1851), pp. 175 ff; (1852), pp. 122 ff.

vantages gained in increasing the quantity of goods marketed and in reducing the time involved.[33]

In the East, this change took place slowly, oxen remaining the characteristic draft animal of the small-scale farm producing only small volumes of marketable products. Oxen also remained important in the earlier stages of frontier settlement, not only because of the poverty of many farm-makers but also because the animals were particularly well-adapted to the tasks of clearing forest lands, breaking prairie sod, and lumbering. In the longer-settled areas of the West, the great distances to be covered, and the need to cultivate large acreages with as little expenditure of human labor and time as possible, made the horse a more useful animal than the ox, while the cost of ownership was reduced below eastern levels by the relative ease with which pasture and feed could be obtained. Oxen were, however, frequently used on farms where a single team of horses was insufficient, and they constituted the common form of supplementary draft power.

After 1830, farmers made increasing use of horses, sometimes instead of, but frequently in addition to, oxen. The growing importance of market contacts was the primary reason for the change, but horses also came to be more widely used for farm work. Greater dependence upon horses became possible with the development of more efficient plows requiring less draft; indeed, the advantages of better plows were fully realized only when horses provided their speedier motive power. Similarly, as other improved implements became available, such as horsepowers and reapers and mowers, their advantages were fully realizable only when pulled by horses. The slow shift from oxen to horses produced considerable though sporadic comment in the agricultural press, most of which insisted upon the greater economy of oxen as contrasted with horses, chiefly because of their value for food at the end of their working life—after four years of work they could be sold for their cost and more.[34]

---

[33] "A majority of western farmers keep but one team. On newly-cleared farms, oxen are probably more profitable than horses, but in the older, settled portions, and where markets and mills are at a distance, horses will be preferred by most, though the expense of keeping is considerably more. Where it is necessary to keep more than a span of horses, we recommend the employment of oxen. The horses can do the road work, while the oxen can be used on the farm exclusively." *Farmer's Companion,* I (1853), 88.

[34] *New England Farmer,* XI (1833), 60; *Farmer and Gardener,* II (1835), 126; *Ohio Farmer and Western Horticulturist,* II (1835), 5; *Genesee Farmer,* IV (1836), 199; IX (1839), 269; *Plough, Loom and Anvil,* II (1849), 263; I (1848), 290-300, 353-

The increasing importance of the horse was left largely to speak for itself, possibly because it was difficult to place a dollar value upon the greater speed in farm operations which that animal made possible.

SELECTION OF PRODUCTS

Effective selection of the products to which to devote resources and energies was a critical task in developing a profitable plan of operations. In 1833 it was pointed out:

the farmer who undertakes to raise all kinds of crops upon one kind of soil misapplies his labor. He had better confine himself to those which make the best return—sell the surplus, and buy with a part of the proceeds that for which his neighbor's soil is better adapted than his own. The adapting of crops to the soil and market are among the first considerations which present themselves to the discreet farmer. The same soil that will produce a profitable crop of one kind, may not repay the labor of cultivating another. The hills and mountains that make the richest pastures, may be illy adapted to the production of grain. And the same farm product that is profitable to the farmer in the vicinity of towns or navigable waters, may be wholly unprofitable in a district remote from them. In newly settled districts, where the opportunities of interchange are precarious, it becomes in a measure necessary that the farmer should adapt his husbandry to the immediate wants of his family, and produce his own bread, meat and clothing. Like causes often render it necessary that he should be his own mechanic—as carpenter, shoemaker, etc. Distance, bad roads, and want of means, leave him no other alternative. But in old settled districts, where the facilities of intercourse and trade are abundant, considerations of economy suggest a wiser course—that the farmer should apply his labor to such objects as will ensure him the best profit.[35]

While this seems obvious, men who had long thought in terms of producing as wide a variety of products as possible to fill the needs of their families, found it difficult to accept the idea of specialization as offering advantages that offset the risks inherent in dependence upon a market. Twenty years after the analysis quoted above, another farmer again found it pertinent to point out:

The farmer who is wide awake to his business should watch, as well as follow, the markets. He should know what crops will sell well. So far as he can form a probable or approximate opinion on this point, he should

---

361; *Valley Farmer*, XIV (1862), 16; Michigan Agricultural Society, *Transactions* (1853), p. 217; Todd, *Young Farmer's Manual*, pp. 49-58.

[35] *Northern Farmer*, I (1833), 101, from *Albany Argus*.

conform his cultivation to it. In some places he can produce milk to advantage; in others, butter and cheese. Again, he may be so situated that neither of these articles will pay him so good a profit as some others. Here, his main crop will be hay; there, fruit; here, potatoes, there, squashes, or other vegetables . . . It is not the crop on which the farmer himself sets the highest value that should be raised by him, but the crops he can produce at the least expense and sell to the greatest profit.

Some farmers are fearful of loss if they diverge from the beaten track. They go on, therefore, cultivating the same products, and often on the same fields, as did their fathers. Other farmers seem to entertain the opinion that unless they raise the heavier products—corn, potatoes and grain and hay,—they are no longer farmers, but a sort of market gardener.

But away with such idle fears and foolish notions. Let our farmers study their true interests. Let them not stand while others are going ahead. Let them be up and doing something to supply the wants of the towns and cities in their vicinity; and not the necessities only, but the tastes also. Let them raise flowers even, if it will pay a profit. Why not?[36]

Such advice reflected the experience of the more aggresive farmers who had early found and pursued their advantage by expanding production of the items most readily and profitably salable in the growing urban markets. The large majority moved toward commercial agricultural production in slow stages, expanding the volume of products intended for sale and discarding one by one such crops intended for home use as interfered with the market objective. These adjustments were not made uniformly by all farmers in any area, and certainly not within so large a region as the eastern seaboard. Distance set limits in terms of transportation costs. Moreover, acceptance of and adjustment to market participation was a highly individual matter. All types of farming, from a high degree of subsistence to complete commercialization, could be found within relatively small areas even those lying within a few hours' travel of the major cities.

The crops from which selections were made for production for sale were generally those proven most useful on the subsistence farm, following long and widespread experimentation with virtually every European-cultivated plant and many others.[37] The market-

---

[36] *Plough, Loom and Anvil,* V (1852), 241.

[37] For listings of the kinds of crops raised on the semisubsistence farm, see New York State Agricultural Society, *Transactions* (1890), p. 5; Illinois State Agricultural Society, *Transactions,* VII (1867-1868), 159-160; Robert L. Jones, "Special Crops in Ohio before 1850," *Ohio State Archaeological and Historical Society Quarterly,* LIV (1945), 127-142.

conscious farmer in any area selected his products by eliminating those crops that offered the poorest prospects of satisfactory returns. In making the decisions he gave weightiest consideration to the nature of the soil and the proximity of markets.[38] The amount of labor that could be applied during critical periods, particularly harvest, and increasingly after 1840, the capital available in the form of implements and machines, placed a limit on the resources applied to the crop selected as the speciality. To secure effective use of labor, attention was given to crops of lesser market importance if their labor requirements did not conflict with those of the principal crop. A major difference between the most advanced farms and the rest was the attention given to crops intended only for family use. A Michigan farmer in 1841 expressed the advanced view: "the best farming is that which produces the most of any one article for which the farm is calculated, and which will command money. If the farm is adapted to wheat, then the cultivation of wheat both in quantity and quality should be the main business. If adapted to grass, then the raising of stock, horses, meat cattle and sheep." But the conflict between older and newer values emerges clearly in the qualification offered by the farmer as he continued: "At the same time, we should have a good dairy and some good Berkshire pigs, the best kind of corn, potatoes, oats, peas, etc., and never neglect a good garden."[39] Such views reflected the general practice. Production for market frequently was superimposed on production for own use. Only in farms near urban centers was production for own use discarded in favor of a full concentration of effort on marketable products.

Whether a single crop or a group of products was established as the market objective, cropping patterns tended to be area-wide.[40] Farmers in a given locality shared the same climate, similar soils, and similar relationships to market. Hence, as a result of their own analysis and experience or by imitation, they tended to arrive at the same conclusions as to the most profitable products, though exceptions existed everywhere. Some farms possessed too few acres of suitable soil to provide a satisfactory income from the crops

[38] *Complete Practical Farmer,* p. 453.

[39] *Western Farmer,* I (1841), 44.

[40] For a more detailed discussion of crops, particularly with regard to local and regional specialties, see Paul W. Gates, *The Farmer's Age: Agriculture, 1815-1860* (New York, 1960), Chs. VIII, X-XII.

found most profitable on larger farms in the area. Other farms might be too large to be fully utilized by the available labor force in cultivating the generally accepted crop, and a more extensive form of land use might then be developed as an alternative to the hiring of labor. Generally, farmers possessing more capital than the average tended to give greater attention to animal production, particularly cattle.

PROBLEMS OF CHOICE

The East. The great diversification of products characteristic of subsistence agriculture was typical of the earlier stages of land settlement on the eastern seaboard, as well as inland when the frontier of settlement pushed westward.[41] Participation in the developing urban markets required that farmers determine the relative advantages of producing or purchasing products for their own use, as well as the crops that might advantageously be produced for sale. Eastern farmers entered markets by increasing the production of those previously cultivated commodities that were most readily salable at remunerative prices. There were, however, serious obstacles. Since agriculture in the East had been long established before a market economy of any significance appeared, the subsistence point of view was deeply entrenched, and the entire pattern of labor utilization and of land ownership and use was adjusted to the objective of supplying family needs. Few farms possessed large acreages, especially in improved land. Most were characterized by small and numerous fields consistent with a high degree of diversification of crops but uneconomic when utilized in the production of a large volume of a single product. Moreover, much of the soil in use was naturally of low fertility and was further depleted by years of exploitative cropping.

Meanwhile, the eastern farmer found the products of the Genesee Valley and of Ohio appearing on his market in a volume sufficiently great to reduce prices below his costs.[42] At the same time, the pressure to secure a larger money income from the sale of farm produce came not merely from the standards established by an increasingly

[41] For a description of the products of such mixed farming, see Maine Board of Agriculture, *Transactions* (1850), p. 54; *New England Farmer*, VIII (1856), 459.

[42] For an analysis of New England costs in relation to prices of western produce, see *Boston Cultivator*, June 13, 1840.

pecuniary society but also from the impact of western competition upon the products raised for own use. To an important degree the relatively low prices at which some western products were available on the seaboard forced commercialization, making production for self-consumption clearly irrational. This development was demonstrated with particular sharpness in wheat-growing in New England, as well as there and farther South in the raising of beef cattle.

While some eastern farmers participated fully in the growing commercialization of farming, many who felt forced to make changes in that direction faced great difficulties in finding a profitable manner by which to accomplish their objective. For a time, some held to a hope that improved cultural practices would permit profitable production of the standard field crops. Others, favorably located near markets, moved to specialize in products such as hay, oats, fluid milk, potatoes, and vegetables which could not be transported over long distances.[43] Those at considerable overland distances from markets faced the most difficult problems. For the majority of these farmers, grass was the most remunerative use of land.[44] The pasture and hay supported dairy herds, which supplied butter and cheese as the marketable products, the cows being purchased from the West and, after a year or two, fattened for the fresh meat markets of the cities.

There were, however, many who, from simple inertia or perhaps a lack of capital or other reasons, clung to the traditional pattern of highly diversified cropping. As late as 1861, the editor of the eastern *Working Farmer* admonished his readers: "There is a great want of discretion . . . on the part of agriculturists in the choice of crops. We often find districts perfectly well suited to the higher priced crops, with adjacent markets, devoted to the raising of low priced staples, and thus continuing from generation to generation. We know of many farms not ten miles distant from New York, devoted to the raising of corn, oats, hay, wheat, rye, etc., in competition with western New York, Ohio, and elsewhere, and on lands, the interest on the value of which is as great as the fee simple of western farms. In our own neighborhood are many farmers who do not realize two

---

[43] On the impact of western produce upon the profitability of farming in southeastern Pennsylvania, see *Farmer's Cabinet,* X (1845-1846), 11; *Quarterly Journal of Agriculture and Science,* III (1846), 110.

[44] Patrick Shirreff, *A Tour through North America* (Edinburgh, 1838), p. 395.

percent upon the value of their farms, while market gardeners in their midst are realizing comparative fortunes."[45]

The failure to adjust to the changing character of the economy afflicted some enterprisers for only a few years, but for many the problems involved remained unsolved for a generation, and perhaps two or three. Such farmers received a relatively declining return for their efforts, a fact that in itself made more difficult the necessary changes should opportunity and desire arise. Other than to give up the enterprise, such farmers could do little but complain of the unprofitability of farming. Many such enterprises were continued with little change from generation to generation, the more enterprising sons and daughters of the family departing in pursuit of the greater opportunities they anticipated in urban occupations or in farming the new lands of the West.

The West. In its earliest stages, agriculture west of the Alleghenies was of necessity rigorously centered within the homestead and focused upon supplying the immediate needs of the farm family. Since the tasks involved in building a productive farm and homestead from wild wooded land made a variety of heavy demands upon labor, and since little capital was usually available, the energies given to cultivation were concentrated upon those products that would satisfy immediate requirements with a minimum of capital and effort. These were usually wheat and corn, oats, perhaps small patches of rye, barley, and potatoes, supplemented by a number of hogs, a few cattle, some bush and tree fruits, and a garden patch.

These differences between East and West arose from differences in opportunities and obstacles, in motives, and in the fact that the period of rapid western settlement occurred at a time when the nation's economic development was experiencing marked change and acceleration. The soils of the West were in general far more productive per unit of labor applied than those of most areas of the East. However, the great distances to markets constituted a serious obstacle to broad commercialization of agricultural production. The growth of the markets of the cotton-producing South and particularly of the eastern cities, combined with the change in the means of transportation, overcome these limitations. Of like importance

[45] *Working Farmer,* XIII (1861), 193; cf. *Plough, Loom and Anvil,* I (1848), 234.

was the fact that for many an emigrant, perhaps most, the impulse toward removal to the West did not arise from a desire to recreate the pattern of the eastern farm left behind, but came from a vision of a rich soil producing an abundant surplus of products readily salable for cash upon markets which, if not immediately available, would certainly develop and could somehow be reached.

In the West, in contrast to the East, this predominantly self-sufficient period was a transitory stage of shorter duration. A rapid shift from semisubsistence to highly specialized and even single-crop farming was characteristic of the development of western farming, particularly as settlement moved onto the prairies. Indeed, on the prairie the new farm-maker frequently reduced subsistence production to a minimum and sought immediately to establish a single-crop, market-dependent operation.

For most such farmers the choice of products was rather limited. The great distances from the major markets demanded crops that were relatively high in value and not perishable. Having typically invested all his capital in land, he required quick returns and lacked the funds to establish herds of cattle, hogs, or sheep. Markets existed for such products as rye, oats, barley, hay, and potatoes, but local demands were relatively small. The principal crops were wheat and corn, both of which could always be sold, though the abundance of western lands and the rapid rate at which they were brought into use meant that prices were frequently low. Wheat was an essential part in the "routine of subduing the prairies." As a Michigan farmer observed in the 1850's, it was "a very natural and obvious move on the part of the first settlers of the West to engage in raising wheat. Possessing a soil rich in the organic and inorganic elements of that noble cereal, and generally having but a small amount of capital remaining, after paying for their farms, they adopted at once that course of husbandry which would yield the readiest returns for the capital and labor bestowed."[46] Capital devoted to the cultivation of wheat provided more immediate and sometimes larger returns than were available in any other way. This being the case, any profits were typically devoted to the cultivation of an even larger acreage in the crop. Wheat followed wheat as the farmer extended his arable fields. The crop was readily salable at the river

[46] *American Agriculturist*, X (1851), 116; cf. *Wisconsin and Iowa Farmer*, II (1850), 254, 263-264.

and lake towns, moving down the Mississippi or across the lakes and the Erie Canal to the markets.

Wheat was also the crop that created the deepest and most universal dissatisfaction. Experiences with unfavorable prices and particularly with crop failures quickly led to the abandonment of wheat as a major commercial crop in the central and southern parts of Ohio, Indiana, and westward. Farther north, wheat remained for a longer time the center of the cropping pattern, but there also declining yields followed continuous cropping. An Illinois farmer noted that, "whether in the North or the South, experience soon teaches that a crop that demands so large an outlay for seed, so many of the best days out of the heart of the season, so much capital in horse flesh and machinery, so much care, so much risk in the crop, so many chances for low prices when the crop is ready for market, as the wheat crop, is not the crop to depend upon." He observed further that the "older and wealthier farmers of Illinois have largely abandoned the practice of growing more wheat than will fully supply them with bread."[47] Wheat was the preeminent crop for exploiting the fertility of new lands with a minimum of capital, achieving a maximum return in the shortest possible time. Once the new farm had been well established and some capital accumulated, alternatives were considered, stimulated by the fact of declining returns.

The chief alternative was corn, which though cultivated everywhere, was less attractive as a crop for sale. As an Indiana observer pointed out:

[corn is] easily cultivated, and almost every farmer has from 20 to 100 acres. A single hand can prepare the ground, plant and attend to and gather from 20 to 25 acres, according to the state of the ground and the character of the season. The product is usually from 35 to 75 bushels an acre, averaging about 45, though most of the land in the state, if properly farmed would produce one-third more than is generally raised. Corn usually sells at from 10 to 30 cents per bushel, millions of bushels being annually sold in the interior to fatten hogs and cattle, at not exceeding the former price. It is the main article of food for man and stock, and can be cooked in a great variety of ways, so as to be equally acceptable at the tables of the poor and rich. The cultivation of corn is admirably adapted to the climate and soil of the State, and to the habits of the farmers . . . with proper cultivation the corn does not often suffer from cold, deluge or drought, and our laborers prefer to work hard in spring and early summer when the corn most needs it, and then relax exertions

[47] Illinois State Agricultural Society, *Transactions* (1859-1860), pp. 84-85.

in the latter part of the season, when they are not required, and the heat is more oppressive.[48]

Corn was most profitable when used on the farm as feed for hogs and cattle. There was, however, in the West a market for corn at the river towns and in the interior. Farmers who had not accumulated adequate numbers of livestock sold their corn to others who had more animals than they could feed from their own plantings.

Corn was less subject to the extremes and uncertainties that accompanied wheat production. Nevertheless, there were frequent grounds for substantial dissatisfaction. The business side of the history of farming in Indiana up to 1850 was summarized by one observer as follows:

The tendency . . . was to produce a surplus of corn, beef, pork, etc., and then when any new article was in demand, every farmer turned his attention to it, and a surplus of that also was soon produced. Low prices at length brought regular customers and now the supply of most kinds of produce has become abundant and uniform and the trader can make his arrangements in advance and calculate with much certainty on carrying them out, wherever there is any access to a market. There are still, however, frequently gluts in the market of some kinds of produce; the farmer often doubts as to the proper objects on which to expend his labor and it has become very desirable that he should have a greater diversity of crops than he has had hitherto. The soil, even when very rich, requires this; and occasionally the wheat is killed in winter or by the fly, or the corn or grass suffers in summer from drought, frost or storms, and to furnish employment for those who wish to labor during the year, it is becoming very important that there should be a greater variety of crops on the farms. Hemp was tried for a few years, but in most instances too much was attempted at first. Flax, tobacco, fruit and various seeds from which oil can be manufactured, may be cultivated to any extent, and often with much profit. Some experiments have been made in beet and corn-sugar, the grape, silk, etc., but in general there has been too much carelessness to decide whether they may not yet be attended to with advantage.[49]

The search for new combinations of crops and more satisfactory methods was vigorous and turned in many directions. Efforts to achieve greater stability of income at satisfactory profit levels were usually directed to the breeding or fattening of hogs or cattle, frequently in a diversified program centering on domestic grasses and corn and including reduced acreages in wheat.

[48] E. Chamberlain, *The Indiana Gazetteer* (Indianapolis, 1850), pp. 55-56.
[49] Chamberlain, *The Indiana Gazetteer,* pp. 34-35.

Cattle were raised principally by those who possessed both large acreages in wild or cultivated grasses and the capital required to establish a herd of significant size. While the value of these animals was low, the investments required for herds of profitable size were large. Many a farmer sought to escape from the unsatisfactory returns of wheat farming by building up a herd of cattle and turning part of his fields into grass. Credit from bankers sometimes made possible the purchase of feeder cattle, these being generally profitable when fattened on corn and providing a way of marketing that crop.

While wheat, corn, grass, cattle, and hogs were the principal interests of western farmers, there were a variety of others. Some farmers developed special interests in raising horses and mules, which even though usually a sideline, might contribute the larger share of their income. Wool, because of its high value relative to weight, had obvious advantages to farmers located at distances from markets. Although the profitability of wool was endlessly urged in the agricultural press, the raising of sheep was among the most hazardous of western farming ventures. Sheep required more care than most farmers were able or willing to give, while prices of wool fluctuated violently. Other farmers ventured into hemp, flaxseed, broomcorn, and fruits, particularly apples. Near the cities they engaged in truck farming and small fruits, especially strawberries.

Throughout this period a few farmers, scattered East and West, were outstanding because of their active interest in improving the effectiveness of their operations. While the typical farmer accepted his circumstances, methods, and routine as given, these emerging leaders looked upon farming as a series of inter-related problems not satisfactorily solved by standard practices. Alternatives were available, requiring a choice. As one farmer pointed out, "there cannot be half a dozen *best ways* of doing the same thing under similar circumstances, requiring different amounts of time, labour, and expense."[50] Satisfactory decisions rested upon broad knowledge of the experience of others, supplemented by their own experimentation. The hope of increased monetary returns was no doubt an important motivating force, but the acknowledgment of leadership that came with success in their endeavors was also a significant stimulus.

[50] *American Agriculturist,* IV (1845), 28.

The search by such men for superior position took numerous directions. They joined in the western migration to find greater opportunities in the larger, richer, and cheaper farms. More important, they directed their activities to enhancing the productivity of a given enterprise, whether in the old East or new West. Superior exploitation of resources might be sought by introducing new and unusual crops, by intensifying advantages through specialization in crops, by acquiring more productive strains and breeds of the standard plants and animals, by using new and improved implements to increase productivity per man, by utilizing techniques to increase or at least maintain the productivity of the soil, and by trying to develop better techniques of management.

An active concern with changing marketing opportunities, with correspondingly appropriate selection of crops, with appraisal and adoption of plant and animal strains promising superior returns for investment, with utilization of new implements in an appropriate plan of cropping, with techniques guaranteeing better results for effort made, with efficient management of hired labor, and with maintenance of soil fertility—these made up the key elements in any plan of operations meriting the designation "superior provision for the raising of crops." Such plans, well executed, with appropriate applications of capital and labor, offered the prospect that a normal application of energy would return a maximum quantity of productions yielding the largest net return for a season's effort. Consistently obtained, such profits held the further attractive possibility, important to farmers with long-range plans, that their farms might be sold at prices representing capitalization of its favorable profit record.

CHAPTER SEVEN

THE MATÉRIEL OF FARM PRODUCTION

Given a decision on the kinds of crops and livestock to be produced, there remained to be determined the specific varieties that promised the greatest returns. At the turn of the century, although regional differences existed, in any locality the plants and animals raised were common to the area and were undifferentiated in variety, sometimes being degenerate forms of old European strains.[1] Distinctions increased rapidly, particularly after 1830. In part this resulted from importations from abroad of varieties that had not previously been known. At the same time, significant work in developing varieties and breeds was taking place in the United States.

PLANT VARIETIES

In the case of field crops, most farmers selected their seed at random from the previous harvest, planting the same stock year after year. Others selected their seed carefully, setting aside choice specimens of corn or wheat or earmarking choice plants growing in their fields. Occasionally, distinct strains of merit were isolated in this manner. A few farmers sought seed supplies elsewhere, both to avoid deterioration from inbreeding, and also to secure by such means whatever promising strains might be developing elsewhere.[2]

A major problem was finding a reputable source of seed supply. Although the better agricultural supply firms sought to handle good stocks, there was much dissatisfaction with commercial seed. Charles L. Flint pointed out that, although farmers paid too little attention to the selection of seeds, "the farmer cannot be sure that he has

[1] For comments on the oat, see Asher Robbins, *Address to the Rhode Island Society for the Encouragement of Domestic Industry* (Pawtuxet, 1822), p. 32.

[2] John H. Klippart, *The Wheat Plant* (Cincinnati, 1860), pp. 512-556; *Michigan Farmer*, VIII (1850), 130, 189-191; *Cultivator*, X (1843), 29; John Nicholson, *The Farmer's Assistant* (Lancaster, Pa., 1820), pp. 46-47; *New York Farmer*, X (1837), 5-6.

good seed unless he raises it for himself or uses that raised in his neighborhood. He too often takes that which has passed through several hands, and whose origin he cannot trace. Bad or old seed may thus be bought, in the belief that it is good and new, and the seller himself may not know to the contrary. The buyer in such cases often introduces weeds which are very difficult to eradicate. The temptation to mix seeds left over from previous years with newer seed is very great, and there can be no doubt that it is often done on a large scale. In such cases the buyer has no remedy. He cannot return the worthless article, and the repayment of the purchase money, even if he could enforce it, would be but poor compensation for the loss of the crop."[3]

The practice of sowing carefully selected seed increased, nevertheless, and represented a clear measure of the commercialization of farming and the development of a rational approach to the problems of maximizing returns. Over the period, the care given to the selection of seed increased greatly as "intelligent" farmers imitated their leaders. A speaker at the first Iowa State Fair in 1855 pointed out that "formerly you paid but little attention to the quality of the seed you sowed or planted. If it was corn—grains of corn were sufficient—if wheat, grains of wheat were sufficient. If potatoes—the semblance of that popular vegetable was sufficient. Now, with what care the intelligent farmer selects his seed corn—desirous of obtaining that variety which is most productive in its nutritive qualities, and produces the largest results from a given quantity of ground."[4]

Wheat. Only a few varieties of wheat were distinguished in colonial times. The efforts of a few American farmers in identifying, isolating, and cultivating wheats with distinct characteristics, together with occasional imports of distinct types, steadily increased the number of named and recognized varieties.[5] While there was much

[3] Charles L. Flint, *Practical Treatise on Grasses and Forage Plants* (New York, p. 141. Problems of this kind persisted for many years. See Earl W. Hayter, "Seed Humbuggery among the Western Farmers, 1850-1888," *Ohio Historical Quarterly*, LVIII (1949), 52-68.

[4] Iowa State Agricultural Society, *Report* (1855), p. 39.

[5] Jared Eliot, *Essays upon Field Husbandry in New England* (Columbia University Press, 1934), pp. 57-58. Nicholson, *Farmer's Assistant*, p. 419, lists the wheats grown about 1820 as spring and winter, the winter including the Bald, Bearded, Cone, Polish, and Smyrna. See also Sereno E. Todd, *The American Wheat Culturist* (New York, 1868), pp. 90-110.

confusion in wheat names—identical varieties bearing different names, and different varieties bearing identical names in various localities—there was nevertheless a growing number of varieties having distinct characteristics. Many of these were the product of obscure developers and gained attention slowly.[6] Others, particularly imports, were well publicized.[7] Interest in new wheats was greatly stimulated when the need arose for a variety resistant to the destructive attacks of the Hessian fly—attacks that made wheat production virtually impossible in some areas and threatened it everywhere. In part, the answer was found in a bearded red wheat of early maturity, the Mediterranean, introduced about 1819. Although the Mediterranean became widely grown because of its resistance to the fly, it was disliked by millers because of its hardness and consequently brought a price well below other wheat.[8]

Other varieties followed. By 1839, in western New York, "the kinds of wheat grown are very various, almost every kind having its warm advocates and eulogists. 'Corn quackery' as the undue extolling of new varieties of grain is called in England is, it is to be feared, not altogether unknown here."[9] At about that date, a survey listed 41 varieties of wheat known in the state, of which nine winter wheats and nine spring wheats were most important.[10] In 1859, a more intensive survey of wheats known in Ohio yielded a list of 135 varieties, including 32 varieties of red bearded winter wheat; 27 varieties of smooth red winter wheat; 20 varieties of bearded white winter wheat; 42 varieties of smooth white winter wheat; and 13 varieties of spring wheat. All of these were or had very recently been cultivated on a significant scale in the state.[11]

[6] Among the more important were Zimmerman's, developed by a Frederick, Maryland, farmer about 1837, and Soule's, a selection of a New York farmer about 1853. Cf. Carelton R. Ball, "History of American Wheat Improvement," *Agricultural History,* IV (1930), 49.

[7] For example, Elkanah Watson's work with American consuls abroad brought fourteen selected varieties of Spanish wheats to this country. Two of them, No. 2 Red Flint and No. 2 White Flint, sometimes known as Watson wheat, became popular in New York. Hugh M. Flick, "Elkanah Watson's Activities in Behalf of Agriculture," *Agricultural History,* XXI (1947), 197. Cf. *Genesee Farmer,* I (1840), 114-115.

[8] *Cultivator,* V (1838-1839), 27; New York State Agricultural Society, *Transactions,* III (1843), 146.

[9] *Genesee Farmer,* IX (1839), 4.

[10] Considerable information on wheat varieties grown in various localities appears in U. S. Patent Office, *Report,* (esp. 1850-1855, 1861-1862, 1865-1866).

[11] Klippart, *The Wheat Plant,* pp. 512-556. See also his "Essay on the Origin, Growth, Diseases, Varieties, Etc., of the Wheat Plant," in Ohio State Board of Agriculture, *Report* (1857), pp. 462-816.

Corn. Although there were relatively few varieties of such crops as oats, rye, or barley, the proliferation of varieties that occurred with wheat was paralleled in the case of corn and potatoes. Before 1820, John Lorain identified five kinds of corn in use in the middle and southern states: Big White, Big Yellow, Little White, Little Yellow, and White Virginia Gourdseed.[12] The first four were flint corns; the gourdseed was a southern dent corn. The maize of the Indian of the northeastern part of the United States was the flint; that of the southeastern Indian was the white southern dent. The two had very different characteristics and origins. Long before 1820 the southern dents had come into use in the northern states, and some hybridization had occurred.[13] The fact that the hybridization yielded highly variable results and produced some mixtures of superior productivity was recognized, notably by John Lorain, who in 1813 reported on experiments in deliberate hybridization of the gourdseed and flint.[14]

The number of varieties that became sufficiently established to continue in use increased rapidly, as farmers followed Lorain's suggestions or discovered for themselves the potential of careful selection and mixing of varieties.[15] Many of the resulting hybrids were of outstanding vigor and productivity, and some were propagated with sufficient care to become recognized as distinct strains of superior characteristics. While most farmers planted corns that were conglomerates of many blendings, care in the selection of the desired strain and in perpetuating it by rational selection of seed was a characteristic of progressive farmers. The heavy yielding and early maturing Dutton corn appeared in New England in the twenties. A survey made in Pennsylvania in the 1830's lists thirty-five varieties, to which Jesse Buel added five more.[16] Selective breeders

[12] John Lorain, *Nature and Reason Harmonized in the Practice of Husbandry* (Philadelphia, 1829), pp. 201-229.

[13] Edgar Anderson and William L. Brown, "The History of the Common Maize Varieties of the United States Corn Belt," *Agricultural History*, XXVI (1952), 2-5.

[14] John Lorain, "Observations on Indian Corn and Potatoes," in Philadelphia Society for Promoting Agriculture, *Memoirs*, III (1814), 303-325.

[15] For example, over a quarter-century Thomas N. Baden of Maryland developed from the White Gourdseed a variety noted for the number of ears that it carried and bearing his name. Cuthbert W. Johnson, *Farmer's Encyclopedia and Dictionary of Rural Affairs* (Philadelphia, 1839), pp. 744-747. For reports on experiments with corn varieties, see *Cultivator*, IV (1837), 148; *Farmer and Gardener*, V (1838), 236-237.

[16] *Farmer's Cabinet*, II (1838), 75-77, 90-92, 123-125, 139-141, 150-152, 187-190;

were particularly active in Ohio. In the late fifties, seventy-one varieties were reported as known in the state, all of them being cultivated to some extent.[17] The outstanding Reid's Yellow Dent was originated by an Illinois farmer in the 1840's.[18] A large number of other varieties of more local significance enjoyed popularity from time to time.

Potatoes. The ease with which new varieties of potatoes could be obtained led to the introduction of many varieties, though only a few achieved wide use. An early source lists sixteen varieties as widely known.[19] Many of these disappeared, to be replaced by others. Farmers first sought varieties that were more productive. After the potato disease had swept the country in the forties, they also sought disease-resistance types. As markets became more significant, they looked for varieties that combined productivity and disease-resistance with high quality. The Mercer was the standard commercial potato over much of the period, but was considered by some as unprofitable compared with a lower quality but more productive variety, such as the Peach Blow.[20] The development of the potato starch industry in the fifties stimulated a search for varieties having the appropriate characteristics.

The multiplication of varieties in the basic crops of wheat, corn, and potatoes was paralleled in other areas, mostly in the tree fruits. Since each named variety possessed special characteristics of value,

---

Cultivator, V (1838-1839), 43. See also *Complete Practical Farmer* (New York, 1839), pp. 88-90.

[17] Excluding popcorns. Klippart, *The Wheat Plant,* pp. 664-673. For further data on corn varieties, see New York State Agricultural Society, *Transactions* (1848), pp. 678-873; (1853), pp. 321-353; (1879), pp. 37-73; Maine State Board of Agriculture, *Report* (1877), pp. 1-21; Indiana State Board of Agriculture, *Report* (1856), pp. 331-355; *Rural New Yorker,* XIII (1862), 118; *Farmer's Register,* III (1835), 16-17; *American Agriculturist,* XXVII (1864), 37. There is considerable information on local use of corn varieties in U. S. Patent Office, *Report* (esp. 1849, 1850, 1852-1855).

[18] Anderson and Brown, "History of Common Maize Varieties," p. 7.

[19] Johnson, *Farmer's Encyclopedia,* p. 927; Willis Gaylord and Luther Tucker, *American Husbandry* (New York, 1840), I, 77. Numerous references to potato varieties appear in U. S. Patent Office, *Report* (1844-1845, 1849, 1851-1855, 1868). In 1851, Chauncey Goodrich of New York imported some potato tubers from South America. This stock was the source of the Garret Chili, popular for a time, and was used for hybridization with established varieties. Redcliffe N. Salaman, *The History and Social Influence of the Potato* (Cambridge University Press, 1949), p. 165.

[20] *Rural New Yorker,* XI (1860), 125, 173; XVI (1865), 101; George Fiske Johnson and W. S. Hagar, *History of the Mercer Potato* (Pennsylvania Department of Agriculture, 1934), mimeo.

farmers were presented with a difficult problem of choice. The wheats differed in their desirability for milling and hence in market value, in their productivity, in hardiness and resistance to disease and insects, in maturity, in adaptability to various soils, in length of straw, and in other characteristics. Corns differed in similar respects, particularly in maturity, storability, and productivity. Because each variety possessed both advantages and disadvantages, choices were critical if the farmers wanted to take full advantage of their particular situations and were willing to assume a risk in pursuing a greater gain. Most farmers were cautious, but a few were aggressive in seeking out the new and unfamiliar in search of greater effectiveness.

LIVESTOCK

The livestock of the colonists—cattle, hogs, horses, and sheep— were the progeny of numerous small importations from Europe, principally the northwestern part. These animals were typically representative of the average common stock of their day and place of origin. Neglect of animal needs for food and shelter in winter was common in most sections of Europe, and was even greater in the United States where it was an unavoidable characteristic of the frontier, although such neglect tended to persist in the United States long after the frontier conditions had disappeared.[21] The scarcity of cleared lands forced the animals to feed in the woods, on lands too wet for cultivation, or on the sparse herbage of fields abandoned because of their low productivity. Winter supplies of hay were obtained from wild grasses. Such hay, as well as other provender, was scarce, even relative to the small numbers of animals kept, so that the winters were trials for survival. Since crops rather than animals were fenced in, the herds ran at large, which

21 As late as 1840 one observer in New York remarked, "it is a very pitiable sight to go about our country and see the condition of multitudes of cattle and sheep which fill almost every farmer's yard in the spring of the year. The severity of our winters, with bad management, are in my opinion the sole cause of so much poverty among our cattle. The fact is, farmers keep too much stock, therefore, some, of course, must look poor in spring." *Genesee Farmer*, I (1840), 19. Adequate supplies of provender were the critical factor. In the West, though shelter was rarely provided, fodder supplies were more abundant. In Iowa, "cows, oxen, young stock, etc., are generally left to shirk for themselves. Rather abusive treatment for winter, yet they invariably look fat and sleek in summer." *Rural New Yorker*, V (1854), 46.

resulted in indiscriminate breeding that not only destroyed such distinct breeds as had been brought from Europe but also produced a further tendency toward the development of those strains whose chief merit was the ability to survive under difficult conditions. This was most true of hogs, though also of cattle, less so of horses, which were too valuable to be greatly neglected, and least true of sheep, which required protection from wolves and dogs.

The ability to survive under very difficult conditions was a most desirable characteristic of animals in an agricultural economy that looked upon them as sources of products needed for home use and obtainable with a minimum of attention. As markets developed and animals came to play a central role in the production plans of many farm enterprises, significant changes occurred in the characteristics considered valuable. Markets placed a premium upon quality products, while the interests of the profit-conscious farmer centered upon securing a maximum return at lowest cost. These changes in the objectives of animal husbandry served to emphasize such traits as early maturity, ease of fattening, quality of flesh, and a high ratio of edible products to gross weight. Heavy fleeces of long staple wool had long been important in selecting sheep, but the selection of dairy cows for milk yield developed only slowly.

Improvements in characteristics were sometimes obtained by providing better care for animals of native stocks. More adequate supplies of animal foods was in fact the central problem in any development of the animal industries, and the period was marked by substantial progress in this respect. One factor was the availability of better plows, which made practicable the preparation and care of land devoted to hay or pasture. The other was the availability of domesticated grasses and legumes, which were far superior to the spontaneous growth that was conventionally relied upon.

Forage Plants. Prior to 1820, interest in cultivating grasses and clovers for pasturage and hay was limited to a relatively few farmers in the longest settled sections of the East. While such farmers claimed that the labor involved was well repaid, the large majority of farmers made no effort to cultivate forage plants. They relied, instead, upon the wild growth of fallow fields, uncultivated or uncleared lands, and roadsides to supply their animals. Marshlands were a principal source of hay.

The desirability of better supplies of cattle roughage, together with the need for a fertility-restoring rotation of crops, served to stimulate a slow increase in interest. The plant materials available included most of the important forage plants of Europe. As a result of numerous importations, some deliberate and some furtive, European plants such as bluegrass, orchard grass, and the white and red clovers had became naturalized in the northern states at an early date. Among others available were timothy and red top, native grasses that had been domesticated in the United States in the eighteenth century.

After 1820 the very active interest in new plants included extensive experimentation with additional imports. Among those that attracted most attention in the agricultural press were certain varieties of alfalfa, sweet scented vernal grass, lespedeza, and Italian rye grass. While the latter had some value, the others either lacked hardiness or demonstrable superiority. As the necessity and profitability of cultivating plants for forage and hay became more widely accepted, a combination of red clover and timothy was nearly universally adopted.[22]

It was typical that farmers only slowly and reluctantly accepted the additional labor and seeding costs involved in establishing stands of domesticated grasses. Initial efforts frequently failed to secure satisfactory stands, which encouraged the belief that followed the frontier westward that the plants could not be grown under the existing conditions. Eventual success was achieved with more carefully prepared seed beds, proper timing, and sometimes the use of lime. Domesticated grasses were standard in the East by 1830, in Indiana in the 1850's, and were being accepted in Iowa in the 1860's.

Improved implements other than the cast-iron plow also played a role. With the adoption of the hay rake in the 1840's and of the mower in the 1850's, a very substantial increase occurred in the capacity of farmers to harvest hay crops. The raising of hogs was stimulated by the development of more efficient plows and tillage devices which made possible large increases in the corn acreage

---

[22] Charles L. Flint, for example, while urging the use of a wider variety of grasses, stated, "the prevailing practice is decidedly against the use of anything but Timothy, redtop, and clover." Flint, *Practical Treatise on Grasses and Forage Plants*, 2nd edition (New York, 1858), p. 144. See also Homer L. Kerr, "Introduction of Forage Plants into Ante-Bellum United States," *Agricultural History*, 38 (1964), 87-95.

cultivated per man. The use of the reaper similarly increased productivity in the case of such crops as oats or rye. The expansion of food supplies that resulted from these developments made it feasible not only to raise animal numbers but also to respond to market demands for animal products of a quality superior to that which was acceptable to the homestead.

An interest in improving the characteristics of the animals bred paralleled the growth of feed-producing capacity. Animals superior to the common American stock were available in Europe, and some of these animals were imported by public organizations, particularly the Massachusetts Agricultural Society. Most of the importations, however, and virtually all of the breeding and publicizing of these animals were carried on as private ventures.

The Breeder. The improvement of livestock required that the services of establishing or securing and of maintaining pure strains of superior animals be performed. The development of a class of farmers who undertook this specialization in the breeding and sale of fine livestock was a significant factor in the growth of the animal industries. Breeders of fine stock were few prior to 1820, and their functions were rarely performed.[23] After 1820, the number of men who conducted some breeding functions increased in number, and their role became not only important but frequently very remunerative. Best known were those who imported fine stock from countries where the development of superior animals was advanced, as in Britain for cattle, or Spain for sheep. A much larger number worked more obscurely, purchasing animals from the importers and the principal domestic breeders, developing their own herds, and selling the progeny and the services of the male animals within their localities. A few sought to develop their own strains by selective breeding, work which in the case of hogs was carried on with particular success but little fanfare.

While the breeder of fine animals appeared partly in response to a demand for his product, the breeder also played the role of promoter, creating interest and willingness to purchase. This task was not an easy one. Improved animals were always very expensive as

---

[23] "Much loss has been sustained by our farmers in not keeping up the purity of blood when possessed, the importance of which has been too little regarded." Gaylord and Tucker, *American Husbandry*, I, 178.

compared with the common stock. It was necessary to convince the prospective purchaser that the substantial investments would be profitable and that it was worthwhile to attempt to upgrade his common stock by introducing the blood of the superior breeds. Since it was frequently argued that the improved breeds had been developed by costly pampering, it was necessary to prove also that these animals would give superior results with reasonably good care and that they would yield a larger money return without significant increases in the raising costs. The breeder's task was simplified by the support of the agricultural journals, which gave the important breeds abundant publicity. Even more important was the fact that the agricultural societies, which had originated as stock shows, universally maintained a great interest in securing exhibits of animals for their fairs and exhibitions. Substantial premiums for the best animals exhibited were frequently offered, thus providing the breeder a not insignificant source of income.[24] The fairs afforded opportunities to publicize fine stock and to demonstrate the animals to more farmers than was possible in any other way.

Sheep. The cultivation of sheep was the first of the major agricultural industries to be strongly influenced by the opportunities provided by the growth of commercial markets. Small flocks of sheep were a standard resource of semisubsistence farming, their wool being the most important fiber used in homespun cloth. The animals available, like other native livestock, were a hardy strain of the common English stock. Their wool was a coarse, short staple, and their meat of a quality for which there was only a limited market.

The woolen industry, emerging in the New England towns in the first two decades of the nineteenth century, required a finer, longer stapled wool than that available from the common stock if it was to meet the competition of the English product. The substantial premiums offered for such wool turned farmer interest to the varieties of sheep characterized by long staple fleeces. Such sheep had been present in the eastern states, particularly New England, for some time without attracting much attention. Substantial numbers of the Spanish Merino had been brought to the northern states be-

---

[24] An example is Peter Melendy of Ohio who in a five-year period won prizes worth over $1,000 by exhibiting fine hogs, cattle, horses, and poultry at Ohio fairs. Ohio Board of Agriculture, *Report* (1855), p. 272.

ginning in 1802, following the breakdown during the Napoleonic wars of the Spanish prohibition against the export of the animals. These animals formed the foundation of a new sheep-raising industry, centering in New England but spreading throughout the northern states. While some farmers maintained flocks of pure-blooded Merinos, the investment required was very large. Many preferred to upgrade the quality of the fleeces of the native stock by a mixture of Merino blood, thereby also securing a hardier, more adaptable animal than the pure-blooded strains.

Dissatisfaction with the Spanish Merino led to experimentations with other European breeds. In 1822 the first specimens of the Saxony, a German development of the Spanish Merino, were being imported. Some years later, a series of importations were made of the Rambouillet strain from France. In the 1820's, efforts to increase returns by combining mutton sales with wool production stimulated the importation of the English Leicester breed by farmers in the Middle Atlantic states. These were followed in the 1830's by the other English mutton, coarse-wooled breeds such as the Southdown and the Cotswold.[25] By the mid-1830's, northern farmers had available all the important European breeds, though the continuing search for superior strains stimulated occasional further imports. The native stock had been substantially, although unevenly, upgraded by infusions of the blood of the European breed, but no American variety had been established.

Viewed superficially, the conditions existing in many parts of the northern states seemed highly attractive to the raising of sheep. The high intrinsic value of wool made distance from market a far less significant factor than was the case for other farm products.[26] Almost every farm had some land adapted to sheep grazing, while wool production seemed an ideal use for land too distant to permit of other uses. A large market obviously existed since the nation

[25] Henry S. Randall, *The Practical Shepherd* (Rochester, N. Y., 1863), is a standard older source. A recent study is Edward Norris Wentworth, *America's Sheep Trails* (Iowa State College Press, 1948). There were numerous reviews of developments in the agricultural press. See, for example, *Genesee Farmer*, XIII (1843), 37-38; *American Agriculturist*, II (1843), 136-138; a series of articles in *Ohio Cultivator*, VIII (1852).

[26] An analysis by a western farmer is illustrative: "At any point two hundred miles from Chicago, this ratio of cost in freighting is well established: that to transport your products to the seaboard on wheat you pay 80 per cent of its value; on pork 30 per cent; on beef 20 per cent; on wool 4 per cent." U. S. Commissioner of Agriculture, *Report* (1862), p. 304.

normally imported a large proportion of its needs of raw wool or fabricated cloth.

In fact, the vicissitudes of sheep farming throughout the period were greater, and the profitability of sheep raising was more widely and persistently debated, than any other objective of farming. Wool production was a remunerative industry in some areas over extended periods, such as New Hampshire and Vermont, and in other areas for shorter spans of time, as in Ohio, southern Michigan, and the western frontier.[27] A major difficulty was the fact that prices fluctuated widely in face of the vigorous competition from European sources. No other farm product was extended the protection of a tariff, but the protection given to wool was never of such a character as to encourage the continuation of sheep raising when alternative uses of resources became available.[28] The introduction of the mutton varieties did little to improve conditions because the demand for lamb and mutton remained limited in view of the abundant supplies of beef and pork. Wheat or beef in the West and dairying in the East were less subject to widely varying returns, less subject to losses from disease, weather, or dogs, and better adapted to the care that farmers felt able to supply.

Beef Cattle. The cattle available to the farmer of 1820 were the native stock descended from numerous importations over the years. While such importations included cattle from all sections of Europe, the English strains predominated in the development of the northern stock almost to the exclusion of the others. In the case of New England cattle, the claim was made that the strain of the English Devons was still discernible, but the Dutch dairy cattle imported into New Amsterdam had long since disappeared into the mixture called the native stock.[29] Although some degeneracy had doubtless occurred, particularly in the middle states, the native cattle were described as very similar to the common stock of Britain.[30]

[27] On the geographic aspects of the sheep industry, see Percy W. Bidwell and John I. Falconer, *History of Agriculture in the Northern United States* (Carnegie Institution of Washington, 1925); Carroll W. Pursell, Jr., "E. I. duPont and the Merino Mania in Delaware, 1805-1815," *Agricultural History*, XXXVI (1962) 91-100; Stephen L. Stover, "Early Sheep Husbandry in Ohio" and "Ohio's Sheep Year: 1868," *Agricultural History*, XXXVI (1962), 101-107; XXXVIII (1964), 102-107.

[28] Chester W. Wright, *Wool-Growing and the Tariff* (Boston, 1910).

[29] Nicholson, *The Farmer's Assistant*, p. 240; *Plough, Loom and Anvil*, XI (1858), 133-146.

[30] The degeneracy was owing chiefly to inadequate food supplies, though also to

The natives were an all-purpose stock, well adjusted to the conditions under which they were raised, and adequate to supply the needs of the older agriculture and the small markets it served. Although highly variable in milking qualities, good cows were common, and excellent ones could be found. The young males, particularly of the New England cattle, made excellent oxen. Both the milking cows when no longer profitable for the dairy, and the oxen at the age of seven or eight years, were fattened and slaughtered, these constituting the supplies of beef. As sources of milk, beef, and draft, the animals fitted well into the economy of the subsistence farm with its characteristic emphasis on multipurpose.

At the same time there was an obvious economic advantage in animals that gave superior returns for "ordinary care." Animals of unusually great weight or high milk productivity were always objects of curiosity, and the establishment of superior breeds was a matter of active interest to at least a few farmers. The principal aim of breeding, however, was to improve the all-purpose animal. A leading breeder of the twenties and thirties, John H. Powell, stated his objective as a "race fitted, at different times, for the production of rich milk and the secretion of fat," meaning that the same animal should have these qualities at different stages of her life.[31] The statement reflected the ideals of breeders throughout this period, though some farmers, particularly in New England, would have added that the breed should also be a source of good oxen. If a choice had to be made, the value of the animal as beef was controlling; there was little interest in animals that might be superior milk producers if they were correspondingly less valuable for fattening as beef.

That one could obtain more desirable animals than the common stock seemed to follow from the occasional appearance of unusually fine specimens and from the improvements sometimes obtained by better than average care. More significant was the work being done in the breeding of superior animals in Great Britain. English cattle about 1800 included a number of distinct varieties, most of them the products of local differentiation. Among the more important were the Galloway, Devonshire, Hereford, Lancashire, Highland

---

careless breeding. Many farmers, for example, sold the largest and best calves for veal because they brought a few cents more. *American Farmer,* II (1820), 304.

[31] Philadelphia Society for Promoting Agriculture, *Memoirs,* IV (1824), 25.

or Kyloes, Alderney, Welsh, and a breed known as the Dutch, Shorthorned, or Holderness, which resulted from crosses with cattle imported from the Low Countries. Importations into the United States of these cattle were not unusual. They entered by way of the fairly numerous though unrecorded sales in American ports of cows that had been kept on shipboard to supply milk on the voyage from England. It is probable that many of these were of the older Holderness race of shorthorns, a popular dairy breed in England. Such importations were undoubtedly of grade rather than superior cattle. They made only local and temporary impressions.[32]

About 1745, Robert Bakewell began his well-known work of breeding the Lancashire cattle, the result being the development of the beef-type Dishley or Longhorn. Although the breed did not establish itself permanently, the failure was insignificant compared with Bakewell's demonstration of the possibilities of selective breeding. About 1780 the Colling brothers began the work that quickly culminated in the improved Shorthorns, a race characterized by comparatively large size, very early maturity, and rapid fattening, while retaining, in some strains, superior milking qualities. When the Collings' herds were dispersed in 1810 and 1818, the breed was well established and highly popular.[33] By that time, numerous other English farmers were engaged in further work with the breed.

The appearance of specimens of Bakewell cattle in the United States within a few years of their development[34] is indicative of the deep interest with which some Americans followed the work of the English breeders. Developments in the breeding of superior cattle were closely pursued not only through the considerable literature but also through contacts with English agriculturists and by personal inspections in Britain. Some argued that cattle with the de-

---

[32] Philadelphia Society for Promoting Agriculture, *Memoirs*, IV (1824), 40.

[33] E. P. Prentice, *American Dairy Cattle* (Harper, 1942), pp. 165-168.

[34] It seems probable that Bakewell cattle were brought into Maine, Connecticut, and Massachusetts at an early date. *Cultivator*, II (1845), 321; VI (1849), 248, 375. In 1783 a number of animals of both Bakewell and the Shorthorn breeds were brought to the United States by H. D. Gough and a Mr. Miller of Maryland and Virginia. In 1785 and again in 1790, animals from this importation were taken to Kentucky by Matthew Patton, Jr. In that state and also in Ohio they were known as the Patton stock. *Western Farmer*, II (1841), 128; *American Farmer*, II (1820), 313; IV (1822), 280; Prentice, *American Dairy Cattle*, p. 175; Charles T. Leavitt, "Attempts to Improve Cattle Breeds in the United States, 1790-1860," *Agricultural History*, VII (1933), 58; George F. Lemmer, "The Spread of Improved Cattle through the Eastern United States to 1850," *Agricultural History*, XXI (1947), 79.

sired characteristics might be obtained by careful selective breeding from the native stock. Others maintained that there already existed in England and on the Continent various breeds far more valuable than the common American stock, and that the importation of such animals was a more economical and certain way of securing superior stock than could be expected from efforts at home. Those who held the latter view followed developments in Europe with particular interest and care. Luther Tucker pointed out in the 1860's that "inobtrusive Yankees had been present at virtually all of the important English livestock sales and that their purchases were a significant factor in making such breeding activities profitable for English farmers."[35]

Interest in the improved English Shorthorns became intense after 1820. A few years earlier, Robert Patterson of Baltimore had begun his long career of breeding cattle, his herds including the Bakewell Longhorns, improved Shorthorns, Devon, and Hereford cattle, all of which had been obtained from the famous English breeder, Thomas Coke of Holkam.[36] Descendants of the Patterson Shorthorns were purchased in the next few years by Maryland as well as New England breeders. John S. Skinner, editor of the *American Farmer* and a strong advocate of improved stock, in 1822 imported three Shorthorns from England. These animals were sold to a leading Shorthorn breeder of Maryland and became a basic source of stock for numerous other breeders.

In 1822, John Hare Powell, a wealthy farmer of Philadelphia County, began the breeding of Shorthorns. For several decades thereafter, Powell was the leading importer and breeder in the middle states, if not in the nation.[37] Powell's vigorous advocacy of Shorthorns was undoubtedly influential in establishing their popularity. His explanation of his careful choice of the breed gives an indication of the development of fine cattle-breeding in the United States. Powell pointed out that, having studied cattle at home and abroad: "I have had cattle bred in Kentucky, Maryland, Virginia,

---

[35] *Prairie Farmer*, XXIV (1861), 41.

[36] *Genesee Farmer*, XVI (1846), 232.

[37] *American Farmer*, X (1828), 55. Powell wrote that he had given an English agent "a standing order to obtain the best animals without limitation as to price, when they could be procured from Mr. Whitaker's fold." J. H. Powell, *Hints for American Husbandmen with Communications to the Pennsylvania Agricultural Society* (1827). On Powell's activities, see George F. Lemmer, "Spread of Improved Cattle," pp. 80-81.

Maine, Massachusetts, Vermont, New York, and Pennsylvania. I have traced every importation of which I have heard. I can distinguish Messrs. O'Donnel's, Patterson's, Gough's, Parkinson's, and Creighton's importations for Maryland; the Holstein, Alderney, Irish, Dutch, Flemish, Brittany, Pie and Short-horn breeds brought into Pennsylvania by Messrs. Sims, Cunningham, Ross, Waln, Hamilton, Ketland, Guest, Massey, and Wurts—families of various degrees of affinity to the Yeeswater race of Short-horns carried to New York by Col. Deveaux, and Mr. Heaton—the Leicestershire, Lancashire, and Hereford cattle taken to Connecticut, Massachusetts, New Jersey, and Maine, by Messrs. Wadsworth, Steward, Edgar, and Vaughn. Of most of these importations I have had individuals and of all have carefully examined some of the progeny either here or at a distance. For some of the animals, which I designate, I had given great prices."[38]

Animals from Powell's herd became the foundation stock of many other breeders scattered throughout the northern states from Maine to Ohio and Kentucky. Some of his successors greatly exceeded his scale of operations, particularly in New York.[39] Possibly the outstanding promoters of fine stock of their period were Lewis F. and A. B. Allen, who were active in western New York in the several decades following 1830.[40] A leading importer of the fifties in New York was Samuel Thorne, who in 1857 was a principal purchaser at the dispersal of one of the finest herds in England, buying fifty-five animals for $35,000. Evidence of the quality of animals developed in the United States appears in the fact that in 1867 animals from a Geneva, New York, herd, when sent to England, brought excellent prices at a sale at Windsor.[41]

Beginning about 1817, the Massachusetts Agricultural Society inaugurated a policy of importing improved cattle, a practice it pursued for half a century.[42] Despite such sponsorship, the recep-

[38] Philadelphia Society for Promoting Agriculture, *Memoirs,* IV (1824), 23; Lewis F. Allen, *History of the Short-Horn Cattle* (Buffalo, 1872), p. 157; Leavitt, "Attempts to Improve Cattle Breeds," p. 58.

[39] Lewis F. Allen, *American Herd Book, Containing Pedigrees of Short Horn Cattle, 1846-1882* (Buffalo, 1883), p. 78.

[40] *Genesee Farmer,* V (1835), 255; VIII (1838), 151; IX (1839), 208; *Cultivator,* IX (1852), 198; *Country Gentleman,* VII (1856), 367-386.

[41] Allen, *American Herd Book,* pp. 175 ff; Prentice, *American Dairy Cattle,* p. 170.

[42] Allen, *American Herd Book,* p. 76.

tion of improved breeds, including the generally popular Shorthorn, was much more restrained in New England than elsewhere. Skeptics were convinced that the animals required better care and food than New England farmers were accustomed or willing to supply. Some claimed that the superiority of the imported animals was due largely to the superior care they had received, a claim that doubtless had some foundation in fact. Some claimed that the native cattle could be similarly improved if such care were provided them, and there was considerable sentiment among some farmers in favor of efforts to develop a superior native breed.[43] Such men argued that the native breed was equal or superior to the Shorthorns in milking qualities and that they made much better oxen.[44]

Interest in the new English breeds developed quickly west of the Alleghenies. In 1817 a group of improved Shorthorns and Longhorns was imported from Britain by Lew Sanders for his bluegrass Kentucky farm. Shorthorns were soon found in Ohio, and specimens were apparently brought into Illinois as early as 1834.[45] Other obscure movements took place across the mountains. Interest in improved animals in Ohio in the early thirties led to the organization of the Ohio State Importing Company, an association of fifty cattlemen. Felix Renick, one of the organizers, traveled to England to make the purchases and there visited every important herd of improved animals. He bought Shorthorns exclusively, sending sixty of them to Ohio where they were sold on the Renick farm at auctions in 1836 and 1838, bringing prices representing substantial profits to the association.[46] These sales inaugurated a boom in Shorthorn cattle in Ohio and the West generally, prices moving to still higher levels.

The interest in foreign cattle was not limited to the Shorthorns but extended on a more restricted scale to other English and Continental breeds. Critics of the Shorthorn turned to breeds with more specialized characteristics. Among the beef breeds, both Devons

[43] This position was strongly held by Timothy Pickering, among others. *Farmer's Library* (1826), p. 148; *New England Farmer*, IV (1825), 81; *Plough Boy*, III (1821), 32.

[44] For an example, see *New England Farmer*, III (1825), 306.

[45] Illinois State Agricultural Society, *Transactions* (1869-1870), p. 252.

[46] Charles S. Plumb, "Felix Renick, Pioneer," *Ohio Archaeological and Historical Quarterly*, XXXIII (1924), 35-36; U. S. Census Office, *Agriculture of the United States in 1860*, p. cxxiii.

and Herefords were in the country prior to 1820.[47] The Devons acquired a degree of popularity in the more northernly sections, and by the late 1840's they were to be found scattered in small herds from New England to Michigan. The Herefords attracted brief attention when Henry Clay and other cattle men of the Ohio-Kentucky area experimented with them in the hope that they would travel better than fattened Shorthorns and would therefore be more profitable to drive the long distances to eastern markets.[48] That hope was disappointed, and until after 1860 the Herefords attracted only a small following, principally in New York and New England.[49]

Although the increase in pure-blooded stock was slow, the imported animals were extensively interbred with the common stock, resulting in a significant upgrading of northern cattle. Upgrading was common in the West, where in Illinois, for example, "nearly all the common cattle have an infusion more or less of Short-horn blood."[50] Though no precise measurements are available, there can be no question that the economic impact of improved beef cattle was substantial. Before 1830, Boston slaughter houses estimated that the improvement in the quality of cattle over the previous ten years had increased the average weight per animal by 10 percent "in consequence of a favorable change in the frame of the animal."[51] Much the same thing was observed in Pennsylvania.[52]

Dairy Cattle. Dairying, which constituted a source of income on almost all farms, became a specialized form of farming in the forties and fifties in parts of New England, in central New York and northern Ohio, and gradually in the vicinity of all the major cities.[53] As was true also in England until near the end of our period, dairy farming combined the production of butter, cheese, and, less frequently, fluid milk with the fattening of beef. Beef was usually the most important product, and even when milk products provided the

[47] *American Farmer,* VII (1826), 416; X (1828), 144; *Genesee Farmer,* I (1831), 145; *Cultivator,* II (1845), 200; V (1849), 120.

[48] Johnson, *Farmer's Encyclopedia,* p. 300.

[49] *Genesee Farmer,* XVI (1846), 281; XVII (1848), 50.

[50] Illinois State Agricultural Society, *Transactions* (1861), pp. 23-24. See also Michigan Agricultural Society, *Transactions* (1857), pp. 101-150; Leavitt, "Attempts to Improve Cattle Breeds," p. 62.

[51] *New York Farmer,* II (1829), 217.

[52] *Cultivator,* VII (1841), 43.

[53] Eric Brunger, "Dairying and Urban Development in New York State, 1850-1900," *Agricultural History,* XXIX (1955), 169-174.

larger part of the income, the sale of beef was a critical factor in the returns of the enterprise. Like those who fattened steers, dairymen frequently did not breed their own stock. Most purchased their cows from passing drovers or at cattle markets, the animals coming from such areas as the cattle-breeding section of southern Ohio, or later from Illinois and farther West. The dairy farmer selected two- or three-year-olds from whatever breeds might be offered, keeping the animals sometimes for only one season, sometimes three or four years. Most of the animals were natives, although Shorthorns and Shorthorn crosses became increasingly popular.

Most farmers accepted such animals as were readily available and made few, if any, efforts to increase the productivity of their herds, except perhaps to send particularly unsatisfactory animals to the butcher earlier than was the usual practice.[54] Although there were good milking strains among the Shorthorns, most of those available were poor milkers, and the breed was so disliked by many farmers in the dairy districts that they preferred to use the natives.[55] There was nevertheless some dissatisfaction with the generally low yield of the cattle used in dairying. A few men developed their own dairying strains. The outstanding example was Samuel Jacques, a breeder of Shorthorns but best known for his work in developing a dairy breed, the Cream Pots, which originated from a cross between a Shorthorn bull and a native cow.[56] Though the Cream Pot strain was to die out, its development stimulated interest in better breeding. Some persisted in the effort to develop superior strains of the native cattle.[57] Others turned to the European dairy breeds,

[54] E. Phinney, speaking for the Trustees of the Massachusetts Agricultural Society, said: "Many farmers in this part of the country, though depending principally for their income upon their milch cows, are not aware, it is apprehended, of the small produce derived from them, and would, no doubt, be surprised on learning that their cows generally do not yield an average daily product of more than from two to four quarts of milk for the year." Massachusetts Agricultural Society, *Abstracts* (1845), p. 185.

[55] On criticisms of the animal, see *New England Farmer*, III (1825), 306; *Country Gentleman*, IX (1857), 449; Ohio State Board of Agriculture, *Report* (1848), p. 32; (1849), pp. 515, 520 ff.

[56] Henry Colman, *Agricultural Survey of Massachusetts*, Second Report (1838), pp. 66-68.

[57] A committee of the Essex Agricultural Society concluded from the experience of the Cream Pots that, "by a judicious choice of the bull, our native breed of cows can be made to do all that cows ought to do, or ever have done anywhere; while the present condition of the cows of our county, at least, proves as clearly that without attention, great attention, to the bull, nothing effectual can ever be done at improving stock." Massachusetts Agricultural Society, *Abstracts* (1850), p. 7.

importing small numbers of such animals and thereby providing a source of supply.[58]

A few Holsteins had been imported before 1820 by farmers near Baltimore and Philadelphia.[59] They were condemned by Powell as unthrifty animals because they would not fatten when dry, hence falling far short of the ideal dual-purpose animal.[60] Moreover, the chief characteristic of the breed was the production of an abundance of milk of relatively low fat content, a quality of little interest to farmers concerned with the production of butter or cheese. The breed attracted little attention until the 1850's when importations of improved strains became the nucleus of the nation's first permanent Holstein herd.[61] However, only farmers selling whole fluid milk had any interest in the breed, and since most of them continued to be committed to beef production, for which the Holstein was clearly inferior, interest never ran high. The Dutch breeds did not establish themselves in economically significant fashion until after 1870.

The Ayrshires underwent great changes during the first half of the nineteenth century, so that the modern race bears little relationship to the Ayrshires of 1800. The improved breed were excellent milk producers, of good size and early maturity, and performed well on scant provender. Specimens were first imported in the early twenties, and other small shipments followed, though they made little impression.[62] Though the Ayrshire might be considered an excellent dual-purpose animal, in Massachusetts in the fifties the best milkers were believed to be crosses of Shorthorns and Ayrshires with natives, although "good milkers can be found in almost every breed."[63] Until the fifties, interest in Ayrshires concentrated mostly in Massachusetts and New York, and they were not numerically

---

[58] Phinney wrote: "What individual farmer has the patience, the skill, the intelligence, and the capital to engage in a task that will require many years and much capital to bring to any considerable degree of perfection. What would be the propriety or the economy of undertaking a work of this kind when, by a little extra expense at the commencement, we may find the work already done to our hands?" Massachusetts Agricultural Society, *Abstracts* (1845), p. 185. See also Lewis F. Allen in New York State Agricultural Society, *Transactions* (1864), pp. 101-110.

[59] Lemmer, "Spread of Improved Cattle," p. 90; *American Farmer*, IV (1822), 122; Holstein Breeder's Association, *Holstein Herd-book* (Boston), I (1872), 17-18.

[60] Philadelphia Society for Promoting Agriculture, *Memoirs*, IV (1824), 25, 54.

[61] Prentice, *American Dairy Cattle*, p. 137.

[62] Lemmer, "Spread of Improved Cattle," p. 89.

[63] *Cultivator*, III (1846), 355; VI (1849), 9-11.

important until after the Civil War, when they spread more rapidly throughout the dairy sections of the East.[64]

Like the Ayrshires, the cattle of the Channel Islands underwent marked changes, particularly about 1835.[65] While the Alderneys of the early part of the century were known as good producers of butter,[66] they were of small size and of little value for beef. Alderney of the early, small type were imported before 1820.[67] Subsequent importations in the thirties were probably of improved strains, since the breed attained some importance about 1840 in the dairy area around Philadelphia.[68] After the middle of the century, the much improved animals came to be distinguished as Jerseys and Guernseys, and importations of both were common, though they did not become popular prior to 1870.

In these developments there were no such men as the Collings or Coke, clearly identified with the improvement of the breed or calling attention to the merits of the animals. Nor did aggressive promoters appear in the United States until after the Civil War to play the role for the dairy breeds that Powell had played for the Shorthorns.[69]

Hogs. The hogs of colonial farmers were mixtures derived from numerous sources, which had degenerated from the lack of care given the animals. The frontier of settlement and the earliest stages of farming were characterized from colonial times until the 1860's by hogs known as the razorback, land sharks, wood hog, and a variety of other names.[70] The principal characteristic of the animal was

---

[64] *Southern Cultivator,* XVI (1858), 251.

[65] Lemmer, "Spread of Improved Cattle," p. 90; Prentice, *American Dairy Cattle,* pp. 234-236.

[66] Prentice, *American Dairy Cattle,* p. 345.

[67] Philadelphia Society for Promoting Agriculture, *Memoirs,* IV (1824), 21; Charles L. Flint, *Milch Cows and Dairy Farming* (New York 1858), p. 27.

[68] *Plough, Loom and Anvil,* I (1848), 55; Charles L. Hill, *The Guernsey Breed* (Kimball Co., Waterloo, Iowa, 1917), Ch. IV; John S. Linsley, *Jersey Cattle in America* (New York, 1885), pp. 483-488.

[69] A noteworthy exception was Colonel John LeCouteur, who played an important role in the development of the Jersey. Prentice, *American Dairy Cattle,* pp. 340 ff.

[70] William Fletcher, *Pennsylvania Agriculture and Country Life, 1640-1840* (Pennsylvania Historical and Museum Commission, 1950), pp. 188-190. As late as 1859 in Vincennes, Indiana, the razorback was still standard. "The hogs are allowed to range at large during the summer, so there is no chance to improve breeds, if there was a disposition among our farmers to do so; and the consequence is that a race of hogs

its ability to fend for itself in securing food and to defend itself from predators. Long-legged, fleet, and narrow-bodied, the razorback served as a semiwild source of animal food for the farm homestead, and when fattened on mast, beechnuts, or corn, it could be slaughtered and packed in brine for such undiscriminating markets as the West Indies or the cotton plantations of the South.

As settlement became more dense and forest disappeared, the food sources of such hogs diminished. Moreover, they were a serious menace to cultivated fields because of their ability to jump over or root under all but the most elaborate fencing. At the same time the razorbacks lost their market significance as buyers became more discriminating, demanding pork of firmer flesh and better cuts than could be obtained from these animals. Although they responded to better care and food, they were at best relatively small in size and slow to reach maturity.

As in the case of cattle, a few individuals turned to foreign sources in search of animals that might better meet American needs. The degeneracy of American hogs was taking place at the same time that English animals were undergoing considerable improvement. About 1800 there were numerous English breeds superior to the American, most of them carrying the names of their locality. Selective breeding had produced animals of heavy weights at early maturity, and distinctions had developed between bacon and lard hogs. Imports of the superior English animals began about 1800 when some specimens of the Woburn breed were sent by the Duke of Bedford, their originator, to George Washington. Known as Bedfords, Woburns, or Parkinsons, these animals were reputed to weigh 400 to 600 pounds at a year of age, two to three times the weight of the razorbacks when slaughtered at the customary eighteen months. The breed was popular in the Baltimore-Philadelphia area for some decades.[71]

After the War of 1812, arrivals of foreign hogs in American ports multiplied. English breeds brought to the United States in the next few decades included the Leicestershire, the Norfolk Thin-rind, the Lincolnshire, Hampshire, Yorkshire, Berkshire, Suffolk, and the

---

with long legs, long noses, and long ears, which after feeding two years and acquiring a weight of two hundred or two hundred and fifty pounds, require a swift dog or rifle to overtake them in the race that usually takes place on the premises of the owner or the public highway on hog killing day." *Ohio Farmer,* VIII (1859), 393.

[71] *Genesee Farmer,* XX (1850), 163-164.

Irish.[72] American merchant men and naval officers, sailing to all parts of the globe, brought back hogs from Spain, Germany, Switzerland, Italy, Russia, India, and China.[73] A few of these found local popularity, and all were used in crosses that produced breeds of local importance.[74] The Chinese animals were particularly important in such crosses, Colman asserting that they had enriched Massachusetts by hundreds of thousands of dollars since they gave "firmness of bone, plumpness and fullness of form, extraordinary thriftiness, and quietness of demeanor."[75]

The foreign breed that secured the widest acceptance was the Berkshire, first imported from England in 1823 by John Brentnall, an English immigrant farmer who settled in Orange County, New York. As the superiority of the breed was recognized—they matured in fourteen months to a weight of from 300 to 500 pounds—a speculative boom sent the prices of Berkshires skyrocketing.[76]

The work of American farmers in developing their own breeds, based on mixtures with and selections from foreign hogs, was noteworthy. Earliest to win substantial recognition was John Mackay, a Boston sea captain, who brought hogs of numerous foreign breeds to his Massachusetts farm. Beginning about 1825, he developed a breed bearing his name which enjoyed a considerable local reputation and was reported as a strong competitor at Massachusetts livestock shows.[77] Mixtures of foreign breeds with native animals were common by 1840, with a few becoming permanently established as recognized breeds. Among the earliest were the Byfields, originating in Massachusetts.[78] The Chester Whites were developed by farmers of Chester County, Pennsylvania, the Bedford stock disappearing into this breed.[79] More important were the Poland-Chinas, based on the Irish Grazier, which gradually emerged as a distinct variety in Warren county, Ohio, the product of numerous developers.[80]

[72] *Complete Practical Farmer*, pp. 490-492.

[73] *Genesee Farmer*, XX (1850), 163-164.

[74] *Complete Practical Farmer*, p. 492.

[75] Henry L. Ellsworth, *The Improvements in Agriculture and the Arts of the United States* (1843), p. 64.

[76] Ellsworth, *Improvements in Agriculture*, p. 63.

[77] *Genesee Farmer*, XX (1850), 163-164.

[78] James W. Thompson, "A History of Livestock Raising in the United States," U. S. Department of Agriculture, Agricultural History Series, No. 5 (1942), p. 136.

[79] Fletcher, *Pennsylvania Agriculture*, p. 190.

[80] U. S. Patent Office, *Report* (1850), p. 417; (1855), p. 61.

Also notable were the Duroc-Jerseys, the product of obscure breeders of Saratoga County, New York.[81]

In the West, the shift from the common razorback to the improved varieties began about 1840 and progressed rapidly. Although the razorbacks were a source of almost costless pork, the animal lost commercial value as hog-packing became a well-organized industry. Since the half-wild animals could not easily be driven, farm slaughtering was necessary. Farmers, however, found it difficult to supply the standardized cuts and brines increasingly demanded by the market, and sales were made only at heavy discounts from the prices offered for the improved breeds.[82] Farmers seeking the profitable conversion of corn into pork were therefore virtually forced to obtain the improved breeds.

Solon Robinson introduced a pair of Berkshires into Lake County, Indiana, in the late thirties, to begin the end of the native stock in that state.[83] The Berkshires were reported in Wisconsin in 1841 and came into Iowa with the early settlers.[84] By the 1850's, the Berkshires and the Poland-Chinas were the two most common hogs in the corn-raising areas, and English travelers were observing that the hogs on western farms were generally superior to those of Britain.[85] In parts of Illinois in the late sixties, "The old-fashioned, flat-sided, sharp-backed, long-bristled, and sharp-nosed hog" was "as great a curiosity . . . as an old fashioned bar-share plow."[86] In Delaware County, Iowa, it was claimed that the "prairie-shark hog had disappeared in a matter of five years with the introduction of the Suffolk."[87]

Horses. The horse of the period was the native animal, of no recognized breed, typically light and small. The animals were excellent for roadwork and useful for light draft tasks but lacked the weight to displace oxen for heavy work. Throughout this period there was

[81] U. S. Commissioner of Agriculture, *Report* (1873), p. 438.

[82] *Western Farmer,* II (1841), 105; *Prairie Farmer,* III (1843), 44; VIII (1848), 52; U. S. Patent Office, *Report* (1849), p. 192.

[83] Indiana State Board of Agriculture, *Report* (1856), p. 191.

[84] *Genesee Farmer,* II (1842), 71. U. S. Patent Office, *Report* (1868), p. 517; (1869), pp. 542, 546.

[85] H. Carman, "English Views of Middle Western Agriculture, 1850-1870," *Agricultural History,* VIII (1934), 17-18.

[86] Illinois State Agricultural Society, *Transactions* (1859-1860), p. 312.

[87] Iowa State Agricultural Society, *Transactions* (1859), pp. 223, 302.

little farmer interest in improved breeds for farm work. A variety was developed in the German area of eastern Pennsylvania, the Conestoga, but it did not spread and dwindled in numbers after 1860. Several Percherons were imported from Europe in 1839 and others in 1850, but the breed enjoyed only a limited popularity. Such breeding activities as were carried on centered upon fast horses for roadwork. The most celebrated breeds were the Narragansett pacers, the Morgans, Hambletonians, and the progeny of Messenger and Black Hawk. Such animals were raised primarily for sale to urban buyers.[88]

Poultry. Prior to 1850, northern farms normally maintained small flocks of chickens, ducks, geese, and perhaps turkeys. All were the common stock of northern Europe. The turkey, though native to North America, had been domesticated in Europe. Returned to the United States, the bird underwent further selective breeding, though it remained of minor economic significance.

About 1848 the agricultural press discovered that the supplying of eggs and poultry to urban markets had grown into an industry of large proportions which promised even more rapid expansion. The trade rested upon the surplus products of the numerous small farm flocks. It seemed possible that larger flocks of more productive chickens would be highly profitable if given good care. The possibilities prompted a search for more productive varieties of chickens, and foreign breeds were imported in substantial numbers from the Mediterranean countries as well as Asia. Interest reached speculative heights in 1849.[89] While the imported varieties proved of little value by themselves, they were widely employed in cross-breeding. Such efforts yielded no significant results prior to 1870. The simultaneous efforts to develop large-scale enterprises in the production of eggs and poultry foundered on the inability to control disease.

Those farmers who led in applying the cost–market price calculus to the planning of their operations were also leaders in seeking ways to increase productivity. Sensitivity to opportunities to secure

[88] *Genesee Farmer,* XVIII (1848), 128; Johnson, *Farmer's Encyclopedia,* p. 642; Thompson, *History of Livestock Raising,* p. 135.

[89] Arthur H. Cole, "Agricultural Crazes," *American Economic Review,* XVI (1926), 622-639.

plant and animal materials that promised an economic advantage was not a widely shared characteristic. Those who did possess it sought to further their objectives by importations from abroad and by efforts to develop at home the characteristics in plants and animals that they desired.

In the case of plants, developments were less publicized though nevertheless significant. It was not possible to control stocks so that revenues could be obtained sufficient to support private breeding operations. On the other hand, the breeding stocks of superior animals could be profitably controlled, and that fact produced the specialized breeder. He was in many ways the epitome of the progressive, highly capitalistic, farm enterpriser. Though his influence spread slowly, this followed chiefly from the naturally slow rate at which his stock could be increased. His influence was widely diffused in that numerous imitators saw advantage to themselves in participating in the development of superior stock.

CHAPTER EIGHT

REACTIONS TO IMPROVED IMPLEMENTS

The major tasks of agriculture—soil preparation, seeding, cultivating, and harvesting—constitute a sequence of operations that must be in balance to maximize the end product and avoid wasted labor. Since the demands made by each operation upon the labor force differ, the man-land ratio and the total product of an enterprise are limited by the labor capacity to perform critical operations on time. About 1820 the ratio of land to men in the technology of northern agriculture was fixed by the capacity to perform the labor of harvesting in the cases of wheat and grass, or of cultivation in the case of corn. This technology had been essentially static for some time.

Changes in the implements available to agriculture gradually provided alternatives to the accepted techniques. No single area of change was by itself of great significance, since the advantages tended to be limited if not neutralized by the labor requirements of other operations. As each improvement fell into sequence, the effect was to establish a new integrated system of operations, which permitted a multiplication of the acreage that could be cared for by one man. In the forty years following 1820 the technology of agriculture was revolutionized by the successful or more effective application of horsepower to every critical task in growing crops. In the West, the abundance of land permitted a ready adaptation of the man-land ratio to the new technological system; in the older sections, adoption of the new system took place more slowly because it was more difficult to make the adjustments in land requirements.

From time to time throughout this period, the attention of progressive farmers was called to claims of improvements in familiar implements, to newly developed tools and machines, and to reports of experiments with them. While many of these innovations quickly disappeared from notice, others were of such merit as to arouse interest in the scattered farmers who were particularly sensitive to opportunities for increasing the productivity of their enterprises.

Few inventions were sufficiently developed at the time of their first introduction to operate reliably or to be effective in reducing costs. In almost all cases a considerable period of time elapsed before they were available in any quantity. Most inventors sought to profit from their patent not by manufacture, since few had such facilities, but by granting licenses to manufacture, usually on the basis of exclusive state or even county rights. Certain plows were successfully marketed in this manner. However, many patented implements placed on the market by licensees disappointed the purchasers and discredited the patent. Virtually all new agricultural implements and machines required skill in manufacture, particularly of their metal parts, to a degree not possessed by the traditional source of supply—the local blacksmith. A successful new implement therefore rested not only upon an idea, patented or otherwise, but also upon the development of manufacturing skills. Over the period there was a marked trend toward the manufacture of agricultural implements in fewer but larger establishments.

The increase in concentration of production also created the need for a more effective system of distribution than the country store or the blacksmith. To meet this need, there developed what were called agricultural warehouses, which retailed and wholesaled all types and makes of implements as well as other agricultural supplies. Appearing earliest in the large eastern seaboard cities—New York, Boston, and Baltimore in the 1830's—such stores were to be found in every important city and in many smaller towns before 1860. Their services were supplemented and sometimes dispensed with by the manufacturers of the more costly implements, such as harvesters, which were typically sold by local agents and traveling salesmen.

These institutional developments, which permitted manufacturers to place an acceptable product before their buyers, were equally important to the farmers who had an interest in utilizing improved implements. Although the agricultural press kept them well informed of new inventions and of patentee's claims, the opportunity to see for themselves and possibly to purchase an implement for trial frequently followed only long after having read of it in some journal. The rate at which new implements were brought into use depended heavily upon success in overcoming manufacturing and distributing difficulties.

Once a new implement had been sufficiently perfected to offer a reasonably certain prospect of increasing the effectiveness of labor, experimental adoption by small numbers of widely scattered farmers occurred. The evaluations of such users sometimes suggested further improvements, while their reports on their experiences to neighbors, agricultural societies, and the press aroused the curiosity of others. Such purchases also enabled manufacturers to increase their capacity to produce and distribute the implement. Improvements in the implement were made as experience in use and in production suggested. Only after a prolonged period of interplay of this type was the typical implement sufficiently perfected and tested to be made available in large enough numbers to attract the consideration of the farmer who was conservatively alert to product-increasing opportunities.

Although some inventors and manufacturers came from farm backgrounds, the role of operating farmers was limited to that of the critical user. The farmer assumed the task of making such adjustments in his operations as the adoption of the machine made necessary, so that full advantage of its features might be obtained. This was rarely an easy undertaking and usually required lengthy experimentation.

During this period, virtually every farm task was affected by the development of improved implements and mechanical aids of some kind. The changes occurred earliest among hand tools, such as hoes, forks, and axes, which were the object of great improvement before 1820. The plow was developed from a crude multipurpose instrument into a variety of special-purpose implements of superior efficiency; the hand rake was replaced by the horse-pulled sulky rake; the hand sowing of grasses and grains gave way to the grain drill and corn planter; the scythe was displaced by the harvester; and the flail was made obsolete by the threshing machine.

THE WOODEN PLOW

The generation that about 1860 was deeding its farms to its sons had witnessed during its lifetime the transformation of the plow from a most primitive wooden implement of limited effectiveness to a modern iron or steel device available in a wide vairety of special-purpose forms, capable of far better work with half the effort. As one Iowa pioneer expressed it:

As a boy I commenced ploughing operations with the long-necked, long-tailed, wooden sided bar share; then came the old fashioned bull plough; and bull ploughs they were with a vengeance; then came on the thousand and one modifications which, being all put together, rendered them but a little better than the ancient Egyptian fork of a tree, with a rude piece of iron on one branch, and the Ox and the Ass attached to the other.

With such ploughs, I learned to plough; next the Peacock, the Cary and the Diamond came up much improved indeed, and we thought then that the acme of perfection had been attained in ploughmaking. But soon the Peoria, the Rough and Ready and the Moline still better adapted to the light soil of our prairie west excelled; still later came the Parkinson light center Draught plough, competing for premium over our broad acres of Prairie, until now . . . we have put in our hands the latest, the last triumph in improvement, in the shape of Parkinson's newly got up Plough.[1]

These were all moldboard plows. More primitive even than the bar-share was the shovel plow, which was probably more widely known throughout the country than any other plow and which continued in use throughout the period.[2] It consisted of a piece of iron shaped like a pointed shovel, attached to a stick, which in turn was attached to a beam with two handles. The hog plow was a similar instrument. The bar-share or bull plow was a wooden moldboard instrument with a flat landside, the work being done by a lance-shaped iron point drawn through the soil.

Stirring versus Turning. In the earlier years of farming in regions cleared of forest, the function of the plow was to stir up the soil sufficiently to provide a seedbed. For this task a harrow was sometimes used, although any simple plow that would loosen and stir the soil was adequate. Under such circumstances a plow that would turn over sod was unnecessary. At that time plowing was avoided as much as possible, particularly the turning of sward. The common cropping sequence of corn and small grain required that the land be plowed (stirred) only once every two years, since the grain was sown either in the standing corn or on the stubble the following spring.[3] Stirring to a depth of three inches was considered adequate for the preparation of a seedbed, and if that were not achieved with one plowing, the farmer might repeat with one or more cross-plow-

[1] *Iowa Farmer*, III (1855), 231. The Peacock and Diamond were cast-iron plows; the Cary was a cast-iron version of an old wooden plow. The other plows mentioned had steel moldboards.

[2] *American Farmer*, V (1823), 1.

[3] *Yankee Farmer*, IV (1838), 266.

ings. For such stirring operations the simple bar-share and shovel plows were practical if inefficient.

Prior to 1820, and to a substantial degree over the next several decades, plows were almost invariably made on the farm or by a local carpenter or wheelwright, with the assistance of the blacksmith:

A Winding tree was cut down, and a mould-board hewed from it, with the grain of the timber running so nearly along its shape as it could well be obtained. On this mould-board, to prevent its wearing out too rapidly, were nailed the blade of an old hoe, thin straps of iron, or worn-out horse shoes. The land side was of wood, its base and sides shod with thin plates of iron. The share was of iron, with a hardened steel point. The coulter was tolerably well made of iron, steel-edged, and locked into the share nearly as it does in the improved coulter plow of the present day. The beam was usually a straight stick. The handles like the mould-board, split from the crooked trunk of a tree, or as often cut from its branches; the crooked roots of the white ash were the most favorite timber for plow handles in the northern States. The beam was set at any pitch that fancy might dictate, with the handles fastened on almost at right angles with it, thus leaving the plowman little control over his implements, which did its work in a very slow and most imperfect manner.[4]

Every plow-maker and blacksmith made implements according to his individual fancy and the exigencies of his materials, but certain general types eventually achieved such widespread acceptance as to constitute patterns, which were more or less exactly imitated. Among these "improved" wooden plows of the period up to 1830, the nationally known Carey was more widely used than any other.[5] Though it varied considerably in details, since it was usually made by the local blacksmith, it was generally constructed of a heavy wrought-iron share, wooden landside and standard, and wooden moldboard plated over with sheet iron, the whole forming a wedge shape.

Other recognized types became more or less standardized. In New England the large and cumbersome Old Colony plow was widely used for breaking grassland. The smaller Sutton was popular in eastern New York. Of it, one contemporary observed:

They were well built and would have no fault if they only had the right construction, and were formed of the right materials. They are not

---

[4] A. B. Allen in New York State Agricultural Society, *Transactions* (1867), pp. 5, 402; *Genesee Farmer*, X (1849), 61.

[5] Charles W. Dickerman, *How to Make the Farm Pay* (Philadelphia, 1869), pp. 71-72.

fit to plough any land which has any kind of sod upon it; your furrows will stand up like the ribs of a lean horse in the month of March. A lazy ploughman may sit on the beam and count every bout of his day's work. Besides the great objection to all these ploughs, that they do not perform the work well, the expense of the blacksmith is enormous. Six of these ploughs cost on an average last year five dollars each to keep the shares and coulters fit for work, and the wear of the other parts could not be less than one dollar more,—six dollars per year for each plough. A man with a pair of oxen will, on an average through the ploughing season, perform with these ploughs, one acre each working day.[6]

In Vermont, a very heavy breaking plow was developed, the Daniel Webster, which was a precursor of the heavy prairie breaker.[7] These plows, as all the other so-called improved plows of wooden construction, were clumsy, heavy, and inefficient, requiring two to four times the draft of the cast-iron plow, with a strong man or even two to hold it and a boy to drive. They turned the sod poorly and could not penetrate the soil more than four or five inches. Their cost of operation was high; perhaps half as much as the full cost of the plow annually.

European plows were no better, with the possible exception of a few English plows, and the occasional importations and comparisons made no impression on American farmers.[8] The development of the turning plow in England had as a primary objective deeper penetration of the soil. In the United States, depth of plowing was not a matter of great interest; to the contrary, there existed a strong prejudice in favor of shallow work. At the same time, the American farmer typically held a strong preference for a multipurpose implement which would serve not only as turning plow but also as a cultivator.

THE CAST-IRON PLOW

The very significant developments that occurred in the plow during this half-century represented the contributions of numerous inventors, manufacturers, and farmers. Jefferson's much publicized

---

[6] *Agricultural Intelligencer,* I (1820), 114.

[7] Dennis Donovan and J. A. Woodward, *History of the Town of Lynderborough, New Hampshire, 1735-1905* (Tufts College Press, 1906), p. 60.

[8] J. B. Bordley, *Essays and Notes on Husbandry* (Philadelphia, 1801), pp. 471-472; *Plough Boy,* II (1820-1821), 3; New York State Agricultural Society, *Memoirs,* IV (1819), Pt. II, pp. 350-352; Philadelphia Society for Promoting Agriculture, *Memoirs,* IV (1815), 13, 163, 169.

application of mathematical techniques to the question of the proper shape of the moldboard, though it did not provide a practical answer, suggested the way in which the problem might be approached and gave emphasis to a matter that was important in the mind of every progressive farmer.[9] An efficient standarized plow could not be attained as long as wood was the material used. Plows that were recognized as excellent instruments had come into existence from time to time, but since they could not be duplicated when worn out, and might even lose their distinguishing characteristics when re-ironed at the blacksmith, such superior plows were irreplaceable. Hence, the importance of inventive activity in the application of cast iron to the plow lay not only in the use of a more resistant material but also in its permitting plow designs to be duplicated and standardized.

There is reference to the use of cast iron in plowshares as early as 1794, and a suggestion that three-part cast-iron plows were on sale in New York City as early as 1800.[10] The first patent on a cast-iron plow was issued in 1797 to a Philadelphia businessman, Charles Newbold.[11] The Newbold plow, cast from a single piece of metal, was offered for sale by a New York plow manufacturer named Curtenius, but it apparently did not prove attractive to farmers.

Newbold was also involved in the promotion of a cast-iron mold-board plow, shaped to conform to Jefferson's suggestion, which was developed about 1800 by Robert and Joseph Smith, farmers in Bucks County, Pennsylvania. This plow seems to have enjoyed an immediate success. The Philadelphia firm that undertook quantity production of the Smith plow was credited with the sale of 1,200 in 1810. The instrument enjoyed considerable use for the next half-century in eastern Pennsylvania and New Jersey but did not achieve significant adoption outside that area.[12]

[9] Thomas Jefferson, "Description of a Mould-Board of the Least Resistance and of the Easiest and Most Certain Construction," in American Philosophical Society, *Transactions*, IV (1799), 312-322. Gideon Davis of Maryland received a patent in 1818 on a single-piece cast-iron plow designed according to Jefferson's suggestions. There is no evidence that it found significant use. New York State Agricultural Society, *Transactions* (1867), Pt. I, pp. 452-462.

[10] New York Society for the Promotion of Agriculture, Arts, and Manufactures, *Transactions* (1794), p. 313. See also New York State Agricultural Society, *Transactions* (1867), Pt. I, pp. 448-449, 479.

[11] For a description and account of the Newbold plow, see New York State Agricultural Society, *Transactions* (1867), Pt. I, pp. 446-448. References to it are frequent in the agricultural literature of the period.

[12] Stevenson Fletcher, *Pennsylvania Agricultural and Country Life, 1640-1840*

Subsequent developments of the iron plow were addressed to the two most important criticisms directed at the Newbold and Smith implements. Cast iron was so fragile that the implement, when made in one piece, was too expensive because of frequent breakage. Moreover, because the shape of the plow conformed to old standards, it was no better suited to the task of fully turning sod.

In 1807 David Peacock patented a cast-iron plow that was designed in three separate parts with the share of wrought iron, to overcome some of the objections to the fragility of cast iron. This plow found users in the neighborhood of New York City.[13] A second patent by Peacock covered improvements on this plow and added a lock colter, a device thereafter extensively used. Meanwhile, Jethro Wood secured patents on a three-part cast-iron plow in 1814 and 1819.[14]

Neither Peacock nor Wood engaged in plow production. Both were successful in exploiting their inventions by licensing use of the patents to manufacturers. In 1817 Gideon Freeborn established a plow manufacturing firm in New York City and included the Peacock plow among his offerings. The following year he began manufacturing the Wood plow under license and soon was engaged in what was for the time very large-scale production. In the first three years, 1817-1819, Freeborn sold 6,750 plows and experienced difficulty in meeting the demand. The plow came to be known as Freeborn's and long enjoyed popularity.[15] Other plow-makers also took

---

(Harrisburg, 1950), pp. 93-94; Ellen D. Smith, "The Smith Plow," in Bucks County Historical Society, *Collections*, III (1909), 11-17; *Farmer and Gardener*, V (1838), 28-29.

[13] A Cayuga County plow manufacturer offered cast-iron models for sale in 1814-1815. *Cultivator*, IV (1847), 378. So did E. Stevens of Hoboken in 1817 and J. Dutcher of New York in 1819. American Institute, *Transactions*, III (1848), 325, 334. "The plows made by Peacock were very extensively used throughout the country, and many of them were to be found in use on farms in this state and in New Jersey and Pennsylvania as late as the year 1850." New York State Agricultural Society, *Transactions* (1867), Pt. I, p. 449; (1846), p. 233; (1867), Pt. I, p. 475.

[14] *Plough Boy*, II (1820-1821), 12; *Cultivator*, IV (1847), 378; Frank Gilbert, *Jethro Wood, Inventor of the Modern Plow* (Chicago, 1882).

[15] *Massachusetts Agricultural Repository*, V (1819), 363; *Plough Boy*, II (1820-1821), 3; *United States Farmer*, I (1842), 134; New York State Agricultural Society, *Transactions* (1867), Pt. I, p. 469; J. Nicholson, *The Farmer's Assistant* (Lancaster, 1814), p. 187; *Cultivator*, IV (1847), 378-379; V (1848), 30. "Freeborn's patent plough is in every material point perhaps as perfect as a plough can be made; all the ground work of it is cast iron; the share weighs about six pounds; and may be of wrought or cast iron; the latter is better than steel, for all but stumpy and rocky land. One of these ploughs may be kept in repairs for about one dollar per year." *Agricultural Intelligencer*, I (1820), 114.

up the licenses of Wood and Peacock. By 1820 it may be roughly estimated that as many as 10,000 cast-iron plows had been manufactured in the United States.[16]

The advantages of the early cast-iron plows over the wooden instruments in use were not so great as immediately to drive out the older types. The money cost of the new cast-iron implement was far greater than that of the wooden one—perhaps twice as much if the wooden plow were purchased, and very much more if the wooden plow were homemade. While the wooden plow required constant and expensive repairs, the early cast-iron plow was also fragile, and though it was so constructed as to be repairable by the farmer, the availability of parts constituted a problem. The question of its operating cost remained to be determined by prolonged experience. In turning over a furrow, these cast-iron plows did better work than many wooden plows, but no better or perhaps not as well as the best. Their great advantage was that they worked with far less resistance and hence required fewer animals: one yoke of oxen could do work equal to two or three with the wooden plow.[17]

The economy in animal power provided by the cast-iron plow had strong appeal to the experimentally minded farmer, particularly if he possessed land beyond his capacity to plow with the old equipment or if he had become convinced of the desirability of the deeper plowing that the cast iron instrument had rendered feasible. There was also, however, considerable resistance to the new implement. Most farmers in the long settled areas of New England and the Middle Atlantic states had achieved some form of balanced operations. Their cropping expectations were based upon their established plowing capacity, and the adoption of a new instrument required a reconsideration of their entire program. Farmers who believed in the benefits of deep plowing were in a small minority; there existed a widespread belief that bringing the subsoil to the surface was very deleterious.

The period from 1820 to 1830 or 1835 nevertheless saw a fairly rapid spread of the manufacture of the cast-iron plow and the consequent adoption of the instrument by the better and more progres-

[16] New York State Agricultural Society, *Transactions* (1867), Pt. I, pp. 464, 470.
[17] *Genesee Farmer*, VIII (1838), 358, where it is further observed: "The reason is very plain, for it is quite certain that we now require not half the team which was found necessary only thirty years ago. It is true that the iron plows are heavy . . . Still they run easy in proportion as friction is reduced."

sive farmers throughout the East. By the end of that period the price of the implement had fallen to a point equaling or only slightly exceeding that of the wooden plow. Experience had proven its economy in operation and maintenance as compared with the older instrument. Moreover, numerous varieties, sizes, and types had become available, and although standardization was far from complete, a purchaser could reasonably anticipate that a plow of a given type from a given manufacturer would perform in a specific manner.[18] It cannot be said that farmers were slow to adopt the cast-iron plow; rather, satisfactory types were made available very slowly.[19] The development of the cast-iron plow in a period of slow and expensive communication and transportation was contingent upon the development of local industries to supply it. The period from 1830 to 1850 witnessed the gradual adoption of the implement by the larger group of more conservative farmers in the New England and Middle Atlantic states, though there were still users of the old wooden implement in the sixties.[20]

Cast-iron plows were in limited use in the area along the Hudson River between New York and Albany and in Saratoga county by 1825, and in Chester County, Pennsylvania, and the vicinity of

[18] For discussion, see *Quarterly Journal of Agriculture,* II (1835), 389; *New England Farmer,* VIII (1829), 281.

[19] S. W. Cole, editor of the *Yankee Farmer* and the *Farmer's Journal,* pointed out that when the cast-iron plow was first introduced, "it was thought that the material was not suitable for so hard usage as a plow received . . . and besides this prejudice, there were at first reasonable objections to the shape and construction of cast iron ploughs." *Farmer's Journal,* I (1841), 1. A more explicit analysis appeared in the *Boston Cultivator,* Mar. 20, 1841: "When the cast iron plows were first introduced it was feared by most of our farmers who are ever prudently cautious of innovations without substantial proofs that they are improvements, that the metal would prove too brittle for service in most of our rocky fields, and for a long time they were shy of giving them a trial. And to avoid as far as possible, this objection, the first manufacturers of the cast iron ploughs made them exceedingly short—and though they were found to run a vast deal better, or rather without half the draft which was formerly required, the extreme shortness of the body of these ploughs was found unfavorable to the complete subversion of the sod—which all good farmers when ploughing green sward are desirous to effect."

[20] Luther Tucker, editor of the *Country Gentleman,* maintained that the cast-iron plow had come into general use by 1830. *Country Gentleman,* XIII (1859), 10. The historical review of agricultural implements in the U. S. Census Office, *Agriculture of the United States in 1860* (Washington, 1864), p. xviii, observed that the cast-iron plow was in limited demand as late as 1836. Leo Rogin, *The Introduction of Farm Machinery in its Relation to the Productivity of Labor in the Agriculture of the United States during the Nineteenth Century* (University of California Press, 1931), pp. 25-26, accepted Tucker's observation as substantially correct, but from the point of view of probable production it could hardly have been.

Baltimore about the same time.[21] The cast-iron plow was coming into general use in eastern Massachusetts in the early 1820's, and by 1841 the editor of the *Farmer's Journal* claimed that the wooden plow was unknown and had not been sold for years in that area.[22] The iron plow came into use in Connecticut between 1825 and 1830, although a few had been known earlier. Production developed on a sufficiently significant scale so that by 1834 it could be said that they were "generally used among the best farmers," which probably also describes the situation in Rhode Island.[23] In Vermont, New Hampshire, and Maine there were apparently no local producers of the implement as late as 1830.[24] But five years later the cast-iron plows of a St. Johnsbury, Vermont, manufacturer were being sold by agents in these states.[25] In 1838 a Portland, Maine, dealer was offering Howard's, Keith's, Hitchcock's, and Prouty and Mears plows, commenting that, "The general use of cast iron ploughs wherever they have been introduced, shows conclusively their superiority over the common kind. It has been correctly observed by intelligent farmers that it requires much less power to draw Cast Iron ploughs than is necessary in the use of other kinds, and as they are repaired at small expense they do not in the course of several years cost more than half as much as the common kind which it is well known cost no small amount annually in repair."[26] The decade of the forties was in Maine the period of rapid adoption; by 1850 the wooden plow had largely been abandoned in that state, as well as throughout New England: "Practical farmers of Massachusetts and all of New England have decided these questions, and 49 in 50 will give their voice in favor of an iron plow in preference to the one with a wooden mold-board. They have already so decided, and you will not find one farmer in a hundred using a plow with a wooden mould-board."[27]

21 New York State Board of Agriculture, *Memoirs*, I (1821), 213; III (1823), 77; *American Farmer*, VII (1825), 174; Pennsylvania Board of Agriculture, *Report*, IV (1880), 211.

22 *Farmer's Journal*, I (1841), 1.

23 *American Agriculturist*, IX (1851), 242; *Genesee Farmer*, II (1832), 8; Richard Fessenden, *The Complete Farmer and Rural Economist* (Boston, 1839), p. 319.

24 At least, none are listed in Louis McLane, *Report on Manufactures*, House Doc. No. 308. 22nd Cong. 1st sess., 1833.

25 C. and T. Fairbanks "warranted" their Patent Cast Iron Plough "for one year with fair usage." *Yankee Farmer*, I (1835), 47, 71; III (1836), 55.

26 *Yankee Farmer*, IV (1838), 312.

27 Maine Board of Agriculture, *Report* (1856), p. 70; (1859), p. 154; *Rural American*, I (1856), 187.

By the early 1840's cast-iron plows in a variety of types and makes were considered standard among the better farmers of New York.[28] Nevertheless, the type of farmer who could report, "I have tried nearly all the plows in use between Albany and Rochester," was the marked exception.[29] The more common situation was described by the comment made in 1842 that "the great mass of farmers are ignorant of the improvements that are making in farm implements and require to have their attention called to the advance of the implements placed before them to understand such improvements."[30] As late as 1860 wooden plows were still on sale in some communities in the eastern part of New York State.[31]

Improved Designs. At the same time that the larger number of more conservative farmers were beginning to accept the cast-iron plow, the more progressive were turning their attention to the new plow types introduced by a small group of aggressive manufacturers. Beginning in the late thirties, plows specifically and carefully designed for definite tasks became available, each in a variety of sizes, with improvements in the quality of metals used. It was claimed that in the period 1840-1850, "more has been done in the United States for the improvement of plows and plowing than had been accomplished since the settlement of the country," and it was estimated about 1850 that "at least 200 different patterns of plows" were being manufactured[32] Such plows not only did better work but could be used with horses instead of oxen. In the hands of the progressive farmer they doubled the acreage that could be plowed, reduced the labor of smoothing the soil by harrowing, and lowered the costs of lost time for repairs.

Perhaps the first improved plow to achieve wide use was the Minor or Peekskill. Introduced in 1836, it was manufactured in

[28] In the county reports on usage of plows in the New York State Agricultural Society, *Transactions* (1842), pp. 139, 148, all references are to the cast-iron plow. A version of the Wood plow known as the "Livingston County" seems to have been most widely used. See also (1841), pp. 134, 142.

[29] New York State Agricultural Society, *Transactions* (1842), pp. 139.

[30] New York State Agricultural Society, *Transactions* (1842), p. 185; (1851), p. 684.

[31] A writer in 1860 noted that the old plow with wooden moldboard and wrought-iron nose was still in use and that, "Not ten years ago, one-handled plows were on sale in a neighborhood on the Hudson River, and it would not be strange if they are still in use in that staid and conservative community." *American Agriculturist,* XIX (1860), 107.

[32] *American Agriculturist,* X (1851), 153; John L. Blake, *The Family Textbook for the Country; or, The Farmer at Home* (New York, 1853), p. 331.

many forms and sizes and by numerous licensees. It was estimated that some one and a half million casts of these plows were produced in the period 1835-1867.[33] Prouty and Mears of Boston in 1841 introduced a plow with a redesigned moldboard intended to secure a more thorough covering of the sod.[34] This implement acquired an enviable reputation and was being sold at a rate of about 5,000 annually in 1850.[35]

Joel Nourse was the most prominent individual in the latter-day development of the cast-iron plow. In the late 1830's he began experimenting with plow design and finally developed the Eagle plows, which became famous and were widely used during the next several decades. Nourse also introduced a plow with a standard moldboard together with a smaller moldboard designed to cut the sod and turn it into the bottom of the furrow, which permitted plowing at a considerably greater depth than was possible with standard implements. Known as the subsoil or Michigan plow, the implement became a symbol of progressive farming in the 1850's. In the late 1850's, the Ruggles, Nourse and Mason firm was offering as many as 150 different forms and sizes of plows and was selling up to 30,000 plows annually; it was credited in the sixties with having sold more plows than any other manufacturer in the country. Manufacturing plows in its own plant, utilizing advanced techniques and management, the Nourse firm was particularly aggressive in advertising and distribution. The plows were publicized in almost every agricultural periodical and were sold by agricutural warehouses in every major city in addition to the warehouse operated by the firm in Boston.[36]

The adoption of such improved forms, though more rapid than the original acceptance of the cast-iron plow, nevertheless was far from immediate. It was claimed in 1855 that "nearly every improvement in the ploughs of the country has been seized upon with eager avidity . . . and very few farmers among us hesitates at making the expenditures necessary to test all such as they think adapted to our

[33] New York State Agricultural Society, *Transactions* (1867), Pt. I, pp. 483-484.

[34] *Boston Cultivator,* Mar. 20, 1841; *Farmer and Gardener,* V (1838), 28-29; Blake, *The Family Textbook,* pp. 331-332.

[35] New York State Agricultural Society, *Transactions* (1867), Pt. I, p. 481.

[36] On Nourse's activities as a plow manufacturer, see New York State Agricultural Society, *Transactions* (1867), Pt. I, p. 471; *Cultivator,* I (1844), 19; VII (1850), 98-100; *Working Farmer,* VII (1855), 229-230; *American Agriculturist,* IV (1845), 374-375.

soil and circumstances."[37] The editor of the *American Agriculturist,* however, commented a few years later that the art of plow-making continued to be far in advance of the art of plowing, adding, "the best plows, some of which have been brought out within the last ten years, are not generally introduced."[38] In 1867 it was observed that plows "which depart very slightly from the principles established by Wood" were still in wide use, although they were considered far inferior to the best available as early as 1848.[39]

West of the Alleghenies, local manufacturers were quick to make supplies of the cast-iron turning plow available, while settlers from the East brought some with them.[40] In southern Ohio, "few cast moldboard ploughs had found their way as far west as Cincinnati" when A. Peacock began business as a plow manufacturer in that city about 1823. The bull plough, a very light wooden instrument, was in general use. Peacock made a few cast-iron moldboard plows of a pattern called the Hackney and then developed plows of his own design. These patterns he sold to blacksmiths and small plow manufacturers, and in this way the Peacock plows were made available widely in the Ohio and northern Mississippi Valley markets. Plows of the Peacock type were being manufactured as early as 1835 in Sangamon County, Illinois.[41] Eastern makes such as the Howard or Prouty and Mears were unknown in northern Illinois as late as 1841, but the latter was introduced into Ohio about 1845.[42] After that date eastern plows rapidly became available throughout the West.

THE STEEL PLOW

The settler on the river bottoms of Ohio and on the open grasslands farther West encountered plowing problems unknown in the East. The sod was extremely heavy and tough, while in many areas

[37] Pennsylvania State Agricultural Society, *Report,* II (1855), 279.

[38] *American Agriculturist,* XIX (1860), 135.

[39] New York State Agricultural Society, *Transactions* (1867), p. 469. The Livingston County plow was such a plow. It seems to have been standard in much of New York State in the 1840's and 1850's. *Cultivator,* V (1848), 97.

[40] Illinois State Agricultural Society, *Transactions,* II (1856-1857), 316.

[41] *Western Farmer,* II (1841), 98, 168; Illinois State Agricultural Society, *Transactions* (1869-1870), p. 255.

[42] *Union Agriculturist,* I (1841), 49; *Western Farmer,* I (1841), 88. For an account of the introduction of the Prouty and Mears plow into the Piqua area of Ohio, see *Farmer's Cabinet,* IX (1844-1845), 243-244.

the ground was occupied with the heavy roots of shrubs and stunted trees. To break such lands, very large wooden breaking plows were developed, which remained in use throughout the period. These were custom-made and hence varied considerably, but typically they cut a wide furrow of 18 to 24 inches or more, and turned it over two and a half or three inches deep. Such plows required three to six yoke of oxen and could break about one and a half acres per day, two men operating the plow.[43] The operation was primitive—"The breaking of American prairies at the west with eight oxen, panting and blowing would even now look quite familiar to an old Roman, could he witness the operation"—but was nevertheless effective; vast areas were cleared by such equipment.[44] In some areas settlers broke their prairie with the larger available cast-iron plows, and that practice was probably common with established farmers who added each year some wild prairie acreage to their tilled lands.[45]

Of far greater importance than breaking to the Western farmer was the fact that his soils were generally of a type which, when moist, clung to the plow moldboard and, when dry, became too hard for plowing. "The plows we had . . . could be made to root through our light soils, but as for plowing them, the matter was out of the question."[46] The editor of the *Prairie Farmer* pointed out that the "cast iron plow will no more scour, or clear itself in most of our prairie soils than a chestnut rail drawn endwise."[47] The task of plowing was described as a "trial to the patience of the farmers of Illinois and Indiana," and some, at least, "averred that they would be compelled to give up farming in the West as they could not cultivate the soil" with the tools they had.[48]

M. L. Dunlap, one of the most progressive farmers of Illinois and editor of the *Illinois Farmer,* wrote:

When we commenced prairie farming in 1839 . . . the plows were made at the blacksmith shops throughout the country, the share was of German or American steel, a small part of the mold board of iron, forged for the purpose, the same as for the old 'bull plow,' the remainder of the board was made of strap iron, about one and three fourths inches wide,

---

[43] Isaac P. Roberts, *The Fertility of the Land* (New York, 1906), pp. 52-54; Nathan H. Parker, *Iowa As It Is in 1856* (Chicago, 1856), p. 76.

[44] U. S. Patent Office, *Report* (1850), p. 70.

[45] *Illinois Cultivator,* I (1840), p. 33.

[46] *Valley Farmer,* III (1851), p. 127.

[47] *Prairie Farmer,* IV (1844), p. 227.

[48] *Scientific Farmer,* X (1854), p. 317; *Rural New Yorker,* XIII (1861), p. 397.

the forward ends of these straps were riveted to the forward part of the mold board and bolted through the right hand handle. The spaces between the straps were a little less in width than the strips. Of course these plows never scoured, and unless the plowman was constant in his attentions to cleaning off the sticky oil with a sort of shovel, they did miserable work, and became very heavy for the team. In fact, anything like good plowing was out of the question; the soil was rooted up into small ridges; the stubble was not covered up; and the labor was of the most laborious and unpleasant kind . . . The cast iron plow, so admirably adapted to sandy and gravelly soils, had proved almost useless, the wooden mold board with iron share being its superior. Notwithstanding the great beauty of our vast stretches of rich prairie, that lay so invitingly open to the emigrant from the stony fields of the east, yet in the very nature of the soil lay an embargo that seemed almost insurmountable.[49]

Since the cast-iron plow presented no particular advantages, such primitive blacksmith-made plows as the bar share and the shovel continued in use into the fifties.[50] An Iowa observer commented in 1853, "No one can tell the varieties of plows used. They are of all patterns from the original type used by Adam to the most finished manufacture of the present day."[51]

Efforts to solve the problems presented by the prairie soils were made by a number of plow manufacturers as well as blacksmiths. They were directed first toward the development of a moldboard shaped so that the problem of scouring was reduced to a minimum. The result was the widespread use of plows with short, sharply-angled moldboards, essentially similar to the old Cary plows of the East.[52] Their moldboards were made both of cast iron and wood covered with strap iron.[53]

Such efforts may have alleviated the difficulties but did not solve them, and in the late thirties and early forties considerable experimentation was carried on with moldboard materials. Iron plate, such as boiler iron, brought to a high polish gave some satisfaction and found some usage. Steel sheet, principally old saws and saw plate,

49 *Illinois Farmer,* V (1860), pp. 131-132.

50 *Iowa Farmer,* IV (1856), p. 123; U. S. Patent Office, *Report* (1852), p. 289. The U. S. Census of 1860 states that the cast-iron plow was in general use at that time in the West. This was probably true for Ohio and Michigan, but elsewhere the wooden instrument did not disappear until full adoption of the steel plow. U. S. Census, 1860, *Agriculture,* I, xxix. Cf. *Western Agriculturist,* I (1851), 17.

51 *Iowa Farmer,* I (1853), 199.

52 New York State Agricultural Society, *Transactions* (1844), pp. 361-362.

53 The popular Jewett's Patent Cary plow was manufactured in Springfield, Ill., St. Louis, and elsewhere, and was extensively used in Illinois by 1840. *Union Agriculturist,* II (1842), 88; I (1841), 49.

was used by a few blacksmiths as early as 1833 for covering wooden moldboards, and a few experimenters persisted in these efforts. In Chicago, Asahel Pierce's experiments resulted in a successful steel self-scouring plow.[54] At the 1841 fair of the Illinois Union Agricultural Society, two plows of sheet steel made by John Lane of Lockport, Illinois, were awarded the first premium.[55] At the fair of the same organization the following year, a consensus was reached that steel was the material from which a successful scouring plow could be made. In 1843, steel plows were placed upon the market in quantity by the Chicago firm of Scovil and Gates, and the Elgin, Illinois, firm of Gifford and Renwick.[56] By 1845 the latter firm was supplying plows made of standardized parts, apparently the first western plow manufacturer to do so.[57]

Among the blacksmiths who experimented most persistently with steel moldboard plows, John Deere of Grand Detour in northern Illinois was particularly successful. His experiments, begun in 1837, progressed to the point that in 1842 he made about 100 plows of sheet steel over a wooden moldboard. In 1847, the Deere firm produced 700 plows, and ten years later its output had reached 10,000 plows annually.[58] There were a number of other manufacturers in Illinois before 1850, and steel plows were being made by local producers in Indiana, Ohio, and Wisconsin by the middle of the decade.[59] Iowa and Minnesota farmers relied largely on Illinois for their supplies.

[54] Alfred A. Andreas, *History of Chicago*, I (Chicago, 1884), 560.

[55] *Illinois Farmer*, V (1860), 131-132.

[56] M. L. Dunlap, editor of the *Illinois Farmer*, wrote, "In 1843, the form of the Steel Clipper may have been considered perfect, and nearly all efforts made since have been to give it durability and strength, the thickness of the wearing parts have been doubled, and cast steel used in place of German and Pittsburgh steel." *Illinois Farmer*, V (1860), 132.

[57] "The Elgin plow was one of the first made in northern Illinois that would scour in prairie muck, and other makers have taken patterns after those made by Mr. Renwick." *Prairie Farmer*, V (1845), 157.

[58] Deere's production was 1,700 plows in 1850; by 1856 he was turning out from 10,000 to 15,000 a year, and his Moline plow had become standard throughout the West. *Rural New Yorker*, XII (1861), 397; Robert Ardrey, *American Agricultural Implements* (Chicago, 1894), p. 176. See also Edward C. Kendall, "John Deere's Steel Plow," in *U. S. National Museum Bulletin*, No. 218 (Washington, 1959), pp. 15-25.

[59] One of the most important steel plow producers was Toby and Anderson of Peoria, Illinois. *Valley Farmer*, II (1850), 365. For others, see *Prairie Farmer*, XI (1851), 10; *Country Gentleman*, X (1857), 129; Rogin, *Introduction of Farm Machinery*, pp. 32-35. Steel plows were being produced on a small scale by at least five manufacturers in Ohio in 1848. Ohio Board of Agriculture, *Report* (1848), pp. 166-167; *Ohio Cultivator*, IV (1848), 40; XIII (1857), 340-341. The best-known Indiana

Farmers in Illinois were quick to adopt the steel plow.[60] Deere's Moline plow became almost standard in Iowa in the late fifties.[61] Similar plows were accepted nearly as quickly in Indiana and Ohio.[62] Not only did the implement offer the possibility of doing better work, but it required far less animal power and effort by the plowman.[63] Farmers were, however, far from satisfied with the steel plow available in the sixties. The implements were expensive, not only in their initial cost but also in use, since they were fragile, given to breakage, and had a much shorter life than the cast-iron plow.[64] Moreover, they did not always give satisfactory service. Complaints that the Moline and other instruments "would not plow" were common, arising from the use of inferior or badly tempered steel and the fact that the shape of the plow could not be controlled in the tempering process.[65]

These problems arose from the limitations of the metallurgical technology of the day. The material used was sheets of spring or blister steel, the best that could be provided by the steel industry at the time. The desired form was obtained by hand hammering on an anvil. Dickerman explains the problems involved as follows: "They could not be uniformly tempered. Many of them, therefore, would not scour perfectly and run clean. The process of hammering, rolling and bending would produce a strain upon the fibre of the steel. It would stay in shape only while it was cold. It would warp

implement manufacturer, Beard and Sinex of Richmond, was offering steel plows in 1851. *Indiana Farmer*, I (1851), 142. In Wisconsin, A. W. Parker of Janesville was producing steel plows before 1855. *Wisconsin and Iowa Farmer*, VII (1855), 118.

[60] *Prairie Farmer*, XI (1851), 130.

[61] Iowa State Agricultural Society, *Report* (1857), pp. 228-229, 236, 243, 257, 323, 331, 390, 400, 438; (1858), pp. 322, 329, 387; (1859), pp. 170, 184, 215-216, 242-243, 250.

[62] Indiana State Board of Agriculture, *Report*, IV (1854-1855), 112, 173. Steel plows seem to have first been introduced into Ohio in 1848. *Ohio Cultivator*, XIII (1857), 340-341. But they were little used until 1855. Ohio State Board of Agriculture, *Report* (1849), pp. 19, 95; (1850), pp. 316, 399; (1851), p. 418; (1856), p. 288; (1862), p. 149.

[63] Steel plows "turn over the soil with an ease to the cattle of about fifty per cent." *Scientific American*, X (1854), 317. See also Indiana State Board of Agriculture, *Report*, IV (1854-1855), 112.

[64] As late as 1867 steel castings cost as much as four times iron ones, though steel plows were not necessarily that much more expensive. *Country Gentleman*, XXIX (1867), 329; *Valley Farmer*, IV (1852), p. 266; Ohio State Board of Agriculture, *Report* (1855), pp. 528-529.

[65] See Iowa State Agricultural Society, *Transactions* (1858), pp. 387, 432. Poorly tempered steel was quickly scratched and lost its scouring ability, whereas proper tempering of the steel interfered with the shape of the plow.

while heating to get the requisite temper, and warp still more while cooling off again. Very few, therefore, could be brought to a sufficient temper for a good scouring plow, so that even if it could stand the heat to produce a proper temper, the warping would ruin the form, so that the sections of the plows could not be duplicated, which is a requisite in order to supply new shares in place of those broken or worn out."[66] For such reasons the cast-iron implement remained in exclusive use among some farmers and was used by others for special purposes.[67] Continued experimentation by manufacturers resulted in the use of cast rather than sheet steel. The eastern firm of Collins Manufacturing Company placed a cast steel plow on the market in 1860, which overcame many of the difficulties though it remained a fragile instrument.[68] Western manufacturers soon were offering this plow, which found a considerable following.[69] Other changes followed, but the solution to the problem of a fully satisfactory plow awaited developments in the technology of the iron and steel industries. The cheap steel and chilled iron plows that were to be the solution did not appear until after 1870.[70]

In the East, the steel plow attracted little attention. So progressive a farmer as John Johnston of western New York did not experiment with the steel plow until 1860, and though he pronounced it a "decided improvement," its superiority over the cast-iron implement in the East was not so great as to offset its disadvantages of higher cost and excessive fragility.[71]

OTHER TILLAGE IMPLEMENTS

In 1820 and for many years thereafter the stirring plow was the all-purpose implement employed by many farmers for virtually any soil tillage operation except the cultivation of corn and similar crops, which might be done altogether by hand hoeing. During this half-century the stirring plow slowly lost its all-purpose application as it

[66] Dickerman, *How to Make the Farm Pay*, p. 85.

[67] Frederick Gerhard, *Illinois As It Is* (Chicago, 1857), p. 317.

[68] Dickerman, *How to Make the Farm Pay*, p. 86. The Ames Plow Company of Worcester also placed cast steel plows on the market. Both firms sold these products largely in the West.

[69] In the ten-county Cedar Valley district of Iowa, "the new patent cast steel plow is considered the best plow ever introduced . . . it is all the go now and should be generally used." Iowa State Agricultural Society, *Transactions* (1863), p. 361.

[70] See Rogin, *Introduction of Farm Machinery*, p. 35.

[71] *Rural New Yorker*, XI (1860), p. 94.

was developed into a variety of specialized forms. The larger breaking or turning plows came to be distinguished from the smaller "stirring" plows both with and without moldboards. Out of this class developed a variety of cultivating implements.

In the preparation of a seedbed, ground that had been plowed with the simple stirring plow was frequently cross-plowed at least once. On land so prepared, farmers commonly broadcast their small grain, covering it with still another shallow plowing. This might be done with the same plow used in breaking, by a shovel plow, or by a cultivator.[72] Alternatively, a harrow might be used to secure the desired pulverization of the soil prior to seeding.[73] The seed would then be covered by the harrow or a light plow. If a moldboard plow had been used to break the soil, a harrow was normally employed further to pulverize the soil and to cover the seed.[74]

The Harrow. Crude harrows were in use to replace or supplement the plow for soil pulverization and seed covering long before 1820. The implements were of two basic types: the brush drag and the straight-tooth harrow. The simple brush implement was made from the crotch of an untrimmed tree, or of brush and small trees, such as cedars or birches, attached to a board. Such instruments were widely used in the East and continued to find advocates up to the Civil War.[75]

The straight-tooth harrow was throughout the period usually a homemade implement. The wooden teeth with which it was equipped about 1820 were replaced in the 1830's with more numerous and smaller iron teeth. Agricultural warehouses were offering steel teeth in the 1850's. In shape and size the implement was highly variable, though of two basic types. The square harrow was simply a square of timbers fixed with teeth on each of its four sides. The triangular harrow was frequently the crotch of a tree set with a few teeth on its two sides. The former covered more ground but because of its fragility could not be used where the soil remained cluttered with stumps and rocks. The design of the crotch or triangular harrow

[72] U. S. Patent Office, *Report* (1851), pp. 373, 381.

[73] Rogin, *Introduction of Farm Machinery,* pp. 59-60.

[74] John L. Blake, *Family Textbook for the Country* (New York, 1853), p. 201.

[75] *Valley Farmer,* XI (1859), 81; Massachusetts Board of Agriculture, *Report* (1854), p. 29.

permitted its operator to avoid such obstacles more easily, and it found wide use where such conditions existed.[76]

The major changes that occurred in the harrow came with the introduction between 1840 and 1845 of the hinged harrow. The triangular instrument made in two parts did better work on rough ground and could more easily be cleaned of trash. The Geddes patent, appearing about 1845, was the most widely manufactured and distributed harrow of this type.[77] An adaptation of the square harrow involved the hinging of two of them together to make an implement that could cover a greatly increased area. The double-hinged square harrow came into use in New York after 1840.[78] A harrow made of wrought iron with steel teeth made in three sections with a sweep of eight feet became available in the next decade.[79] Its cost was $20.00, which may explain the farmers' failure to substitute it on any large scale for their locally made implements. Probably no agricultural implement experienced less improvement than the harrow during this half-century. In Maine in 1856 it was reported: "The harrow is an instrument which every farmer manufactures for himself, to suit his own taste, but I do not think it has attained a perfection proportionate to its importance as an agricultural implement or to its great number of manufacturers. The old fashioned crotch, the double crotch, and the square harrow in some form, make up the principal patterns in this implement."[80] From western New York at the same time came the report: "The square hinged thirty-tooth harrow is perhaps more generally used than all others . . . The Geddes harrow has been introduced to a limited extent, but has been generally abandoned after a short trial. The triangular harrow, single and double, (one behind and within the other) has also had its day here. The Scotch harrow is now coming into use, and is very well liked on smooth land; but it is difficult to turn, clogs badly on rough land, and is not, on the whole, so well adapted to all kinds of work as the first named above."[81]

It was not that progressive farmers were satisfied with their im-

[76] Massachusetts Board of Agriculture, *Report* (1854), p. 29.

[77] See New York State Agricultural Society, *Transactions* (1841), pp. 134 ff; (1842), pp. 148 ff; Ohio State Board of Agriculture, *Report* (1848), pp. 169-171.

[78] New York State Agricultural Society, *Transactions* (1841), pp. 147, 159-160, 165, 174.

[79] *American Agriculturist*, XVIII (1869), 126.

[80] Maine Board of Agriculture, *Report*, I (1856), 72.

[81] *Genesee Farmer*, XIX (1858), 220.

plements.[82] J. J. Mapes argued in 1854 that harrow teeth should be curved and not straight.[83] The problem of clogging and consequent heavy drag was met in part by the introduction of a colter harrow about 1855, which attained a limited popularity after the Civil war.[84] Although a disk harrow had been introduced as early as 1847, and another form was on the market after the Civil War, these implements found little use.[85]

Corn Cultivation. Among the crops that required cultivation and weed control for success, corn was by far the most important on northern farms, with potatoes, roots, tobacco, and others having lesser significance. The areas planted to corn seem to have been limited only slightly by the ability to plow land and not at all by the problems of harvesting. Although planting was a time-consuming task, it was more subject to the hazards of weather than to the availability of labor. The problem of adequately caring for the growing crop was the major consideration limiting the acreage planted and hence production.

To control weeds and to maintain a mulch for corn, four hoeings were considered necessary, each involving about one and a half days of labor—a total of six days of labor per acre. Where mixed farming was practiced, the demands of the corn crop competed for labor with the harvesting of hay and wheat. The time allocated to such harvesting was a further factor limiting the corn acreage and, more broadly, the acreage per farm.

In the earlier part of the period, the hoe was employed exclusively in the cultivation of corn by most farmers. However, the harrow and the stirring plow came to be used for at least part of the cultivation tasks, which reduced the amount of hand hoeing necessary. The harrow was usually applied only to the first cultivation, though in some areas smaller types of harrows were also employed for subsequent work.

[82] The harrow "has not seemed to obtain the attention which it deserves. Indeed, while constructed in the manner in which most of them are now used, they will gain few golden opinions from intelligent men." Massachusetts Board of Agriculture, *Report* (1851), p. 526. See also *Genesee Farmer,* XIX (1858), 220.

[83] *Working Farmer,* VI (1854), 102.

[84] On Share's Patent Coulter Harrow, see Rogin, *Introduction of Farm Machinery,* p. 65.

[85] U. S. Commissioner of Agriculture, *Report* (1865), pp. 250-251; *Country Gentleman* (1866), p. 336; New York State Agricultural Society, *Transactions* (1867), Pt. I, p. 2.

The search for a device that would better substitute for the hoe turned to the plow. Throughout this period the most common form of horse-cultivation instrument was the simple shovel plow which, after the development of the turning plow, was employed principally for cultivation. This plow, in addition to destroying weeds, provided a deep stirring of the soil and also hilled the plants by turning the soil against them.

Some farmers, believing in the beneficial effects of deep cultivation and hilling, continued to use the shovel plow even after other implements became available. Others thought the use of the shovel plow for corn cultivation an undesirable expedient, which applied an old and familiar implement to a task for which it was not specifically designed. They severely criticized the use of the shovel plow as a cultivator on the ground that it worked too deeply, cutting the plant roots and reducing the crop.

The horse hoe, based upon Jethro Tull's designs, had been introduced from England to cultivate wheat by 1820, though it found little use for that purpose.[86] To meet the need for cultivating corn in widely separated rows, a one-horse cultivator equipped with five shovels, resembling the modern duck-feet, was in use as early as 1820.[87] In subsequent years a variety of similar implements appeared, as well as substitutes for the harrow in pulverizing soil and in covering seed. These were initially one-horse devices with the operator walking behind.[88] In the fifties, wheeled devices including two-horse, two-row sulky cultivators became available.[89] The substitution of steel for iron teeth was an important advance at this time.

The variety in implements, the varying circumstances under which corn was produced, and the differences in ideas about the needs of the plant resulted in a number of different techniques in its cultivation. It seems likely that in no crop did there exist greater differences in methods employed or greater uncertainties as to their effectiveness. The result was a wide range in costs of production.

[86] The horse hoe was nevertheless reported in Michigan in 1848. U. S. Patent Office, *Report* (1848), p. 545; (1849), p. 180.

[87] *American Farmer*, VIII (1826), 55; *Agricultural Intelligencer*, I (1820), 113.

[88] *Working Farmer*, IX (1858), 73; *Iowa Farmer*, V (1857), 7; Maynard's—*American Farmer*, XI (1853-1854); Wetherwell's—*Ohio Farmer*, VII (1859), 154; Share's—*American Agriculturist*, XIX (1860), 162; *Homestead*, I (1856), 711; *Cultivator*, V (1848), 65.

[89] The earliest riding cultivator apparently was introduced in 1843. Rogin, *Introduction of Farm Machinery*, p. 66.

Some of the cultivation differences were regional, depending upon the importance of corn in the cropping pattern, but the full range of techniques seem to have been employed within most neigborhoods, both East and West.[90] The major differences involved hill versus row planting and the cultivation techniques employed.

In New England's agriculture, crops requiring cultivation of the soil during growth occupied relatively small acreages per farm. Few farmers undertook to cultivate more than four or five acres of corn, the small grains and grasses being the principal crops, with hogs raised largely on the waste products of the dairy and orchard. Corn occupied somewhat larger acreages in the southern parts of the Middle Atlantic states. But it was west of the Alleghenies that corn vied with wheat for first rank in acreage planted. There, after farmers had built up their herds of cattle and hogs, the acreage in corn determined the income from the enterprise.

In the East generally the hoe remained the essential tool in corn cultivation at least until 1860. Frequently it was the only tool used, although farmers planting large acreages were employing horse cultivators to ease the work of hoeing.[91] It was claimed in 1845 that the horse cultivator reduced the labor requirement in corn cultivation to one-third of a day's labor per acre. Throughout the fifties the editors of eastern agricultural journals considered it news-worthy that corn was raised in the West without the use of the hand hoe, and urged their readers to discard that instrument in favor of harrows and cultivators.[92] In corn production there is no question that New England's difficulties in competing with the West were intensified by the fact that the small fields characteristic of its farms were worked by hand and that her farmers were unwilling or unable to adapt their operation to the newer implements.

In those eastern areas where corn occupied substantial acreages, as in eastern Pennsylvania, Delaware, and parts of New York,

[90] New York *Tribune*, June 18, 1845; U. S. Patent Office, *Report* (1845), p. 446; *Indiana Farmer*, I (1852), 228, 291-292; U. S. Patent Office, *Report* (1850), pp. 208, 309, 409.

[91] The *Yankee Farmer*, II (1836), 111, noted the cultivator was then "coming into general use in all parts of the country." Yet in 1850 it was observed that "many farmers within fifty miles of New York are without a cultivator" and "it is far from being in general use." *Valley Farmer*, II (1850), 124-125. Cf. U. S. Patent Office, *Report*, (1845), pp. 307, 436; (1856), p. 269; (1852), pp. 238, 244; New York State Agricultural Society, *Transactions* (1859), p. 330.

[92] See *Rural New Yorker*, I (1850), 216; *New Hampshire Journal of Agriculture*, Sept. 8, 1859; *Indiana Farmer*, V (1856), 245; *Genesee Farmer*, XVII (1856), 175.

farmers seem early to have resorted to horse-drawn implements to reduce the hand-hoeing task at least in part and sometimes altogether. Familiar implements were used at first and continued to be employed after specialized machines had been introduced. There and in the West, as in Ohio, by the late thirties the common method of cultivating corn was by the harrow and the shovel plow. A two-horse triangular harrow, the front tooth removed to straddle the row, was used for the first cultivation when the corn was a few inches high. Further cultivation was sometimes accomplished by a one-horse harrow drawn between the rows, but much more frequently by the shovel plow, or perhaps a small moldboard plow.[93] Such instruments required two trips to cultivate each row, but also served to hill up the corn, which was considered important by the majority of farmers. The cultivator, however, found some adherents as early as the middle forties.[94]

On the prairies, fields that were well broken of their virgin sod tended to remain relatively weed-free for some years, and corn did well if the soil was merely stirred. No supplementary hoeing was needed. In the early fifties in the West, particularly in Indiana, Illinois, and Iowa, a common practice in corn culture was to harrow once and then plow three or four times, no use being made of the hoe. In the late fifties in Iowa, cultivators and the stirring plows, usually single or double shovels, were the standard implements, although on some farms it was still "plow, harrow and hoe."[95] In the late sixties in eastern Iowa, as elsewhere in the corn-growing West, cultivators were displacing stirring plows, while the most aggressive farmers were adopting two-horse, two-row sulky cultivators.[96] These, though crude and relatively expensive, were important labor-savers. Corn cultivation remained characterized by wide differences in the techniques used and consequently in costs of production.

93 U. S. Patent Office, *Report* (1845), p. 307; (1852), pp. 217, 254, 259, 289; *Farmer's Journal*, II (1843), 140-141.

94 The cultivator was in use in Ohio by 1834. See *Cultivator*, I (1834), 73. On early adoptions elsewhere, see U. S. Patent Office, *Report* (1850), pp. 143, 409; (1851), pp. 244 ff; (1852), pp. 217, 229.

95 See Iowa Agricultural Society, *Transactions* (1858), p. 229; (1865), p. 530.

96 In Page County in 1866: "A two-horse Shanghai cultivator which is highly prized by our farmers and with which most of the cultivation of corn and other plowed crops is attended in this region." Clinton County reported one hundred two-horse corn cultivators in use. Iowa State Agricultural Society, *Transactions* (1863), pp. 444, 453; (1865), pp. 420, 509, 516; (1866), pp. 301, 409.

SEEDING MACHINES

Prior to 1840 small grains were universally sown broadcast by hand, and the seed was then covered with soil by drawing a harrow over the ground or, as was thought better by some, by cross-plowing with small plows.[97] Though wheat was sometimes sown on freshly plowed ground, it was a very common practice to sow it on land already in corn, usually before the corn crop had been harvested. Almost all wheat sown was winter wheat.

In the 1840's wheat producers in the older areas of the East faced serious problems of low and declining yields per acre, uncertain crops, and the competition of western wheat exerting heavy pressure upon prices. Generally two and a half bushels of seed were applied to an acre, from which as little as ten, and an average of something like fifteen, bushels were harvested. There was general agreement that production was well below what had been obtained earlier. Exhaustion of the soil from continuous cropping and inadequate fertilization was partially blamed, but even where soil was of a superior fertility the wheat grower frequently found his returns disappointing. Winter-killing was an important source of loss, while insects and diseases were added hazards.

In 1843, a farmer of New Castle County, Delaware, an area "where farming is carried to a greater perfection than perhaps anywhere else in the United States,"[98] wrote: "At the present moment, when the price of agricultural produce of every description is so reduced, it becomes of great importance to the farmer to look around and see whether he cannot increase the produce of his soil without increasing his expenses. This is particularly needful in raising wheat. From some causes, perhaps not well understood, the wheat crop has become, in the Eastern and Atlantic states, exceedingly precarious." He noted that the current method of planting or sowing wheat was not likely to ensure the largest yield and then recounted his own experiments with broadcast sowing versus drill seeding of wheat, having been furnished with a drill by "our enterprising neighbor, John Jones of Bohemia Manor, who owned the only wheat drill in the state of Delaware."[99] The experiment was sufficiently in favor

[97] *Genesee Farmer,* IX (1839), 41.
[98] *Working Farmer,* IV (1852), 244.
[99] U. S. Patent Office, *Report* (1843), pp. 180-182.

of wheat sown with the drill to lead him to purchase a machine for his own use.

The drill he used had been manufactured by Moses and Samuel Pennock of Chester County, Pennsylvania.[100] The Pennocks' drill, which was based upon English models,[101] was patented in 1841 and was apparently the first to be manufactured in the United States. It proved successful in use in the area about Kennett Square, including Lancaster and Chester Counties, Pennsylvania, New Castle County, Delaware, and nearby sections of Maryland.[102] For some years Samuel Pennock performed custom seeding with the machine, which aided in proving its worth to the farmers of the area.[103] Its early adoption by John Jones was also undoubtedly a factor in encouraging widespread use, since he was one of the larger wheat growers of the area, with 160 acres in wheat in 1847. He wrote a few years later:

When I commenced drilling, and for two or three years, I was ridiculed by my neighbors; some would advise me to take the implement home, break it up and cook my dinner on it.

I, however, disregarded their jeers and persevered. And now the best evidence that I can possibly bring forward in support of the drill over the broadcasting system, is the fact that all my neighbors have adopted the drill for sowing their wheat and most other small grain; and that we have three or four drill builders besides M. W. Pennock . . . all of whom could not supply the demand for drills for Newcastle County the last season. I think I am warranted in saying that three-fourths of all the wheat that will be grown in New Castle County the next year, will be sown with the drill.[104]

[100] For a description of the Pennock and other drills and a history of the technical development of the machine, see Russell H. Anderson, "Grain Drills through Thirty-Nine Centuries," *Agricultural History*, X (1936), 157-205.

[101] The English experiments with drills were known, having been discussed in the *Memoirs* of the Philadelphia Society for Promoting Agriculture and the *Transactions* of the Society of Arts in New York. Henry Colman reviewed the use of drills in seeding wheat in his *Agriculture of Massachusetts, Third Report* (1840), Appendix, pp. 173-175. See also John Lorain, *Nature and Reason Harmonized in the Practice of Husbandry* (Philadelphia, 1819), pp. 362-363. Drills were available upon order from agricultural warehouses as early as 1821. References to the importation of English drills appear in *American Farmer*, I (1846), 245-246; III (1848), 217.

[102] *Plough, Loom and Anvil*, I (1848), 96; II (1849), 355-361. By the early fifties, the drill was in "almost universal use" in this area. *Pennsylvania Farm Journal*, IV (1854), 382.

[103] Pennock's usual charge for the service was $4 per day or 50¢ per acre. Cuthbert W. Johnson, *Farmer's Encyclopedia and Dictionary of Rural Affairs* (Philadelphia, 1839), p. 423.

[104] U. S. Patent Office, *Report* (1848), p. 467. See also *American Farmer*, VIII (1852), 5-8.

Wheat growers in western New York were faced with essentially similar problems. The Pennock drill was introduced into western New York in 1848, and the following year was being manufactured in Rochester.[105] The availability of the implement, aided by the substantial publicity accorded it in the agricultural press, seems to have induced a number of farmers to purchase and experiment with it.[106] Their receptivity was sufficient to set off a small-scale manufacturing boom, so that by 1851 the product of at least eight manufacturers as well as Pennocks' were available in the area. Thereafter the drill spread rapidly throughout the wheat growing area and in scattered portions of northern and western New Yorker.[107]

Well before 1850, wheat had been abandoned as a basic crop in New England; such as was produced was generally in plots of a few acres in the rotation of corn, wheat, and grass. As a consequence, the drill received no attention there, with the exception of Maine. The editor of the *Maine Farmer* was urging its value by 1850, and a few were reported in use before 1853. One was exhibited in the rotunda of the State House in Portland in 1852, so that farmers might see it.[108]

The drill was introduced into Ohio about 1844, but manufacturers seem to have been slower to undertake production there, and not until about 1850 did a supply of any consequence become available.[109] In southern Michigan the scattered open prairies offered the necessary conditions for use of the drill, while the lake and rail transportation facilities enabled New York manufacturers to reach that market. Before 1850 every county in Michigan traversed by the Michigan Central Railroad had reported the successful use of the drill.[110] A few farmers were experimenting with the implement before 1850 in Illinois and Iowa, and before 1855 in Wisconsin, Missouri, and Kentucky.[111]

[105] *Genesee Farmer,* VIII (1848), 93; XI (1850), 39-40.

[106] The drill was in use before 1850 in Tomkins, Yates, Wayne, and particularly Monroe County, where four or five makes were reported. *Rural New Yorker,* I (1850), 87, 202.

[107] *Western Farmer,* IV (1852), 176; New York State Agricultural Society, *Transactions* (1853), p. 527.

[108] *Maine Farmer,* July 25, 1850; March 18, 1852; Sept. 1, 1853.

[109] *Cultivator,* I (1844), 44; *Journal of Agriculture,* II (1847), 486; Ohio Board of Agriculture, *Report* (1846), pp. 4, 27.

[110] *Michigan Farmer,* VIII (1850), 229, 244 ff; IX (1851), 106; XI (1853), 154.

[111] *Prairie Farmer,* X (1850), 279; XI (1851), 39; *Genesee Farmer,* XII (1851), 173.

The reaction of the enterprising farmers who risked the substantial sum of $75 or $100 in the purchase of a drill was almost universally favorable.[112] It was claimed that the drill saved up to half the seed grain, which in itself repaid the cost of the machine in a single season if the acreage planted to wheat amounted to sixty or more acres. The savings in seed were held to justify the cost of the machine even for plantings as small as ten or fifteen acres because of its long life.[113] Also important was the general belief that use of the drill reduced winter-killing of the plant, so that the increased crop might return the investment from a relatively small acreage.[114] There was some disagreement as to its significance as a labor-saving implement. Where wheat was sown on unplowed corn or fallow land and harrowed in, the seed drill required more labor in preparing the soil. But the type of farmer who accepted the drill was also one who argued that careful soil preparation was essential for a wheat crop, and for such individuals the drill facilitated the sowing task.[115] In the first decade or so of its use, this aspect of the matter received little attention. It was commonly observed, however, that the drill was not a machine for slovenly farmers— that fields had to be well prepared for its successful use.[116]

The experimental period of the drill had ended by 1855, within ten years of its introduction. Reports of dissatisfaction were negligible. After 1855 it may be assumed that manufacturers and dealers in agricultural warehouses everywhere east of the Mississippi were able to meet the demands for the machine.[117] The agricultural press had published countless reports on experiments and during the fifties took up the cause of machine drilling with considerable enthusiasm, as did some of the state agricultural organizations.[118] This did not mean, however, that the machine came into universal use. In 1852 it was asserted: "Not one farmer in ten ever heard of such a labor-saving crop-increasing machine, not one in fifty ever saw

[112] *Ohio Cultivator,* XV (1859), 19.
[113] On objections to the machine, see, *Genesee Farmer,* XVIII (1857), 279; *Rural Register,* II (1860), 229.
[114] On the claimed saving of seed, see *American Agriculturist,* XVI (1857), 198; *Indiana Farmer,* V (1858), 249; *Western Farm Journal,* I (1856-1857), 122.
[115] *Ohio Farmer,* VIII (1852), 234; *Germantown Telegraph,* Aug. 13, 1851.
[116] *Illinois Farmer,* I (1856), 245; *Valley Farmer,* XII (1860), 267; *Michigan Farmer,* X (1852), 201.
[117] *Genesee Farmer,* XI (1850), 112; *Valley Farmer,* II (1850), 112.
[118] *American Agriculturist,* IX (1850), 314.

one, not one in a hundred believes in the advantage of using them, and not one in a thousand will buy one within the next ten years."[119]

As far as the country as a whole was concerned, the comment was no doubt correct, but it was unduly pessimistic in areas where wheat was the important money crop. In the area of its initial introduction the drill seems to have attained a high degree of popularity by 1855 and to have been in use by virtually all significant growers of wheat before 1860.[120] From there it spread into other wheat-growing sections of Pennsylvania and New Jersey, but was far from universal in 1870.[121] The observation made at a "Legislative Agricultural" meeting in Boston in 1856 that "very few farmers in New York now broadcast" was something of an exaggeration, unless the reference was to the most progressive farmers.[122] New York farmers still expressed misgivings about the utility and economy of the machine.[123] Available data on production of the drill in New York, allowing for exports, suggest clearly that only a small percentage of the state's farmers could have had one in their possession. But the drill had achieved acceptance as an essential element of the best farming techniques and during the 1860's seems clearly to have become recognized as indispensable in the production of wheat when undertaken on a significant scale. In western New York the drill experienced a high rate of adoption, particularly after 1855, though it seems doubtful that more than 10,000 drills could have been manufactured in the state prior to 1865, and many of these were probably sold in the West.

It was in Ohio that the drill achieved broadest acceptance in the period prior to 1870. The machine was reported "in widespread and general use" by 1850,[124] and it was known in almost every county

---

[119] *American Agriculturist*, X (1852), 191.

[120] *Pennsylvania Farm Journal*, II (1852), 156. The editor of the *Ohio Cultivator*, X (1854), 308, on a trip through Lancaster and Chester Counties, noted that the young wheat showed the "almost universal use of the drill."

[121] Pennsylvania State Agricultural Society, *Report*, I (1852), 200; *Pennsylvania Farm Journal*, I (1851-1852), 297.

[122] *New England Farmer*, VIII (1856), 181.

[123] Henry Murray, in traveling through the Genesee area, noted that the wheat was sometimes sown broadcast, sometimes drilled. Murray, *Lands of the Slave and the Free*, I (New York, 1849), p. 43; New York State Agricultural Society, *Transactions* (1859), p. 326.

[124] Ohio State Board of Agriculture, *Report* (1859), p. 534; *Ohio Cultivator*, XVI (1860), 296.

in the state before 1855.[125] Thereafter drill manufacturing became an important industry in many of the state's smaller cities. Dayton, for example, had four establishments which in 1857 made 2,900 drills. [126]

Fortunately, we have at least one check on the meaning of the phrases "widespread," "general," and "universal" which appear so frequently in the literature of the time. These adjectives were applied to the use of the drill in Colombiana County, Ohio, where a tax assessor in the spring of 1859 took the trouble to note the condition and mode of seeding each wheat field in his township. Of the 228 fields observed, 104 had been drilled, 124 sowed broadcast.[127] We may safely assume that "general" and "universal" are usually to be understood as applying only "to the more intelligent farmers in our community" or to the more enterprising class. [128]

The early experiments with the drill in southern Michigan were highly successful, followed by significant adoption in the more settled areas, the reports being that the drill was "commonly" or "extensively" used.[129] It seems probable that by 1860 the drill was as widely used in this area as in Ohio or western New York. In Indiana and Illinois, the early users of the drill likewise became its advocates, although their advocacy was not followed by the widespread acceptance experienced elsewhere.[130]

The situation was similar in Iowa and Missouri. Experimentation had begun about 1850 in Iowa, but adoption was slow.[131] In part this was due to the unavailability of the machine in local communities; as late as 1856 the editor of the *Iowa Farmer* replied to an inquiry that he did not know where a drill might be purchased.[132] The relative scarcity of capital and the slovenly cultivation tech-

[125] There are numerous references to the drill in Ohio State Board of Agriculture, *Report* (1850-1854).

[126] *Ohio Cultivator,* VII (1851), 115.

[127] *Ohio Cultivator,* XV (1859), 167.

[128] "In traveling from New York to St. Louis, about the first of October (1864) when the newly sown wheat was nicely up, almost every field of it, on well improved farms was observed to be in drills." Missouri State Board of Agriculture, *Report,* I (1865), 101.

[129] Michigan State Agricultural Society, *Transactions* (1851), pp. 190-191; *Michigan Farmer,* XI (1853), 258.

[130] Michigan State Board of Agriculture, *Report* (1864), pp. 14 ff.

[131] *Iowa Farmer,* I (1853), 148; II (1863), 4.

[132] *Iowa Farmer,* IV (1856), 88. But a factory for making drills was established in Mt. Pleasant in 1857.

niques employed were doubtless more important factors. Certainly by 1860, with the growth of the agricultural implement industry in Illinois and the Mississippi River towns and the spread of agricultural warehouses, the drill could be purchased as easily as the reaper or steel plows. By 1865 conditions had changed sufficiently to encourage the use of the machine in the eastern part of the state along the Mississippi River. Further west it was still in use largely on an experimental basis and was viewed with considerable skepticism.[133]

Manufacture of the drill was an important item in St. Louis by 1857.[134] That the machine might be expected to fill a need may be indicated by the following comment on wheat production in Missouri: "Winter-killing is the great source of uncertainty in wheat raising here—more owing to broad-cast sowing than any other human cause. Those who drill their wheat lose least of all from climate, those who plow it in are the next most successful; and those who harrow it unluckiest of all. Drill seeding might be altogether practiced on prairie land and it is most needed there. It would not surprise me if drilling and plowing became the universal mode in a few years as the farmers are fast learning their superiority for such climate as this, where we have some very cold weather in the winter with very little snow."[135]

However, over the next decade drilling hardly became the universal mode. Although a few drills had been used since 1854, in 1865 many county respondents reported to the Missouri State Board of Agriculture that the machine had not yet been tried in their localties, and even where it was in use, the numbers employed were small.[136]

The suggestions from a number of agricultural correspondents that groups purchase and use drills cooperatively may be taken as evidence that the capital required presented a more serious obstacle in the West than in the East.[137] The $75 or $100 involved were likely to go first into the purchase of a reaper or mower, more cattle

---

[133] As in Clinton and Davis Counties. Iowa State Agricultural Society, *Transactions* (1868), pp. 320-323, 357, 361. In the reports from the counties in the same volume, pp. 320-323, a number of respondents merely stated that the drill had its proponents and one commented that "drilling has some advocates, especially by those interested in the sale of drills."

[134] *Valley Farmer,* X (1858), 60.

[135] Letter from Lewis County, Missouri, in *Rural New Yorker,* X (1859), 366.

[136] *Valley Farmer,* VI (1834), 293-295; IX (1857), 174, 175, 185.

[137] *Michigan Farmer,* XIII (1855), 264; *Indiana Farmer,* III (1853), 361; *Iowa Farmer,* V (1857), 49-50; Iowa State Agricultural Society, *Report* (1858), p. 371.

or hogs, or perhaps even more land—all of which were more important to a prairie farmer than the production of more wheat per acre.

The editor of the *Illinois Farmer* claimed in 1857 that "drills have fairly fought their way into public favor," which meant that farmers generally conceded the machine's advantages, not that their use was universal or even might become so.[138] Though some held that the drill was more appropriate to the broad, level, stone-free fields of the prairies than to the East, a careful, objective analysis of the situation in the *Cultivator* was doubtless more accurate: "It certainly cannot be questioned at this day, but that drilling in wheat possesses many valuable claims over the broadcast system of sowing grains . . . This, however, like most other branches of improvement, requires great care in its management. It ought not to be attempted by a slovenly farmer— and unless the ground be previously fitted for the process, it would be unwise to attempt to use the machine . . . The use of the drill is strongly recommended, but no slovenly farmer need expect to derive any advantage from it."[139]

Unlike other agricultural implements, such as the plow or the harvester, the grain drill underwent no substantial technical changes during the thirty or forty years after its introduction. Although several less elaborate and hence less expensive forms were offered by manufacturers, Pennock's and Seymour's machines were considered standard throughout the period. Adoption of the implement, thus depended solely upon the advantages it offered as compared with the costs of the superior soil tillage required and the cost of the machine itself. In areas where farming had become stabilized, where individual farmers had brought their farms to a high standard of cultivation, where costs and profits were calculated within a fairly narrow margin, and where capital was available, the drill was forced upon the attention of farmers. Failure to adopt it in such areas represented a rigid adherence to techniques which the drill had rendered obsolete.

Where farming had been undertaken more recently, however, other considerations operated. At least a generation was required to bring farming on the prairie to what may be termed a stabilized level, with all land in use, soil and climate factors at least reasonably

138 *Illinois Farmer*, II (1857), 145; Gerhard, *Illinois As It Is*, p. 326.
139 *Cultivator*, IX (1852), 38-39.

well understood, and profit calculations reduced to a fairly narrow margin. In Iowa and Illinois, wheat was generally considered a much less profitable crop than corn and hogs, or grass-corn and cattle. There the objective of many farmers was to accumulate sufficient capital so that they could acquire adequate herds of these animals and reduce their dependence on the wheat crop. Under such circumstances, capital was not readily invested in an implement that would merely make wheat production somewhat more certain and possibly more profitable. Since the farmer had strong inducement to reduce his acreage in wheat as quickly as possible, the adoption of the drill would be postponed until such time as adequate investments had been made in other items and until the gains that might be made from the purchase of a drill would appear as attractive as an equal investment elsewhere.

Corn Planting. Until well after 1820, about ten acres of corn per man constituted a season's task, though in cases where hay and wheat were important, four or five acres were more usual. The hill culture adopted from the eastern Indians remained everywhere the basic method. A hole was scooped out of the plowed soil, fertilizer, if any, dropped into it, a little dirt added, then six to eight corn kernels dropped in and covered. This was hoe work—from one half to one acre constituting a day's work, depending upon the condition of the soil. In most parts of the northern United States the period of time within which corn should be planted did not exceed three weeks, while the maximum period was four to five weeks. Since hand planting of corn required approximately a day's labor per acre, the planting of twenty acres per laborer was possible but not common prior to 1830 or 1840. It was the hoe-work—thinning the seedlings, weeding, stirring the soil, and hilling the plants—that set limits on the acreage cultivated.

In the East some slight reduction in the amount of time spent with the hoe followed the introduction of horse-drawn implements. However, it was west of the Alleghenies that the availability of large acreages of fertile soil invited efforts to increase the corn acreage per man and where horse-drawn tillage implements quickly replaced the hoe. The use of these implements stimulated a variety of modifications in the traditional practices of hill planting, the earliest changes relating to methods used to locate the hills so that cross cultivation was possible.[140] Probably the most common method used before 1830 involved a shovel plow drawn across the previously plowed field at intervals of three to four feet. The process was repeated at right angles, and the corn was dropped at each furrow intersection and covered, usually with a hoe.[141] Some planters saved time by omitting the right-angle furrowing, dropping the corn at intervals, and laying out the field in the desired orderly hills by visual inspection. Eventually the common method involved the use of a simple homemade horse-drawn marker that laid out three or four shallow furrows simultaneously and, with cross-dragging, gave the desired pattern.[142]

Occasionally the covering of the corn was done, not by the hoe, but by a small plow. In the West it was common practice to plant on sod land at the same time that the plowing was done, which required the assistance of a "small boy" who dropped the kernels into every second or third furrow, where they were then covered by the succeeding furrow.[143]

The persistence of the hill-culture technique of corn cultivation was evidenced in the ridge culture that remained important in New England well into the forties. Under this system, the plow was used to throw two furrows against one another, the corn being planted on the ridge, about three feet apart.[144] Although this technique was being discarded in New England about 1850, it was still in use under certain conditions, such as a wet soil.[145] A similar method was occasionally used in the West where it was known as listing.[146]

The task of planting corn by hand and hoe was not only time-consuming but also arduous. To ease the labor involved, a variety of hand planters had been offered the farmer from time to time. When inserted into prepared soil, these dropped a few kernels, which were then automatically covered. Although they achieved some acceptance when introduced in the early part of the 1850's, none found any significant degree of adoption, with the possible exception of

[140] In the East, particularly New England, corn leaves were frequently used as cattle feed; occasionally the young green corn plant was fed entire. See U. S. Patent Office, *Report* (1843), p. 75; (1845), p. 207.

[141] Numerous reports on this type of planting are found in U. S. Patent Office, *Report* (1852-1854).

[142] Iowa State Agricultural Society, *Transactions* (1868), p. 322.

[143] U. S. Patent Office, *Report* (1852), p. 313.

[144] U. S. Patent Office, *Report* (1854), p. 125.

[145] Solon Robinson, *Facts for Farmers* (New York, 1865), I, 273.

[146] On the listing technique, see U. S. Patent Office, *Report* (1852), p. 292.

Randall and Jones' Double Hand Planter which planted two hills simultaneously.[147] In the general view, these implements made too small a hill and were not saving of labor.[148]

The appearance and success of the wheat drill suggested the possibility that this method of seeding might be applied to corn also. Seeding corn in straight rows with the plants nine to twelve inches apart was not altogether unknown in the early fifties. Before 1850, Pennock had both modified and added attachments to his wheat drill so as to enable it to sow corn at the desired distance. Similar machines were available from other makers. Such machines eliminated the seeding task as a limiting factor in corn production. The method was employed extensively though by no means exclusively in Chester and Lancaster Counties in southeastern Pennsylvania, as well as in a few other scattered areas.[149] It became important in the West after 1855.

Despite the efforts of manufacturers to induce farmers to use these drills in planting corn, and general agreement that the machines operated satisfactorily, the mass of farmers adhered to the traditional hill technique, arguing that culture in uninterrupted rows required more hand hoeing than did hill culture, which permitted horse cultivation in both directions.[150] The fact that the hand planting and covering of the seed was "boy's" work was also a consideration.[151]

The insistence of farmers upon pursuing hill culture aroused a good deal of inventive activity, but only a partial solution was achieved before 1870. Most successful in securing farmer acceptance was a two-row horse planter placed on the market by George Brown in 1853 and soon followed by others. If the ground was furrowed in one direction and the machine operated by two men, one driving and the other operating the planting mechanism, it could plant in hills at a rate of fifteen to twenty acres per day.[152] This type of machine was slowly accepted in the late 1850's and with much greater

[147] *Valley Farmer*, VII (1855), 107. "There was considerable experimentation with these devices in Ohio in the early fifties. See Ohio State Board of Agriculture, *Report* (1851-1852).

[148] *Valley Farmer*, VIII (1856), 179; *Prairie Farmer*, X (1850), 116.

[149] *Pennsylvania Farm Journal*, III (1853), 117; IV (1854), 93.

[150] *Indiana Farmer*, I (1851), 264; *Iowa Farmer*, IV (1856), 185.

[151] See the appraisal in U. S. Patent Office, *Report* (1861), p. 283.

[152] For a brief description, see Waldemar Kaempffert, *A Popular History of American Invention*, II (Scribner's, 1924), pp. 260-264; *Valley Farmer*, XIII (March 1860), 340.

rapidity in the 1860's. It was claimed that in 1866 more corn was planted by machine than by hand in Illinois, and seems certain that the machine also had achieved wide acceptance in the older, eastern parts of Iowa and possibly Missouri.[153] Of the 21,000 corn planters reported as produced in 1869, more than three-fifths were credited to Illinois, though it is not certain whether hand planters were included.[154] Acceptance of the machine was also important in Michigan and Ohio.[155] East of the Allegheny River the corn planter remained almost unknown. Progressive farmers in some sections continued to use the drill, but its use did not spread extensively. In part this was owing to the relatively small acreages planted in corn, but even more to resistances against changing long-established customs.[156]

[153] Illinois State Agricultural Society, *Transactions* (1859-1860), p. 312; Iowa State Agricultural Society, *Transactions* (1866), p. 340; (1867), p. 420; (1868), pp. 320-323.
[154] U. S. Census Office, 9th Census, 1870. *The Statistics of Wealth and Industry of the United States*, III (Washington, 1872), 588-589.
[155] Michigan State Board of Agriculture, *Transactions* (1864), pp. 18, 22, 26, 47, 55.
[156] U. S. Commissioner of Agriculture, *Report* (1866), p. 263.

CHAPTER NINE

FURTHER REACTIONS TO IMPROVED IMPLEMENTS

The short periods of time during which most crops had to be harvested and the arduous labor involved set limits on the total product of a farm enterprise. In Europe, these problems had long stimulated considerable inventive activity, directed toward improving the tools used and substituting horse power for human labor. Such efforts were intensified under American conditions. The horse-powered rakes, threshers, reapers, and mowers were the more important developments of the half-century. There were others of lesser significance, as hay-loading equipment, balers, potato diggers, corn shellers, straw and root cutters, feed cookers, hay tedders, and fanning mills. The introduction of the hay rake, the thresher, and the harvester is analyzed in the following pages because those tools illustrate the sources and nature of the changes that occurred in harvesting operations, the problems encountered, and some of the consequences of their solution.

THE HAY RAKE

The first important success in applying horse power to the tasks of farming, other than in plowing and harrowing, was in gathering mown grass. Although cutting the grass with a scythe was the most difficult and time-consuming operation in hay-making, gathering the cut hay further reduced the time that could be applied to cutting, while the whole operation demanded much labor at a season when numerous other tasks called for attention. Hay production was everywhere an important concern, the quantity gathered determining the number of animals that could be fed over the winter or, if the hay were sold, the money income of the farm enterprise.

A simple form of horse-drawn rake had found its way to the

United States from Europe prior to 1800.[1] This was merely an enlarged version of the common hand rake, equipped with shafts and a handle thereby serving as a drag rake. Because operation of the rake required that it be stopped and lifted with the completion of each windrow, little if anything was gained by its use. The drag rake was considered to have some advantage in gleaning grain and hay fields after normal hand raking, but there was little interest in such operations.

An implement was required that would readily drop its contents, and one became available shortly before 1820 in the form of the revolving horse rake. This was a simple device—merely two rows of wooden teeth set opposite on a beam to which were attached a shaft and handle in such a manner that the beam could be tripped to slide over a load of accumulated hay, bringing the second set of teeth into position to commence a new windrow.

With such an instrument and a horse to draw it, one man could accomplish work equivalent to that of five to ten men with hand rakes. This substantial gain in productivity was available at little expense. The revolver could be made by most farmers with materials readily available or could be purchased from commercial sources at a cost of about ten dollars. The capital required was therefore small and the investment attractive, since the cost of the implement might be returned in a single season from its utilization on as little as five acres of meadow.

Despite the fact that the revolver received much publicity in the agricultural journals in the 1830's and 1840's, was available from commercial sources after 1823, offered significant possibilities for reducing production costs, and represented a modest investment whether made or purchased, widespread adoption took place only slowly. The implement came into use earliest in areas where hay was a cash crop or where large acreages supported sizable dairy herds. In these areas dependence upon native grasses had been abandoned, and the meadows were devoted to cultivated forage plants. During the 1840's the revolver was in extensive use on farms along the Ohio and Hudson rivers, in southeastern Pennsylvania, and similar areas that sent hay to market by water. The implement was by this time in use by scattered farmers in every state. Although

[1] This discussion is based on Clarence H. Danhof, "Gathering the Grass," *Agricultural History*, XXX (1956), 169-173.

cultivated meadows were common throughout New England and central New York by the 1840's, the scant evidence available suggests that the revolver was only slowly brought into use.

No doubt the slow acceptance of the revolver followed from resistance to new ideas and an inability to visualize the gains from the application of horse power to a traditionally human task. Rejection might be rationalized by attaching importance to the special skills needed, to the reduction in quality of the product, such as that the revolver increased the dust and dirt in the hay, and to the delays and uncertainties that followed from the need to make repairs. More important was the fact that the revolver intruded upon a system of production which represented a rough balance between the various resources applied within each farm unit. Effective use of the revolver required that hay fields be reasonably level and free of obstacles such as rocks and stumps. If preparatory work of this kind were unnecessary or minimal, the revolver was quickly adopted. Where significant adjustments in land use or in the plans for labor application were necessary, adoption was postponed until such adjustments had been made. For many farmers the advantages to be gained from the revolver were insufficient to stimulate them to make the arrangements needed to employ it effectively.

The revolver had not achieved acceptance as a standard implement before it was being displaced by the wheeled riding or sulky rake. The first such implement to gain substantial use was Calvin Delano's, patented in 1849. The wooden teeth with which Delano's rake was equipped were superseded in the late 1850's by other patented rakes equipped with wire teeth. Such implements were two or three times more efficient than the revolver, ten to twenty times more productive than men with hand rakes. After about 1850 references to the horse rake frequently fail to distinguish between the old revolver and the riding form, though it is clear that the new type was displacing the older version.

Meanwhile, efforts to develop a machine which would cut either grain or grass by horse power were increasingly successful. As the mower was improved, it provided a cutting capacity that also rendered hand raking obsolete, besides making uneconomical the size of meadow that had been practical for hand harvesting operations. The mower and the sulky rake together thus made highly attractive, if not essential, those adjustments in the acreages devoted to mowing and in tillage practices necessary to their effective utilization.

THE THRESHER

About 1820, the farmer who spent something like twenty man-hours in the work of cutting, binding, and shocking an acre of wheat, gave as much or more time to the tasks of threshing, winnowing, and bagging.[2] When the acreage in wheat was small, the shocked grain was stored in a barn and the threshing postponed until winter. When time permitted, the flail was used to separate the grain kernels from the straw, the straw removed by rakes and forks, and the grain screened and fanned to clean it of dust and chaff. Productivity with the flail was from five to ten bushels per man day. Traditionally, the hired labor employed in this operation received one-tenth of the product. Threshing by the flail provided useful employment during the winter. The procedure involved, however, the storage of large quantities of wheat shocks for considerable periods with accompanying risks of loss from insect pests and rodents as well as from changing market prices.

On farms where wheat was cultivated in larger acreages, more expeditious threshing methods were employed. Treading was common in the Middle Atlantic states and was also practical in some areas in the West in the earlier stages of development. Treading floors were sometimes used, but more frequently the grain was piled on hardened earth or perhaps on frozen ground. In a few areas a groundhog thresher was employed, a loglike device that was drawn by a horse over the shocks scattered on the barn floor.[3] This method economized on the animal power needed, as well as serving to reduce injuries to the animals. While these methods were satisfactory for certain small grains, they yielded a wheat well mixed with dirt, difficult to clean, and frequently salable only at a discount.

[2] Leo Rogin, *The Introduction of Farm Machinery in Its Relation to the Productivity of Labor in the Agriculture of the United States during the Nineteenth Century,* University of California Publications in Economics, IX (1931), 234-235. Rogin assumes a yield of 20 bushels to the acre.

[3] J. Leander Bishop, *History of American Manufacturers from 1608 to 1863* (Philadelphia, 1866), II, 102; John Nicholson, *The Farmer's Assistant* (Lancaster, Pa., 1820), p. 379; Edward Carpenter, "The Groundhog Thresher: An Enigma," *Wisconsin Magazine of History,* XXXVII (Summer 1954), 217-218.

Simple threshing machines, hand- or horse-operated, had been in use in Scotland well before 1820. A few of these found their way to the United States, and both they and similar devices manufactured locally were used in New England and in the New York and Virginia wheat areas.[4] They were simple beating devices of low capacity and subject to the objection that the straw and grain were inadequately separated, permitting a high percentage of loss. Those that were hand-operated offered little if any advantage over the flail; others operated by means of a horse-powered sweep found some use.

Cleaning the grain of chaff, dust, and dirt was a slow process when done by hand methods. When large quantities of grain were handled, greater speed was sought through the use of fanning mills. Imported machines from Europe were known throughout the East but were little used before 1820. Though the history of the development of these devices is obscure, the period of the 1830's and 1840's was one of considerable improvement and adoption. Most such mills were made by small manufacturers for local markets, and information on their production and use is slight.

Development of the Machine. The technical history of the threshing machine is a complex one, in which improvements upon the beating device, the separator, the winnower, and the power source played interdependent roles. As it finally developed, the machine was a combine which performed all these operations. The power source similarly evolved from the hand crank, through horse-powered sweeps, tread mills, and finally to steam. Inventive activity concerned with these various factors became noteworthy after 1830.[5]

In the thirties and forties, substantial improvements were made in threshing machinery, both in the threshing mechanism and in the devices to supply power. The sweep or lever type of power, with two to eight horses walking in a circle operating a geared arrangement, was made available in improved forms. It remained popular throughout the period for operating the larger threshing machines

[4] *American Farmer,* II (1820), 168, 109; *New York Farmer,* II (1829), 161-163; *New England Farmer,* I (1822-1823), 363; *Yankee Farmer,* II (1836), 4; *Northern Farmer,* II (1833), 23; *Western Farmer,* I (1839), 90; *Cultivator,* I (1834), 52-53; *Genesee Farmer,* I (1831), 285.

[5] For European development of threshers and the most important of the 350 patents issued in the United States prior to 1860, see U. S. Census, 1860, *Compendium,* p. 90; R. L. Ardrey, *American Agricultural Implements* (Chicago, 1894), pp. 103-114.

but was cumbersome to move and expensive.[6] During the forties another type of power became popular, a treadmill generally referred to as a railway horse-power. This was available in sizes for operation by one to four horses and was readily portable. It quickly superseded the older lever powers on all but the largest farms.[7]

Numerous inventors and manufacturers contributed to the development of practical and economical threshing machinery. Among the earliest and most successful were the brothers John and Hiram Pitts of Maine. Their first contribution was a railway or treadmill type of horse power intended for use with the older simple thresher, which with subsequent improvements became very popular. In 1837 the Pitts patented a machine which for the first time successfully combined the operations of threshing, separating, and fanning. It was portable and relatively inexpensive, a two-horse model, with a capacity of one hundred bushels per day, selling for about $200. Hiram Pitts manufactured his machine for some years in Maine, moving his operations in 1847 to Alton, Illinois, and in 1851 to Chicago. John Pitts in 1837 moved his manufacturing activities to Albany and then successively to Rochester, Springfield, Ohio, and Buffalo. The Pitt machines achieved extensive distribution and were popular over a wide area in the years following 1840.[8]

Numerous other manufacturers sought to supply threshing machines, many of them offering equipment closely patterned after the Pitts'. Small-scale production to order or for sale through local agricultural warehouses was typical. However, in the 1840's and 1850's some of these suppliers developed into substantial, nationally known firms producing a thousand or more threshers annually. Among the better known thresher manufacturers in the fifties were Emery & Co., Wheeler, A. B. Allen, M. Russell, Westinghouse, Case, and Cox and Roberts.[9] All provided machines considered effective, though difficulties resulting from the poor quality of metal parts and the reliance upon wood construction for parts subjected to heavy vibration plagued both manufacturers and users.[10] The period

---

[6] *American Farmer,* XI (1829), no. 1.

[7] Ohio State Board of Agriculture, *Report* (1859), p. 527.

[8] *Genesee Farmer,* V (1835), 372.

[9] For data on these firms, see Ardrey, *American Agricultural Implements,* pp. 105-114, 323-326.

[10] There were complaints, for example, that the imperfect balance of the cylinder, which traveled with great velocity, produced accidents and breakdowns. *Plough, Loom and Anvil,* III (1851), 185.

was one of constant technical improvement, particularly in increasing the efficiency of the machines in separating grain from the waste straw.

Adoption of Mechanical Threshing. Threshing by machine rapidly superseded the older methods during the 1830's in New York.[11] By the 1850's the machine was widely used among commercial producers of grains throughout the northern states.[12] Much of the spread of mechanical threshing derived from development of the practice of custom service. The earlier threshers had been stationary, intended for permanent installation in a barn or shed and powered by cumbersome lever-type movements. With the development of more compact and efficient machines, portability was achieved, furthered by the introduction of treadmill horse powers, likewise easily mounted on wheels. The cost of the machines was substantial, and their capacity well beyond the needs of most farmers.[13] Providing the services of such a machine together with the additional labor required was a profit opportunity that in most neighborhoods found takers—frequently nonfarmers.[14] The farmer employing such a custom machine supplied teams and some of the labor required and thus secured the threshing of his grain immediately after harvest at a cost of 3¢ or 4¢ up to 10¢ per bushel.[15]

Custom threshing became popular after 1840, employing the

[11] New York State Agricultural Society, *Transactions* (1842), p. 30; (1850), pp. 171, 518, 530; (1852), pp. 125, 130; (1854), 383; *Genesee Farmer*, I (1831), 132; III (1833), 178; II (1841), 97; *Cultivator*, I (1834), 52; Patrick Shirreff, *Tour Through North America* (Edinburgh, 1835), p. 25.

[12] New York State Agricultural Society, *Transactions* (1850), p. 518, 530; (1852), p. 130; (1854), p. 383; *Agricultural Survey of Massachusetts, Second Report* (1838), p. 144; *Connecticut Valley Farmer and Mechanic*, I (1854), 147; *Northern Farmer*, V (1858), 323; *Rural New Yorker*, II (1851), 151; V (1854), 261; VIII (1857), 286-301; U. S. Patent Office, *Report* (1851), p. 214; (1854), p. 197.

[13] The large, eight-horse-power machines were priced at about $275. The small Wheeler two-horse-power thresher and separator was priced at $128 in Albany; the two-horse-power thresher combined with winnower was $245. With all attachments, including feed cutter, saw mill, and clover huller, the thresher was $316 in Albany, $366 in St. Louis.

[14] It was reported that "often three active and experienced men, generally handy mechanics, often blacksmiths, would purchase one." Nathan H. Parker, *Iowa As It Is in 1857* (Boston, 1857), pp. 253-254.

[15] U. S. Commissioner of Agriculture, *Report* (1863), pp. 432-433; Illinois State Agricultural Society, *Transactions* (1869), p. 225; *American Agriculturist*, XVIII (1858), 364; *Northwestern Farmer*, VI (1861), 206, 97-98; Percy W. Bidwell and John I. Falconer, *History of Agriculture in the Northern United States* (Washington, 1925), p. 338.

larger Pitts, Emery, Westinghouse, and Case machines.[16] In western New York custom work was common as early as 1843, and it was available soon thereafter throughout the East.[17] In New England and eastern New York, however, wheat was less frequently grown in quantity for market with the result that the older methods of threshing persisted.[18]

West of the Appalachians, threshing machines were brought into use almost as rapidly as they became available. They were introduced into northern Ohio in 1831 and were standard by the 1850's, custom work with the larger machines being common.[19] By that date, machine threshing was common in parts of Illinois, Indiana, Wisconsin, and Michigan.[20] Much and perhaps most was custom work. In Iowa by the middle of the 1850's, "eight horse-power-threshers . . . almost monopolized the threshing business."[21] The

[16] Emery & Co. reported that sales of its Overshot Thresher and Cleaner were nearly always intended for use in custom threshing. *Genesee Farmer*, XIII (1852), 169. Westinghouse cited the case of one of its two-horse-power machines being used by eighty different farmers in one season. *Illustrated Annual Register* (1858), p. 130; American Institute, *Transactions* (1860-1861), p. 538.

[17] *Rural New Yorker*, VIII (1857), 386; *Maine Farmer*, Feb. 17, May 5, 1853; April 2, 1857; New York State Agricultural Society, *Transactions* (1843), p. 454; (1850), p. 518; New Jersey State Agricultural Society, *Transactions* (1859), pp. 6-9; Pennsylvania State Agricultural Society, *Report* (1854), p. 200.

[18] The flail was still in use in the 1860's in New England "when the crop is only 200 to 500 bushels." *Working Farmer*, XIV (1862), 132. See also New York State Agricultural Society, *Transactions* (1841), p. 155; (1842), p. 160. "The use of the hand hoe instead of the plow, in some parts of our southern country, is not more ridiculous than the use of the hand flail instead of the threshing mill in the north, and still we hear the sound of the flail in almost every county in New York and New Jersey." *Valley Farmer*, II (1850), 124.

[19] Ohio State Board of Agriculture, *Report* (1848), p. 106; (1847), p. 98; (1868), p. 202; *Cultivator*, VIII (1850), 308; *Ohio Cultivator*, XI (1855), 100; *Southern Planter*, XVIII (1859), 233; Robert L. Jones, "Introduction of Farm Machinery in Ohio Prior to 1865," *Ohio Historical Quarterly*, LVIII (1949), 1-20. References to the use of threshers are numerous in Ohio Board of Agriculture, *Report* (1849), and succeeding volumes.

[20] In Illinois, Robert Russell reported in the early fifties that, "there is still a large quantity of grain trodden out by horses." *North America: Its Agriculture and Climate* (Edinburgh, 1857), p. 115. William V. Pooley notes that threshers were not in general use there at that date. Pooley, *Settlement of Illinois* (University of Wisconsin Press, 1908), p. 350. See also U. S. Patent Office, *Report* (1850), pp. 198, 403; Ohio State Board of Agriculture, *Report* (1846), p. 27; *Prairie Farmer*, V (1845), 157. On Indiana, see Indiana State Board of Agriculture, *Report* (1852), pp. 114-115, 304-305; (1854-1855), p. 82; (1856), p. 241. On Wisconsin, see Benjamin H. Hibbard, *History of Agriculture in Dane County, Wisconsin* (Bulletin of the University of Wisconsin, 1904), p. 123; U. S. Patent Office, *Report* (1854), p. 148. On Michigan, see Michigan State Board of Agriculture, *Report* (1864), pp. 22, 26 ff.

[21] *Northwestern Farmer*, VI (1861), 97-98. See also *Country Gentleman*, VI (1855), 143; *Prairie Farmer*, X (1850), 129; Rogin, *Farm Machinery*, pp. 184-185. Numerous

same was true in Minnesota: "half a dozen threshing machines were in operation in 1859 in the neighborhood of Plainview, an area which received its first settler in 1855."[22]

Criticism of the Thresher. Threshing by flail continued to have adherents, however, and not only among farmers who raised just a few acres of grain. The machine was considered wasteful of the grain, while it left the straw and chaff in a useless condition. Some believed that the machine killed the wheat germ and was thus responsible for poor crops.[23] The *American Agriculturist* observed that "many good wheat growers thresh all their seed wheat with a flail, to avoid crushing the kernels by use of a threshing machine, which often cracks or bruises at least a tenth part of the very best kernels."[24]

More interesting was the argument based upon costs. It was urged that the flail was cheaper than the machine because grain could be threshed by hand at the low wages prevailing during the winter season and the straw made available as needed by the farm animals.[25] As late as 1857 the relative economy of flailing versus mechanical threshing was debated by the members of the American Institute, Solon Robinson arguing that reliance upon the flail "enabled the farmer to keep a hand over winter without loss, whereas if grain were threshed by machine there would be no work for the hired help in winter."[26]

The issue was resolved in favor of the machine partly because of the desirability of getting wheat to market as quickly after har-

references to the machine appear in Iowa State Agricultural Society, *Report* (1857-1865).

[22] *Ohio Farmer,* VIII (1859), 289. References to itinerant threshers are numerous in *Minnesota Farmer and Gardener,* I (1860).

[23] "Another fact, which should not be left unobserved, is that seed wheat should never be threshed with a machine, but should be carefully shelled to prevent its cracking; from a continued use of threshed wheat for seed, it becomes more and more degenerate each year." Frederick Gerhard, *Illinois As It Is* (Chicago, 1857), p. 327. See also *Rural New Yorker,* I (1850), 202; *American Agriculturist,* IX (1850), 156; *Ohio Cultivator,* XV (1859), 246; U. S. Patent Office, *Report* (1850), p. 249; (1851), pp. 402-403; (1852), p. 126; (1854), p. 143.

[24] *American Agriculturist,* XIII (1854), 198. But a Michigan farmer reported, "from actual count . . . my wheat was not injured by the machine more than it would have been to have been flailed." *Michigan Farmer,* XII (1854), 142.

[25] American Institute, *Report* (1857), pp. 505, 543-544.

[26] *American Agriculturist,* XVIII (1858), 333; *Homestead,* IV (1859), 30; *Rural New Yorker,* VIII (1857), 286, 301.

vest as possible, partly by the disappearance of laborers who were willing to do the arduous work of flailing for the traditional one-tenth.[27] An Ohio farmer wrote in 1859: "The fact is that very few agricultural labor-saving machines do save anything on the first cost of performing labor—always except the horse-rake—yet many of them have become imperatively necessary. We cannot do without the threshing machine; laborers cannot be found to do by hand its work; yet every farmer knows that one hundred bushels of wheat or oats can be more cheaply threshed with a flail in the winter season, than by machine."[28]

Power Sources. The sweep and railway horse-powers left much to be desired since the amount of energy that could be applied was very limited, highly variable, and difficult to control, while valuable animals were endangered by the hard, continuous labor required. The increasing application of steam to ships, railroads, and industry during this time suggested the utilization of such power in agricultural tasks. The greatest interest and most dramatic experimentation dealt with the employment of steam in plowing.[29]

Successful use of steam power, however, was achieved earliest by a few scattered farmers who undertook modest experiments with the stationary steam engine as a substitute for horse power in threshing, pumping water, operating churns, and similar tasks.[30] Such efforts were stimulated in the early fifties when a few manufacturers placed on the market small mobile steam engines mounted on wheels and hence mobile.[31] By the latter part of the 1850's, the steam engine gave promise in the hands of experimentally minded farmers of becoming an agricultural machine, particularly in operating threshers.[32] Improvements in mobile steam engines appeared

[27] *Farmer and Gardener,* I (1834), 19-20.

[28] *Ohio Farmer,* VIII (1859), 218.

[29] Among the experimenters were the harvester manufacturers Obed Hussey and P. Manny. Hussey constructed a steam plow in 1855. Manny, after constructing a machine, wrote in 1858 that he had abandoned his efforts because the steam plow was impractical and too costly. *Valley Farmer,* VIII (1856), 118; *Soil of the South,* VI (1856), 35-36; *Plough, Loom and Anvil,* XI (1858), 15; *Scientific American,* XII (1856), 341; XIV (1858), 54, 333.

[30] For example, a farmer of West Boxford, Mass., used a small stationary engine before 1850 to pump water and operate churns. *New England,* II (1850), 377.

[31] Reynold M. Wik, *Steam Power on the Farm* (University of Pennsylvania Press, 1951), Chs. II-III.

[32] A mobile steam engine brought into operation near Chillicothe, Ohio, was so

so rapidly that the *Country Gentleman* reported editorially in 1869, "the success which is found to attend the use of steam for thresh-ing grain is resulting in the rapid introduction of their power for farm purposes."[33]

THE MECHANICAL HARVESTER

The harvesting of small grains and grass was the most difficult as well as the most critical task known to northern farming. The ability to command labor at wheat harvest or at haying time de-termined the acreage of those crops that could be raised and the number of animals that could be supported, which effectively estab-lished limits on the total product of an enterprise.

Until the 1850's the hand-swung scythe was the instrument by which the chief task of harvesting—cutting the grain and grass—was accomplished. The cradle, which somewhat facilitated the work of gathering the cut grain, was known before 1820, but the advan-tages it offered were debated and it was by no means in universal use thirty years later.[34]

A solution of the problem of harvesting was early felt to be a critical need of agriculture. Jonathan Roberts, President of the Pennsylvania Agricultural Society, wrote in 1823 that "nothing is more wanted than the application of animal labor in the cutting of grain. It is the business on the farm which requires the most ex-penditure and it is always the most expensive labor."[35] The pos-sibility of achieving that goal had attracted much effort before 1830, by which date eleven reaper and mower patents had been issued to American inventors, and a number of European devices had been given trials.[36] The 1830's witnessed the introduction of several machines that answered the need. Most important were those patented by Obed Hussey (1833) and Cyrus McCormick

---

successful that in 1857 it was scheduled to thresh the grain from 1,500 acres. *Ohio Cultivator,* XIII (1857), 357; *Rural New Yorker,* XIV (1863), 294.

[33] *Country Gentleman,* XXIV (1869), 34.

[34] Rogin, *Farm Machinery,* p. 71.

[35] *American Farmer,* V (1823), 307.

[36] On the history of harvesting machinery patents, see William T. Hutchinson, *Cyrus Hall McCormick: Seed-Time, 1809-1856* (Century Co., 1930), pp. 49-73; M. F. Miller, *The Evolution of Reaping Machines,* U. S. Department of Agriculture, Office of Ex-periment Stations, Bulletin No. 103; Ardrey, *American Agricultural Implements,* Chs. 6-9.

(1834).[37] The next decade witnessed extensive inventive and developmental activity, with the issuance of numerous other patents relating to harvesting machinery.[38] The one issued to Ketchum in 1847 for a mower was to prove particularly successful.

The early machines were crude in design, rude in workmanship, and unreliable in performance. Although they were sufficiently effective to draw the attention of small numbers of farmers and to encourage continued experimental activity, the reaper-mower was not fully developed from an experimental device into a practical and economical machine until midcentury. Such men as Hussey, McCormick, Ketchum, and Manny were the leading figures, but numerous others also contributed as inventors, manufacturers, sales promoters, and especially users. The success of the harvester derived in large part from the zeal of the widely scattered farmers who purchased the machines as they were offered and operated them under difficult conditions of poor design, awkward and crude construction, inadequate maintenance and repair facilities, and their own lack of familiarity with mechanical devices.[39] Sometimes they had to face the strenuous objections of farm laborers.[40] Such purchasers contributed not only essential financial support but also encouragement, and if their criticisms were not always welcome, they nevertheless constituted important elements in the developmental process.

[37] For other harvesters that reached the exhibition and trial stage but then disappeared from notice, see *Genesee Farmer,* IX (1839), 317; *Farmer and Gardener,* III (1836), 236, 371; IV (1837), 127, 165; American Institute, *Journal* (1836), pp. 85, 92; *Farmer and Gardener,* II (1836), 377; Ardrey, *American Agricultural Implements,* p. 40.

[38] As employed here, the term harvester is applied to any device designed to cut either grass, grain, or both. The more specific use of the term for machines that did more than merely cut grain originated with the Marsh harvester after 1858.

[39] Edward Ruffin, the distinguished Virginia farmer and agricultural editor, wrote in 1850 that although the reaper was in use in his neighborhood, "because of their great liability to get out of order, the difficulties of working them, and especially my own ignorance of machinery, I have feared to attempt the use of reaping machines." U. S. Patent Office, *Report* (1850-1851), p. 104. Such a lack of familiarity with mechanical devices and consequent inability to use them as intended by the manufacturer represented a serious difficulty not only in selling the machines but also in securing proper use and care. *Homestead,* I (1855), 597; *American Agriculturist,* XIV (1855), 243.

[40] In Franklin County, Pa., "Our cradlers here were so opposed to the reaping machines that they refused to follow after one, and that helped to make hands scarce." *Rural Register,* I (1859), 68. For a similar situation in Lehigh and Northampton Counties, Pa., see *Prairie Farmer,* X (1850), 175; *American Agriculturist,* XIV (1855), 340.

Farmer Specifications. As inventors and manufacturers labored to improve the performance of their machines and to develop and supply a market for them, farmers became increasingly specific about the characteristics required of a satisfactory mower or reaper. An important specification was quality of performance, equal to that of a good human cradler or mower. Under favorable conditions even the earliest Hussey and McCormick machines worked equal to or better than the best human harvester, performing much faster and with a saving of grain. However, heavy or matted grass and heavy, wet, or blown grain presented problems requiring prolonged experimentation for solution.

A second requirement of the farmers was certainty of operation. The manufacturer's task was to build a machine that would not only operate under ideal conditions but stand up under the stresses of ordinary harvesting operations. It was in machines so proven that farmers were interested, and it was against machines which failed in ordinary use that a large volume of complaints about quality of construction were directed.[41] The criticism of a southern Illinois farmer with regard to a Hussey was applicable to almost all manufacturers: "The workmanship in the making of these machines was very imperfect, and they were built with bad timber and brittle iron castings where there should have been hardened steel, and faults concealed which I could not discover until the machines were put in use."[42] Breakdowns were frequent, and while a wooden part might be replaced on the farm with little loss of time, the breakage of metal parts was much more serious since a supply of replacements was rarely readily available. The local blacksmith might be called upon to make repairs, but these were frequently unsatisfactory, and replacement from the distant manufacturer or even his more accessible agent might render the machine useless during the critically short harvesting period.

Some of these difficulties arose from the farmer's ignorance of the use and care of mechanical devices and from the equal ignorance and carelessness of manufacturers, particularly the failure of licensed manufacturers of a proven machine to follow the specifi-

---

[41] Very detailed specifications were sometimes laid down by agricultural society committees supervising mower and reaper trials. See, e.g., Massachusetts Board of Agriculture, *Transactions* (1859), pp. 190-191.

[42] *American Farmer,* IX (1853), 40.

cations and standards of workmanship established by the original builder.[43] A more important source of problems was the limited technological skill of iron workers generally. As one farmer pointed out: "The implements for the most part now made, are so slight, and in too many cases of such poor material, that the use of them for one season, is about as long as they will last in credit; the bars, bolts, and screw-heads, after that time, will need constant repairing, and this is the case with nearly all the farming implements now made."[44] The uncertainties surrounding the technical adequacy of a harvester were compounded by questions as to the quality and precision of manufacture of the particular machine under consideration.

Yet another demand of the farmers was for interchangeability of mowers and reapers. No sharp distinction between the reaper and the mower was made in the developmental stage of the machines. While both Hussey and McCormick were primarily interested in developing grain reapers, their machines were also employed for cutting grass. The similarity of reapers and mowers and their high cost fostered the goal of an interchangeable machine for many years, with the advertising claims of many manufacturers emphasizing this feature.

Hussey's machine, with its rear delivery arrangement, proved to be a good mower and was offered as a combined machine. As McCormick's machine was less adaptable to mowing, the manufacturer early dropped the interchangeable concept. His efforts to supply an acceptable single-purpose mowing machine proved unsuccessful, however, although after 1855 the McCormick reaper was available with attachments to convert it into a mower. Most other manufacturers followed a similar policy, and from 1850 until after the Civil War the machines were intended to perform both operations.

[43] *American Farmer,* IX (1855), 286; Massachusetts Board of Agriculture, *Transactions* (1856), p. 289; *Homestead,* II (1856), 330-331. McCormick's difficulties in securing acceptable machines from licensees are described in Hutchinson, *Cyrus Hall McCormick: Seed-Time,* pp. 195, 305.

[44] *Rural Register,* I (1859), 169-170. Such complaints persisted. In 1866 a New York farmer wrote: "The main defect in farm machinery is want of simplicity in construction. They are more trouble than profit. Pieces of complex mechanism that will answer for the shop and factory, where they are stationary, and have trained operatives to manage them, are unfitted for the farm where the opportunity for practice is limited. Something that boys and hired hands can manage is wanted. Inventors need not expect to introduce largely among farmers any labor-saving machine which a plain man cannot operate, or no one but an engineer keep in order." New York State Agricultural Society, *Transactions* (1867), Pt. 2, p. 684.

Meanwhile, W. F. Ketchum patented in 1844 and 1847 a single-purpose mower, which along with a few others, such as Danford's, achieved wide use in the fifties. These machines served to emphasize the fact that the problems of mowing were quite different from those of reaping, and their development drew a distinction between the two machines that sharpened with time. Close-cutting over rough ground was unimportant in reaping but essential in mowing. Rear delivery was desirable in mowing but side delivery, preferably in gavels, was necessary in a reaper. A series of patents after 1854 substantially improved upon the Ketchum machine and marked the development of a two-wheeled mower equipped with a flexible rather than a rigid cutter bar. In the form of the Buckeye and Kirby, the mower was established by 1860 as a specialized instrument superior to the dual-purpose machine. At the same time, the major inadequacy of the simple reaper—the necessity of human raking of the cut grain—was solved by the appearance of mechanical raking devices.[45] Such relatively complex devices served to destroy whatever advantages lay in combined machines, although they remained the most popular form until after the Civil War.

Finally, the farmers desired a machine with low draft. Most of the earlier machines were very heavy, with severe side drafts, and had poor maneuverability. When the problems of side drafts and maneuverability were solved, the machines remained comparatively heavy, partly because the wood and cast iron used in their construction required weight to withstand the stresses of use. Some of the machines required a minimum of four horses to operate. Others, though intended for a single team, quickly exhausted the animals, requiring that a second team be available if a day's machine work was to be performed. The need for several teams militated against the machine in the eyes of countless farmers who possessed only one team, or perhaps a lone horse. A one-horse machine was considered by many to be a highly desirable objective. The one-horse mowers that were placed on the market proved unsatisfactory. Both farmers and manufacturers learned from experience[46] that machinery built to give satisfactory service from the materials avail-

[45] Ardrey, *American Agricultural Implements,* pp. 78-95, pp. 86-95.

[46] By 1856 manufacturers were discovering that light-weight machines were so unsatisfactory as to lose them business, and the trend was back to heavier machines. *The Farm Journal and Progressive Farmer,* VI (1856), 258-260.

able required weight, and the user of reaper or mower discovered that in this respect as in others he was forced to adjust his operations to the characteristics and requirements of the machine.

All these specifications of the farmers could be satisfied without achieving any advantages in harvesting costs because of investment requirements. In the early 1850's the smallest and cheapest mowers sold for $100, the simpler reapers brought $115, while combined machines were priced at $150 and upward. Such sums were unprecedentedly large compared with the investments required for other types of farm equipment. The mere size of investment led to predictions that the harvester could never be profitably utilized.[47]

While substantial labor savings were early claimed, the question of cost advantages of harvesters was long debated.[48] Comparisons with harvesting costs by hand labor were frequently made to the disadvantage of machine work, taking into account interest and depreciation.[49] Others claimed that such doubts would be resolved with the machine's increasing perfection. Well before the question was clearly answered, however, significant numbers of individuals had seen the harvester's value as a substitute for labor that was frequently not available with certainty and in the amounts desired.[50] Some recognized early that the economy of the machine was not properly evaluated in terms of the acreages planted to grain and grass with human harvesting in mind. To men whose operations

[47] John W. Oldmixon, *Transatlantic Wanderings* (London, 1855), p. 49.

[48] "Hussey's Reaper, which costs $100, will pay for itself in one year, in a crop of 1500 to 2000 bushels, in the saving of grain alone, to say nothing of the greater saving in labour, and the neatness with which it does its work." *Plough, Loom and Anvil*, II (1849), 11. A useful analysis of the costs of the reaper compared with the cradle appears in Paul A. David, "The Mechanization of Reaping in the Ante-Bellum Midwest," in Henry Rosovsky, ed., *Industrialization in Two Systems: Essays in Honor of Alexander Gerschenkron* (Wiley, 1966), Ch. I. These cost differences were widely acknowledged at the time. If adoption of the reaper can be judged as being slow, it was principally because of the technological immaturity of the machine. Once the farmers were assured of a satisfactory machine of reasonable reliability, their ability to adapt their operations and to secure a machine of their choice was the determining factor in adoption.

[49] *Genesee Farmer*, XIX (1858), 27, 115, 147; *American Agriculturist*, XIX (1860), 201; *Boston Cultivator*, Nov. 22, 1851; *Miner's Rural American*, I (1856), 243. For analyses favorable to the machine, see *Connecticut Valley Farmer and Mechanic*, II (1855), 53; *Genesee Farmer*, XII (1851), 27, 15; *Scientific American*, X (1854), 366; XI (1855), 30; *American Agriculturist*, XIV (1855), 168; *Rural New Yorker*, XII (1861), 206.

[50] *Ohio Farmer*, VIII (1859), 218; *Michigan Farmer*, X (1852), 87; *Prairie Farmer*, X (1850) 175; *American Agriculturist*, XII (1854), 164; *Farmer's Companion*, III (1853), 126.

were not closely integrated with the existing technology and who had suitable unused or underutilized land, the harvester represented an opportunity to increase grain and grass plantings beyond the capacity of available hand labor and up to the capacity of one or more machines.[51] So viewed, the machine offered substantial advantages even in its earlier and cruder forms. An upward tendency of agricultural wages served as a further incentive to adoption.[52]

The years 1848-1852 brought to an end the first or experimental period of harvester development. In 1848 the basic patents held by Hussey and McCormick expired, encouraging the efforts of numerous inventors and manufacturers to enter the field. Although both Hussey and McCormick secured patents on improvements on their original machines, there can be little question that the increased competition hastened the development and adoption of the machines in the following years. Of equal importance was the fact that manufacturing skills had been developed to a sufficiently high degree to ensure consistent production of satisfactory machines. Most important, by 1852 the harvester had been developed into a useful, reasonably reliable, and cost-saving machine. At the first publicly sponsored trials of reaping machines held by the New York State Agricultural Society at Buffalo in 1848, the performance of the machines had been judged unsatisfactory. All machines were found to clog badly and were extremely heavy with excessive side drafts, while their overall performance compared unfavorably with the scythe or cradle.[53] Four years later the same society held another trial at Geneva with quite different results.[54] The judges now found that though important defects remained, both reapers and mowers now did work equal in quality to that of a scythe and that they possessed advantages assuring substantial economies from their use.[55]

For many years after 1852, harvester trials were a standard fea-

---

[51] Estimates of the acreage required for profitable use of a mower ranged from 30 to 50; of a reaper, from 20 acres up. *Northern Farmer*, V (1858), 207; Massachusetts Board of Agriculture, *Transactions* (1859), pp. 190-191; *Valley Farmer*, IX (1857), 141; *American Agriculturist*, XIV (1855), 340.

[52] *Northern Farmer*, V (1858), 212.

[53] New York State Agricultural Society, *Transactions* (1849), p. 109.

[54] See New York State Agricultural Society, *New York State Agricultural Society's Trial of Implements at Geneva, July, 1852* (Albany, 1852). There were numerous other trials, the most important being that of the Ohio State Board of Agriculture.

[55] *Farmer's Companion*, IV (1854), 271.

ture of almost every agricultural fair. Though doubts of the practicability of the machines persisted, they were displaced during the fifties by uncertainties as to the claims made for their machines by the numerous manufacturers. The trials served both to acquaint an increasing number of farmers with the practicability of the harvesters and to afford opportunity to compare the effectiveness of the products of competing firms. The major trial of the decade was held at Syracuse in 1857 by the United States Agricultural Society, with more than forty machines entered.[56] Though the question of the merits of the various machines was not settled at this or any other trial, the occasion demonstrated the considerable progress made in perfecting the harvester and decided conclusively their economic practicability.

The large number of manufacturers entering machines in the 1852 trials represented but a small fraction of the firms engaged in harvester production. Hussey had established production of his machine in Baltimore in 1837, with additional arrangements in Ohio. McCormick had undertaken small-scale production of his machine in Virginia. He made production arrangements in Cincinnati, Brockport, New York, and on a smaller scale in Illinois, Wisconsin, and Iowa. Eventually McCormick canceled all licenses and concentrated production in his own plant in Chicago. By 1852 the manufacture of harvesters was focused on three major centers: northern New York, particularly Brockport and Buffalo; Ohio, principally Cincinnati and Canton; northern Illinois, principally Chicago, which soon was supplemented by Rockford. Hussey's production in Baltimore had already passed its peak: he was one of the numerous scattered producers who sprang up merely to exploit patents or serve local needs. While each of the major centers served an obvious marketing area, competition was national. Chicago and Rockford manufacturers sold their machines in Ohio, New York, and on the eastern coast. Brockport and Canton machines were marketed in the prairie states as well as on the eastern coast.

After 1852 the number continued to expand, some of them achieving large size. Many manufacturers operated under licenses from patentees, though they frequently added "improvements" of their own so that machines were identified by both patent and manufacturer. Other firms secured patents on machines that more

---

[56] *Northwestern Farmer,* I (1856), 157.

or less closely resembled those of Hussey and McCormick. The editor of the *Prairie Farmer* observed in 1850 that harvesters "are now constructed in almost every town and village in the West where implements of any sort are manufactured." Two years later he listed seventeen manufacturers within the state of Illinois, pointing out that the machines, of one style or another, accounted for only a small proportion of those actually in existence.[57] The same picture held for such areas as Ohio and New York. In New England, where no harvesters of any kind were being manufactured in 1850, ten years later there were "some sixty houses manufacturing mowing machines, each claiming superiority."[58]

Prior to 1850 about 7,000 harvesters had been produced.[59] The number in use was a fraction of that figure because of rapid obsolescence, the discarding of machines as failures, and the short life of the wooden and cast-iron implement (the average useful period then being estimated at two years).[60] In the following years, production mounted rapidly, with the demand frequently exceeding the ability of manufacturers to supply it. Between 1851 and 1857 somewhat in excess of 22,000 machines were manufactured by the two largest firms, McCormick and Manny. According to contemporary estimates, this number was less than one-fifth of the total produced in the period.[61] Approximately 100,000 reapers and mowers were purchased by farmers in the decade of the fifties. By 1864 annual production was estimated to be from 87,000 to 100,000.[62] In 1869 the federal census returns indicated production of 60,000 reapers, 39,486 mowers, and 3,566 harvesters.[63]

General familiarity with the character and nature of the new machines was a prerequisite to inspection and purchase. There were

[57] *Prairie Farmer*, X (1850), 293; XII (1852), 88.

[58] *New England Farmer*, XII (1860), 280.

[59] Hutchinson, *Cyrus Hall McCormick: Seed-Time*, pp. 366, 377; L. C. Flint in U. S. Department of Agriculture, *Report* (1872), p. 289.

[60] One editor wrote that a well-cared-for machine "should last at least eight years," but because of neglect, the average life was only two years. *Rural New Yorker*, XII (1861), 382; XIII (1862), 390.

[61] *Scientific American*, XII (1856), 293; *Genesee Farmer*, XVIII (1856), 34; New York State Census, *Report* (1855), p. 322.

[62] Rogin, *Farm Machinery*, p. 78; Massachusetts Board of Agriculture, *Transactions* XXI (1873-1874), 32-37; William T. Hutchinson, *Cyrus Hall McCormick: Harvest, 1856-1884* (Appleton-Century, 1935), p. 97.

[63] U. S. Census Office, 9th Census, 1870, *The Statistics of Wealth and Industry of the United States*, III (Washington, 1872), 588-589.

a few farmers who, stimulated only by a reading knowledge, had the initiative to travel or send funds over considerable distances to secure a machine. However, adoptions on a significant scale occurred only as the machines were made available for demonstration, sale, and delivery within the farmer's immediate area, and then only if guaranteed to perform to certain standards and sold on long credits. The problems of the inventor thus did not cease with the development of an operative machine but extended to the establishment of satisfactory production, demonstration, sales, financing, and servicing procedures. The harvester differed from other new implements in that it required a heavy investment and unfamiliar skills. It also called for a care and precision in production that were new to the agricultural implement industry. The need to adjust to these requirements to achieve widespread adoption of the machine was not at first clearly seen by McCormick and even less by Hussey. With very limited resources, both men sought to forward acceptance of the harvester by techniques that had served but poorly in the past and which would be not at all satisfactory in the future.

Initial adoptions of the reaper occurred on a significant scale almost simultaneously in western New York, Ohio, and Illinois. The rate of subsequent acceptance depended on the quality and usefulness of the machines made available, the economic conditions affecting agriculture from year to year, and the readiness with which the machine could be integrated into the farming pattern.

Adoption in the East. There were good reasons to expect that farmers in the area surrounding Philadelphia and Baltimore, including the northern part of the Delaware peninsula, would lead the nation in adoption of harvesting machinery. In the forties and fifties the region was one of the most progressive in the nation; it enjoyed active agricultural societies and press; and grain and grass were important crops. Moreover, the machine was early publicized and made available. Hussey demonstrated his reaper in Talbott County, Maryland, in 1836 and at numerous other points in the region in the following years,[64] conducting his activities from his factory in

[64] *Farmer's Register,* III (1836), 413-414; *American Farmer,* III (1836), 113, 168, 181; VIII (1852), 57, 102-103, 275; IX (1853), 40, 114; *Farmer's Cabinet,* I (1836), 174-175; *Genesee Farmer,* VI (1836), 376; VII (1837), 293-294; *New England Farmer,* VI (1837), 204; XIV (1836), 52; Henry W. Ellsworth, *Valley of the Wabash* (New York, 1838), pp. 67-78.

Baltimore until his death in 1860.[65] McCormick reapers were in use on scattered wheat fields in Virginia, from which some found their way north across the Potomac in the forties. Although the reaper won substantial recognition in the area from Queen Anne's County, Maryland, northward to New Castle County, Delaware, the number involved was nonetheless small.[66] Until the early 1850's the machine used was almost exclusively Hussey's, which was never produced in large quantity.[67]

Farther north the reaper found acceptance more slowly. In Chester and Delaware Counties, Pennsylvania, it had been only "partially tested" by 1854.[68] By then the machines of Manny, Atkin, and Ketchum as well as McCormick were available, but acceptance was accompanied by criticism directed at their poor workmanship.[69] Reapers and mowers were also coming into use about the middle of the decade in northeastern Pennsylvania as well as New Jersey.[70] In western Pennsylvania the prospect of a heavy hay crop in 1856 stimulated adoption of the mower in the Pittsburgh area, while in Franklin County the reaper-mower was by 1859 considered "as necessary as the plough."[71]

Both wheat and grass were important crops in western New York. In the rest of the state, as in New England, grass occupied the largest acreage of any crop. The wheat area of western New York included among its farmers some of the most progressive in the nation—men who in the forties, after decades of considerable prosperity, found themselves searching for solutions to the problems of increasing costs and declining profits that had resulted from declining soil fertility, insect depredations, and the pressure on prices coming from western competition. They reacted with a lively interest in new implements.

[65] Hutchinson, *Cyrus Hall McCormick: Seed-Time,* pp. 167 ff.

[66] The machine was particularly important in New Castle County. *American Farmer,* II (1846), 84; *American Agriculturist,* IX (1853), 223. John Jones in 1851 had two Husseys, "which had been used a dozen years." *Plow,* I (1852), 303.

[67] From 1839 to 1847, Hussey manufactured 248 reapers. Thereafter production increased to a peak of 521 in 1855, followed by a sharp decline. Hutchinson, *Cyrus Hall McCormick: Seed-Time,* pp. 202, 420-421.

[68] Pennsylvania State Agricultural Society, *Report,* I (1854), 180.

[69] *Pennsylvania Farm Journal,* IV (1854), 276; *Prairie Farmer,* X (1850), 175.

[70] *Pennsylvania Farm Journal,* II (1852), 181; Pennsylvania State Agricultural Society, *Report,* I (1854), 264; *American Agriculturist,* IX (1850), 333; XII (1854), 192; *New Jersey Farmer,* V (1860), 351.

[71] *Western Farm Journal,* I (1856), 43; *Pennsylvania Farm Journal,* II (1852),

Hussey had successfully demonstrated his reaper in Livingston County in the heart of the wheat area in 1834.[72] In 1840 his brother, T. R. Hussey, began manufacture of the Hussey machine in Auburn, New York, and a small number were henceforth available in the state.[73] McCormick demonstrated and sold one of his machines in Genesee County in 1844, at which time he made arrangements for their manufacture in Brockport.[74] In 1845 John Delafield of Geneva imported a Hussey machine from Baltimore, which he later endorsed with the report that it had cut ninety-one acres of wheat at a cost of 41¢ per acre for reaping, binding, and shocking.[75] A Hussey was in use in Seneca County in 1843, and several more by 1848, the users claiming that they were thus able to produce wheat at a total cost of from 26¢ to 30¢ per bushel.[76]

The Hussey and McCormick machines were in use in most of the important wheat counties of New York before 1850. Other manufacturers entered the field, among them Ketchum with a mower and Burral with a combined machine.[77] The reaper's popularity increased rapidly after 1852. In 1853 it was to be found on widely scattered farms throughout the wheat areas and was being employed in some counties to harvest substantial portions of both wheat and grass crops.[78] By the late 1850's the reaper had become

---

95. The reaper was reported as known but not in general use in Allegheny County in 1855. U. S. Patent Office, *Report* (1855), p. 197; *Rural Register,* I (1859), 68.

[72] *New York Farmer,* VII (1835), 13; Hutchinson, *Cyrus Hall McCormick: Seed-Time,* p. 165; *Cultivator,* V (1848), 162; *Genesee Farmer,* XI (1850), 173.

[73] *Cultivator,* VIII (1841), 81, 196-197; IX (1842), 174; *Genesee Farmer,* II (1841), 97, 155.

[74] The sale was to Ansel Chappell who, after acting as McCormick's sales agent for a few years, founded in Brockport the firm of Seymour, Chappell & Co., later Seymour & Morgan, which manufactured McCormick's machine until 1851 and thereafter its own. *Genesee Farmer,* IV (1844), 238-239; U. S. Patent Office, *Report* (1851), p. 202; Hutchinson, *Cyrus Hall McCormick: Seed-Time,* pp. 210-233, 243, 283, 318-319.

[75] *American Agriculturist,* IV (1845), 300.

[76] *Genesee Farmer,* V (1845), 134-135; XI (1850), 149; New York State Agricultural Society, *Transactions* (1850), p. 528; U. S. Patent Office, *Report* (1848), pp. 422-423. But the cradle was still important in the county in 1853. U. S. Patent Office, *Report* (1853), p. 144.

[77] T. D. Burral was a farmer of Geneva, New York, who possessed considerable mechanical as well as business ability. His improvements upon the primitive threshing machine available in the 1820's led him into its manufacture, producing some 4,000 threshers from 1830 to 1850. He also entered upon plow manufacture and later undertook production of a reaper, which achieved substantial popularity in western New York by 1851. *Cultivator,* VI (1849), 178; U. S. Patent Office, *Report* (1848), pp. 422-423; *Rural New Yorker,* III (1852), 222.

[78] U. S. Patent Office, *Report* (1851), pp. 202, 230; *Genesee Farmer,* XII (1851),

a standard item of farm equipment and had superseded the cradle on most farms where wheat occupied a significant acreage.[79]

Although most of the machines in use at the end of the decade were combinations, the earlier reaper was not a good mower, and mechanization of the hay harvest in New York developed parallel to but independent of the introduction of the McCormick and Hussey machines. It was with the appearance in the late forties of the Ketchum mower that a practical device became available. Adoption of this machine was rapid, evidenced by the sale of about 500 mowers for the harvest season of 1853, most of them in New York. Other makes were appearing by this date, though Ketchum retained leadership, with total sales of 12,000 up to 1856, most of them in New York and New England.[80] By 1852, mowers were finding extensive use on Long Island, encouraged by the fact that hand mowers were asking $2.00 a day for their labor.[81] Though doubts of the economy of mechanical mowing long persisted,[82] J. J. Mapes, on a trip through the state of New York in 1854, found Ketchum's machine at work everywhere.[83] By then the mower had found its way into northerly St. Lawrence County and was being extensively used in adjoining Lewis County.[84]

Although the agricultural press of New England closely followed the development of the harvester, the opinion was widely held that the machine was of little significance to the area. This was owing in part to the emphasis placed upon reaping rather than mowing,

---

31. In Monroe County in 1850 wheat "was mostly cut with McCormick's reaper." New York State Agricultural Society, *Transactions* (1850), p. 171. In Ontario County in 1852 "a great part of the grain . . . is cut with the reaper . . . with great satisfaction," and "mowing machines are now used on most of our fields that are smooth enough to admit of their use. They work exceeding well." U. S. Patent Office, *Report* (1852), pp. 210-211; (1853), p. 140; (1854), p. 192.

79 *Genesee Farmer*, XX (1859), 178-179; *American Agriculturist*, XIV (1855), 362; *Valley Farmer*, V (1853), 189; *Cultivator*, IX (1852), 109.

80 *New Jersey Farmer*, II (1856), 320.

81 *Uncle Sam's Large Almanac* (Philadelphia, 1853), p. 34; *Scientific American*, X (1854), 387.

82 *American Agriculturist*, XIV (1855), 362; *Genesee Farmer*, XIX (1858), 27, 115, 147, 210; XX (1859), 178, 274-275. But one editor in 1854 pointed out that, since labor was not available to accomplish haying and harvesting: "Farmers who count their acres of grass and grain by twenties, fifties and hundreds, can not only afford to own and use the most improved labor-saving machine, but will find it nearly indispensable." *Rural New Yorker*, V (1854), 196. See also *Northern Farmer*, V (1858), 207.

83 *Working Farmer*, VI (1854), 121.

84 *American Agriculturist*, XII (1854), 228; *Rural New Yorker*, V (1854), 254. Cf. *Genesee Farmer*, XX (1859), 178-179.

but more to a belief that the machine could never be profitably utilized on the small, rough, rocky, hilly fields of the region.[85] To judge from their lack of attention to the area, Hussey and McCormick shared this belief.

W. F. Ketchum, however, entertained no such doubts and as early as 1848 sought to introduce his mower on the meadows of New England.[86] It was in use in Massachusetts by 1850 and within the next two years was introduced in each state, total sales in New England in 1854 being estimated at three hundred.[87] By that date the machines of a number of other manufacturers, particularly Allen's and Manny's, were available in Boston and elsewhere.[88]

The results of these early adoptions were sufficiently satisfactory to attract wide attention. However, although the ability of the machine to operate under New England conditions had been demonstrated, and it could be asserted that "no farmer can afford to cut his grass with a scythe," the economy of the machine remained a subject of long continued debate.[89] Only on relatively few farms were meadows sufficiently large and adequately prepared for effective use of the mower. On most farms profitable utilization required leveling of the ground, removal of stones, and enlargement of fields by removal of stone walls.

Farmers of some of the river bottom lands of Massachusetts were leaders in accepting the mower. In 1855 it was asserted that the "meadows of the Hoosic are now annually cut with horsepower."[90] Elsewhere reactions were more cautious, though a scattering of farmers were soon experimenting with the machine.[91] A survey by the Massachusetts Board of Agriculture in 1856 indicated that one or more mowers were in use in every county in the state.[92] How-

---

85 *New England Farmer*, V (1853), 395-396; Massachusetts Board of Agriculture, *Report* (1855), p. 127.

86 Ketchum sought for some time to secure a New England manufacturer for his mower. *New England Farmer*, V (1853), 457-458.

87 Massachusetts Board of Agriculture, *Report* (1854), pp. 233, 238; (1856), p. 178.

88 Massachusetts Board of Agriculture, *Report* (1856), pp. 176-180.

89 Massachusetts Board of Agriculture, *Report* (1857), p. 249; *American Agriculturist*, XV (1856), 26; *New England Farmer*, VIII (1856), 386-387; *Miner's Rural American*, I (1856), 243; *Country Gentleman*, XI (1858), 175, 206-207. As late as 1869 it was being pointed out that the cost of hay cut by scythe and raked by hand was equal to half its value, while with mowing machines and horse rakes the cost "need not be one fourth." *Rural Affairs*, III (1869), 180.

90 *American Agriculturist*, XV (1856), 2.

91 *Maine Farmer*, July 23, 1857.

92 Massachusetts Board of Agriculture, *Report* (1856), pp. 178-180; (1858), pp. 237-

ever, though some farmers of Norfolk County were among the earliest users, "in more than half of the towns . . . there is not a mowing machine, and there is a common prejudice against its introduction."[93] Evidence of slow acceptance exists in the fact that a year earlier the board had believed it desirable to stimulate interest in mowing machines by offering a premium of $600 to the person cutting not less than fifty acres of grass by a machine moved by horses or oxen.[94] Two years later a mowing contest in Essex County drew numerous spectators who "came miles to learn what kind of things these mowing machines are—some doubting whether they could be worked at all by horse power."[95]

The situation in Connecticut was similar,[96] but in New Hampshire and Vermont acceptance on a significant scale was even slower.[97] Shortly before 1860, local manufacturers appeared to supplement imported supplies,[98] but doubts as to the usefulness and economy of the machine persisted. Widespread adoption did not come until well into the sixties.[99]

The first mowing machine to be successfully used in Maine was a Ketchum, which was employed in 1853 by Seth Storer on his thousand-acre farm near Scarboro.[100] Storer expressed himself highly satisfied but had few immediate imitators,[101] despite the

---

241; (1859), pp. 190-191; *New England Farmer,* VII (1855), 320, 420; XI (1859), 64, 82, 245, 249.

[93] Massachusetts Board of Agriculture, *Report* (1856), pp. 173-174; *American Agriculturist,* XIV (1855), 352.

[94] The following year the Massachusetts Board of Agriculture offered a $1,000 premium for the best mowing machine. The prize went to the Heath machine, manufactured by Ruggles, Nourse, Mason & Co., which did not prove successful. *American Agriculturist,* XV (1856), 165; *Plough, Loom and Anvil,* XI (1858), 663-664.

[95] Massachusetts Board of Agriculture, *Report* (1857), p. 243.

[96] *Homestead,* I (1856), 580; II (1857), 651; *Country Gentleman,* II (1853), 102; *Connecticut Valley Farmer and Mechanic,* II (1854), 53; *New England Farmer,* V (1853), 416; *American Agriculturist,* XIV (1855), 243; Connecticut State Agricultural Society, *Transactions* (1856), p. 93.

[97] *New England Farmer,* IX (1857), 155; *Northern Farmer,* IV (1857), 208-209; *Farmer and Visitor,* VIII (1856), 49.

[98] Russell's Mower was made at Manchester and the New England Mower made at Hinsdale. *New Hampshire Journal of Agriculture,* May 5, 1860; June 9, 1859.

[99] *New Hampshire Journal of Agriculture,* June 9, 30, July 21, 28, Aug. 4, 25, 1860; *New England Farmer,* XII (1860), 374, 487.

[100] *Farmer and Artizan,* II (1853), 130; *Maine Farmer,* Aug. 25, 1853; June 15, 1854. One editor, who was a strong advocate of experimental use of mowers, did not see one of them in operation until 1855. *Maine Farmer,* July 12, 1855; see also *Wisconsin Farmer,* IX (1857), 260.

[101] Maine Board of Agriculture, *Report* (1855), pp. 16, 25, 120-124; (1856), pp. 70-75; *Maine Farmer,* May 15, July 3, 1856.

urgings of the editor of the *Maine Farmer* that most old farms could be adapted to use of the machine with little extra land preparation and that it would solve the labor problem at harvest. In 1856 this periodical observed that "mowing machines have been tried in Maine, but cannot be said to be fully introduced among us." However, three years later about fifty mowers were introduced into northern Somerset County,[102] evidence that the machines were rapidly becoming a standard item in Maine farming.

Adoption in the West. While interest in the harvester was matched elsewhere, in no other region did adoption of the harvester take place as quickly as in central Ohio, the Indiana-Michigan prairie openings, northern Illinois, and southern Wisconsin. These were all primarily wheat areas, with many farmers holding suitable acreages in excess of those they could harvest with available labor supplies. Moreover, the concept of mechanical reaping was well established. Southern Ohio was the scene of Hussey's development and successful trial in 1833 of the machine he patented. McCormick in 1844 shipped a few of his machines from Virginia to the West and demonstrated them on a tour that took him from the Genesee Valley of New York through southern Michigan, southeastern Wisconsin, northern Illinois, and eastern Missouri. There were also independent inventive efforts in the West, resulting in the development of a practical header.[103] Headers found some use, but widespread adoption was frustrated by lack of techniques for handling the high moisture content of wheat so harvested.

Although both Hussey and McCormick sought to exploit their patents and to establish sources of supply of their machines by licensing local manufacturers, prior to 1845 only a few machines

102 *Maine Farmer,* July 14, 1853; May 1, 1856; July 1, 1859; June 30, 1860; Maine Board of Agriculture, *Report* (1860), p. 25.

103 Experimentation with headers persisted, and they found a number of users among the large wheat-growers on the Indiana-Michigan prairies, fewer in Illinois, Wisconsin, and Iowa. Some of the machines operated satisfactorily, but they did not become established because of difficulties in handling the grain. Since the grain was not dried in the field, its moisture content was high, and as a consequence tended to be salable only at a discount. Illinois State Agricultural Society, *Transactions,* I (1862), 11; *Prairie Farmer,* XV (1855), 225; XXV (1862), 258. See also Joseph Schafer, "Hiram Moore, Michigan-Wisconsin Inventor," *Wisconsin Magazine of History,* XV (1931), 234-243; Mentor L. Williams, "Cooper Lyon and the Moore-Hascall Harvesting Machine," *Michigan History,* XXXI (1947), 26-34; F. Hal Higgins, "John M. Horner and the Development of the Combine Harvester," *Agricultural History,* XXXII (1958), 14-24.

were made in Ohio and the West under such arrangements.[104] Renewed efforts by Hussey to make licensing arrangements about that date were successful only in Ohio. A Chicago partnership with J. S. Wright, editor of the *Prairie Farmer,* was terminated in 1852 with few machines produced. The Hussey reaper was never available in significant numbers to prairie farmers, though a number of manufacturers undertook to supply Hussey-type machines, the Atkins being one of the more successful.[105] McCormick also made efforts to establish licensing arrangements, with similarly unsatisfactory results.[106] However, while Hussey remained in Baltimore, McCormick established himself in Chicago where, after terminating all licenses, he undertook manufacture of his machine in his own plant and aggressively promoted its sale.

After 1850 other manufacturers brought out machines, some of which for one reason or another were found superior to McCormick's. The importance of grass in farming tended to be inverse to that of wheat; hence, farmers who did not cultivate enough wheat to have a strong interest in McCormick's machine might nevertheless be attracted to an implement that was a good mower, particularly one that was also a satisfactory reaper. Ketchum's mower found purchasers in Illinois, as did other mowing machines,[107] but the combinations had greater appeal. Many appeared, but none were more important than the machines of J. H. Manny. Presented as the first successful dual-purpose machine, it almost immediately proved attractive to farmers. By 1853 Manny's production in Illinois equaled McCormick's, and from that time onward his machine played an important role both in the East and the West.

Beginning in 1847 in Ohio, the firm of Monturn and Allen of Champaign County, north of Springfield, made Husseys of good

[104] *Prairie Farmer,* V (1845), 258; VI (1846), 69, 103; *Ohio Cultivator,* I (1845), 40. At least one Hussey was in use in Iowa in 1846. *Prairie Farmer,* VI (1846), 285; see also IX (1849), 214, 216; *Genesee Farmer,* XI (1850), 173.

[105] Edward Stabler, *A Brief Narrative of the Invention of Reaping Machines; and an Examination of the Claims for Priority of Invention* (Chicago, 1897), pp. 3-47; Hutchinson, *Cyrus Hall McCormick: Seed-Time,* p. 326; *Prairie Farmer,* X (1850), 146; XII (1852), 305.

[106] Hutchinson, *Cyrus Hall McCormick: Seed-Time,* p. 213.

[107] *Prairie Farmer,* XV (1855), 151. Marsh's harvester, built at Geneva, Kane County was one of many that acquired local reputations. *Prairie Farmer,* XIII (1853), 399; XIV (1854), 321; XV (1855), 151.

quality at a rate of twenty-five to fifty per year.[108] The farmers of the area promptly became leaders in experimentation and adoption of the reaper. By 1850 "a great many reaping machines were used in the county," chiefly Husseys.[109]

Meanwhile, from 1844 through 1847, McCormick reapers were manufactured in Cincinnati by a licensee. The machines so produced were poor in quality and performance and early acquired an unfavorable reputation.[110] By 1850, however, the machines were coming into use in the surrounding area, and other machines were appearing on the market, particularly in the area around Canton.[111]

Acceptance elsewhere in Ohio was erratic during the early fifties. In the area about Columbus by 1854 reapers were "on almost every farm," and they were being rapidly introduced around Youngstown.[112] However, in the northwestern part of the state, where reapers manufactured in Chicago or Brockport were readily available, adoption was slow.[113] In 1854 in the area west of Toledo the scythe was still the standard harvesting tool.[114] In 1855 a traveler in the area between Zanesville and Columbus reported a heavy loss of wheat due to "lack of hands to cut and secure the crops in due season," and pointed out that reapers were almost unknown.[115] Nevertheless, reapers and mowers were being tried by farmers scattered about the state. The results were such that by 1857, 10,000 machines were claimed to be in use—enough, if properly distributed, to cut most of the wheat grown in the state. Two years later the number of machines owned by Ohio's farmers had increased to an estimated 18,000.[116]

---

108 Hutchinson, *Cyrus Hall McCormick: Seed-Time*, p. 200; *Ohio Cultivator*, VI (1850), 216; U. S. Patent Office, *Report* (1850), p. 397.

109 *Ohio Cultivator*, V (1849), 2, 70, 214, 217; VI (1850), 216, 227, 243, 315; XII (1856), 231; U. S. Patent Office, *Report* (1850), p. 397; *Scientific American*, III (1847), 266.

110 Hutchinson, *Cyrus Hall McCormick: Harvest*, pp. 220-221; 232.

111 Other areas of use were Miami, Preble, Butler, Stark, and Warren Counties. Ohio State Board of Agriculture, *Report* (1851), pp. 245, 377, 418, 437, 442, 476; *Cultivator*, VII (1850), 308.

112 Ohio State Board of Agriculture, *Report* (1854), pp. 106, 127, 134.

113 *Ohio Cultivator*, VI (1850), 26. Seymour & Morgan sold much of its early production of McCormick reapers in the Great Lakes ports.

114 *American Agriculturist*, XII (1854), 297. See also *American Farmer*, XI (1855), 106; Ohio State Board of Agriculture, *Report* (1854), p. 162.

115 Ohio State Board of Agriculture, *Report* (1853), pp. 160, 93; (1854), p. 106; (1855), pp. 160, 214; (1857), pp. 510-514; (1859), pp. 526 ff.

116 Ohio State Board of Agriculture, *Report* (1859), p. 535.

When in 1846 and again in 1847, Illinois farmers purchased all the machines McCormick had to offer, they gave the mechanical reaper its warmest reception up to that time. In place of the cautious curiosity, rarely reaching the point of purchase, McCormick had found elsewhere, here was a willingness to purchase on minimal evidence.

In 1846, McCormick readily sold in Chicago about 90 reapers manufactured by his Brockport, New York, licensee. The following year another 250 of the Seymour, Chappel & Company machines were sold in Chicago, plus 100 made by a Chicago licensee.[117] These sales were chiefly to farmers in the three counties immediately west and southwest of the city. That area in 1848 represented the most concentrated acceptance of the reaper in the nation. Conditions were especially favorable in that wheat prices were attractive and many farmers held land suitable for wheat far in excess of what they could harvest by the cradle.

Within a few years the machine could be found in every section of Illinois, although acceptance in quantity tended to be concentrated.[118] Almost all those sold by McCormick in 1846 and 1847 were disposed of to farmers in three counties—DuPage, Kendall, and LaSalle—lying to the west and southwest of Chicago. Up through 1857 almost two-thirds of the 7,000 machines sold by McCormick in Illinois went to farmers in a fourth of the state's counties, chiefly in the northern, north-central, and west-central areas. The pattern of adoption as revealed by McCormick sales differed widely.[119] In counties such as DuPage and McHenry, a

---

[117] Ohio State Board of Agriculture, *Report* (1859), pp. 234, 243.

[118] The farmers of southern Illinois were slow to accept the reaper. They had the opportunity, however, to become familiar with it, since one farmer of Egypt purchased three Husseys in Chicago—for himself and two neighbors. He reported that "they did tolerably well. We would not part with them unless we could obtain better machines. With four horses they could cut from eight to twelve acres in a day's time and cut the grain very clean." *Prairie Farmer*, XI (1851), 266. See also XIII (1853), 414; Hutchinson, *Cyrus Hall McCormick: Seed-Time*, p. 234.

[119] Note the differences in McCormick sales in selected counties:

County	1849	1856	1857	1849-1957
Bureau	13	95	126	312
La Salle	8	33	97	163
Macoupin	2	108	59	213
Du Page	46	—	—	70
McHenry	51	14	7	87

Data from Hutchinson, *Cyrus Hall McCormick: Seed-Time*, facing p. 468.

high degree of acceptance occurred within a year or two, virtually eliminating the cradle, with demand for machines limited to improved types.[120] In other counties a delay of roughly five years occurred between the first purchase of a machine and its widespread acceptance in a county. Elsewhere acceptance was longer delayed, owing in part to a noncommercial attitude toward farming.[121]

Rapidity of adoption of the reaper elsewhere in the West depended primarily upon the importance of wheat as a market product. In his promotional tour of 1844, McCormick demonstrated and sold one of his reapers in Monroe County in southern Michigan.[122] A few Cincinnati-built machines were purchased in Indiana as early as 1845.[123] As the machines became available in significant quantities, the wheat farmers on the open prairies dotting northern Indiana and southern Michigan adopted the machines as readily as did the farmers of northern Illinois. By 1850 McCormicks were common in this grain-producing area, as evidenced when the editor of the *Michigan Farmer* observed twenty McCormicks in use on the forty square miles of Terracopia Prairie in St. Joseph County.[124] In adjoining La Porte County in 1854, "the crops were secured principally by machinery," and while "reapers of a great variety of patterns were employed, that most extensively used was the product of a local patentor and manufacturer."[125]

---

[120] In 1854, when McHenry County farmers had purchased fifty-six McCormicks and possibly some other makes, "nearly all our harvesting is done by machinery, the grain being secured in shocks and threshed in the field." U. S. Patent Office, *Report* (1854), p. 139; *Prairie Farmer*, XI (1851), 410.

[121] Both the Hussey and McCormick reapers were in use in Bond County by 1850 but aroused little interest, the majority of the farmers being described as viewing deep plowing and "the use of machinery . . . as an innovation, while they pursue their old course, and manage to raise corn enough to do them." U. S. Patent Office, *Report* (1850), p. 198.

[122] A Hussey was in use on Prairie Ronde in southeastern Michigan by 1847. *Prairie Farmer*, XIV (1854), 83.

[123] Hutchinson, *Cyrus Hall McCormick: Seed-Time*, pp. 211, 233.

[124] The editor continued: "John Reynolds, Esq., who with his brother owns a farm upon the prairie, embracing twenty-two hundred acres, said to us that he had harvested forty-five acres in two days . . . and that he averaged generally about 15 acres per day. The cost per acre is about 80 cents, and that of harvesting with the cradle about $1.18, the difference being about three shillings per acre. And then it is estimated that this machine will pick up the crinkled grain enough cleaner than the cradle, to make a further difference of fifty cents per acre, which, added to the other will about pay the entire expense of harvesting." *Michigan Farmer*, VIII (1850), 226; see also 269; *Ohio Cultivator*, VI (1850), 298; U. S. Patent Office, *Report* (1851), p. 435; (1852), p. 288; *Valley Farmer*, V (1853), 352.

[125] Indiana State Board of Agriculture, *Report* (1854-1855), p. 82.

Elsewhere the reaper or mower was adopted most readily in areas enjoying advantages of transportation to markets for either wheat or hay, as was the case along the Wabash and Ohio rivers in Indiana as well as Marion, Wayne, and Scott Counties.[126] Although stumpy and rough ground delayed utilization of the machines, increasing accessibility to markets together with a shortage of harvest labor induced many farmers to prepare their fields for using the machines. In both Michigan and Indiana widespread acceptance occurred toward the end of the fifties.[127]

Because wheat was of major importance in the development of farming in Wisconsin, the reaper received an initial reception in that state virtually as enthusiastic as that received across the border in Illinois. McCormick claimed the sale of 190 of his machines in southern Wisconsin in early 1849.[128] In 1853 the editor of the *Prairie Farmer* found that the reaper was "mostly employed" in harvesting wheat on the level prairies of the state, although the cradle continued in use on rough ground, such as that near the lake shore.[129] By then mowers were also in wide use. A rough estimate placed purchases of harvesters within the state in 1856 at 2,000, half of them Mannys.[130]

Settlement of the territories of Iowa and Minnesota was gaining momentum as the reaper came into use farther East. With an abundance of smooth and fertile land, the new farms needed no major adjustments to adapt to the reaper. The editor of the *Ohio Cultivator*, after a trip through Iowa in 1849, reported, "A large proportion of the farmers are men of intelligence and of some pecuniary ability, who have become familiar with the means of improvement which are in successful operation in other States; hence we find

---

[126] U. S. Patent Office, *Report* (1851), p. 435; (1852), pp. 288, 290; *Valley Farmer*, V (1853), 352; Indiana State Board of Agriculture, *Report* (1853), p. 163. In Warren County, mowers were introduced between 1850 and 1852, wheat culture being abandoned for corn on the prairies, while in the timbered sections wheat was considered "a poorly remunerating crop owing to the high price of labor and the inability to use the reaper in fields not yet clear of stumps."

[127] *Indiana Farmer*, VII (1858-1859), 338; Indiana State Board of Agriculture, *Report* (1856), pp. 188, 241; see also II (1852), 156; *Ohio Cultivator*, XIII (1857), 244; U. S. Patent Office, *Report* (1852), p. 304; *Michigan Farmer*, XII (1854), 271; XIV (1856), 263; XV (1857), 300; *Genesee Farmer*, XIX (1858), 183; Michigan Board of Agriculture, *Report* (1863), p. 237.

[128] *Genesee Farmer*, XI (1850), 173.

[129] *Prairie Farmer*, XIV (1853), 284-285. See also *Cultivator*, VIII (1851), 82-83.

[130] *Wisconsin Farmer*, VIII (1856), 423.

already the most improved kinds of implements and machinery introduced there, such as steel plows, seed drills, rollers, mowing and reaping machines, etc."[131] By then "the introduction of a large number of machines (McCormick's, Hussey's, and others) enabled the farmers to complete their work in an unusually short span of time.[132] Indeed, but for these machines, great delay and probably much loss would have taken place owing to the large amount of grain to be cut and the scarcity of hands."[133] The machines were in wide use throughout the state by 1857, with mass adoption following in the next decade.[134] Much the same was true in Minnesota. In the Plainview area, which saw its first settler in 1855, "nine self-raking reapers were received at the river at once" in 1859, "to fill orders from this and one adjoining town, and several others have been received since, and without which the harvesting could not have been done."[135] About 1,000 reapers were purchased by Minnesota farmers in 1860, marking the start of universal adoption.[136]

OTHER IMPLEMENTS

There were other implements that cost-conscious farmers found useful.[137] Corn shellers were on the market before 1850, mostly of the hand-operated type, though large horse-powered forms found limited use, particularly in the West on farms selling the grain. Feed cutters were well known in the East in the forties and reached the West during the fifties.[138] Hand- and horse-operated mills for grinding feed grains had long been known but came into wider use

---

[131] *Iowa Farmer*, I (1853), 90.

[132] A few Husseys were sold in Iowa in 1849. *Prairie Farmer*, IX (1849), 214, 216; *Genesee Farmer*, XI (1850), 173. McCormick licensed a manufacturer in Iowa in 1845, but no machines were produced. By 1849, McCormick salesmen were covering the settled part of the state. Hutchinson, *Cyrus Hall McCormick: Seed-Time*, pp. 65, 69, 320.

[133] *Ohio Cultivator*, V (1849), 298. See also *Iowa Farmer*, IV (1856), 59, 122, 319. In reply to a query, one Iowa farmer reported that McCormick's reaper worked cleaner and better "than any other way I know of on wheat sown on ground on which cornstalks had been left standing." *Prairie Farmer*, IX (1849), 378; see also X (1850), 294.

[134] Iowa State Agricultural Society, *Report* (1857), p. 170; (1858), pp. 217 ff; (1863), pp. 344 ff; (1865), pp. 417 ff; (1866), pp. 357 ff.

[135] *Ohio Farmer*, VIII (1859), 289.

[136] *Minnesota Farmer and Gardener*, I (1860), 267.

[137] A survey is in R. L. Allen, "Advancement in Agricultural Machinery within the Present Century," U. S. Agricultural Society, *Journal*, II (1854), 91-100.

[138] Jay B. Brownlee and Leon W. Chase, *Farm Machinery and Farm Motors* (New York, 1908), p. 187.

in the mid-fifties. Hay-baling presses were similarly known prior to 1850, but afterwards became available in standardized forms from agricultural implement manufacturers. The increasing demand for hay in the cities stimulated their adoption.[139] Horse-powered hay- and straw-stacking equipment was also acquiring users.[140] All these articles supplemented and extended the gains in productivity provided by the basic implements, but their significance prior to 1870 is difficult to assess.

Change in the techniques of farming, in terms of implements, was a highly complex process, to which the inventor, the manufacturer, the innovating farmer, and his imitators, each made indispensable contributions. The farmer who experimented with an invention possessed marked innovating characteristics himself—investing time, energy, and capital, besides accepting the uncertainty of a device of usually crude design and construction and of doubtful utility or economy. The interaction between innovator and manufacturer was of great significance, with the innovator supplying leadership to those who shared his faith in the possibility of improvement upon the familiar. The imitator, though less aggressive and less imaginative than the innovator, nevertheless assumed risks in the hope that the device might immediately or in time be of advantage to him.

By 1860 the application of horse power to many farm tasks and utilization of the new agricultural implements had been thoroughly established as the superior farming system. In the West, the man-land ratio necessary for profitable use of the system was readily available. In the East, adjustments were somewhat slower, since changes occurring in objectives required changes in land use. The rapidity of diffusion now depended principally on the attractiveness of market prices for crop alternatives. The 1860's were a period of rapid diffusion, stimulated by the attractive prices of the war period, and perhaps influenced by the shortage of labor attendant upon the war service of a large proportion of farm youth.

[139] *Prairie Farmer,* VIII (1848), 335; *American Agriculturist,* XVI (1857), 153; XIX (1860), 94.

[140] *Rural New Yorker,* XII (1861), 93, 278; *Working Farmer,* XIV (1862), 12; XV (1863), 157; XXII (1870), 179; Solon Robinson, *Facts for Farmers* (New York, 1865), p. 774.

CHAPTER TEN

UTILIZATION OF THE SOIL

 Over this period the application of fertility-maintaining practices as a farming routine was characteristic of progressive farmers, imitated only slowly by the large majority, many of whom persisted in the traditional practices long after they had clearly lost any justification from a cost-profit point of view.[1] Long-continued cropping resulted in declines in productivity under semisubsistence as well as under market conditions, but reactions differed. Although some diversity was inherent in a cropping program controlled by family needs, eventual reductions in fertility were inevitable. The farmer's reaction might be to bring new lands into use if they were available, to accept smaller crops, or to emigrate. In farming for market, locational factors were sufficiently important to encourage many farmers to adopt the simple procedures that would aid in maintaining or rebuilding the fertility of their soils.

The approach to soil utilization pursued by the majority of farmers was a product of the circumstances in which early settlers had found themselves.[2] The known fertility-maintaining practices had been almost completely discarded early in the process of farm-making as neither necessary nor practical. They were unnecessary since the soils yielded a satisfactory product for some years without such effort. They were impractical because it was typical in the early years of farm-making that the available labor was fully occupied to more immediate advantage with the numerous tasks of the frontier homestead, specifically including the clearing of new land. Furthermore, all the tillable land available, even that yielding only

---

[1] A correspondent, discussing the use made of the numerous "old fields" in Massachusetts, pointed out: "the common practice is to sow rye once in three years; fallow plowing in June and again plowing and sowing early in September. No grass seed is sown, nor is it expected the ground will produce anything during the two intervening years." This practice, he held, "impoverishes both the soil and the tiller." *New England Farmer,* V (1853), 426.

[2] *Cincinnnatus,* I (1856), 7-8.

a small return, was needed in crops to maintain the production of the farm. The general paucity of animals on new farms also meant a scarcity of fertilizing materials, while the labor necessary for their effective utilization was required for other tasks. The maximum returns desired were obtained by cultivating with a minimum of labor the largest possible acreage planted in the most immediately valuable crops. When both corn and wheat were equally valuable, they were alternated, not as a soil conservation measure, but because labor was thereby economized. The wheat was sown in the standing corn, which saved one plowing task in each two-year sequence.[3]

Inevitably the yield of fields so tilled declined, sometimes rapidly, sometimes very slowly.[4] Most farms were established with acreages that required many years to bring into cultivation, and as long as virgin land remained available, the breaking of new land was the reaction to declining fertility. Fields so reduced in fertility that they no longer returned a worthwhile quantity of product were allowed to lie fallow for some years or were turned into pasture, frequently without being seeded.[5] While a number of years and perhaps a generation were required to clear the land held within a farm in forested areas, declines in productivity on the shallow upland soils of the East were sometimes so rapid that the rate at which new land could be brought into cultivation could barely sustain the total product of the farm.

In most areas, fertility declined slowly, and evidence of reduced productivity was easily missed or misunderstood in the normal vagaries of farming.[6] Disappointing crops were readily blamed upon unfavorable weather, insect damage, and other uncontrollable

[3] *New Jersey Farmer,* III (1857), 8-9.

[4] "We have more land than we can till, and when one department of one field becomes exhausted and worn out by a succession of crops, we generally prefer 'turning it out to pasture'—the ordinary system adopted by most cultivators—and commence the same system of cropping on another section." *Germantown Telegraph,* Sept. 3, 1851.

[5] Connecticut State Agricultural Society, *Transactions* (1854), pp. 20-22.

[6] "The first business of clearing new farms, is almost necessarily exhausting; because a virgin soil seldom receives manures, and because the farmer has but little leisure to apply them, or room to alternate his crops. Necessity is then the supreme law; but it does not continue to be so after the farm is cleared up and well stocked. Yet the pioneer habit becomes so established by usage, as to be persisted in long after the necessity of the practice of it has ceased. The deterioration is so imperceptible to the cultivator, and his reasoning upon the matter so superficial that his farm becomes worn out before he is aware of it, or thinks of adopting means of renovating its fertility. In this way, most of the lands upon the seaboard and in the old settled states were impoverished." *Cultivator,* IV (1837), 141. See also *Maine Farmer,* Feb. 19, 1857.

influences. Usually the routines were continued until the evidence of reduced fertility had accumulated unmistakably. By then it was frequently too late for economic adoption of techniques that, applied earlier, might have maintained fertility at little cost. The utilization of depleted fields for pasture or mowing was almost universal, but was generally an unsatisfactory solution. Grass was difficult to establish on impoverished land.[7] Moreover, as usually managed, these pastures and meadows likewise suffered from slow but significant declines in productivity.[8] The crisis thus ultimately presented might have been prevented had available techniques been applied. Foresight was necessary, but hardly difficult, since the experience of slightly older regions was well known. The consequences of depleted fertility was a part of the experience of most farmers. Agricultural journals were filled with accounts of the ominous effects of soil exploitation and with suggestions regarding its avoidance. Though there were important exceptions, most farmers, once established in a routine of cultivation, continued it unchanged throughout their careers. Among those who did attempt to apply fertility conservation and renovating techniques, many found returns inadequate, so that they too joined the search for new lands. There, despite their experiences, they renewed the exploitative approach.[9]

Everywhere behind the frontier of settlement land lay shorn of its productivity. Significant declines in the yield of the staples—corn and wheat—tended to appear within a decade or so of settlement on

[7] *Boston Cultivator,* July 26, 1851.

[8] Note the observations of three New Hampshire farmers regarding the effects of bad management: "pastures cannot sustain half the stock they could thirty years ago." "Our ability to grow stock has diminished greatly in the last thirty years, and consequently a smaller amount of manure and a less crop, the next less stock, and so on." "If the pastures held their own from year to year, it would be much easier rejuvenating the plowlands. But the amount of stock on them must be reduced equal to one fourth every twenty years, if not more." *Cultivator,* VII (1859), 82; *New Hampshire Journal of Agriculture,* Sept. 15, 1860; Feb. 5, 1859. See also *Maine Farmer,* Jan. 8, June 25, 1857.

[9] J. J. Mapes reported, "Ohio no longer surprises the seaboard farmers by large crops, and the same course of cropping, and modes of tillage, which have impoverished the land of the older states, are daily producing similar results in the far West. Many farmers are still living and carting manures upon their poor farms, who in the Mohawk and Genesee vallies threw their manures into the river when younger . . . the same practices are now followed in the Wabash valley, and the tributaries of the Mississippi, and other rivers, are suffered to drain the very essence of our future prosperity and to convey it to the ocean." *Working Farmer,* II (1850), 271. Cf. *American Agriculturist,* X (1851), 75; *Genesee Farmer,* XVI (1855), 333-334.

the poorer lands, within twenty years on richer lands, although some bottom lands seemed inexhaustible. By 1800 the depletion of fertility was characteristic of all the cultivated regions along the coast, with marked declines in crops noted in the fertile Connecticut and Mohawk valleys.[10] Reduced fertility was perhaps most serious and certainly most apparent in Delaware and Maryland. The practice of turning fields abandoned for tillage into pasture was somewhat more successful North than South, although returns were low, and the decline in fertility by no means eliminated by the practice.

Thousands then turned to the West, where they continued the familiar exploitative routines. Such methods soon exposed the notion of inexhaustibility as a myth, in some cases within a decade and at most within a generation. By the 1840's, declines in productivity were serious in many parts of Ohio, and it was predicted that the state would soon resemble "the sterility of the tobacco sands of the Eastern shore."[11] In the next decade the problem of declining yields and worn-out lands attracted comment in every western state.[12] In Iowa a few farmers were observing the signs of depletion before 1860.[13]

The techniques required to meet the problem were well known from European, particularly English, experience. These were given abundant publicity in the agricultural press and at the meetings of the agricultural societies. Firsthand knowledge was brought by

[10] An excellent survey is in William Stickland, *Observations on the Agriculture of the United States of America* (London, 1815).

[11] *Cultivator,* VI (1849), 28. See also *Ohio Farmer,* VIII (1859), 105. Lewis C. Gray states, "By 1850 a large proportion of Virginia and Maryland east of the Blue Ridge was a waste of old fields and abandoned lands covered with under-brush and young cedars." Gray, *History of Agriculture in the Southern United States to 1860* (Carnegie Institution of Washington, 1933), p. 910. See also Avery O. Craven, *Soil Exhaustion as a Factor in the Agricultural History of Virginia and Maryland, 1606-1860,* University of Illinois Studies in the Social Sciences, XIII (1925).

[12] In Michigan the effect of alternating wheat with corn "is such that land which has not been more than twelve years cleared from its primitive forest has, if not run out, become at least thoroughly run down." *Cultivator,* V (1848), 121. According to another report, "nine-tenths of Wisconsin farms are being skinned as rapidly as sharp knives and folly can do it." *Wisconsin Farmer,* IX (1857), 381. See also *Ohio Cultivator,* V (1849), 71.

[13] An Iowa farmer estimated that twenty years of cultivation "have reduced the average yield of crops by one-third to one-half." *Prairie Farmer,* XI (1851), 579. See also *Cultivator,* VII (1850), 369; *Indiana Farmer,* II (1852), 208; *Wisconsin Farmer and Iowa Farmer and Northwest Cultivator,* II (1850), 214-215; *Rural New Yorker,* XVI (1865), 110; *Homestead,* IV (1858), 129; *Genesee Farmer,* XVI (1855), 333-334.

recent immigrants from Europe. However, the shift from a frontier to a permanent point of view toward soil use lacked the drama associated with clearing the forest and breaking prairie sod. Those who chose to change their attitudes and methods rather than their locations, who purchased the worn-out lands left behind by the migrant to the West and sought to establish permanent, remunerative farming on such soils, were pioneers in a less publicized but no less important area of activity.

About 1800, a few farmers in eastern Pennsylvania, southern New York, and eastern Massachusetts were undertaking soil use programs based upon English practices as a solution to the serious depletion of their soils. Substantial successes were experienced, and the new approach found ardent advocates among virtually all those who had a concept of progressive agriculture. The new system was described by Jesse Buel as consisting of "draining, manuring, alternating crops, the culture of roots and artificial grasses, the substitution of fallow crops for naked fallows, the application of lime, marl, and other earthy matters to improve the mechanical condition and the fertility of the soil, and the blending of tillage and grass husbandry—of cattle and grain."[14]

Of the components Buel lists in the new system, the most important were the use of manures, the cultivation of domesticated grasses, and the adoption of rotations, including the planting of clover. Open ditch draining of swampy areas and wet meadows became common in New England after 1830 and in the West somewhat later.[15] The underdraining of cultivated soils to improve their productivity had some earnest advocates but was too expensive to find much application.[16] The cultivation of roots on any significant scale was rejected everywhere except in New England because corn was a far more certain and profitable crop, requiring less labor for larger returns, while the fact that it was a hoed crop, like roots,

[14] *Cultivator*, IV (1837), 141.

[15] *Boston Cultivator*, April 13, 1850; U. S. Patent Office, *Report* (1855), p. 128; *Rural New Yorker*, III (1852), 138; *Homestead*, 1850 issues. On such drainage in the West, see *Ohio Cultivator*, XIII (1857), 90.

[16] The principal promoter of tile drainage was John Johnston of Geneva, New York. Under his leadership "almost every county in western New York is now doing more or less at tile drainage." *Ohio Cultivator*, IX (1853), 3-4. See *Homestead*, II (1856), 169; New York State Agricultural Society, *Transactions*, XV (1855), 258.

served the purpose of clearing the land of weeds.[17] Buel does not mention deeper and subsoil plowing, which received a great deal of attention as a method of increasing soil productivity after suitable plows had become available.[18]

By the 1820's, elements of the new system had formed the basis of a permanent, fertility-maintaining agriculture in certain areas, such as those centering about Chester County, Pennsylvania, Dutchess County, New York, and Suffolk County, Massachusetts. As applied in those areas, it consisted of the conservation and careful use of animal manures and a rotation of crops centering on red clover, the growth of this plant being made possible and profitable by applications of lime and sometimes gypsum to the soil.

From these areas the techniques spread, following the westward movement of the frontier by a generation or so. However, adoption was scattered and selective, and throughout the period the techniques were restricted to progressive farming. In 1850, for example: "of the 12,000,000 acres of improved land in the State of New York, 1,000,000 are so cultivated as to become richer from year to year—being in the hands of 40,000 farmers who read agricultural journals and nobly sustain the state and county societies of that commonwealth. 3,000,000 acres barely sustain their fertility and are cultivated by a class of farmers who read not, but do their best to follow the practices of the best. 8,000,000 acres are in the hands of 300,000 cultivators who follow the old practices of exhausting the soil."[19] Support for this estimate comes from the fact that in New York total crops did not increase comparably with the rise in improved acreages. Although 700,000 acres were added to that state's improved farm lands between 1850 and 1855, the census returns of crops showed no increase between these two dates.[20]

---

[17] U. S. Patent Office, *Report* (1861), p. 263. The importance of rutabagas, turnips, and carrots for cattle food increased in most New England states after the failures of the potato crops. In 1855 root crops exceeded wheat in acreage in Massachusetts. U. S. Patent Office, *Report* (1850), pp. 378, 386; (1851), p. 658, (1855), pp. 140-149; Maine Board of Agriculture, *Report* (1856), p. 102.

[18] See, e.g., *New York Farmer*, II (1829), 54; Pennsylvania Agricultural Society, *Memoirs* (1824), p. 225; *American Agriculturist*, XII (1854), 20.

[19] U. S. Patent Office, *Report* (1852), pp. 7-9; (1860), 14-21. See also *Country Gentleman*, II (1853), 38; *Working Farmer*, V (1854), 159.

[20] American Institute, *Reports* (1856), p. 426. Although comparisons of census data are inconclusive, in this case there is considerable supporting evidence of declines in productivity.

ESCAPE AND REPEAT

Once depletion was far advanced, not only was a substantially different approach to soil use required, but also a different type of management, a longer time perspective, and an investment of capital and labor that would yield relatively low returns, at least for a few years. Usually the necessary renovation was accomplished by establishing and then plowing under a stand of clover and grasses. Such a stand was frequently obtained only after purchasing and spreading lime and plaster; it also required both the purchase of the seed and the labor of preparing the seedbed and plowing under the sod. The process required several years to restore a measure of fertility. Once achieved, the maintenance of a higher level of fertility required a permanently higher application of labor and capital per acre.[21] Although returns could be increased, there always existed uncertainty as to whether the labor and capital applied would be adequately remunerated. Many farmers succeeded in gradually converting their routines from the old to the new methods, but many others were unwilling to make the change. Even among those who did attempt to apply fertility-conserving and renovating techniques, many found the returns inadequate and joined the movement to the West.

Resort to new lands was the popular solution to the problem of maintaining farm production; migration to the West to establish new farms was the drastic solution. While highly significant and dramatic, such migration was an escape from problems that had emerged from, but could not be overcome by, established habits of work and thought. For many, migration took place only when the failure of their techniques could no longer be ignored; characteristically it was "the old story . . . of the skinning system—little manure on much land—small crops growing smaller by degrees and beautifully less—an empty purse, and emigration."[22] Geographic mobility served as a cover for mental inadaptability.

UTILIZATION OF THE KNOWN TECHNOLOGY

Farm Materials. In the earliest stages of soil use, manures were everywhere almost completely neglected as a factor in crop cultiva-

---

[21] For an analysis, see *New Jersey Farmer*, III (1857), 8-9.
[22] *American Agriculturist*, XVI (1857), 163.

tion.[23] Supplies of manure were usually small since livestock were few and rarely housed. As animals increased in number, accumulations of manure came to be considered a nuisance rather than as materials of value in maintaining soil fertility. Considerable ingenuity was frequently displayed in arranging for the cheapest possible disposal of the animal wastes that amassed in barns and barnyards. Barns and sheds were sometimes removed as a less expensive procedure than transporting the accumulations of years. Sometimes barns were built over streams and gullies or on slopes so as to achieve easy disposal of animal wastes. When there was no other way, the material was disposed of in the cheapest rather than the most effective way: on the nearest field if that was the least laborious; or into ditches, roads, or streams.[24] Straw, which had come to be highly valued in the East as animal bedding and then as manure, long continued to be burned in the West. It was estimated that in the fifties, "manures worth more than one hundred million dollars are annually thrown away in the United States."[25]

This attitude was characteristic of land use in the farm-making and early farming stages throughout the northern states. It characterized Eastern farming prior to 1800, perhaps longer. Thereafter a change took place, at least among the more progressive farmers. By 1820, in areas such as southeastern Pennsylvania, southern New York, and eastern Massachusetts, farm supplies of manure were recognized for their value in maintaining soil productivity and were considered essential for use on corn lands or pastures. By the fifties in the older sections of New England and the Middle Atlantic states the attitude toward animal manures was one of complaint about their insufficiency.[26] Not only were readily available supplies put to careful use, but in succeeding years interest developed in techniques designed to increase on-the-farm supplies as well as off-farm sources of fertilizing materials.

To increase such supplies, progressive farmers in these areas were

[23] *American Farmer*, VIII (1826), 122; X (1828), 66, 114; *New England Farmer*, III (1825), 100; Henry Colman, *Agriculture of Massachusetts, Report*, II (1838), 80; IV (1841), 131.

[24] U. S. Patent Office, *Report* (1852), p. 198; (1851), 404; *Working Farmer*, XI (1859), 232; *Illinois Farmer*, V (1860), 204; Michigan State Board of Agriculture, *Report* (1864), p. 35.

[25] *Plough, Loom and Anvil*, V (1852-1853), 304.

[26] U. S. Agricultural Society, *Journal*, I (1852), 129; *Maine Farmer*, Feb. 19, 1857; *New Hampshire Journal of Agriculture*, Mar. 24, May 12, 1859.

by the 1840's building barns with cellars to store manure without loss, and in some cases old barns were fitted with such cellars, it being thought that up to 50 percent of the value of the manure might thus be saved.[27] Some farmers close to towns or cities undertook the considerable task and expense of purchasing and hauling manure from livery stables and similar sources. Others went to the trouble and cost of supplementing supplies by making composts of manure, muck, straw, and cornstalks, to which were sometimes added fish and seaweed.[28] Methods of making composts from various materials were offered prize awards at fairs and were commonly discussed at meetings of agricultural societies.

By 1850 there were few places east of the Alleghenies and north of Virginia, except for the Maine frontier,[29] where animal manures were not spread on cultivated lands in a rational manner, with even the most negligent farmers removing accumulated manures to the fields at a favorable opportunity. For New England farmers, handicapped by intrinsically poor soils that had now been shorn of their virgin productivity, manures were essential. "Without it we can do nothing, with it we can succeed in raising fine crops by careful attention."[30] So important were manures considered in this region that the prominent agriculturist R. T. Pell remarked in reference to cattle raising that the "daily product of manure is of as much importance to the farmer as the yield of milk."[31]

The farmer who moved West to escape the problems confronting him in the East did not seek to prevent these same difficulties from reappearing but instead renewed the familiar exploitative routines or, if he had been forced to make some changes in his eastern farming, reverted to the routine of unremitting cropping, ignoring the needs of the soil. In western New York, Pennsylvania, Ohio, and Indiana in the 1840's, as in the East a generation earlier, attention was principally directed to disposing of manure with a minimum of

[27] *Northern Farmer,* I (1852), 115; *Homestead,* IV (1859), 107-108.

[28] *Connecticut Valley Farmer and Mechanic,* I (1853), 135; U. S. Patent Office, *Report* (1850), pp. 415, 431-432; (1853), p. 84; (1854), p. 115.

[29] There was some increase in the utilization of manures in the 1840's and 1850's in the older sections of Maine, but the more recently settled sections were characterized by typical frontier neglect. Maine Board of Agriculture, *Report,* I (1856), 9-17; *Maine Farmer,* Feb. 19, 1857.

[30] *New England Farmer,* X (1858), 259.

[31] American Institute, *Transactions* (1857), p. 490; Connecticut Agricultural Society, *Transactions* (1854), p. 114.

effort.[32] Although the usefulness of manure in securing a satisfactory stand of grass on land worn-out by continuous cropping had been demonstrated in Ohio as early as 1840,[33] there was little general interest in such procedures.

Changes occurred, however, as declining productivity became more apparent. By the fifties in Ohio, "the unavoidable accumulation in stables and barnyards" was removed "to the garden or to some poor spot in the fields."[34] In Indiana, in an area that was classified as "done making farms and beginning to farm," "when manure accumulates about our barns and stables so as to be in the way, we generally remove the nuisance to our fields instead of pulling down our buildings."[35] A survey by the Indiana State Board of Agriculture in 1857 on the utilization of manure aroused little response, but those who did answer indicated that although waste was still typical, a change was taking place and manures were increasingly applied to the fields.[36] In general, if any lands remained to be cleared on a farm, or if in fact there were any other tasks to be done, manuring was the last chore to be undertaken and the first to be given up, as showing the least immediate cash return. The situation was described in a report to the U.S. Patent Office on the customary procedures in southeastern Michigan: "But little attention is paid to saving or applying manure; we are aware of its utility, we haul it to our fields if we find time; the low price of lands and the high price of labor will not warrant the operation in all cases."[37] Essentially this remained true throughout the area until after 1870.

On the prairies, farmers in the 1850's were carrying on the practices of their eastern ancestors of half a century earlier, "deeming it unnecessary to pay any regard to the land," being "under the im-

[32] *Farmer's Register,* III (1835), 319; *Country Gentleman,* I (1853), 210; New York State Agricultural Society, *Transactions* (1850), pp. 153-160; (1852), p. 198.

[33] *Cultivator,* VII (1841), 144.

[34] *Boston Cultivator,* Aug. 10, 1850; Ohio Board of Agriculture, *Report* (1859), pp. 164, 184; U. S. Patent Office, *Report* (1852), p. 263. However, there were in Ohio "very few if any farmers who manure their lands regularly, and perhaps it would be difficult to find a single individual who makes a business to attend to his barnyard with a view to the accumulation and preservation of manure." *Ohio Cultivator,* V (1849), 114; VII (1851), 129; *Wool Grower,* I (1849), 59.

[35] U. S. Patent Office, *Report* (1850), p. 373; (1852), p. 334.

[36] U. S. Patent Office, *Report* (1857), pp. 214-216. See also *Plow,* I (1852), 179. But a few farmers used manure with considerable care. *See Indiana Farmer,* IV (1854), 115-116; VII (1858), 148.

[37] Michigan State Agricultural Society, *Transactions* (1852), p. 160; Michigan State Board of Agriculture, *Report* (1864), pp. 11 ff.

pression of best guarding their interests by exclusively cultivating that which commands the highest price at the time."[38] "There is not," wrote a traveler, "one lot in ten on the prairies that has ever been manured. It would surprise some of you eastern folks, to travel through the country, and see the large piles of manures about the barns and yards. This I am glad to inform you, is not the case generally, but it is true in a great many cases. Some farmers consider the manure heaps a nuisance, and are of the opinion that manures would spoil lands by causing the straw to grow so large as to fall and not fill."[39]

In Illinois this was the case, one farmer writing in explanation: "Land devoted to corn-growing gets pretty thoroughly manured. The stalks are seldom cut-up; the corn is picked from the hill, and the stalks are left to the herds of cattle to be eaten and trampled into the earth. In this manner the supply of vegetable mold is kept up, and rather increases than diminishes from year to year. But wheat, coming in for a liberal share in the rotation of crops with us, removes all its product from the soil and thus tends to impoverish it. It pays to manure for corn with common back-yard manure; but the growth of straw is ample for wheat, unaided by any such stimulant . . . It is the common opinion here that manure is not worth the saving, and straw is almost universally burned."[40]

Although a few Illinois farmers had arrived at the point where they found the use of manures desirable, "not more than one in a thousand of the farmers in Iowa take any pains to make or preserve manure. Instead of using upon their land what is made by their horses, cattle, and hogs, it is suffered to waste about the stables. Many make it a point to place their stables and yards near a ravine, so that all the liquid manure, and as much as possible of the solid, will wash away by heavy rains."[41] Another observer commented: "Every one admits that manure is useful and would do good even here—but I have seen more straw drawn onto the prairie to be wasted than manure to the fields. Fields that have been planted without intermission for the last ten or twelve years still yield their

38 Frederick Gerhard, *Illinois As It Is* (Chicago, 1857), p. 313.

39 *Country Gentleman,* VI (1855), 273. See also *Valley Farmer,* VIII (1856), 272.

40 *Genesee Farmer,* XX (1859), 85. To the contrary, see *Illinois Farmer,* V (1860), 204; *Prairie Farmer,* II (1858), 326; *Cincinnatus,* I (1856), 219.

41 *Indiana Farmer,* III (1853), 52; *New England Farmer,* IX (1859), 513.

golden harvests, as unmindful of failures as their owners."[42] Much the same was true in Wisconsin, until the decline in productivity and profitability of wheat had forced a shift to cattle and it became desirable to manure for the purpose of securing satisfactory stands of grass.[43] In western Wisconsin in the early fifties it was a matter of note that the English immigrant farmers hauled their manures onto their fields, thereby raising the best crops in the area.[44]

Gypsum and Lime. While the usefulness of manures was easily explained—something that had been taken away from the soil was returned—the operation of other fertilizers and soil amendments was not easily understood. Nevertheless, the success of English farmers with gypsum and lime led to the use of these materials by a few American farmers in the latter part of the eighteenth century.[45] The earliest experiments with gypsum occurred in New York, but in the southeastern part of Pennsylvania it most quickly came into popular use.[46] There under the leadership of Richard Peters, gypsum attained great popularity as a soil additive, being used by some farmers as a substitute for stable manure. Even though initially imported from Nova Scotia, it gave marked results inexpensively, the material being placed in corn hills or scattered over fields of wheat or clover at the rate of one or two bushels per acre.

Gypsum quickly achieved a similar popularity in eastern New York, where local quarries were developed to supply the demand. It became popular on Long Island and along the Hudson, particularly in Dutchess County, while "it was familiarly said that plaster has made Putnam County."[47] Enthusiasm for the material ran so high that Jesse Buel chided his readers in 1828: "I perceive that many of our farmers, although slow to adopt this or any other innovation upon old habits, now that they have become satisfied of the benefit of plaster in *some* cases, seem to infer that it is useful in *all,* and to apply it without 'rhyme or reason.' "[48] There followed

[42] *Iowa Farmer,* I (1853), 102; IV (1856), 310; *Rural New Yorker,* V (1854), 46; XII (1861), 62.
[43] *Rural New Yorker,* VI (1855), 182.
[44] U. S. Patent Office, *Report* (1852), p. 332. On Minnesota, see *Country Gentleman,* II (1852), 103.
[45] *Rural Economist,* I (1861-1862), 9.
[46] *Farmer and Gardener,* II (1835), 132; *Plough, Loom and Anvil,* I (1848), 102.
[47] *Northern Farmer,* II (1855), 173.
[48] *New York Farmer,* II (1855), 173.

a debate over the properties and uses of the material, which led to a more discriminating application.[49]

New England farmers also experimented with gypsum but with less spectacular results than in Pennsylvania. Nevertheless, it was used in small quantities by a scattering of farmers throughout the period.[50] It was "universally used" in sections of Massachusetts, and was credited with renovating the worn-out fields of Litchfield, Connecticut.[51] In Maine and New Hampshire, gypsum came into fairly extensive use in the fifties. The development of railroad connections made the use of gypsum possible in some areas where it had been previously untried.[52]

Gypsum, readily available from local sources, came into use in the wheat regions of western New York in the late thirties.[53] In the fifties it was the most widely used soil additive in the state, exceeding all others in both tonnage and value.[54]

In the West, no widespread interest in the material developed in this period except in southern Michigan and sections of Ohio. Gypsum was employed by some farmers near Sandusky, Ohio.[55] In Michigan, extensive use was made of the gypsum quarries in Van Buren County. The material was being utilized in the eastern part of the state in the forties, and in the following decade became important throughout the southern tier of counties in maintaining wheat production and securing the stands of clover that were essential in renovation programs.[56] Farther west, gypsum aroused little interest, except for slight utilization among scattered farmers in Wisconsin.[57]

Although gypsum proved to be a valuable corrective on some soils, it was found to have no effect on others. Moreover, renewed

[49] *Farmer's Register,* I (1833), 228-229; New York State Agricultural Society, *Transactions* (1843), pp. 462-464; (1852), p. 865.

[50] *Farmer's Register,* III (1835-1836), 16-17; Massachusetts Board of Agriculture, *Transactions* (1856), p. 175.

[51] U. S. Patent Office, *Report* (1852), p. 178; (1853), pp. 34, 82-89.

[52] *Maine Farmer,* Jan. 8, June 25, 1857; June 20, 1850; June 29, 1854; *Farmer and Artizan,* II (1837), 67; *Journal of Agriculture* (Boston), I (1851), 4; New Hampshire Agricultural Society, *Transactions* (1856), p. 335.

[53] *Cultivator,* II (1835-1836), 184; *Genesee Farmer,* XII (1856), 105, 266.

[54] New York State, *Census* (1855), p. 327.

[55] *Ohio Cultivator,* VII (1851), 83, 98; U. S. Patent Office, *Report* (1849), pp. 301-302.

[56] *Michigan Farmer,* VIII (1850), 101 ff; 1851 and 1854 volumes. See also Michigan State Board of Agriculture, *Report* 1850, 1853, 1856, and subsequent volumes.

[57] *Wisconsin and Iowa Farmer,* II (1850), 29; VII (1855), 226.

applications were disappointing because the original effect failed of repetition. In eastern Pennsylvania, where the interest in gypsum had been most intense, by 1820 returns had become so disappointing that its use was being abandoned. Farmers turned instead to lime, which also stimulated the growth of red clover but had a longer period of effectiveness. While the demand for lime increased, its cost was reduced as anthracite displaced wood as the fuel for burning the stone.[58] By 1830 the practice of liming land was spreading rapidly among all but the most conservative of southeastern Pennsylvania farmers.[59] Lime was credited with restoring the worn-out lands of Chester and Delaware Counties to a permanently remunerative productivity.[60] The farmers of this area set a standard of soil use for the rest of the nation. They were quickly imitated throughout the limestone areas of both eastern and western Pennsylvania.[61]

In the thirties, burnt lime from Pennsylvania as well as crushed shells came into use in Maryland and Delaware. The material formed the basis of a revolution in the agriculture of the area, as it had a decade earlier in Pennsylvania.[62] In New Jersey, meanwhile, some of the more progressive farmers were making use of the marl deposits available. That material was credited with increasing land values "twenty-fold" in parts of Monmouth County.[63]

Lime was coming into use in western New York in the forties, as in Cayuga and Genesee Counties, and in the Springfield area of Ohio

[58] *Farmer's Register,* III (1835), 281-282; New York State Agricultural Society, *Report* (1841), p. 167.

[59] The German farmers of York, Lancaster, and neighboring counties enjoyed reputations as excellent farmers, but they were not progressive in the use of lime or gypsum or in accepting other innovations. They did not participate in the spirit of agricultural advancement "flourishing in Chester and Delaware" in the forties. New York State Agricultural Society, *Transactions* (1841), p. 167. A few years later they were described as relying on manual labor with little aid from science and "preferring to hold fast to the time-honored principles and examples of their ancestors; they plow, plant and reap as did their fathers before them. Year after year they follow the same unbroken round of duties, only striving that each year may leave them richer than it found them, and generally, by frugality, industry and close application to their affairs, they secure a competence, which in due time is left to their children, who will follow in the same path." *Genesee Farmer,* XVI (1855), 15-16. A similar observation is made by Mathew S. Henry, *History of the Lehigh Valley* (Easton, 1860), p. 246.

[60] U. S. Patent Office, *Report,* (1850), 419; (1853), 86.

[61] *Cultivator,* II (1836), 117; I (1844), 272. *Pennsylvania Farm Journal,* III (1853), 129-134; Pennsylvania State Agricultural Society, *Report,* I (1854), 181-196, 308-309.

[62] *Cultivator,* V (1838-1839), 77; *American Agriculturist,* X (1853), 91; *New England Cultivator,* I (1853), 26; *American Farmer,* XIII (1857), 15.

[63] *Cultivator,* III (1835), 21; *New Jersey Farmer,* II (1856), 234-235; *Homestead,* III (1858), 444-445.

in the fifties, but found little application elsewhere in the West prior to 1870.[64]

Guano. The interest in securing additional sources of fertilizing materials that had become active by the 1840's is strikingly illustrated in the case of guano. After the German chemist Justus Liebig had noted the value of this material as a fertilizer, it was introduced in England in 1840 and in the United States a few years later, quickly achieving popularity in both countries.[65] Importations into the United States totaled about 1,000 tons in 1848, climbed to 21,000 tons in the following year, and reached 163,622 tons in 1856, the peak year.[66] Imports for the decade of the fifties totaled 843,000 tons.[67] Farmer interest in securing an honest product led the states of Connecticut and Maryland to establish the posts of State Chemists, charged with examining for adulterants the products offered for sale.[68] An increase in prices brought demands for congressional action, which resulted in exploration of sources in the West Indies and eventually the annexation of Jarvis and Baker Islands in the Pacific.[69]

Guano was most enthusiastically received by the farmers of Maryland and Delaware, Baltimore being the largest importing center.[70] Experimentation with the material was widespread in the late forties. Considerable quantities were being used in Dorchester County, Maryland, and New Castle County, Delaware, by 1850. Within a few years the material was considered indispensable to the production of wheat and corn by many farmers on the worn-out lands of those two states.[71] Farmers who had long neglected stable

[64] New York State Agricultural Society, *Transactions* (1844), pp. 140, 164; *Genesee Farmer*, IX (1839), 34-35; *Cultivator*, I (1834), 59-60; IV (1847), 211.

[65] Solon Robinson, *Guano, A Treatise of Practical Information for Farmers* (New York, 1853); J. E. Tesehemacher, *Essay On Guano* (Baltimore, 1852); American Institute, *Transactions* (1856), pp. 217-218, 221-228.

[66] John Jay, *Statistical View of American Agriculture* (New York, 1859), p. 56; *Hunt's Merchant Magazine*, XLI (1859), 645.

[67] U. S. Commissioner of Agriculture, *Report* (1872), p. 303.

[68] Connecticut State Agricultural Society, *Transactions* (1858), pp. 35-87; *Rural Register*, II (1860), 104.

[69] *Working Farmer*, VI (1855), 102-103.

[70] American Institute, *Transactions* (1858), pp. 342-343; (1859), 219-220; *Farm Journal and Progressive Farmer*, VI (1856), 214-215; *American Agriculturist*, XIV (1855), 296; XV (1856), 131.

[71] On purchases of guano in Newcastle County, see G. Emerson, *Address*, Agricultural Society of Kent County, Delaware, 1857; *Rural Register*, II (1860), 215.

manures used guano freely, while some who had begun to use lime abandoned it in favor of the Peruvian dust.[72]

Farther north, guano found its principal users among the farmers of Long Island, the market gardeners about Philadelphia, and in sections of New Jersey and Connecticut. Elsewhere there was considerable experimentation with the material. Farmers in Orange and Ulster Counties of New York employed guano on a small scale on grass, and it was used experimentally on wheat in the Genesee Valley, while some Maine and Vermont farmers employed it on potatoes.[73]

Other Materials. Along New England's seacoast and on Long Island, fish were second in importance only to barnyard manures as a soil-enrichment material.[74] In the forties, commercial fishermen supplied nonedible fish such as menhaden at prices approximating one dollar per thousand.[75] Fish were frequently applied in the traditional method, a few to each hill of corn at planting time. They were also scattered on the land and plowed under, while some farmers mixed them with muck to make a compost.[76] Applied in quantities as high as 10,000 to 12,000 per acre, such fish were an extremely valuable source of soil productivity.[77] However, distances of more than five or ten miles from the coast constituted the feasible limits of hauling such materials.

In the fifties, a few firms, following French experience, began the manufacture of oil from menhaden, the solid residue finding ready sale as a fertilizer.[78] By 1860 such plants were operating in Rhode Island, Connecticut, near Boston, and on Long Island, and the material was finding a widening area of users.[79]

Chemical fertilizers appeared early in the fifties in the form of superphosphate of lime. J. J. Mapes was the most aggressive pro-

[72] *American Farmer,* VIII (1852), 1.

[73] *American Agriculturist,* XIV (1855), 387; *American Quarterly Journal of Agriculture and Science,* III (1846), 28; *Maine Farmer,* Jan. 22, 1857; *Connecticut Valley Farmer and Mechanic,* II (1854), 3.

[74] U. S. Patent Office, *Report* (1852), pp. 166-167; *Indiana Farmer,* V (1856), 129.

[75] *Cultivator,* VI (1849), 30-31.

[76] *Cultivator,* IV (1847), 240; V (1848), 345-346; *Working Farmer,* IV (1852), 268; VI (1855), 70.

[77] Connecticut State Agricultural Society, *Transactions* (1857), pp. 209-213; *Cultivator,* VI (1849), 30-31.

[78] American Institute, *Transactions* (1855), pp. 345, 537.

[79] American Institute, *Transactions* (1857), p. 564; Connecticut State Agricultural Society, *Transactions* (1859), p. 35.

moter of the material, but other manufacturers soon appeared, the chemist of the Connecticut State Agricultural Society reporting on eight brands in 1857.[80] The material was considered expensive, and its use was confined to the truck farms near the major cities.[81]

There were numerous other materials that had local uses.[82] Wood ashes were generally too valuable for commercial or domestic soap-making purposes, but spent soap-maker's lye was frequently applied to the soil.[83] Bone meal was popular on Long Island, and seaweeds were used along the coast.[84] Salt had some advocates.[85] Among other materials occasionally used as fertilizers were slaughterhouse wastes, spent tanbark, leather turnings, woolen wastes, brewery's refuse, and charcoal dust from the spark catchers of railroad locomotives. Efforts to process night soil into easily usable form achieved some success though not an important role in agriculture.[86] At the same time, an interest developed in the analysis of soils so that deficiencies might be determined with accuracy and better use made of artificial fertilizers.[87]

ROTATIONS

Increasing the nitrogenous and humus content of the soil and hence rebuilding its fertility might be accomplished by applications of manure and other fertilizing materials, such as gypsum and lime,

[80] *Working Farmer*, VII (1856), 265; *Rural New Yorker*, V (1854), 196.

[81] New York State, *Census* (1855), p. 327; *Agriculture of Massachusetts*, (1868-1869), pp. 93, 124; *Plough, Loom and Anvil*, IV (1851), 300.

[82] For surveys of the other materials used, see John Nicholson, *The Farmer's Assistant* (Lancaster, Pa., 1820); Samuel L. Dana, *A Muck Manual for Farmers* (Lowell, 1842); D. J. Browne, *The Field Book of Manures* (New York, 1856); American Institute, *Transactions* (1860), pp. 320 ff.

[83] *Farmer's Register*, III (1835-1836), 136; U. S. Patent Office, *Report* (1844), p. 384; (1861), p. 208.

[84] On the use of bone meal, see *New England Farmer*, XXIV (1845), 19; American Institute, *Report* (1853), pp. 313-314. On the use of seaweed, see Maine Board of Agriculture, *Report* (1861), p. 43; *New Hampshire Journal of Agriculture*, Oct. 13, 1859.

[85] A combination of salt and lime, under the name of "Baummer's plan," was widely promoted as a rejuvenator of soils. U. S. Patent Office, *Report* (1850), p. 254; American Institute, *Transactions* (1854), p. 407, and subsequent volumes.

[86] Night soil was manufactured in New York by the Lodi Manufacturing Company, under the name of "Poudrette," and in Connecticut by the Liebig Manufacturing Co. *Cultivator*, VI (1839), 120-121; VIII (1840), 144; I (1844), 263; Connecticut State Agricultural Society, *Transactions* (1851), 77-81.

[87] Rhode Island Society for the Encouragement of Domestic Industry, *Transactions* (1856), pp. 31-32; U. S. Agricultural Society, *Journal*, IV (1856), 69.

or the plowing under of red clover. The economical maintenance of the soil of a farm required, however, what a contemporary called a "convertible husbandry," "a regular change . . . constantly going on from aration to pasturage and vice versa."[88] Such a rotation involved not only the alteration of a few crops but a rational use-sequence involving all the tillable land within the farm boundaries. It required a substantial break with established practice, since one characteristic of early American farming in the East was to divide lands into crop and grass and treat the two as distinct. About 1800 "a man would have been considered rash who should have hazarded the assertion that the same lot could be used successively for plowing and meadow land."[89]

Fertility-maintaining programs involving a planned alternation of grass and crop were sometimes established before depletion was severe, but except for areas such as southeastern Pennsylvania, this occurred more frequently after mid-century in the West than in the East. Eastern farmers typically turned to rotations for the purpose of renovating seriously depleted lands. Frequently the individual responsible for the reduced fertility turned over his farm to someone else who undertook the rebuilding task.

Leadership in the establishment of fertility-maintaining rotations came before the opening of the century from small groups of men in such organizations as the Philadelphia Society for the Promotion of Agriculture, the New York Board of Agriculture, and the Massachusetts Agricultural Society. Their general approach was to urge that the principles of the English Norfolk system, adapted to American conditions, be applied to agriculture. Some of them did so experimentally on their own lands and concluded that red clover should be used as the essential renovating crop.[90] While their influence was felt in their own localities, it was in southeastern Pennsylvania that progress in the adoption of red clover rotations was earliest and most effective.

About 1820 the farmers of Chester County began to employ an eight- to ten-year rotation, with the land customarily manured once

[88] *Complete Practical Farmer* (New York, 1839), p. 72.

[89] Connecticut State Agricultural Society, *Transactions* (1854), p. 22.

[90] References to clover are invariably to red clover. Other legumes, such as alfalfa, lucerne, and varieties of peas, were known but not extensively planted. See *New York Farmer*, I (1828), 17-18; *Massachusetts Agricultural Journal*, X (1827), 13-14; *New England Farmer*, VIII (1830), 309; *Cultivator*, I (1844), 86.

and, after 1825, limed once in each sequence.[91] The usual sequence of crops was corn—oats or barley—wheat or rye—clover and timothy, with the latter being mown for two years and pastured for two to five years more.[92] This system, which came to be known as the Chester system, was widely imitated in eastern Pennsylvania.[93] Clover, together with lime, came into use in Lehigh and Northampton Counties to the north, where they were employed in what was essentially the Chester system and "saved the second and third rate lands from being deserted for the far west."[94] There were many variations, such as the more strenuous sequence designed to maximize wheat production: wheat and clover—clover—wheat and clover—clover—wheat—rye and clover—corn—fallow.[95] Throughout the region, however, clover and timothy formed the foundation of progressive land-use programs and set a pattern that spread throughout the northern United States during the half-century.[96] A major difference did develop in the treatment of the clover-grass sod: in the forties and fifties the practice of turning it under as a green manure became popular with farmers who were undertaking thoroughgoing renovation programs.[97]

A few miles to the south of Chester County, in Maryland and Delaware, lay some of the most exhausted lands in the nation. Until the early 1840's the farmers of the area remained unaffected by the example of their northern neighbors.[98] A traveler reported of northern Delaware that "the abandoned condition of many of the farms, dilapidated fences, fields thrown out to common as worthless, tottering houses, and starved cattle, jarred upon our nerves like the discordant music of a mill file on duty." Returning fifteen years later, in 1852, all was changed: "farms are everywhere well looked after,

91 *American Farmer*, III (1821), 309; VII (1825), 163; *Farmer's Cabinet*, V (1840), 94; *Genesee Farmer*, XVI (1855), 15-16; *Tippecanoe Farmer*, I (1854), 20; *Rural Economist*, I (1861-1862), 38.
92 U. S. Patent Office, *Report* (1847-1855), contains much information on rotation practices not specifically cited in text.
93 *American Agriculturist*, XV (1856), 154.
94 *Farmer's Register*, III (1835), 281-282.
95 *Cultivator*, IV (1847), 144.
96 See Daniel Lee, "Theory of Rotations," in U. S. Patent Office, *Report* (1850), pp. 125-126.
97 The beneficial effects of red clover were limited by constant mowing and grazing. Its use as a green manure was uncommon in the East until the forties; later in the West. Rye and buckwheat were occasionally employed as green manure crops. See *Michigan Farmer*, XII (1854), 225; *Western Farmer*, II (1846), 130.
98 *Cultivator*, I (1844), 202.

fences up, fields enclosed, and covered with luxuriant crops, and everyone you meet looks sleek, prosperous and happy, and lands that a few years since went abegging at $10 or $15 an acre, now command $50, $75, and sometimes $100."[99] The change resulted from the example set by a few men who had used lime purchased in Pennsylvania and guano obtained from Baltimore to establish clover and grass.[100] The sod so obtained was frequently neither mown nor pastured but plowed under as green manure. This procedure reestablished wheat growing and cattle grazing as profitable uses of the land, the Chester system or some variation being then followed.[101] The technique achieved satisfactory results in other sections of the two states, though by no means universally.[102] By the thirties much of the soil of New Jersey had also been seriously depleted, and returns were generally unfavorable. The reaction of the progressive farmers of the state followed the usual pattern. The land was dressed with lime or marl and a clover—wheat—timothy rotation was followed as a foundation for the adoption of the Chester system.[103]

Although the practice of alternating crops was generally established early in the older sections of New England, efforts to establish true fertility-maintaining rotations came more slowly. Henry Colman found that "little of systematic husbandry prevails in any part of Massachusetts; and the crops which are cultivated, and the manner in which they succeed each other, are dictated rather by accident or convenience than by any well-considered principle of vegetation."[104] On the richer soils, such as those of the Deerfield meadows, an exhaustive alternation of crops, such as corn with winter rye-peas and oats, was a common sequence.[105] Facing serious disadvantages in the production of cereal crops, farmers tended to occupy the land with grass for much longer periods than elsewhere,

[99] *Plow*, I (1852), 303. See also *American Agriculturist*, X (1851), 91; *Rural Register*, I (1860), 249.

[100] *Cultivator*, IV (1847), 95; *Southern Cultivator*, XVIII (1860), 307.

[101] *American Agriculturist*, IX (1850), 138; *American Farmer*, XII (1856), 17-18.

[102] *American Farmer*, VII (1851), 237; IX (1853), 236-237; XI (1855), 209; *Country Gentleman*, XXVI (1865), 43.

[103] *American Agriculturist*, IV (1845), 177-178; *Plow*, I (1852), 370; *New Jersey Farmer*, VI (1861), 237.

[104] Henry Colman, *Agriculture of Massachusetts, Fourth Report* (1841), p. 133.

[105] James F. W. Johnston, *Notes on North America* (Boston, 1852), I, 961.

the land being exploited in this way almost as effectively as if it had been continuously cropped in grain.[106] Maintenance of the productivity of grasslands received scant attention, for they were held in permanent meadows that received little if any care.[107] Some of these meadows had been turned to grass only after exhaustive cropping. The idea that these lands should be included in a tilled rotation and that clover might be plowed under to advantage won acceptance very slowly.[108] Many New England farms were cultivated throughout this period by methods that, though beneficial to parts of the farm, did not maintain the productivity of all of it.

Although the need for some alternation of crops was unquestionable, the systems varied according to individual and local evaluations of market opportunities, utilization of labor, and needs of the soil.[109] Rotations stressing the maintenance of fertility were in use in the thirties and earlier.[110] Nevertheless, in the sixties the most common rotation followed in Massachusetts was described as "cultivating smoother land as long as it would bear a remunerating crop, applying as little manure as could be gotten along with, then laying it down to rye, oats, or barley, then a crop or two of hay, then pasture for a number of years."[111]

Rotations on New England farms most frequently consisted of a small grain, then a hoed crop, followed by grass that remained from three or four to ten and more years. There was, however, considerable diversity. Among the more popular sequences were corn—oats or wheat—grass, corn—potatoes—grain—grass, corn—potatoes—grass, wheat—corn—grass, barley—oats—peas—grass, or rye—corn—oats—clover.[112] Many of the grazing farms of Vermont fol-

106 One editor averred that there were few instances of truly systematic rotations in Massachusetts. "The succession, if we have any, is dictated by convenience rather than any conviction that the soil needs a change of crops, and that the interests of the owner demands it." *Homestead,* III (1857), 232. See also Massachusetts Board of Agriculture, *Report* (1853), p. 264; (1861), p. 99.

107 *Maine Farmer,* Feb. 1, 1849.

108 *Country Gentleman,* II (1853), 231.

109 *Maine Farmer,* Dec. 4, 1850; *New York Farmer,* VII (1835), 134.

110 The corn—oats or flax—wheat—clover rotations were popular in the Pittston and Hoosic region. *New York Farmer,* VII (1835), 132.

111 Massachusetts Board of Agriculture, *Report,* IX (1861), 81.

112 Massachusetts Board of Agriculture, *Report* (1854), p. 446; *Plough, Loom and Anvil,* VII (1854), 720.

lowed a wheat—grass—oats—grass system. In the northern parts of New England, including the older sections of Maine, a popular rotation was oats—corn—grass, though sometimes the land was planted in a hoed crop for one year and then in grass for four or five.[113]

In New England areas where potatoes were an important market crop, a potatoes—wheat—grass—grass sequence had been established before the appearance of the potato rot, and it was being resumed in the mid-fifties. In areas near lumber camps, where oats were readily salable, they were frequently planted continuously, though sometimes being replaced by an oats—corn—grass or oats—corn or potatoes—wheat—grass rotation.[114]

The development of improved agricultural practices in New York centered in Duchess County. Events followed essentially the same pattern as in southeastern Pennsylvania, with the usual rotation being corn or buckwheat—oats—wheat or rye—grass—grass. The results were such that in the thirties agriculture in the county was held to exceed "in improvement and profit that of any other portion of the union."[115] Rotations centering about grass were well established in the southern part of the state by the forties. The Chester system, with potatoes taking the place of wheat, was common, though sometimes reduced to corn—wheat—grass, with the grass remaining as long as profitable. This cropping system was being followed on Long Island and in Westchester by 1825, and it was still in use in the 1850's.[116]

In the Mohawk Valley continuous cropping was still common in the early forties, but rotations consisting of a hoed crop—barley, spring wheat, peas, or oats—wheat—grass were coming into general use. In the hill country to the north continuous cropping persisted longer, but about 1850 in Essex County "skillful farmers" were following a rotation of a hoed crop for one or two years, small grains for one or two years, then grass. Rotations were only slowly adopted

---

113 *Granite Farmer*, II (1851), 282; Maine Board of Agriculture, *Report* (1857), pp. 76-77.

114 *Maine Farmer*, Nov. 25, 1852; Nov. 4, 1855; American Institute, *Transactions* (1857), p. 265.

115 *Cultivator*, I, (1844), 107; IV (1847), 211; III (1838), 30. The reputation of the county for fine farming was short-lived, declining markedly after 1840. *Working Farmer*, XII (1860), 44.

116 *Cultivator*, I (1834), 62; *American Agriculturist*, III (1844), 163-164; New York State Agricultural Society, *Transactions* (1842), pp. 187, 220; (1843), pp. 462-464.

in the central part of the state, where cattle were the chief interest. However, corn—spring wheat—oats—grass—grass—grass was a sequence in use in Madison County in the late forties.[117]

In the wheat country of western New York continuous cropping, broken only by summer and occasional year-long fallows, was the rule in the earliest years and was continued in some areas until the 1850's.[118] In the interval between harvest and reseeding of winter wheat, the land was usually allowed to lie fallow. In the 1840's this procedure was being abandoned as wasteful. In its place, some adopted the labor-saving but equally exploitative sequence of corn —wheat, or corn—barley—wheat.[119] A common routine after 1835 involved the sowing of clover or clover and timothy with wheat, which substituted a grass cover for the usual fallow and establishing a wheat—clover rotation.[120]

As soils became less productive and competition from the products of newer farms farther West increased, continuous cropping became less common and animals took a larger place in farm operations. During the forties more complex rotations became common, and the necessity of rotating became widely accepted. A wheat— corn, peas, or barley—wheat—wheat—grass—grass—grass rotation was in use in Genesee County in the forties, and similar sequences were followed elsewhere in the grain areas.[121] Corn—wheat—grass —grass was probably the most common cropping sequence in the fifties, but there were a wide variety of others, usually adding a grain crop or two.[122] In the sixties the most widely used rotation was the Chester system of corn—oats or barley—wheat—grass—grass. This was critized, however, as "no longer productive of the larger returns sought for," particularly where the grass was sold off the farm as hay, and there was a tendency to abandon the wheat

---

[117] New York State Agricultural Society, *Transactions* (1842), p. 365; (1852), p. 865; (1851), p. 722; *Cultivator,* III (1846), 95.

[118] *Cultivator,* VII (1850), 195; *Rural New Yorker,* VI (1855), 357. For a defense of the naked fallow, see *Cultivator,* I (1834), 23.

[119] The New York State Census of 1855 reported 506,030 acres, or 3.7% of the improved lands of the state, lying fallow in 1854. Fallowing had by then fallen into disuse throughout the North.

[120] See, e.g., *Ohio Farmer and Western Horticulturist,* II (1835), 19; *Rural New Yorker,* V (1854), 413.

[121] *Rural New Yorker,* IV (1853), 405; New York State Agricultural Society, *Transactions* (1851), p. 722; (1852), p. 565; (1842), p. 164; (1843), p. 451.

[122] *Genesee Farmer,* XVIII (1857), 81; *Northern Farmer,* I (1854), 162.

crop.[123] Soils that required rebuilding were cultivated with fewer cereal crops and kept in clover for two or three years.

The sequence of continuous cropping to the point of substantial soil exhaustion and then renovation based on clover was followed everywhere in the West, although the sowing of domesticated grasses was undertaken earlier there than in the East. By the fifties, all "good" farmers in Ohio were employing red clover in some rotation.[124] In the northern wheat areas of the state, clover had become necessary to a good crop of wheat by mid-century, and continuous cropping was giving way rapidly to the wheat—clover—clover sequence common in the Genesee country a decade or more earlier.[125] In some areas clover was plowed under in the early summer, the land then lying in naked fallow until seeded to wheat in the fall.[126] Rotations such as corn—corn—wheat—wheat—wheat—clover and various modifications were employed, particularly on new or very fertile land. In the next decade greater diversification, more complex rotations, and longer intervals between wheat crops became common.

In the corn areas of the southern part of the state, continuous cropping remained characteristic of the richer lands, particularly the bottoms. On the uplands, continuous cropping in corn was being replaced in the fifties by an alternation of corn—wheat—oats, which in turn was modified to include one or more years in clover, eventually resulting in the adoption of the Chester type of rotation. Rye was sometimes sown with corn as a green manure crop.[127]

Indiana farmers were a decade or so behind those of Ohio in turning to crop rotations. On new land continuous cropping of corn, for up to fifteen years or more, might be followed by an alternation of wheat and corn, then wheat and clover, followed by longer rotations such as corn—wheat—clover or wheat—corn—wheat—clover.[128] In the wheat areas summer fallows were still practiced in the fifties, though a few farmers recognized the importance of clover

---

[123] *Rural New Yorker,* XIV (1863), 333; *Country Gentleman,* XXVI (1865), 11.

[124] Ohio State Board of Agriculture, *Report,* V (1850), 279.

[125] *Ohio Cultivator,* VI (1850), 371.

[126] *Cultivator,* VIII (1851), 258; *Ohio Cultivator,* V (1849), 195-196.

[127] *Valley Farmer,* IX (1857), 6; XI (1859), 264; *Ohio Cultivator,* V (1849), 251; IX (1853), 243; XI (1855), 212; XVI (1860), 426; *Western Agriculturist,* I (1851), 198; *Indiana Farmer,* VII (1858-1859), 311-314.

[128] *Ohio Valley Farmer,* I (1856), 56.

to satisfactory wheat crops.[129] In the southern sections lands that had been continuously cropped in corn for a generation were occasionally "rested" by a year in wheat.[130] In the fifties an alternation of corn and wheat was common in the Wabash Valley, but except for such modifications, continuous cropping remained the rule. In the following decade, however, better farmers were adopting rotations similar to those employed in Ohio.[131]

Continuous cropping of wheat broken only by summer fallows was practiced in some sections of Michigan into the fifties, though abandoned in others.[132] Early attempts to establish clover in the state had failed, but by the fifties rotations based on clover were more widely established in the southern part of the state than anywhere else in the West. The cropping sequence was typically designed to secure remunerative crops of wheat, utilizing clover to maintain soil fertility at a high level. A rotation of wheat—corn—oats—buckwheat—clover—clover was widely considered as remunerative, since it maintained the tilth and fertility of the soil while at the same time permitting good use of labor. Sometimes oats were discarded, or a third year of clover substituted. Simple wheat—clover or wheat—corn—wheat—clover rotations were in use, although prairie land was considered too rich to permit wheat to follow clover.[133] More strenuous rotations were wheat—wheat—wheat—clover or corn—oats or barley—wheat, the latter on land plowed deep to bring up the old clover sod.[134]

Continuous cropping remained the rule in Illinois: "most farmers, deeming it unnecessary to pay any regard to the land, are under the impression of best guarding their interests by exclusively cultivating that which commands the highest price."[135] New land was ordinarily cropped in wheat or corn for the first ten years or until the yield fell to unprofitable levels.[136] Wheat and corn might be alternated,

129 U. S. Patent Office, *Report* (1850), pp. 374, 426.
130 *Ohio Cultivator*, XIII (1857), 67.
131 Indiana State Board of Agriculture, *Report* (1857), pp. 212-214.
132 *American Agriculturist*, X (1851), 117; *Michigan Farmer*, XII (1854), 193; Michigan State Agricultural Society, *Transactions* (1851), p. 272.
133 *Michigan Farmer*, IX (1851), 150; XI (1851), 8; XIII (1855), 362; XV (1857), 361-362; XVI (1858), 294; *Genesee Farmer*, XIX (1858), 86; Michigan State Agricultural Society, *Transactions* (1851), pp. 294-295.
134 Gerhard, *Illinois As It Is*, pp. 312-313.
135 *Michigan Farmer*, XV (1857), 139-140; XI (1853), 266; XII (1855), 44.
136 This sequence was described by one farmer as "corn—corn and weeds—weeds and corn—weeds." *Prairie Farmer*, XI (1851), 270.

or a more complex sequence followed, such as wheat—corn—corn—oats or wheat—corn—barley—oats—corn.[137] In southern Illinois "the general practice of farming is to plant and sow the same seed on the same ground, from year to year. If a man puts in a piece of meadow, he will cut the grass for fifteen to twenty years without manuring, scarificing or reseeding. There are farmers here who have planted corn on the same ground ever since they commenced farming, say for twenty-five years, without changing their seed or ploughing deeper than at first. Corn—corn, without manure, is their rotation. Corn is their motto from beginning to end, barely splitting the rows. And should anyone presume to do differently he would be denounced as a book-farmer, and thought to be incapable of getting a living by farming."[138]

By the mid-fifties, a few scattered farmers were risking denunciations and turning to book-farming to maintain productivity. In the northern part of the state, clover was becoming necessary to profitable crops of wheat, so that continuous cropping or the alternation of corn—wheat was being displaced by such rotations as corn—oats—clover—wheat, and gradually by others less taxing, such as wheat—clover—clover.[139] The wheat—corn—oats—grass—grass rotation, popular in the East, was also coming into use.[140] In general, after 1855 timothy and clover were increasing rapidly in importance. In the central stock-raising section of the state the native grasses were giving way to blue grass in some sections and to clover and timothy in others. The demand for domesticated hay, particularly timothy, in the markets of the lower Mississippi Valley was a factor in the shift. Change occurred much more slowly in the southern part of the state.[141]

The usual sequence—first continuous cropping, then resting the land by planting it in an alternate grain crop, finally slowly turning to a clover-grass rotation—was characteristic of Iowa and Wisconsin as well. In both areas a few farmers had reached the third stage about 1855, but not until after 1860 did rotations achieve even a slight significance in those states.[142]

[137] *Prairie Farmer*, XII (1852), 36, 286.
[138] U. S. Patent Office, *Report* (1850), p. 199. See also *Valley Farmer*, VIII (1855), 37.
[139] *Valley Farmer*, XI (1859), 264.
[140] *Northern Farmer*, III (1856), 120; *Genesee Farmer*, XVII (1856), 84.
[141] *Illinois Farmer*, V (1860), 76, 188.
[142] *Country Gentleman*, II (1853), 183; *New England Farmer*, VII (1855), 377;

As the record shows, in this area of agriculture, as in others, the large majority of farmers were insensitive to change and inflexible in the management of their affairs. Changing circumstances forced changes in the routine of production. Adaptation of the techniques of soil use so as to maintain or renew fertility called for a routine based upon settled agriculture and a longer time perspective— qualities that a farm-making generation rarely possessed.[143]

Large numbers, forced to a decision when the returns from their worn-out farms fell to unacceptable levels, preferred to move West, where they could renew the familiar pattern of destructive soil exploitation. It was left to men of superior foresight and energy to assume leadership and to demonstrate the profitability of operational plans that with little more capital but with substantial long-range planning would assure the maintenance and even increase of fertility. Their work was imitated by those who had purchased worn-out lands at prices and market locations that made the effort at renovation economically feasible. Those who succeeded in changing their attitudes and methods rather than their locations, who purchased the worn-out lands left behind by the Western migrant and sought to etablish permanent and remunerative farming enterprises upon depleted soils, were pioneers in an unsung but fundamentally important area.

Wisconsin Farmer, IX (1857), 277; XVI (1864), 59; *Prairie Farmer,* X (1850), 344-345; XIV (1854), 252; Wisconsin State Agricultural Society, *Transactions* (1851), p. 106.

143 *Rural New Yorker,* VI (1855), 22; *Cultivator,* VIII (1851), 359; *Indiana Farmer,* VII (1858), 12.

CHAPTER ELEVEN

CONCLUSION

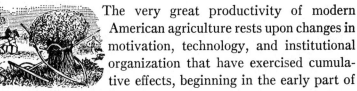 The very great productivity of modern American agriculture rests upon changes in motivation, technology, and institutional organization that have exercised cumulative effects, beginning in the early part of the nineteenth century. As farmers responded to the increasing size and accessibility of markets, the established, traditional approach to production was slowly eroded. In its place appeared a new rationalistic approach to farm operations, applied by only a few, but spreading sufficiently to stimulate dramatic changes in agricultural technology. These changes contributed to successive increases in aggregate production, identified the barriers to still further increases in efficiency, and established the broad approaches that would make change a continuing characteristic of a new system in a new and complex society.

Each factor involved in this process required time and effort to develop, test, perfect, and adapt it as needed for effective utilization. Opposition, and more frequently indifference, deterred participation. Meanwhile, early gains in productivity were offset by continuing declines in the fertility of soils that had long been cultivated. Available statistical data do not permit adequate measurement, but the interdependent nature of the changes and their slow adoption suggest that net gains in productivity did not become substantial until after 1840.

By 1850, changes that had occurred in every important sector of the technology had merged to create a new set of farming systems. The land area of the progressive farmer had been adjusted so that it was adequate or, given the abundance of land, more than adequate to permit effective use of the new plows, cultivators, reapers, mowers, threshers, horse rakes, drills, and corn planters, all unknown in 1820. He planted the more productive strains of corn and wheat, and his hogs, cattle, and sheep were significantly superior to those of half a century earlier. Pasture and hay were available in adequate amounts for efficient livestock growth and were provided by domesticated grasses and clovers raised in rotation with other crops, which could be regulated to maintain or rebuild the fertility of his soil. Those who fully applied the best techniques available in 1850 were able to secure perhaps two to four times more product per man than had their predecessors in 1820. Few, however, did so well, since in 1850 few had fully adopted the new system in all its aspects.

Although many factors contributed to increased productivity, the effective application of horse power to numerous farming tasks was of central significance. The successful use of horse power in harvesting, by the reaper and mower, removed a serious bottleneck and completed the technology based on animal power. The resulting integrated technology of agriculture was well balanced in its labor requirements for the successive steps of cultivation. Adoption of the new system depended upon availability of the implements and upon the advantages that could be obtained from their use. Both availability and advantage increased during the 1850's. During the years of the Civil War, the combination of high prices for farm products, shortage of farm labor, and increasing supplies of agricultural implements, particularly reapers and mowers, substantially accelerated the rate of farmer acceptance.[1] Although agriculture surrendered at least a third of its labor force to military service, available evidence suggests that production was maintained and may even have increased.[2]

Acceptance of an innovation tended to be limited and slow. To some extent the barriers to change were physical: many farmers, for example, did not have enough tilled acreage to justify the use of a new implement. Although capital requirements were rarely a significantly inhibiting factor, they no doubt delayed the spread of new breeds of cattle and the use of clover and domesticated grasses. For the most part the barriers were less tangible. The agricultural society of 1820 and for many years following was characterized by a rigid adherence to routines founded on and sanctified by past experience. The customary practices of an area governed what should be produced, how much should be attempted, and the way operations should be conducted. These customs represented the community consensus as to the best objectives and procedures; alternatives

[1] For an analysis that places somewhat greater emphasis on the stimulus of the Civil War, see Wayne D. Rasmussen, "The Civil War: A Catalyst of Agricultural Revolution," *Agricultural History*, XXXIX (1965), 187-195.

[2] See Paul W. Gates, *Agriculture and the Civil War* (Knopf, 1965), Ch. 9.

were rarely considered, and even the existence of alternatives worthy of consideration was doubted.

Considerable differences existed between individuals in the effectiveness with which they discharged their responsibilities for resource use. Prior to 1820 and for some time thereafter, farmers were classified as good or poor, careful or slipshod, prompt or dilatory, economical or extravagant, intelligent or ignorant, "snug" or "slack." Such designations reflected judgments as to conscientiousness; they were evaluations of the performance of routine operations by standards that included little or no allowance for deviation from established patterns. Whereas pecuniary standards were applied, they were not the primary element.

Stereotyped routines characterized most segments of the agricultural society, and the technology and economic organization were static. In northern agriculture this was the case until events outside agriculture—a rising urban population, development of transportation facilities, expansion of external markets—prompted some farmers to take the fullest possible advantage of the new conditions in hopes of enhancing their position. Their actions risked social disapproval and possible suppression unless in some way the defenders of the status quo could be made to feel uncertainty about their own attitude. A small body of rational, market-oriented farmers provided the leadership, while western and urban migration served to weaken the inhibiting forces. Nevertheless, the normal inertia of human beings and the inherent conservatism of the society constituted strong defenses of its habitual patterns of action. The institutional structure, supported by public opinion and buttressed by spokesmen for the status quo, served to defend what was known and understood and to oppose what was not the common and hence the respected experience.

The basic characteristics of the type of farmer who provided leadership were a sensitivity to market conditions as guides to determining products and a constant re-evaluation of routines of production in the light of new alternatives, followed by a willingness to make whatever adjustments appeared advantageous. Changes in the technology occurred because the social system failed to discourage deviations from the customary pattern. Private ownership of the means of production made possible, without necessarily encouraging, experimentation by the producer. The presence of unused resources, an equalitarian social system, and a democratic government were of significance, as were all circumstances or situations that tended to minimize control over the individual by others or by the group. Such conditions provided a favorable environment for change.

Changes in agricultural enterprise, occurring at an accelerated rate after 1820, were evidenced by the increasing prominence of new standards by which to judge performance. Although the older values by no means disappeared, they tended more and more to be subordinated to judgments relating to the probability of pecuniary success, giving recognition to the fact that the objective of maximizing money income had come to control the farmer's entrepreneurial actions. The emphasis on care, economy, and doing everything for oneself gave way to the question, "Does it pay?" The symbols of pecuniary success increased in importance. "Big" farming, although not a new objective, took on a new character as it came increasingly to be judged in terms of the net money income secured, not just the number of acres cultivated or the number of farms owned.

A farmer who was good by the old standards—that is, careful, economical, and primarily self-sufficient—might by the new standards be called conservative, stubborn, tradition-bound, miserly, ignorant, or blind to self-interest. The answers to the question, "Does it pay?" were no longer to be found through adherence to the routine of production that had served well to achieve the older objectives. The pursuit of agriculture as a source of an attractive net money income required frequent and precise re-evaluation of the appropriateness of the uses to which all resources, including the owner's labor, were being put. Such re-evaluation was accomplished under the guidance supplied by the market, not by the contents of the family's larder. The system of values now being applied, though centered on money profits, accorded recognition to farmers who qualified as "intelligent," "scientific," or "progressive." The phrase "book farmer," once unquestionably derogatory, lost its effectiveness as a weapon of derision and control.

This new kind of farmer acted in the light of what he saw on his travels, on the farms of like-minded neighbors, or read in periodicals and books. Stimulated by observation of activities varying from normal routines, such a farmer experimentally applied his own ideas or undertook to imitate what he saw or learned. The ultimate test of his activities became the impersonal one of pecuniary return, in which subjective judgments of neighbors played a less important role.

In the words of a contemporary observer, no feature of the husbandry of the 1850's showed greater contrast with earlier times than the farmer himself: "He looks at his business from a new standpoint. It is no longer a stereotyped routine, in which man uses as little mind as the dumb cattle he drives over his fields. Among the more intelligent class of cultivators, husbandry is no longer considered a perfected art. Its methods are not so well established that it is deemed a waste of time and labor to try anything new. It is a tentative art, in which every man feels that he has much to learn, and experiments in new tools, crops, fertilizers, and modes of tillage are everywhere the order of the day."[3]

This description applies to the farmers who were the leaders of their day. The attitudes and activities of the rest, the large majority, covered a wide range. Their differences led one observant farmer to suggest an explanatory classification. He wrote:

As a farmer I have lived among farmers, without a change of residence thirty-six years; and during that period of time have had opportunity to observe the development of several generations of farmers. One generation I can trace from infancy to mature age; another which first came under my notice at manhood, are now old men; and others, according to several ages have had time more or less to exhibit what they are able to accomplish. The result of my observations, in one direction, has been that the individuals composing these several generations constantly range themselves under one of four classes. Class No. 1 is composed of those who are always poor; Class No. 2 includes those who barely make a living all their lives long; Class No. 3 numbers those who acquire a comfortable and a constantly increasing competence; and Class No. 4 is composed of those who acquire wealth. Numerically, each class diminishes as we advance in the classifications. I have said that the individuals of each generation range themselves under one or other of these heads—and I believe that I am correct in saying so, notwithstanding the constant averment of Classes Nos. 1 and 2 that their want of success is to be attributed to the circumstances surrounding them. The man himself, and what he is made of, determines to what class he will belong. It is true, surroundings are sometimes favorable and sometimes unfavorable, but the energetic and skillful will dodge the unfavorable obstacles and avail themselves with great dexterity of all that will assist their progress.[4]

---

[3] *American Agriculturist,* XVI (1857), 145.
[4] *Rural New Yorker,* XIII (1862), 2.

Financial success is, however, not necessarily an indicator of contributions to significant change. Leadership in the development of agricultural technology and of a new role for agriculture in the society was provided by those who most frequently and readily departed from familiar routines in reacting to shifting circumstances or new knowledge. Most such departures were in imitation of others. A few represented enough originality to be considered true innovations. It is thus useful to classify farmers according to the imaginativeness and promptness with which they reacted to change.[5] They fall into four principal groups: the innovative, the imitative, the gradualist, and the traditionalist.

Innovative farmers over this half-century were those very few who originated significant changes that became integral parts of the routine of farm operations. The farmer's role as innovator was not to invent and develop new implements or economic arrangements—although many who did undertake such efforts had come from farms. A few farmers made innovative contributions to the technology in areas closely related to their day-to-day operations—as in developing new plant and animal materials as well as new techniques of dealing with plants, animals and soils. More often the innovative farmers were distinguished by their success in efforts to test a new material or method that offered promise but for which they had little or no evidence of technical effectiveness, not to mention economic advantage. Among them may be mentioned John H. Powell who set out to determine the most profitable breed of cattle, tested many, selected the Shorthorns as conforming to his criteria, and followed up his findings with aggressive development and promotion of the animals; Samuel Jacques, who developed his own strain of dairy cattle; the anonymous farmers who first purchased cast-iron plows, grain drills, or mechanical harvesters of uncertain performance and doubtful economy; the Massachusetts farmers who before 1820 determined that row was superior to hill culture for corn; and the Pennsylvania and Massachusetts farmers who demonstrated that red clover could be grown profitably although

[5] For an earlier version of this analysis, see Clarence H. Danhof, "Observations on Entrepreneurship in Agriculture," in *Change and the Entrepreneur* (Harvard University Press, 1949), pp. 20-24. See also Arthur H. Cole, *Business Enterprise in Its Social Setting* (Harvard University Press, 1959), and Everett M. Rogers, *Diffusion of Innovations* (The Free Press, 1962).

folklore had asserted that it could not. These men broke in one way or another with the stereotyped pattern of activity.

Perhaps the chief characteristics of these innovators were their dissatisfaction with some aspect of routine procedure, their willingness to look upon their operations as involving unsatisfactorily solved problems, and their persistent search for and experimentation with solutions. Aware of the possibility of improvement, with the hope of acquiring financial gain for themselves, such men sought out ideas by observing farm operations outside their normal range of experience. Perhaps even more effective as a source of stimuli was the knowledge they obtained from wide reading, thereby securing not only an acquaintance with farming practices elsewhere and with experiments being carried out but also familiarizing themselves with matters only indirectly relating to farming routines. It was through the imaginative abilities of these men that developments outside agriculture, as in industry and transportation, in science and government, whether in the United States or Europe, were brought to bear upon their problems.

The available information on these men suggests that they were good managers; that is, they appeared on the whole to have been highly successful in applying the standard routines of production to their operations. Most of them employed both labor and capital more effectively than did the average farmer; their management was of such a quality that they secured from the labor of hired hands a profitable return on the wages paid. Superior abilities in management were of basic importance, since these men were thus able to free themselves from preoccupation with routine details and could give time and energy to critically reviewing their operations and evaluating alternatives.

To a large extent the efforts of innovative farmers involved only minor deviations from established patterns. Their search for excellence led them to experiment with novel techniques, implements, and plant and animal materials. Failures were frequent, but the accumulation of knowledge from such failures, persistently explored, produced occasional successes. Rarely did a single innovator achieve a true contribution unassisted. In almost every instance, groups of men, working independently but utilizing the information gained from the experiments of others, must be credited with the achievements. Their dissatisfaction, curiosity, and imagination resulted in changes in the technology that were ultimately imitated widely by others.

True innovations, though they range from small changes in technique, such as depth of cultivating corn, to such drastic changes as mechanical harvesting, are never numerous. Even when they occurred in this period, they tended to remain unknown and insignificant unless, long before being perfected and proven, they were adopted by men willing and anxious to test their feasibility in normal operations, to adapt routines so as to derive their full advantage, and to make or suggest improvements. Men who readily accepted changes that came to their attention and incorporated them into their routines may be classed as imitative farmers. These were the ones who tested claims of both a technical and an economic nature, who undertook to determine the value of a novelty in their particular circumstances, who adapted their thinking and procedures so as to secure the most effective results, and who thereby contributed to the cumulative process of improving the technology.

Few innovations in agriculture achieved significant impact before undergoing prolonged experimentation in operating routines. Most innovations incorporated contributions from many experimental users by the time they were sufficiently perfected to be considered proven and necessary. In agriculture it was typical for innovations first to appear and then to fall into dormancy, later to be revived, further developed, and finally widely accepted. In such cases it was usually the failure of imitators to contribute to development that was responsible for the delay. The imitator performed the essential function of testing the new idea under a wide variety of conditions, blending the change into a new sequence of productive operations, and frequently suggesting minor but important adjustments.

Although more numerous than the innovators, the imitators comprised only a fraction of all farmers. Like the innovators, they were widely and thinly scattered about the country. The early adoption of an innovation, whether a crop, method, or tool, did not in the American experience necessarily or even usually occur near the point of origin, nor did it usually spread from a point in widening circles, as would have been the case if early imitations had been solely the product of closely observed evidence of feasibility and desirability.[6] A center of general acceptance did occasionally de-

6 Jesse Buel quoted William Coke to the effect that "his example in farming only

velop about the place of origin, as in the case of the Smith plow or the McCormick reaper in Illinois. But it was more typical for early imitators to be scattered and at a distance from the source of the innovation. Numerous secondary centers of adoption tended to develop about the imitative farmers.

The number of imitators determined the rate at which change spread. Since in the case of agriculture, conditions on one farm differ slightly from those on others, in spite of superficial similarities, the imitative process frequently required a significant amount of imagination, as well as some adaptative skill. Like the innovator, the imitator possessed an ability to deal imaginatively with a problem. Though the solutions considered were clearly borrowed, he nevertheless undertook the task of acquainting himself with alternatives and of visualizing the results when incorporated in his own routine. He possessed the willingness to work experimentally with a new technique, tool, or material, even though the economic results were uncertain. In so doing, his conviction of the desirability of exploring changes was sufficiently strong to overcome the powerful social restraints operating to discourage deviations. These imitators, together with the innovators, are to be credited with the increases that occurred in the productivity of American agriculture.

It remains necessary to account for the great majority of farmers during this period. It is again useful to distinguish them, as we have the innovator and the imitator, by the degree to which they exercised their functions as users of resources, according to which they were either gradualists or traditionalists.

Most farmers were characterized by strong prejudices in favor of their long-established routines of production. They looked upon possible change with great caution and skepticism and typically had convincing reasons for refusing to imitate changes that were proving themselves elsewhere. They nevertheless adjusted their routines when it became perfectly and sometimes painfully clear that continued rejection of such opportunities would result in a decline in the relative position of their enterprise. These were the gradualists.

While innate conservatism was the special characteristic of this group, it also included some who had succeeded in applying the

---

enlarged the circle of their influence about a mile a year." Coke's influence was, in fact, far greater among a few scattered and aggressive imitators in the northern United States than in the immediate vicinity of his farm in England. *New York Farmer,* VII (1834), 143.

old technique with great efficiency, achieving an operation in which all resources were in fine balance. There were some significant changes that could not readily or advantageously be made in such situations. Whereas an operation in which resources were not well balanced—in which, for example, there was excessive or poorly utilized land—might incorporate certain changes without difficulty and with advantage, in a finely balanced operation changes could be made only by a thoroughgoing adjustment of the factors involved. A farmer, for example, who could profitably produce small acreages of wheat with hand-harvesting methods, and who had avoided holding land in excess of the capacity of his technology, was unable to gain a cost advantage by adopting the harvester. Such a man found that those who did adopt the harvester achieved a volume of product per unit of labor far greater than he could hope for, whether he continued harvesting by hand or used the machine. As long as the price of wheat was maintained at the same level, he could continue his established practices even though he failed to share in the increased net income of others. But if the price fell in response to the generally higher output of those employing the harvester, he was forced either to abandon wheat production or to secure more land. In any case, the general acceptance of a change involving substantially reduced costs forced many farmers into a drastic adjustment of their operations, either in products sought or in methods employed. These problems were not easily or quickly solved, partly because adjustments in land resources could not readily be made. Decisions on such problems were frequently postponed as long as possible.

Not only did a well-adjusted operation tend to be insensitive to change, but so also did an enterprise that possessed unused resources if control over those resources was insecure. Many an enterpriser in this period placed all his financial resources in land, motivated by speculative considerations and relying on credit for the material and equipment needed over and above his own labor. Since many changes in the technique of production involved the investment of liquid capital, enterprisers of this type found themselves unable to participate, even though they had every reason for doing so, because of their lack of capital and credit. It was only as the new materials and devices were made available on generous credit that they could be employed.

The traditionalists, the fourth group, exhibited a great inertia in appraising the possibilities of changing their production routines and an even greater resistance to adopting such changes. Some, no doubt, lacked the capacity to deal with the more complex kind of production characterizing some of the new methods. Others delayed the acceptance of changes until well after they had become standard and then found themselves with an enterprise so low in productivity that their total returns were below common wages. Under such conditions only sweeping changes, possibly including substantial refinancing, could revitalize the enterprise through a replacement of the obsolete production techniques with the new standard ones. In many instances the area of tillable land held by the enterprise was inadequate to justify such changes, while financing was unavailable to an enterpriser who had demonstrated his incompetence. In other cases the growth of the transportation system bypassed whole groups whose resources, though adequate for an earlier economy, were unsuitable or poorly located for utilization by the newer techniques. Many of the hill-country farmers of New England found themselves in circumstances where they were unable to make adjustments, even if willing. Such men lived out their careers in an economic backwash, away from the main stream of events, in which they took no part and to which they made no contribution. Insofar as the resources they controlled were of substantial value, they constituted an obstacle, though minor, to economic progress.

The American rural society produced over this half-century many men who in various ways and differing degrees sought to improve upon the methods of securing economic objectives. Some, it is true, were drawn into urban occupations, but their energies indirectly supported the essential growth of both the market and the institutions which integrated agriculture with that market. Many others remained on their farms, to apply their energies to the problems of those enterprises. This group was sufficiently influential to change drastically the nature of the agricultural economy within a span of scarcely more than a generation.

The emergence in significant numbers of aggressively innovating and imitating farmers was one aspect of the ferment working in the American society as a whole. The growth of an urban market for farm products beyond the capacity of the subsistence farm to satisfy; the appearance of urban occupations and of an urban way of living disruptive of rural standards; the development of water and then of railroad transportation, breaking down barriers to the movement of people, goods, and ideas; the close relationships maintained with Europe and the rest of the world, which led to the borrowing of innovations in agriculture, industry, and, more broadly, science; the egalitarian society developing its own status structure and motivational patterns; the mingling of ideas that occurred as migrants from various sectors came together in the cities and on the frontiers—these were among the factors that served to stimulate imagination, to establish patterns of thought and action, and to neutralize the forces discouraging deviation from the status quo.

The ability of northern farmers to meet the needs and respond to the challenges presented by the Civil War demonstrated the accomplishments of the preceding decades. From this success sprang an optimistic faith that continued efforts would assure even more dramatic achievements. A speaker at the New York State Agricultural Society Fair in 1867 assured his audience: "Fond of experiments, and untrammeled by habit, we are advancing to a highly scientific agriculture, which shall more than double the productive power of our soils. We shall learn how to create artificial climates by controlling the action of the sun and atmosphere, and how to replenish the soil by restoring the vital forces which are annually withdrawn from it. With a perfected agriculture, we shall have cheaper food, clothing and lodging; manufacturers will be encouraged; labor and raw materials becoming cheaper, commerce will flourish, and we shall have more time for education and travel."[7]

If it was possible to imagine objectives unthinkable several decades earlier, the barriers to continued change and progress were also significantly different from those dealt with earlier. Some were, of course, in familar areas, and could be solved along established lines. The nation's manufacturing industries, for example, were responding to the farmer's desires for better implements and machines, although there was some concern over the concentration of production in fewer and fewer firms. Other barriers called for new approaches. It was clear that the common experience had exhausted its usefulness. Questions about agricultural materials and practices were being raised for which conventional sources could provide no

[7] W. W. Averill in New York State Agricultural Society, *Transactions* (1867), Pt. 2, p. 752.

answer. Solutions were sought through the reorganization of the federal government's role as a source of information and through the new institution of the land grant college. With sources of technical information thus assured, the farmer's interest turned to his relationships with the larger economy. Out of touch with the development of deposit banking in the eastern cities, he sought a supply of money that "would keep overnight" and more adequate sources of credit. He also sought to improve the methods of shipping and marketing his products, for which he turned to the state legislatures for regulation of railroads, elevators, commission merchants, and the commodity exchanges. The change in the character of the farmer's conception of his primary problems is a measure of the evolution of northern farming over this half-century.

BIBLIOGRAPHY   INDEX

SELECTED BIBLIOGRAPHY

The pioneer historical study of the northern United States is Percy W. Bidwell and John I. Falconer, *History of Agriculture in the Northern United States, 1620-1860* (Washington, D.C.: Carnegie Institution of Washington, Publication No. 358, 1925). It remains particularly useful for the period prior to 1820. A more detailed examination of the period to 1860, with particular emphasis on land policy and the characteristics of the major agricultural products, is Paul W. Gates, *The Farmer's Age: Agriculture, 1815-1860* (New York: Holt, Rinehart & Winston, 1960). The years following 1860 are dealt with in Fred A. Shannon, *The Farmer's Last Frontier: Agriculture, 1860-1897* (New York: Farrar and Rinehart, 1945).

The extensive bibliographies in these volumes may be supplemented by Everett E. Edwards, "A Bibliography of the History of Agriculture in the United States," *U. S. Department of Agriculture Miscellaneous Publications*, no. 84 (Washington, D.C.: U. S. Government Printing Office, 1930), which, though old, remains useful. A more recent and specialized bibliographical aid is Carroll W. Pursell, Jr., and Earl M. Rogers, *A Preliminary List of References for the History of Agricultural Science and Technology in the United States* (University of California, Davis, Cal., 1966).

A. AGRICULTURAL PERIODICALS

This study draws heavily upon the contemporary agricultural periodicals listed below as well as the reports and transactions of agricultural societies and state boards of agriculture. Stephen C. Stuntz, "List of the Agricultural Periodicals of the United States and Canada Published during the Century July, 1810, to July, 1910," *U. S. Department of Agriculture Miscellaneous Publications*, no. 398 (Washington, D.C.: U. S. Government Printing Office, 1941), is a useful guide employed in conjunction with the *Union List of Serials*. Stuntz records numerous titles that seem never to have reached publication or were local newspapers of limited value.

The agricultural press has deservedly attracted considerable scholarly attention. Albert L. Demaree, *The American Agricultural Press, 1819-*

1860 (New York: Columbia University Press, 1941), is a valuable introduction to this literature, particularly for its biographical sketches of the editors. It supplants the pioneer study, Gilbert M. Tucker, *American Agricultural Periodicals: An Historical Sketch* (Albany: privately printed, 1909). Important specialized book-length studies are George F. Lemmer and Norman J. Lemmer, *Colman and Colman's Rural World: A Study in Agricultural Leadership* (Columbia: University of Missouri Press, 1953); John T. Schlebecker and Andrew W. Hopkins, *History of Dairy Journalism in the United States, 1810-1950* (Madison: University of Wisconsin Press, 1957); and Richard Bardolph, "Agricultural Literature and the Early Illinois Farmer," *University of Illinois Studies in Social Science*, XXIX (1948). Among articles published in *Agricultural History* are: Claribell R. Barnett, "The Agricultural Museum: An Early American Periodical," II (1928), 99-102; Harold T. Pinkett, "The American Farmer: A Pioneer Agricultural Journal, 1819-1834," XXIV (1950), 146-151; George F. Lemmer, "Early Agricultural Editors and Their Farm Philosophies," XXXI (1957), 3-22; and John T. Schlebecker, "Dairy Journalism: Studies in Successful Farm Journalism," XXXI (1957), 23-33.

Agricultural Intelligencer and Mechanic's Register, I, 1820. Boston.
American Agriculturist, I-XXIX, 1842-1870. New York.
American Cabinet. See *New York Farmer and Mechanic*.
The American Farmer, I-XV, 1819-1834. Baltimore. Continued as *Farmer and Gardener and Livestock Breeder and Manager*, I, 1834-1835. *Farmer and Gardener*, II-VI, 1835-1839. *American Farmer and Spirit of the Agricultural Journals of the Day*, 3rd ser., I-VI, 1839-1845; 4th ser., I-VI, 1845-1850; 4th ser., VII-XIV, 1850-1859; 5th ser., I-III, 1859-1861; 6th ser., I-V, 1866-1870.
The American Farmer's Companion or Cabinet of Agricultural Knowledge, I, 1840. Philadelphia.
The American Farmer's Magazine. See *The Plough, the Loom and the Anvil*.
The American Gardener's Magazine and the Register of Useful Discoveries and Improvements in Horticulture and Rural Affairs, I-II, 1835-1836. Boston. Continued as *The Magazine of Horticulture, Botany, and All Useful Discoveries and Improvements in Rural Affairs*, III-XXXIV, 1837-1868.
The American Quarterly Journal of Agriculture and Science, I-IV, 1845-1846. Albany and New York. Continued as *The American Journal of Agriculture and Science*, V-VII, 1847-1848.
The American Ruralist, I, 1858. Springfield, Ohio.
Boston Cultivator, I-XXXI, 1839-1870. Boston.
The Central New York Farmer, I-III, 1842-1844. Rome.
The Cincinnatus, I-V, 1856-1860. Cincinnati. Continued as *The Cincinnatus and Journal of the American Patent Company*, I, 1861.
Colman's Rural World. See *Valley Farmer*.
The Connecticut Farmer and Gazette and Horticultural Repository. See *The Farmer's Gazette*.

The Connecticut Farmer's Gazette. See *The Farmer's Gazette.*

Connecticut Homestead. See *The Homestead.*

The Connecticut Valley Farmer and Mechanic, I, 1853-1854. Springfield and Amherst, Massachusetts. Continued as *The Connecticut Valley Farmer,* II, 1854. *The Farmer,* n.s. I, 1855.

The Country Gentleman, I-XXVI, 1853-1865. Albany. Continued as *The Cultivator and Country Gentleman,* XXVII-XXXVIII, 1866-1872.

The Cultivator, I-VI, 1834-1839. Albany. Continued as *The Cultivator: A Consolidation of Buel's Cultivator and The Genesee Farmer,* VII-X, 1840-1843. *The Cultivator,* n.s. I-IX, 1844-1852; 3rd ser. I-XIII, 1852-1965.

The Cultivator and Country Gentleman. See *The Country Gentleman.*

Delaware Register and Farmer, I, 1828. Wilmington.

Delaware Register and Farmer's Magazine, I-II, 1838-1839. Dover.

The Dollar Farmer, I-IV, 1842-1846. Louisville.

Emery's Quarterly Journal of Agriculture, I, 1856-1857. Chicago. Continued as *Emery's Journal of Agriculture and Praire Farmer,* II, 1858-1859. See also *The Union Agriculturist.*

Evan's Rural Economist, I-II, 1861-1862. West Chester.

Farm and Garden, I, 1853. New York.

The Farm and Shop, I-II, 1853-1855. Indianapolis.

The Farm Journal and Progressive Farmer. See *Pennsylvania Farm Journal.*

The Farmer. See *The Connecticut Valley Farmer and Mechanic.*

Farmer and Artizan, I-II, 1852-1853. Portland.

Farmer and Gardener. See *The American Farmer.*

The Farmer and Gardener, I-V, 1859-1863. Philadelphia. Continued as *The Pennsylvania Farmer and Gardener,* VI, 1864.

Farmer and Gardener and Livestock Breeder and Manager. See *The American Farmer.*

Farmer and Mechanic, I-II, 1852-1853. Lewiston.

Farmer and Mechanic. See *The New York Farmer and Mechanic.*

The Farmer and Mechanic and American Cabinet of Mechanics, Manufactures, New Inventions, Science, Agriculture and the Arts. See *The New York Farmer and Mechanic.*

Farmer's Cabinet, I-IV, 1836-1840. Philadelphia (also, at times, Pittsburgh and Wilmington). Continued as *The Farmer's Cabinet and American Herdbook,* V-XII, 1840-1848.

The Farmer's Companion and Horticultural Gazette, I-IV, 1853-1854. Detroit.

The Farmer's Gazette, I, 1840. New Haven. Continued as *The Connecticut Farmer's Gazette,* I-IV, 1840-1844. *The Connecticut Farmer and Gazette and Horticultural Repository,* I, 1844.

The Farmer's Journal and Magazine of Useful Arts, I-II, 1841-1843. Boston.

The Farmer's Library and Monthly Journal of Agriculture, I-II, 1845-1848. New York. (*The Farmer's Library* was a serial reissue of agricultural books; the *Monthly Journal* included original articles. The two parts were issued with separate title pages.) Continued as *Monthly Journal of Agriculture,* II-III, 1846-1848.

The Farmer's Monthly Visitor, I-XIII, 1839-1849, 1852-1853. Concord and Manchester, N. H. (XII-XIII, 1852-1853, published at Manchester, was a different publication although continuing title and volume numbering.)

The Farmer's Register, I-X, 1833-1842. Shellbanks, Garysville, and Petersburg, Va.

The Franklin Farmer, I-IV, 1837-1840. Frankfort, Ky.

Genesee Farmer. See *New Genesee Farmer and Gardener's Journal*.

Genesee Farmer and Gardener's Journal, I-IX, 1831-1839. Rochester. Also entitled *Monthly Genesee Farmer*, 1836-1839.

Granite Farmer and Visitor, I-VXI, 1850-1857. Manchester.

Granite State Farmer. I-II, 1857-1858. Manchester.

The Green Mountain Farmer, I, 1852. Bradford. Continued as *The Green Mountain Culturist*, I, 1852. Middlebury.

The Homestead, I-VII, 1855-1861. Hartford.

Illinois Cultivator, I-II, 1841-1842. Stephenson.

The Illinois Farmer, I, 1841-1842. Springfield.

———, I-IX, 1856-1864. Springfield.

Indiana Farmer and Gardener, I, 1845. Indianapolis. Continued as *Western Farmer and Gardener*, II-III, 1846-1847.

———, I-VIII, 1851-1859. Springfield, Richmond, and Indianapolis. Also entitled *Indiana Farmer's Guide*.

The Iowa Farmer and Horticulturist, I-V, 1853-1857. Burlington, Fairfield, Mt. Pleasant, and Des Moines. Continued as *Pioneer Farmer and Iowa Home Visitor*, I-II, 1858-1862.

The Iowa Farmer's Advocate, I, 1847-1848. Burlington.

Iowa Homestead. See *Northwestern Farmer and Horticultural Journal*.

The Journal of Agriculture, I-IV, 1851-1854. Boston. See also *The Farmer's Library*.

Journal of the American Institute, I-IV, 1835-1839; I, 1850-1851. New York.

The Journal of the United States Agricultural Society, I-V, 1852-1855. Washington, D.C., and Boston. Continued as *Transactions and Monthly Bulletin of the United States Agricultural Society*, VI, 1858. *The Quarterly Journal of Agriculture*, VII-X, 1859-1862.

Kennebec Farmer and Journal of Useful Arts, I, 1833. Winthrop and Augusta, Me. Continued as *Maine Farmer and Journal of the Useful Arts*, II-IX, 1833-1841. *Maine Farmer and Mechanics Advocate*, X-XII, 1842-1844. *Maine Farmer*, XIII-XXXVIII, 1845-1870.

The Magazine of Horticulture, Botany and All Useful Discoveries and Improvements in Rural Affairs. See *The American Gardener's Magazine*.

Maine Farmer. See *Kennebec Farmer*.

Massachusetts Ploughman, I-XXVI, 1841-1866. Boston. Continued as *Massachusetts Ploughman and New England Journal of Agriculture*, XXVII-XXXI, 1867-1871.

The Michigan Farmer. See *The Western Farmer and Record of General Intelligence*.

Minnesota Farmer and Gardener, I-II, 1860-1861. Minneapolis.

Monthly Bulletin of the United States Agricultural Society. See *The Journal of the United States Agricultural Society*.

Monthly Genesee Farmer. See *Genesee Farmer and Gardener's Journal*.

Monthly Journal of Agriculture. See *The Farmer's Library*.

Moore's Rural New Yorker. See *Rural New Yorker*.

Morris' Rural Advertiser, I-III, 1864-1866. Philadelphia. Continued as *The Practical Farmer and Rural Advertiser*, IV-VII, 1867-1870.

New England Cultivator, I-IV, 1852-1853. Boston.

The New England Farmer, I-V, 1822-1827. Boston. Continued as *New England Farmer and Horticultural Journal*, VI-XII, 1827-1834. *New England Farmer and Gardener's Journal,* XIII-XVII, 1834-1839. *New England Farmer and Horticultural Register,* XVII-XXIV, 1839-1846. *New England Farmer,* I-XIV, 1848-1864; n.s. I-V, 1867-1871.

New Genesee Farmer and Gardener's Journal, I-V, 1840-1844. Rochester. Continued as *Genesee Farmer,* VI-XXVI, 1845-1865.

New Hampshire Journal of Agriculture, I-V, 1852-1862. Manchester.

The New Jersey Farmer, I-VI, 1855-1861. Freehold, Trenton.

The New York Farmer and Horticultural Repository, I-V, 1828-1832. New York. Continued as *The New York Farmer and American Gardener's Magazine,* VI-X, 1833-1837.

The New York Farmer and Mechanic, I-IV, 1844-1846. New York. Continued as *Farmer and Mechanic,* III-VII (n.s., I-V), 1847-1851. *The Farmer and Mechanic and American Cabinet of Mechanics, Manufacturers, New Inventions, Science, Agriculture and the Arts,* VII-X (n.s. V-VI), 1851-1852. New York and Boston.

The Northern Farmer, I-II, 1852-1853; I-II, 1854-1855; I-V, 1856-1861. Utica and Clinton.

The Northern Farmer and Practical Horticulturist, I-II, 1832-1834. Newport, N. H.

Northwestern Farmer and Horticultural Journal, I-VI, 1856-1862. Dubuque. Continued as *Iowa Homestead and Horticulturist,* VII-XIII, 1862-1868. *Iowa Homestead and Western Farm Journal,* XIII-XVIII, 1868-1873.

The Ohio Agriculturist, I, 1851. Tiffin.

Ohio Cultivator, I-XVIII, 1845-1862. Columbus.

Ohio Farmer, I-XVIII, 1852-1870. Cleveland.

Ohio Farmer and Western Agriculturist, I-II, 1834-1835. Batavia and Columbus.

Ohio Valley Farmer, I-VI, 1856-1861. Cincinnati.

Pennsylvania Farm Journal, I-V, 1851-1855. Lancaster, West Chester, and Philadelphia. Continued as *The Farm Journal and Progressive Farmer,* VI-VII, 1856-1857.

Pennsylvania Farmer and Gardener. See *The Farmer and Gardener.*

Pioneer Farmer and Iowa Home Visitor. See *The Iowa Farmer and Horticulturist.*

The Plough, the Loom and the Anvil, I-X, 1848-1857. Philadelphia and New York. Continued as *The American Farmer's Magazine,* XI-XII, 1858-1859.

Plough Boy, I, 1818-1820. Albany, N.Y. Continued as *Plough Boy and Journal of the Board of Agriculture,* II-III, 1820-1822. *Plough Boy,* IV, 1822-1823.

The Plow, I, 1852. New York.

The Practical Farmer. See *Morris' Rural Advertiser.*

The Practical Farmer and Scientific Gardener, I-III, 1863-1964. New York.

The Prairie Farmer. See *The Union Agriculturist.*

Progressive Farmer, I, 1855. Philadelphia.

The Quarterly Journal of Agriculture. See *The Journal of the United States Agricultural Society.*

Ruffin's Farmer's Register. See *The Farmer's Register.*

Rural Advertiser. See *Morris' Rural Advertiser.*

The Rural American, I-II, 1856-1857. Utica and Clinton.

Rural New Yorker, I-XX, 1850-1870. Rochester.

The Rural Register, I-IV, 1859-1863. Baltimore.

Tippecanoe Farmer, I, 1854-1855. Lafayette, Ind.

The Union Agriculturist, I, 1840. Chicago. Continued as *The Union Agricul-*

turist and Western Prairie Farmer, I-II, 1841-1842. *The Prairie Farmer*, III-XVIII, 1843-1858. *Emery's Journal of Agriculture and Prairie Farmer*, XVII, 1858-1859. *Prairie Farmer*, XIX-XXXI, 1859-1871.

United States Farmer and Journal of American Institutes, I, 1842. New York.

Valley Farmer, I-XVI, 1849-1864. St. Louis and Louisville. Continued as *Colman's Rural World and Valley Farmer*, XVII-XIX, 1865-1867. *Colman's Rural World*, XX-XXIV, 1868-1872.

Vermont State Agriculturist, I, 1848-1849. Burlington.

Western Agriculturist, I-II, 1851-1852. Columbus.

Western Agriculturist and Fireside Companion, I-II, 1855-1856. Pittsburgh.

Western Agriculturist and General Intelligencer, I, 1829. Brookville, Ind.

Western Farm Journal, I-II, 1856-1857. Louisville.

The Western Farmer, I, 1839-1840. Cincinnati. Continued as *The Western Farmer and Gardener*, II-III, 1840-1842. *The Western Farmer and Gardener and Horticultural Magazine*, IV-V, 1843-1845.

The Western Farmer, I-II, 1841-1842. Detroit.

Western Farmer and Gardener. See *Indiana Farmer and Gardener*.

The Western Farmer and Record of General Intelligence, I-II, 1841-1843. Detroit and Jackson. Continued as *The Michigan Farmer and Western Agriculturist*, I, 1843-1844. *The Michigan Farmer and Western Horticulturist*, II, 1844-1845. *The Michigan Farmer*, III-XVI, 1845-1862 (n.s. 1-4, 1859-1862).

The Western Plow Boy, 1853. Fort Wayne.

Western Reserve Farmer and Dairyman, I, 1852. Jefferson.

Wisconsin Farmer and Northwestern Cultivator, I, 1849-1850. Racine and Madison. Continued as *Wisconsin and Iowa Farmer and Northwestern Cultivator*, II-VII, 1850-1855. *Wisconsin Farmer and Northwestern Cultivator*, VII-XI, 1855-1859. *Wisconsin Farmer*, XII-XX, 1860-1867.

The Wool Grower and Magazine of Agriculture and Horticulture, I-IV, 1849-1852. Buffalo. Continued as *The Wool Grower and Stock Register*, IV-X, 1852-1856.

Working Farmer, I-XIV, 1849-1862. New York. Continued as *Working Farmer and United States Journal*, XV-XVI, 1862-1864.

Yankee Farmer, I-V, 1835-1839. Cornish and Portland. Continued as *Yankee Farmer and New England Cultivator*, VI-VII, 1840-1841. Boston.

In addition to the agricultural periodicals, many other publications include material relating to farming. Among the more important are *De Bow's Review* (New Orleans); *Hazard's Commercial Register* (New York); *Hunt's Merchants' Magazine and Commercial Review* (New York); *The National Magazine and Industrial Record* (New York); and *The Scientific American*, vols. 1-14 (1854-1859), n.s. I-XXI (1859-1870, New York).

Newspapers are also important sources of information. Among those utilized in the preparation of this study are the *Germantown Telegraph*, Germantown, Pa., the *Journal of Commerce*, New York, and the *New York Tribune*.

B. PUBLICATIONS OF PRIVATE, QUASI-PUBLIC AND GOVERNMENT ORGANIZATIONS

The numerous separately published reports of county and local agricultural organizations, having little value, are not listed.

Connecticut.
    State Agricultural Society. *Transactions,* 1854-1860. Hartford.
    State Board of Agriculture. *Annual Report of the Secretary of the State
        Board of Agriculture,* I-IV, 1866-1871/1872. Hartford.
Illinois.
    State Agricultural Society. *Transactions,* I-VIII, 1853-1870. Springfield.
    ———. *Journal,* I-II, 1862-1863. Springfield.
Indiana.
    State Board of Agriculture. *Report,* I-IX, 1851-1867. Indianapolis.
Iowa.
    State Agricultural Society. *Report,* I-XVI, 1854-1870. Des Moines.
Maine.
    Transactions of the Agricultural Societies of Maine, I-IV, 1850-1855. Augusta.
    Board of Agriculture. *Annual Report of the Secretary,* I-XV, 1856-1870.
        Augusta.
Maryland.
    *The Agricultural Report of James Higgins, State Chemist, to the House of
        Delegates of the State of Maryland,* I-VI, 1850-1858. Annapolis.
Massachusetts.
    Massachusetts Society for Promoting Agriculture. *Massachusetts Agricultural
        Repository and Journal,* III-X, 1815-1827. Boston.
    ———. *Transactions,* I, 1856; n.s. I, 1858-1861. Boston
    Secretary of the Commonwealth. *Abstracts from the returns of the Agricul-
        tural Societies in Massachusetts,* 1845-1846, 1846-1847. Boston.
    Board of Agriculture. *Transactions of the Agricultural Societies of Massachu-
        setts,* 1847-1852. Boston.
    ———. *Annual Report of the Secretary,* I-XVIII, 1853-1870. Boston. (In-
        cludes abstracts of the transactions of the county agricultural societies,
        separately paged, and cited in the text as "Abstracts.")
Michigan.
    State Agricultural Society. *Transactions,* I-XI, 1849-1859. Detroit.
    ———. *Journal,* I, 1853-1854. Detroit.
    State Board of Agriculture. *Annual Report of the Secretary,* I-VIII, 1862-
        1870. Lansing.
Missouri.
    State Board of Agriculture. *Annual Report,* I-II, 1865-1866; III-VII, 1867-
        1871. St. Louis.
New Hampshire.
    State Agricultural Society. *Transactions,* I-IX, 1850/1852-1860. Manchester,
        Dover, and Concord.
    State Board of Agriculture. *The New Hampshire Agricultural Repository,*
        No. 1, 1822. Concord.
New Jersey.
    Agricultural Society. *Proceedings,* 1839. Trenton.
    State Agricultural Society. *Report,* I-XVII, 1855/1856-1867. Trenton.
New York.
    Board of Agriculture of the State of New York. *Memoirs,* I-III, 1821-1826.
        Albany.

State Agricultural Society. *Transactions,* I-XXX, 1841-1870. Albany.
———. *Journal,* I-XXIII, 1850-1873. Albany.
New York State Agricultural Society's Trial of Implements at Geneva, July, 1852. Albany.
Second National Trial of Mowers, Reapers, Horse Powers, etc., by the New York State Agricultural Society at Auburn, July, 1866. Albany.
Report of the Trial of Plows, held at Utica by the New York State Agricultural Society, commencing September 8, 1867. Albany.
New York Secretary of State. *Census of the State of New York for 1845.* Albany, 1846.
———. *Census of the State of New York for 1855.* Albany, 1857.
———. *Census of the State of New York for 1865.* Albany, 1867.
National Convention of Farmers and Gardeners and Friends of Agriculture. *Proceedings.* 1844. New York.
National Convention of Farmers, Gardeners, and Silk Culturists. *Proceedings.* 1846. New York.

American Institute of the City of New York. *Journal,* I-IV, 1835-1839; I, 1850-1851. New York.
———. *Transactions,* I-XXX, 1841-1871. New York and Albany.

Ohio.
Ohio Commissioner of Statistics. *Annual Reports to the Governor of the State of Ohio.* Vols. 1-14, 1857-1870. Columbus.
State Board of Agriculture. *Annual Report,* I-XXV, 1846-1870. Columbus.

Pennsylvania.
Agricultural Society. *Hints for American Husbandmen, with Communications to the Pennsylvania Agricultural Society,* 1827. Harrisburg.
———. *Memoirs.* 1823/1824. Harrisburg.
State Agricultural Society. *Proceedings,* I-III, 1823-1825. Harrisburg.
———. *Report of the Transactions,* I-VII, 1854-1857/1858; 1859-1870. Harrisburg.
Philadelphia Society for Promoting Agriculture. *Memoirs,* I-V, 1808-1827. Philadelphia.

Rhode Island.
Society for the Encouragement of Domestic Industry. *Transactions,* 1850-1870. Providence.
Report on the Industrial Statistics of the State of Rhode Island from Materials Collected by the Rhode Island Society for the Promotion of Domestic Industry in Accordance with a Resolution of the General Assembly, January session, 1860. Providence.

United States.
Census Office. *Census for 1820.* Washington, D.C., 1821.
———. *The Seventh Census of the United States: 1850.* Washington, D.C., 1853.
———. *Compendium of the Seventh Census, 1850.* Washington, D.C., 1854.
———. *Agriculture of the United States in 1860.* Washington, D.C., 1864.
———. Population of the United States in 1860. Washington, D.C., 1864.
———. *Ninth Census of the United States, 1870. Statistics of Population.* Washington, D.C., 1871. *Agriculture.* Washington, D.C., 1872. *Statistics of Wealth and Industry.* Washington, D.C., 1872.

Bureau of the Census. *Sixteenth Census of the U. S.: 1940.* Vol. I: *Population.* Washington, D.C., 1942.

————. *Sixteenth Census of Population: Comparative Occupation Statistics of the United States, 1870-1940.* Washington, D.C., 1943.

Commissioner of Patents. *Annual Report,* 1839-1845, 1847-1861. Washington, D.C. (The report on agriculture was included as part of a single-volume report through 1848. Thereafter it appears as a separate volume.)

Commissioner of Agriculture. *Report,* 1862-1889. Washington, D.C.

(A useful guide to the Reports of the Commissioner of Patents and the Commissioner of Agriculture is Handy, R. B., and Minna A. Cannon. "List of titles of Publications of the United States Department of Agriculture from 1840 to June, 1901." *U.S.D.A. Bulletin No. 6.* Washington, D.C., 1902.)

Department of Agriculture. *Yearbook of Agriculture,* 1894-   . Washington, D.C.

United States Agricultural Society. *The American Quarterly Journal of Agriculture and Science,* I, 1852. Washington, D.C.

————. *Annual Meeting . . . President's Address,* I-VI, 1853-1858. Washington, D.C.

Vermont.

Vermont State Agriculturist, I, 1848-1849. Burlington.

State Agricultural Society. *Proceedings,* 1862. Windsor.

Wisconsin.

State Agricultural Society. *Transactions,* Vol. I-XIX, 1851-1870. Madison.

Agricultural and Mechanical Association. *Bulletin,* 1860. Milwaukee.

C. TRAVEL AND GUIDE BOOKS

Andrews, Christopher C. *Minnesota and Decotah: Letters Descriptive of a Tour Through the Northwest in the Autumn of 1856.* Washington, D.C., 1857.

Baird, Robert. *Impressions and Experiences of the West Indies and North America.* Philadelphia, 1850.

————. *View of the Valley of the Mississippi or the Emigrant's and Traveler's Guide of the West.* Philadelphia, 1835.

Barclay, Captain. *Agricultural Tour in the United States and Upper Canada.* Edinburgh, 1842.

Beste, J. Richard. *The Wabash: or Adventures of an English Gentleman's Family in the Interior of America.* 2 vols. London, 1856.

Birkbeck, Morris. *Notes on a Journey in America, from the Coast of Virginia to the Territory of Illinois.* Philadelphia, 1818.

————. *Letters from Illinois.* Philadelphia, 1818.

Bishop, Harriet E. *Minnesota: Then and Now.* St. Paul, 1869.

Bond, John Wesley. *Minnesota and Its Resources.* New York, 1853.

Borret, George Tuthill. *Out West: A Series of Letters from Canada and the United States.* London, 1866.

Burlend, Rebecca. *A True Picture of Emigration.* Chicago: Lakeside Press, 1936.

Caird, James. *Prairie Farming in America.* New York, 1859.

Carlisle, George William. *Travels in America.* New York, 1851.

Casey, Charles. *Two Years on the Farm of Uncle Sam. With Sketches of His Location, Nephews, and Prospects.* London, 1850.

Chamberlain, E. *The Indiana Gazetteer.* Indianapolis, 1850.

Chambers, William. *Things as They Are In America.* London, 1854.

Chevalier, Michael. *Society, Manners and Politics in the United States: Being a Series of Letters on North America.* Boston, 1839.

Cobbett, William. *The Emigrant's Guide: In Ten Letters.* London, 1829.

———. *A Year's Residence in the United States of America.* New York, 1818.

Colman, Henry. *European Agriculture and Rural Economy from Personal Observation.* 2 vols. Boston, 1844.

———. *Agriculture and Rural Economy in France, Belgium, Holland, and Switzerland.* New York, 1851.

———, *European Life and Manners in Familiar Letters to Friends.* 2 vols. Boston, 1849.

Cunynghame, Arthur. *A Glimpse of the Great Western Republic.* London, 1851.

Curtiss, Daniel S. *Western Portraiture and Emigrant's Guide: A Description of Wisconsin, Illinois, and Iowa; With Remarks on Minnesota and Other Territories.* New York, 1852.

Dicey, Edward. *Six Months in the Federal States.* London, 1863.

Drake, Benjamin, and E. D. Mansfield. *Cincinnati in 1826.* Cincinnati, 1827.

Dwight, Theodore, Jr. *Things as They Are: Or Notes of a Traveller Through Some of the Middle and Northern States.* New York, 1834.

———. *The Northern Traveller.* New York, 1841.

Ellsworth, Henry William. *Valley of the Upper Wabash, Indiana, with Hints on its Agricultural Advantages: Plan of a Dwelling, Estimates of Cultivation, and Notices of Labor-Saving Machines.* New York, 1838.

Emigrant's Guide to Minnesota, by an Old Resident. St. Anthony, 1856.

Farnham, Eliza W. *Life in Prairie Land.* New York, 1856.

Fearon, Henry Bradshaw. *Sketches of America, A Narrative of a Journal of 5,000 Miles Through the Eastern and Western States.* London, 1818.

Ferguson, William. *America by River and Rail.* London, 1856.

Ferris, Jacob. *The States and Territories of the Great West.* New York, 1856.

Flint, James. *Letters from America.* 1822. Reprinted in R. G. Thwaites, *Early Western Travels,* vol. IX. Cleveland, 1907.

Flint, Timothy. *Recollection of Ten Year's Residence in the Valley of the Mississippi.* Boston, 1826.

Gerhard, Frederick. *Illinois As It Is: Its History, Geography, Statistics, Agriculture.* Chicago, 1857.

Gregory, John. *Industrial Resources of Wisconsin.* Milwaukee, 1855.

Hall, James. *Letters from the West.* London, 1828.

———. *Notes on the Western States.* Philadelphia, 1838.

———. *Statistics of the West at the Close of the Year 1836.* Cincinnati, 1836.

———. *The West: Its Commerce and Navigation.* Cincinnati, 1848.

———. *The West: Its Soil, Surface and Production.* Cincinnati, 1848.

Holmes, Isaac. *An Account of the United States of America.* London, 1823.

Hunt, John W. *Wisconsin Gazetteer.* Madison, 1853.

Johnston, James F. W. *Notes on North America: Agricultural, Economical, and Social.* 2 vols. Boston, 1852.

Jones, Abner D. *Illinois and the West.* Boston, 1838.

Lyell, Charles. *Travels in North America in the Years 1841-1842.* 2 vols. New York, 1855.

————. *A Second Visit to the United States of North America*. 2 vols. New York, 1849.

Mackay, Charles. *The Western World*. 2 vols. Philadelphia, 1849.

————. *Life and Liberty in America*. 2 vols. London, 1859.

McClung, John W. *Minnesota As It Is in 1870*. St. Paul, 1870.

Marshall, Josiah T. *The Farmer's and Emigrant's Handbook*. Utica, 1852.

Minnesota: Its Advantages to Settlers. St. Paul, 1869.

Mooney, Thomas. *Nine Years in America*. Dublin, 1850.

Murray, Henry A. *Lands of the Slave and Free: Or Cuba, the United States and Canada*. 2 vols. London, 1855.

Newhall, John B. *Sketches of Iowa: Or the Emigrant's Guide*. New York, 1841.

Oldmixon, John W. *Transatlantic Wanderings or a Last Look at the United States*. London, 1855.

Oliphant, Laurence. *Minnesota and the Far West*. London, 1855.

Oliver, William. *Eight Months in Illinois, with Information to Immigrants*. Newcastle Upon Tyne, 1843.

Parker, Nathan H. *Iowa As It is in 1855*. Chicago, 1855.

————. *Iowa As It Is in 1856*. Chicago, 1856.

————. *Iowa Handbook for 1857*. Boston, 1857.

————. *Kansas and Nebraska Handbook for 1857-58*. Boston, 1857.

————. *Minnesota Handbook for 1856-57*. Boston, 1857.

————. *Missouri Handbook*. St. Louis, 1865.

————. *Missouri As It Is in 1867*. Philadelphia, 1867.

————. *Illustrated Handbook of the Great West*. New York, 1869.

Peck, John M. *A Guide for Emigrants*. Boston, 1831.

————. *A Gazeteer of Illinois*. Philadelphia, 1837.

————. *A New Guide for Emigrants*. Boston, 1836.

————. *A New Guide for Emigrants in the West*. Boston, 1837.

————. *A New Guide to the West*. Cincinnati, 1848.

————. *Forty Years of Pioneer Life*. Philadelphia, 1864.

Regan, John. *The Emigrant's Guide to the Western States of America*. Edinburgh, 1852.

Ritchie, James S. *Wisconsin and Its Resources with Lake Superior, Its Commerce and Navigation*. Philadelphia, 1857.

Russell, Robert. *North America: Its Agriculture and Climate, Containing Observations on the Agriculture and Climate of Canada, the United States, and the Islands of Cuba*. Edinburgh, 1857.

Seymour, E. S. *Sketches of Minnesota, the New England of the West*. New York, 1850.

Shirreff, Patrick. *A Tour Through North America Together with a Comprehensive View of the Canadas and the United States as Adapted for Agricultural Emigration*. Edinburgh, 1835.

Smith, Sidney. *The Settler's New Home*. London, 1850.

Strickland, William. *Observations on the Agriculture of the United States of America*. London, 1815.

Stuart, James. *Three Years in North America*. Edinburgh, 2 vols. 1833.

Thomason, D. R. *Hints to Emigrants*. Philadelphia, 1848.

Thomson, E. H. *The Emigrant's Guide to the State of Michigan*. n.p., 1849.

Tocqueville, Alexis de. *Democracy in America*. 2 vols. New York: A. A. Knopf, 1948.

————. *Journey to America*, ed. J. P. Mayer. London: Faber & Faber, 1960.

Tudor, Henry. *Narrative of a Tour in North America.* 2 vols. London, 1834.

Wakefield, Edward S. *England and America: A Comparison of the Social and Political Life of Both Nations.* 2 vols. London, 1833.

Wales, W. W. *The Immigrant's Guide to Minnesota in 1856.* St. Anthony, 1856.

Weld, Charles Richard. *A Vacation Tour in the United States and Canada.* London, 1855.

Wetmore, Henry C. *Rural Life in America.* New York, 1856.

Wilkie, Franc B. *Davenport, Past and Present.* Davenport, 1858.

Wilson, William D. *Description of Iowa and Its Resources.* Des Moines, 1865.

Woods, John. *Two Years' Residence in the Settlement on the English Prairie in the Illinois Country, United States: With an Account of Its Animal and Vegetable Productions, Agriculture, Etc., Etc., A Description of the Principal Towns, Villages, Etc., Etc., With the Habits and Customs of the Backwoodsmen.* London, 1822.

Wyse, Francis. *America: Its Realities and Resources.* 2 vols. London, 1846.

D. OTHER CONTEMPORARY MATERIALS

The list includes only the most useful of the numerous manuals and textbooks on agriculture published prior to 1900.

Allen, James T. *Digest of Plows, with Attachments, Patented in the United States, 1789-1883.* Washington, D.C., 1883.

──────. *Digest of Agricultural Implements Patented in the United States from A.D. 1789 to July 1881.* New York, 1886.

──────. *Digest of Seeding Machines and Implements Patented in the United States from the Year 1800 Up To and Including June 1878.* Washington, D.C., 1879.

Allen, Lewis F. *American Cattle, Their History, Breeding and Management.* New York, 1868.

──────. *History of the Short-horn Cattle; Their Origin, Progress and Present Condition.* Buffalo, 1872.

──────. *The American Herd Book, Containing Pedigrees of Short Horn Cattle, 1846-1882.* New York, 1883.

Allen, Richard L. *Brief Compendium of American Agriculture.* New York, 1846.

──────. *Domestic Animals.* New York, 1847.

Andreas, Alfred A. *History of Chicago.* 3 vols. Chicago, 1884-1886.

Andrews, Israel D. *Report on the Trade and Commerce of the British North American Colonies and Upon the Trade of the Great Lakes and Rivers.* Washington, D.C., 1853.

Ardrey, Robert L. *American Agricultural Implements: A Review of Invention and Development in the Agricultural Implement Industry in the United States.* Chicago, 1894.

Benton, Thomas Hart. *Thirty Years' View: A History of American Government for Thirty Years, from 1820 to 1850.* 2 vols. New York, 1864.

Bishop, John Leander. *A History of American Manufacturers from 1608 to 1860.* 3 vols. Philadelphia, 1866.

Blake, John L. *A Family Textbook for the Country, or The Farmer at Home.* New York, 1853.

──────. *The Farmer's Cyclopedia of Modern Agriculture.* New York, 1852.

————. *The Modern Farmer.* New York, 1854.

————. *The Farm and the Fireside, or the Romance of Agriculture.* Auburn, N. Y., 1852.

Bordley, John B. *Essays and Notes on Husbandry.* Philadelphia, 1801.

Brown, Abram E. *Faneuil Hall and Faneuil Hall Market.* Boston, 1900.

Browne, Daniel J. *The Field Book of Manures; or the American Muck Book.* New York, 1856.

Buel, Jesse. *The Farmer's Companion, Essays on American Husbandry.* Boston, 1839.

————. *The Farmer's Instructor: Essays and Hints on the Management of the Farm and Garden.* 2 vols. New York, 1840.

Burrows, J. M. D. *Fifty Years in Iowa.* Davenport, 1888.

Chickering, Jesse. *A Statistical View of the Population of Massachusetts from 1765 to 1840.* Boston, 1846.

Colman, Henry. *Letter to the Farmers of Massachusetts on the Subject of an Agricultural Survey of the State.* Boston, 1837.

————. *Agriculture of the United States, Address Before the American Institute of the City of New York.* New York, 1841.

Complete Practical Farmer. New York, 1839.

Curtis, Josiah. *Report of the Special Committee on the Census of Boston, 1855.* Boston, 1856.

Cutler, Julia F. *Life and Times of Ephrain Cutler.* Cincinnati, 1890.

Dana, Samuel L. *An Essay on Manures.* New York, 1852.

————. *A Muck Manual for Farmers.* Lowell, 1842.

De Voe, Thomas. *The Market Book, Containing a Historical Account of the Public Markets in the Cities of New York, Boston, Philadelphia, and Brooklyn.* New York, 1862.

Dickerman, Charles W. *How to Make the Farm Pay.* Philadelphia, 1869.

Eliot, Jared. *Essays Upon Field Husbandry in New England,* ed. Harry J. Carman and Rexford G. Tugwell. New York: Columbia University, 1934.

Ellsworth, Henry L. *Improvements in Agriculture, Arts, Etc., of the United States.* New York, 1843.

————. *The American Swine Breeder.* Boston, 1840.

Emmons, Ebenezer. *Agriculture of New York.* 5 vols. Albany, 1846-1854.

Enfield, Edward. *Indian Corn: Its Value, Culture, and Uses.* New York, 1866.

Fessenden, Thomas G. *The Husbandman and Housewife.* Bellows Falls, Vt., 1820.

————. *The New American Gardener.* Boston, 1828.

————. *The Complete Farmer and Rural Economist.* Boston, 1834.

Flagg, W. C. "The Agriculture of Illinois, 1683-1876." *Transactions of the Department of Agriculture of the State of Illinois, 1875.* Springfield, 1876.

Flint, Charles L. *Practical Treatise on Grasses and Forage Plants,* 2nd ed. New York, 1858.

————. *Milch Cows and Dairy Farming.* New York, 1858.

————. "Agriculture in the United States," in Thomas P. Kettel, ed. *Eighty Years' Progress of the United States,* 2nd ed. New York, 1861.

Flower, George. *The Western Shepherd.* New Harmony, Ind., 1841.

Fox, Charles. *The American Textbook of Practical and Scientific Agriculture.* Detroit, 1854.

Freedley, Edwin T. *Practical Treatise on Business.* Philadelphia, 1854.

Gaylord, Willis, and Luther Tucker. *American Husbandry*. 2 vols. New York, 1840.

Gilbert, Frank, *Jethro Wood, Inventor of the Modern Plow*. Chicago, 1882.

Greeley, Horace. *What I Know of Farming*. New York, 1871.

Hammond, J. H. *The Farmers' and Mechanics' Practical Architect and Guide in Rural Economy*. Boston, 1858.

Hartley, Robert M. *An Historical, Scientific, and Practical Essay on Milk, As an Article of Human Sustenance; With a Consideration of the Effects Consequent Upon the Present Unnatural Methods of Producing It for the Supply of Large Cities*. New York, 1842.

———. *The Cow and the Dairy*. New York, 1851.

Henry, Mathew S. *History of the Lehigh Valley*. Easton, 1860.

Hollister, Hiel. *Pawlett for One Hundred Years*. Montpelier, 1867.

Iowa, Secretary of State. *Iowa: Historical and Comparative Census, 1836-1880*. Des Moines, 1883.

Jay, John. *Statistical View of American Agriculture with Suggestions for the Schedules of the Federal Census*. New York, 1859.

Johnson, Cuthbert W. *Farmer's Encyclopedia and Dictionary of Rural Affairs*. Philadelphia, 1839.

Klippart, John H. *The Wheat Plant*. Cincinnati, 1860.

Lorain, John. *Hints to Emigrants*. Philadelphia, 1819.

———. *Nature and Reason Harmonized in the Practice of Husbandry*. Philadelphia, 1819.

MacLane, Louis. *The Manufacturers of the United States*, vol. I. Executive Documents, First Session, 22nd Congress, Washington, D.C., 1833.

Marshall, Josiah T. *The Dignity of the Agricultural Occupation. An Address*. Watertown, N.Y., 1838.

Milburn, M. M. *The Cow, Dairy Husbandry, and Cattle Breeding*. New York, 1852.

Mitchell, Donald G. *My Farm of Edgewood*. New York, 1863.

Moore, Thomas. *The Great Error of American Agriculture Exposed*. Baltimore, 1801.

New York, Secretary of State. *Census of the State of New York for 1845*. Albany, 1846.

———. *Census of the State of New York for 1855*. Albany, 1857.

———. *Census of the State of New York for 1865*. Albany, 1867.

Nicholson, John. *The Farmer's Assistant*. Lancaster, Pa., 1820.

Ohio, Commissioner of Statistics. *Annual Reports to the Governor of the State of Ohio*. Columbus, 1858.

Pitkin, Timothy. *A Statistical View of the Commerce of the United States of America*. New Haven, 1835.

Prairie Farmer Annual. Chicago, 1868-1871.

Randall, Henry S. *The Practical Shepherd*. Rochester, N. Y., 1863.

Robbins, Asher. *Address to the Rhode Island Society for the Encouragement of Domestic Industry*. Pawtucket, 1822.

Robinson, Solon. *Guano, A Treatise of Practical Information for Farmers*. New York, 1853.

———. *How to Live: Saving and Wasting*. New York, 1860.

———. *Facts for Farmers; also for the Family Circle*. 2 vols. New York, 1865.

Rural Affairs. A Practical and Copiously Illustrated Register of Rural Economy and Rural Tastes. Albany, 1855-1870.

Seaman, Ezra. *Essays on the Wealth and Progress of Nations.* New York, 1868.

Skinner, John S. *Book of the Farm.* 2 vols. New York, 1859.

Stephens, Henry. *The Farmer's Guide to Scientific and Practical Agriculture.* New York, 1852.

Teschemacher, J. E. *Essay on Guano.* Baltimore, 1852.

Thomas, John J. *Farm Implements and the Principles of Their Construction and Use.* New York, 1854.

Todd, Sereno E. *The American Wheat Culturist.* New York, 1868.

Tucker, George. *The Progress of the United States in Population and Wealth in Fifty Years.* Boston, 1843.

Watson, Elkanah. *History of the Rise, Progress and Existing Conditions of the Western Canals in the State of New York, from September 1788 to . . . 1819. Together with the Rise, Progress and Existing State of Modern Agricultural Societies on the Berkshire System.* Albany, 1820.

Wells, David. *Yearbook of Agriculture or the Annual of Agricultural Progress and Discovery for 1855 and 1856.* Philadelphia, 1856.

E. SECONDARY SOURCES

Adams, Thurston M. *Prices Paid by Vermont Farmers for Goods and Services and Received by Them for Farm Products, 1790-1840; Wages of Vermont Farm Labor, 1780-1940.* Bulletin 507. Burlington: Vermont Agricultural Experiment Station, 1944.

Anderson, Edgar, and William L. Brown. "The History of the Common Maize Varieties of the United States Corn Belt," *Agricultural History,* XXVI (1952), 2-8.

Anderson, Russell Howard. "Grain Drills Through Thirty-nine Centuries," *Agricultural History,* X (1936), 157-205.

Atherton, Lewis E. "The Pioneer Merchant in Mid-America," *University of Missouri Studies,* XIV (1939).

Baldwin, Leland D. *The Keelboat Age on Western Waters.* Pittsburgh: University of Pittsburg Press, 1941.

Ball, Carleton R. "The History of American Wheat Improvement," *Agricultural History,* IV (1930), 48-71.

Basset, T. D. Seymour. "A Case Study of Urban Impact on Rural Society: Vermont, 1840-1880," *Agricultural History,* XXX (1956), 28-34.

Beaver, R. P., and Joseph Hough. "An Early Miami Merchant," *Ohio State Archaeological and Historical Quarterly,* XLV (1936), 27-45.

Becker, Carl M. "Entrepreneurial Invention and Innovation in the Miami Valley During the Civil War," *Cincinnati Historical Society Bulletin,* XXII (1964), 5-28.

Berry, Thomas S. *Western Prices Before 1861.* Cambridge, Mass.: University Press, 1943.

Bidwell, Percy W. "Rural Economy in New England at the Beginning of the Nineteenth Century," *Transactions of the Connecticut Academy of Arts and Sciences,* XX (1916) 258.

Billington, Roy Allen. "The Origin of the Land Speculator as a Frontier Type," *Agricultural History,* XIX (1945), 204-212.

Bogue, Allan G. "Farming in the Prairie Peninsula," *Journal of Economic History,* XXIII (1963), 3-29.

————. *From Prairie to Corn Belt.* Chicago: University of Chicago Press, 1963.

————. *Money at Interest: The Farm Mortgage on the Middle Border.* Ithaca: Cornell University Press, 1955.

————. "Pioneer Farmers and Innovation," *Iowa Journal of History,* LVI (1958), 1-36.

————, and Margaret Beattie Bogue. "Profits and the Frontier Land Speculator," *Journal of Economic History,* XVII (1957), 1-24.

Bogue, Margaret Beattie. "Patterns from the Sod: Land Use and Tenure in the Grand Prairie, 1850-1900," *Collections of the Illinois State Historical Library Land Series,* XXXIV, vol. 1 (1959).

————. "The Swamp Land Act and Wet Land Utilization in Illinois, 1850-1890," *Agricultural History,* XXXV (1951), 169-180.

Brady, Dorothy. "Relative Prices in the Nineteenth Century," *Journal of Economic History,* XXIV (1964), 172-185.

Bruchey, Stuart. *The Roots of American Economic Growth, 1607-1861.* New York: Harper & Row, 1965.

Brunger, Eric. "Dairying and Urban Development in New York State, 1850-1900," *Agricultural History,* XXIX (1955), 169-174.

Buley, R. Carlyle. *The Old Northwest: Pioneer Period, 1815-1840.* 2 vols. Indianapolis: Indiana Historical Society, 1950.

Carlson, Theodore L. "The Illinois Military Tract: A Study of Land Occupation, Utilization and Tenure," *Illinois Studies in the Social Sciences,* XXXIII (1951).

Carman, Harry J. "Jesse Buel, Early Nineteenth Century Agricultural Reformer," *Agricultural History,* XVII (1943), 1-13.

————. "Jesse Buel, Albany County Agriculturist," *New York History,* XIV (1933), 214-219.

————. "English Views of Middle Western Agriculture, 1850-1870," *Agricultural History,* VIII (1934), 3-19.

Carriel, Mary T. *The Life of Jonathan Baldwin Turner,* 2nd ed. Urbana: University of Illinois Press, 1961.

Carrier, Lyman. *The Beginnings of Agriculture in America.* New York: McGraw-Hill Book Company, 1923.

————. "The United States Agricultural Society, 1852-1860: Its Relation to the Origin of the United States Department of Agriculture and the Land Grant Colleges," *Agricultural History,* XI (1937), 278-288.

Carson, Gerald. *The Old Country Store.* New York: Oxford University Press, 1954.

Cavanagh, Helen M. *Funk of Funk's Grove: Farmer, Legislator and Cattle King of the Old Northwest, 1797-1865.* Bloomington: University of Indiana Press, 1952.

Clark, John G. *The Grain Trade of the Old Northwest.* Urbana: University of Illinois Press, 1966.

Clark, Victor. *History of Manufactures in the United States.* 3 vols. New York: McGraw-Hill for the Carnegie Institution of Washington, D.C., 1929.

Clemen, Rudolph A. *American Livestock and Meat Industry.* New York: Ronald Press, 1923.

Cole, Arthur H. *The American Wool Manufacture.* 2 vols. Cambridge: Harvard University Press, 1926.

————. "Agricultural Crazes: A Neglected Chapter in American Economic History," *American Economic Review,* XVI (1926), 622-639.

————. *Business Enterprise in Its Social Setting.* Cambridge: Harvard University Press, 1959.

Cooper, Glenn T. Barton, and Albert P. Brodell. "Progress of Farm Mechanization," *Department of Agriculture Miscellaneous Publication,* 630 (1947), 5-7.

Cox, LaWanda F. "Tenancy in the United States, 1865-1900: A Consideration of the Validity of the Agricultural Ladder Hypothesis," *Agricultural History,* XVIII (1944), 97-105.

Craven, Avery O. "Soil Exhaustion as a Factor in the Agricultural History of Virginia and Maryland, 1606-1860," *University of Illinois Studies in the Social Sciences,* XIII (1925).

Cummings, Richard O. *The American and His Food.* Chicago: University of Chicago Press, 1940.

Curti, Merle. *The Making of an American Community: A Case Study of Democracy in a Frontier Community.* Stanford: Stanford University Press, 1959.

Danhof, Clarence H. "Gathering the Grass," *Agricultural History,* XXX (1956), 169-173.

————. "The Fencing Problem in the Eighteen-Fifties," *Agricultural History,* XIX (1956), 169-173.

————. "Farm Making Costs and the Safety Valve," *Journal of Political Economy,* XLIX (1941), 317-359.

————. "American Evaluations of European Agriculture," *Journal of Economic History, Supplement,* IX (1949), 61-71.

David, Paul A. "The Mechanization of Reaping in the Ante-Bellum Midwest," in Henry Rosovsky, ed. *Industrialization in Two Systems: Essays in Honor of Alexander Gerschenkron.* New York: John Wiley & Sons, 1966, pp. 3-39.

————. "The Growth of Real Product in the United States Before 1840: New Evidence, Controlled Conjectures," *Journal of Economic History,* XXVII (1967), 151-195.

Davis, Joseph. "Agricultural Fundamentalism," in O. B. Jesness, ed. *Readings on Agricultural Policy.* Blakiston, 1949, pp. 1-17.

Dupree, A. Hunter. *Science in the Federal Government.* Cambridge: Harvard University Press, 1957.

Easterlin, Richard A. "Interregional Differences in Per Capita Income, Population, and Total Income, 1840-1950," in *Trends in the American Economy in the Nineteenth Century.* National Bureau of Economic Research, Studies in Income and Wealth, vol. 24. Princeton: Princeton University Press, 1960, pp. 73-140.

————. "Regional Income Trends, 1840-1950," in Seymour Harris. *American Economic History.* New York: McGraw-Hill, 1961, pp. 525-547.

Edwards, Everett E. "American Agriculture: The First 300 Years," *Yearbook of Agriculture,* U. S. Department of Agriculture. Washington, D.C.: Government Printing Office, 1941, pp. 171-276.

Ellis, David M. *Landlords and Farmers in the Hudson-Mohawk Region: 1790-1850.* Ithaca: Cornell University Press, 1946.

Erdman, H. E. "The Associated Dairies of New York as Precursors of American Agricultural Cooperation," *Agricultural History,* XXXVI (1962), 82-90.

Fabricant, Solomon. "The Changing Industrial Distribution of Gainful Workers: Some Comments on the American Decennial Statistics for 1820-1940," *Stud-*

ies in Income and Wealth, vol. 11. New York: National Bureau of Economic Research, 1949.

Feller, Irwin. "Inventive Activity in Agriculture, 1837-1890," *Journal of Economic History*, XXII (1962), 560-577.

Felton, Isaac K. "Coming and Going of Ohio Droving," *Ohio Archaeological and Historical Quarterly*, XVII (1908), 247-253.

Fish, Carl Russell. *The Rise of the Common Man, 1830-1850*. New York: Macmillan & Company, 1937.

Fishlow, Albert. *American Railroads and the Transformation of the Ante-Bellum Economy*. Cambridge: Harvard University Press, 1965.

Fite, Gilbert C. "The Historical Development of Agricultural Fundamentalism in the Nineteenth Century," *Journal of Farm Economics*, XLIV (1962), 1,203-1,211.

Fletcher, Stevenson W. *Pennsylvania Agriculture and Country Life, 1640-1840*. Harrisburg: Pennsylvania Historical and Museum Commission, 1950.

———. *Pennsylvania Agriculture and Country Life, 1840-1940*. Harrisburg: Pennsylvania Historical and Museum Commission, 1955.

———. *The Philadelphia Society for Promoting Agriculture, 1785-1955*. Philadelphia, 1959.

Fogel, Robert W. *Railroads and American Economic Growth: Essays in Econometric History*. Baltimore: Johns Hopkins Press, 1964.

Gallman, Robert E. "Commodity Output, 1839-1899," in *Trends in the American Economy*. National Bureau of Economic Research, Studies in Income and Wealth, vol. 24. Princeton: Princeton University Press, 1960, pp. 13-71.

———. "Gross National Product in the United States, 1834-1909," in *Output, Employment and Productivity in the United States after 1800*. National Bureau of Economic Research, Studies in Income and Wealth, vol. 30. New York: Columbia University Press, 1965.

Gates, Paul Wallace. *The Illinois Central and Its Colonization Work*. Cambridge: Harvard University Press, 1934.

———. *Agriculture and the Civil War*. New York: Knopf, 1965.

———. *Frontier Landlords and Pioneer Tenants*. Ithaca: Cornell University Press, 1945.

———. "Cattle Kings of the Prairies," *Mississippi Valley Historical Review*, XXXV (1948), 379-412.

———. "Charles Lewis Fleischmann, German-American Agricultural Authority," *Agricultural History*, XXXV (1961), 13-23.

———. "The Disposal of the Public Domain in Illinois, 1848-1856," *Journal of Economic and Business History*, III (1931), 216-240.

———. "Frontier Estate Builders and Farm Laborers," in Walker D. Wyman and Clifton B. Kroeber, ed. *The Frontier in Perspective*. Madison: University of Wisconsin Press, 1957, pp. 143-164.

———. "The Homestead Law in Iowa," *Agricultural History*, XXXVIII (1964),, 67-68.

———. "Land Policy and Tenancy in the Prairie States," *Journal of Economic History*, I (1941), 60-82.

———. "Hoosier Cattle Kings," *Indiana Magazine of History*, XLIV (1948), 1-24.

———. "Large Scale Farming in Illinois, 1850 to 1870," *Agricultural History*, VI (1932), 14-25.

————. "Role of the Land Speculator in Western Development," *Pennsylvania Magazine of History and Biography,* LXVI (1942), 314-333.

Gilchrist, David T., ed. *The Growth of the Seaport Cities, 1790-1825.* Charlottesville: University Press of Virginia. 1967.

————, and W. David Lewis, eds. *Economic Change in the Civil War Era.* Greenville, Del.: Eleutherian Mills-Hagley Foundation, 1965.

Goodrich, Carter, and Sol Davison. "The Wage-Earner in the Westward Movement," *Political Science Quarterly,* L (1935), 161-185; LI (1936), 61-116; LIII (1937), 299-314.

Gould, R. E. *Yankee Storekeeper.* London: Whittlesey, 1946.

Graue, Erwin. "Agriculture Versus Urban Enterprise," *Journal of Farm Economics,* XI (1929), 609-622.

Gray, Lewis C. *History of Agriculture in the Southern States to 1860.* 2 vols. Washington, D.C.: Carnegie Institution of Washington, 1933.

Griswold, A. Whitney. *Farming and Democracy.* New York: Harcourt Brace, 1948.

Hammond, Bray. "Banking in the Early West: Monopoly, Prohibition, and Laissez-Faire," *Journal of Economic History,* VIII (1948), 1-25.

————. *Banks and Politics in America from the Revolution to the Civil War.* Princeton: Princeton University Press, 1950.

Handlin, Oscar, and John Burchard, eds. *The Historian and the City.* Cambridge: M.I.T. and Harvard University Press, 1963, pp. 45-64.

Hayter, Earl W. "Mechanical Humbuggery Among the Western Farmers, 1860-1890," *Michigan History,* XXXIV (1950), 1-18.

————. "Livestock-Fencing Conflicts in Rural America," *Agricultural History,* XXXVII (1963), 10-20.

————. "Seed Humbuggery Among the Western Farmers, 1850-1888," *Ohio State Archaeological and Historical Quarterly,* LVIII (1949), 52-68.

Hedrick, Ulysses Prentiss. *A History of Agriculture in the State of New York.* Albany: New York State Agricultural Society, 1933.

Henlein, Paul C. *The Cattle Kingdom of the Ohio Valley.* Lexington: University of Kentucky Press, 1959.

————. "Early Cattle Ranges of the Ohio Valley," *Agricultural History,* XXXV (1961), 150-154.

Hibbard, Benjamin H. "The History of Agriculture in Dane County, Wisconsin," *Bulletin of the University of Wisconsin,* Economics and Political Science Series, no. 2. (1904).

————. *A History of Public Land Policies.* New York: Macmillan, 1924.

Higgins, F. Hal. "John M. Horner and the Development of the Combined Harvester," *Agricultural History,* IV (1930), 1-9.

Hirsh, A. H. "French Influence on American Agriculture in the Colonial Period," *Agricultural History,* IV (1930), 1-9.

Hunter, Louis C. *Steamboats on the Western Rivers: An Economic and Technological History.* Cambridge: Harvard University Press, 1949.

Hutchinson, William T. *Cyrus Hall McCormick: Seed-Time, 1809-1856.* New York: Century Co., 1930.

————. *Cyrus Hall McCormick: Harvest, 1856-1884.* New York: Appleton-Century Co., 1935.

Jackson, Sidney L. *America's Struggle for Free Schools: Social Tension and Education in New England and New York, 1827-1842.* Washington, D.C., American Council on Public Affairs, 1941.

Jarchow, Merrill E. *The Earth Brought Forth: A History of Minnesota Agriculture to 1885.* St. Paul: Minnesota Historical Society, 1949.

Johnstone, Paul H. "In Praise of Husbandry," *Agricultural History,* XI (1937), 80-95.

———. "Turnips and Romanticism," *Agricultural History,* XII (1938), 224-255.

Jones, Fred M. "Middlemen in the Domestic Trade of the United States, 1800-1860," *Illinois Studies in the Social Sciences,* XXI, no. 3. University of Illinois, 1930.

Jones, Robert Leslie. "The Beef Cattle Industry in Ohio Prior to the Civil War," *Ohio Historical Quarterly,* XLIV (1955), 168-194, 287-319.

———. "Special Crops in Ohio Before 1850," *Ohio Historical Quarterly,* LIV (1945), 127-142.

———. "Introduction of Farming Machinery in Ohio Prior to 1865," *Ohio Historical Quarterly,* LVIII (1949), 1-20.

Jordan, Terry G. "Between the Forest and the Prairie," *Agricultural History,* XXXVIII (1964), 205-216.

Kellar, Herbert Anthony. *Solon Robinson, Pioneer and Agriculturist: Selected Writings.* 2 vols. Indianapolis: Indiana Historical Collections, XXI-XXII, 1936.

Kemmerer, Donald. "The Pre-Civil War South's Leading Crop, Corn," *Agricultural History,* XXIII (1949), 236-239.

Kendall, Edward C. "John Deere's Steel Plow," *U. S. National Museum Bulletin,* no. 218. Washington, 1959, pp. 15-25.

Kerr, Homer L. "Introduction of Forage Plants into Ante-Bellum United States," *Agricultural History,* XXXVIII (1964), 87-95.

Kirkland, Edward C. *Men, Cities and Transportation: A Study in New England History, 1820-1900.* 2 vols. Cambridge: Harvard University Press, 1948.

Klose, Nelson. *America's Crop Heritage: The History of Foreign Plant Introduction by the Federal Government.* Ames: Iowa State College Press, 1950.

Knoblauch, H. E., E. M. Law, and W. P. Meyer. "State Agricultural Stations: A History of Research Policy and Procedure." *U. S. Department of Agriculture Miscellaneous Publication,* no. 904. Washington, D.C.

Kuhlman, Charles B. *The Development of the Flour-milling Industry in the United States.* Boston: Houghton Mifflin Co., 1929.

Ladin, Jay. "Mortgage Credit in Tippecanoe Country, Indiana, 1865-1880," *Agricultural History,* XLI (1967), 37-43.

Lampard, Eric E. *The Rise of the Dairy Industry in Wisconsin: A Study in Agricultural Change, 1820-1930.* Madison: State Historical Society of Wisconsin, 1963.

———. "The History of Cities in the Economically Advanced Areas," *Economic Development and Cultural Change,* II (1955), 81-136.

Larson, Henrietta M. *The Wheat Market and the Farmer in Minnesota.* New York: Columbia University Press, 1962.

Leavitt, Charles T. "Attempts to Improve Cattle Breeds in the United States, 1790-1860," *Agricultural History,* VII (1933), 51-67.

———. "Transportation and the Livestock Industry of the Middle West to 1860." *Agricultural History,* VIII (1934), 20-33.

Lebergott, Stanley. *Manpower in Economic Growth: The American Record Since 1800.* New York: McGraw-Hill, 1964.

———. "Wage Trends, 1800-1900," in *Trends in the American Economy in the Nineteenth Century*. National Bureau of Economic Research, Studies in Income and Wealth, vol. 30. Princeton: Princeton University Press, 1960, pp. 449-498.

————. "Labor Force and Employment, 1800-1960," in *Output, Employment and Productivity in the United States after 1800*. National Bureau of Economic Research, Studies in Income and Wealth, vol. 30. Princeton: Princeton University Press, 1966, p. 140.

————. "The Pattern of Employment Since 1800," in Seymour E. Harris, ed. *American Economic History*. New York: McGraw-Hill (1961), 16-32.

LeDuc, Thomas. "Public Policy, Private Investment, and Land Use in American Agriculture, 1825-1875," *Agricultural History*, XXXVII (1964), 3-9.

————. "History and Appraisal of U. S. Land Policy to 1862," in Howard W. Ottoson, ed. *Land Use and Problems in the United States*. Lincoln: University of Nebraska Press, 1963, pp. 3-27.

Lee, Guy A. "The Historical Significance of the Chicago Grain Elevator System," *Agricultural History*, XI (1937), 16-32.

Lemmer, George F. "Farm Machinery in Ante-Bellum Missouri," *Missouri Historical Review*, XL (1946), 467-480.

————. "The Spread of Improved Cattle through the Eastern United States to 1850," *Agricultural History*, XXI (1947), 79-83.

Lemon, James T. "Household Consumption in Eighteenth-Century America and Its Relationship to Production and Trade: The Situation Among Farmers in Southeastern Pennsylvania," *Agricultural History*, XLI (1967), 59-70.

Lippincott, Isaac. "Internal Trade of the United States, 1765-1860," *Washington University Studies*, IV, pt. II, no. 1. St. Louis, 1916.

Loehr, Rodney C. "Influence of English Agriculture on American Agriculture, 1775-1825," *Agricultural History*, XI (1937), 3-15.

————. "Self-Sufficiency on the Farm," *Agricultural History*, XXVI (1952), 37-41.

McDonald, Angus. "Early American Soil Conservationists," *Department of Agriculture Miscellaneous Publication*, no. 449. Washington, D.C., 1941.

McNall, Neil A. *An Agricultural History of the Genesee Valley, 1790-1860*. Philadelphia: University of Pennsylvania Press, 1952.

Malin, Donald F. *The Evolution of Breeds: An Analytical Study of Breed Building As Illustrated in Shorthorn, Hereford and Aberdeen Angus Cattle, Poland China and Duroc Jersey Swine*. Des Moines: Wallace Publishing Co., 1923.

Martin, Edgar. *The Standard of Living in 1860: American Consumption Levels at the End of the Civil War*. Chicago: University of Chicago Press, 1942.

Murray, William G. "An Economic Analysis of Farm Mortgages in Story County, Iowa, 1854-1931," *Agricultural Experiment Station Research Bulletin*, no. 156. Ames: Iowa State College of Agriculture and Mechanic Arts, 1933.

Neely, Wayne Caldwell. *The Agricultural Fair*. New York: Columbia University Press, 1935.

Nettels, Curtis P. *The Emergence of a National Economy, 1775-1815*. New York: Holt, Rinehart & Winston, 1962.

North, Douglass C. *The Economic Growth of the United States, 1790-1860*. Englewood Cliffs, N. J.: Prentice-Hall, 1961.

Odle, Thomas E. "Entrepreneurial Cooperation on the Great Lakes: The Origin of the Methods of American Grain Marketing," *Business History*, XXXVIII (1964), 439-455.

Parker, George E. *Iowa Pioneer Foundations*. Iowa City: University of Iowa Press, 1940.

Parker, William N. "Sources of Agricultural Productivity in the Nineteenth Century," *Journal of Farm Economics*, XLIX (1967), 1,455-1,468.

——, and Judith L. V. Klein. "Productivity Growth in Grain Production in the United States, 1840-1860 and 1900-1910," in *Output, Employment, and Productivity in the United States after 1800*. National Bureau of Economic Research, Studies in Income and Wealth, vol. 30. New York: Columbia University Press, 1965.

Pooley, William V. *Settlement of Illinois, 1830-1850*. Madison: University of Wisconsin Press, 1908.

Potter, David. *People of Plenty, Economic Abundance and the American Character*. Chicago: University of Chicago Press, 1954.

Pred, Allen R. *The Spatial Dynamics of U. S. Urban-Industrial Growth, 1800-1914*. Cambridge: M. I. T. Press, 1966.

Prentice, E. P. *American Dairy Cattle: Their Past and Future*. New York: Harper & Sons, 1942.

Price, Robert. "Travel in the 1830's," *Ohio State Archaeological and Historical Quarterly*, LIV (1945), 40-45.

Primack, Martin L. "Land Clearing Under Nineteenth Century Techniques: Some Preliminary Calculations," *Journal of Economic History*, XXII (1962), 484-497.

Pursell, Carroll W., Jr. "E. I. du Pont and the Merino Mania in Delaware, 1805-1815," *Agricultural History*, XXXVI (1962), 91-100.

Ramsey, Elizabeth. "The History of Tobacco Production in the Connecticut Valley," *Smith College Studies in History*, XV (1930), 139-146.

Rasmussen, Wayne D. "The Impact of Technological Change on American Agriculture, 1862-1962," *Journal of Economic History*, XXII (1962), 578-591.

——. "The Civil War: A Catalyst of Agricultural Revolution," *Agricultural History*, XXXIX (1965), 187-195.

Robbins, Roy W. *Our Landed Heritage, the Public Domain, 1776-1936*. Princeton: Princeton University Press, 1942.

Rogin, Leo. "The Introduction of Farm Machinery in Its Relation to the Productivity of Labor in the Agriculture of the United States during the Nineteenth Century," *University of California (Berkeley) Publications in Economics*, IX (1931).

Ross, Earle D., ed. *Dairy of Benjamin F. Gue in Rural New York and Pioneer Iowa, 1847-1856*. Ames: Iowa State University Press, 1962.

Ross, Earle D. "The United States Department of Agriculture during the Commissionership," *Agricultural History*, XX (1946), 129-143.

——. "Retardation in Farm Technology before the Power Age," *Agricultural History*, XXX (1956), 11-18.

Rothstein, Morton. "America in the International Rivalry for the British Wheat Market," *Mississippi Valley Historical Review*, XLVII (1960), 401-418.

——. "Ante-bellum Wheat and Cotton Exports: A Contrast in Marketing Organization and Economic Development," *Agricultural History*, XL (1966), 91-100.

Ryerson, Knowles. "History and Significance of the Foreign Plant Introduction

Work of the United States Department of Agriculture," *Agricultural History,* VII (1933), 110-128.

Salaman, Redcliffe N. *The History and Social Influence of the Potato.* Cambridge: Cambridge University Press, 1949.

Schmidt, Louis B. "Internal Commerce and the Development of the National Economy Before 1860," *Journal of Political Economy,* XLVII (1939), 798-822.

———. "The Internal Grain Trade of the United States, 1850-1860," *Iowa Journal of History and Politics,* XVIII (1920), 94-124.

———. "The Westward Movement of the Wheat Growing Industry in the United States," *Iowa Journal of History and Politics,* XVIII (1920), 396-412.

Severson, R. F., Jr. "The Source of Mortgage Credit for Champain County, 1865-1880," *Agricultural History,* XXXVI (1962), 150-155.

Smith, Ellen D. "The Smith Plow," *Bucks County Historical Society Collections,* III (1909), 11-17.

Stilwell, Lewis D. "Migration from Vermont, 1776-1860," *Proceedings of the Vermont Historical Society,* New Series, no. 2 (June 1937), 62-245.

Stover, Stephen L. "Early Sheep Husbandry in Ohio," *Agricultural History,* XXXVI (1963), 101-107.

———. "Ohio's Sheep Year, 1868," *Agricultural History,* XXXVIII (1964), 102-107.

Taylor, George Rogers. *The Transportation Revolution, 1815-1860.* New York: Rinehart, 1951.

———. "American Economic Growth before 1840: An Explanatory Essay," *Journal of Economic History,* XXIV (1964), 427-444.

———. "American Urban Growth Preceding the Railway Age," *Journal of Economic History,* XXVII (1967), 309-339.

Taylor, Henry C., and Anne D. Taylor. *The Story of Agricultural Economics in the United States, 1840-1932.* Ames: Iowa State College Press, 1952.

Thompson, James W. "A History of Livestock Raising in the United States, 1607-1860," *U. S. Department of Agriculture Agricultural History Series,* no. 5 (1942).

Thompson, John G. "The Rise and Decline of the Wheat Growing Industry in Wisconsin," *Bulletin of the University of Wisconsin, Economics and Political Science Series,* V, no. 3 (1909).

Thorne, Mildred. "Southern Iowa Agriculture, 1833-1890: The Progress from Subsistence to Commercial Corn-belt Farming," *Agricultural History,* XXIII (1949), 125-127.

———. "Book Farming in Iowa, 1840-1870," *Iowa Journal of History,* XLIX (1951), 117-142.

Towne, Marvin W., and Wayne E. Rasmussen. "Farm Gross Product and Gross Investment During the Nineteenth Century," in *Trends in the American Economy in the Nineteenth Century.* National Bureau of Economic Research, Studies in Wealth and Income, vol. 24. Princeton: Princeton University Press, 1960, pp. 255-312.

True, Alfred Charles. "A History of Agricultural Experimentation and Research in the United States," *U. S. Department of Agriculture Miscellaneous Publication,* no. 251 (1937).

———. "A History of Agricultural Education in the United States, 1785-1925," *U. S. Department of Agriculture Miscellaneous Publication,* no. 36 (1929).

True, Rodney H. "The Early Development of Agricultural Societies in the United States," *Annual Report of the American Historical Association for the Year 1920*. Washington, D.C.: Government Printing Office, 1925, pp. 293-306.

Tryon, Rolla M. *Household Manufactures in the United States, 1640-1860*. Chicago: University of Chicago Press, 1917.

U. S. Department of Agriculture. *Century of Service: The First Hundred Years of the United States Department of Agriculture*. Washington, D.C.: Government Printing Office, 1963.

Van Wagenen, Jared, Jr. *The Golden Age of Homespun*. Ithaca: Cornell University Press, 1953.

Wade, Richard. *The Urban Frontier: The Rise of Western Cities, 1790-1820*. Cambridge: Harvard University Press, 1959.

Wentworth, Edward Norris. *America's Sheep Trails*. Ames: Iowa State College Press, 1948.

Wik, Reynold M. *Steam Power on the American Farm*. Philadelphia: University of Pennsylvania Press, 1953.

Wilson, Harold Fisher. *The Hill Country of New England: Its Social and Economic History, 1790-1930*. New York: Columbia University Press, 1936.

Woodward, Carl R. *The Development of Agriculture in New Jersey, 1640-1880*. New Brunswick, N. J.: Rutgers University Press, 1927.

Wright, Chester W. *Wool-Growing and the Tariff*. Boston: Houghton Mifflin, 1910.

INDEX

Agricultural book publishers, 55

Agricultural entomologist, 63

Agricultural exports, 9

Agricultural fairs, 62-63

Agricultural fundamentalism, 24

Agricultural information in newspapers, 58

Agricultural ladder, 89n

Agricultural organizations: as fair sponsors, 62-63; financial support, 61; functions of commissioners and secretaries, 64, 69

Agricultural periodicals: circulation, 56-57; correspondents of, 59; editors, 58-59, 64, 69

Agricultural schools and colleges, 71-72

Agricultural staples, northern lack of, 11

Agricultural warehouses, 183, 193, 209

Alfalfa, 162

Allen, A. B., 54, 170

Allen, L. F., 44, 54, 170

Almanacs, 136

Bakewell, Robert, 53, 168

Bakewell cattle in U. S., 168

Balers, 218

Banking system, as source of agricultural credit, 85-86

Barter, 29

Beef-packing industry, 33

Bills of exchange, 86

Blacksmiths, 182, 185-186, 187, 194, 197, 224n, 230

Bogue, Allan G., 126n

Book farming, 72, 276

Botany, 68

Boutwell, George S., 139

Breaking plows, 195

Brentall, John, 177

British agricultural influence on America, 52

British cattle, American imports of, 52, 168-169

Buel, Jesse, 54, 56, 61, 255-256, 262

Butter, marketing of, 40

Buyers of agricultural products, 28

Canals, effect on agriculture, 5, 108-109

Capital: ability to accumulate, 76, 78; criticism of inadequate, 139; investment of, 139; need for working, 15-99; requirements for in East compared to West, 113, 125; sources of, 75, 81; waste of, in agriculture, 139n

Capital gains: how sought, 103; importance of, 103-104, 109; realization of, 127. See also Speculation

Capron, Horace, 86, 98

Cattle breeders, 168-175

Cattle: dairy breeds, 173-175; native, 166-167; neglect of, 160-161, 166n; sources, significance, and criticism of improved breeds, 164, 171-172, 174n; in West, 153, 171

Cattle marketing, 34-35

Cheese factories, 41, 64

Chemistry, agricultural, 54, 63, 68, 265

Chester system of crop rotation, 269

Civil war, effect on northern agriculture, 279, 289

Clay, Henry, 172

Clearing land: costs of, 118; hired labor for, 118-119; methods, 117-118; rate of, 118; value of lumber and cordwood, 119

Clover, 162, 256

Coke, Thomas, 175, 285n

Cole, Samuel W., 54

Colman, Henry, 54, 270

Commission merchants, 28, 39, 46; use in selling butter, 40

Competition, East versus West, 51

Connecticut: adoption of improved plows, 191, 198; of mowers, 242; farm problems in, 108, 110-112; farm renting in, 89; gypsum and lime, 263

Conservatism, 17, 23, 286. See also Motives

Consulting agriculturists, 69n

Consumption levels, 9, 18-20

Cooperative purchases of wheat drill, 212

Corn: cultivation in hills, 215-216; use of corn planter, 216-217; of hoe, 202, 204, 214; of horse cultivation, 203-205; profitability of, 151-152; varieties of, 158

Corn shellers, 218, 249

Country merchant, as buyer of agricultural products, 29, 30, 38-40

Craftsmen, village, 9

Crawford, William H., 66

Cream Pots, 173

Credit: cost of, 86; extensive use of, 78; in purchasing implements, 85; role of, 87, 287; types of, 84

Crop rotation: adapted from English practice, 268; Chester system, 269; effects of, 269-270; Pennsylvania leadership in, 268; use of red clover, 268; variations in, 270-276

Crops: on homestead, 4; selection of, 144-147; specialization in, 148, 150-154

Custom work: threshing, 224-225; wheat drilling, 207n

Customary practices, 132, 279

Dairying, 172

Davy, Humphry, 54

Dean, Saul, 54

Debt: approval of, 81; extent of, 79; fear of, 79, 81; of merchants, 85n; sources of, 80

Deere, John, 197

Delafield, John, 239

Delano, Calvin, 220

Delaware: adoption of drill, 206; crop rotations, 269-270; farm renting in, 89; guano, 265; gypsum and lime, 264; urban growth, 8

Devons, 169, 171

Dickerman, Charles W., 198

Draining, open ditch and tile, 255

Drovers: functions of, 28, 35-38; as dealers in horses, 35n; scale of operations, 38n

Dunlap, M. L., 195

East, effect of western farm production on, 15, 20n, 108, 147

Eastern farms, advantages of, 109

Ellsworth, Henry L., 66-67

Employment in farming, 73-74

Enterprise in agriculture compared to industry, 25n

Entomology, 68

Erie Canal, 5, 14, 108; effect on farm values, 109

European criticism of American agriculture, 52

European immigrants, 128

European plant materials, 52

Experimental farms, 71

Experiments, 53, 69

Experience, exhaustion of common, 69

Exports: growth of markets, 12; value of farm, 10

Fairs, agricultural, 24

Fallowing, 273n

Fanning mills, 218, 222

Farm accounts, 110

Farm acquisition, 107

Farm consumption objectives, 3

Farm labor: earnings, 77; force, 10

Farm-making: animals in, 122; breaking, 123; capital requirements, 114-116, 120-121, 125; crops raised, 124; disadvantages of, 123; delayed returns, 124; exhaustive nature of, 252n; selecting location for, 114-121

Farm management: choices in, 131-132; common approach, 132-133; criticism of, 133, 134-135; by imitation, 23, 51; leadership in, 136

Farm owners, mobility of, 101n, 126

Farm ownership, capital required, 125-129

Farm products: markets for, 9-11, 12-13; selection of, 4, 144, 155; sold as a percentage of production, 2, 11

Farm purchase: considerations in, 102-103; cost of, 101-102; selection in East, 107-113; in West, 126-128; supply of farms available for, 101, 126-127

Farm surpluses, 17-18

Farm wages, 77

Farmers: characteristics of, 280; classification of, 280; criticism of, 135; differences among, 17; by entrepreneurial types, 283; objectives of, 102; standards by which judged, 281-283

Farming: commercial, 13, 18, 21-22; differences in, 130; entering, 73; knowledge necessary, 75; for own use, 130; in lumbering areas, 119-120; problems of, 130, 289; profit-motivated, 22-23, 95; profitability of, 134; skills, 74-75; subsistence, 13; unprofitability of, 51, 141; urban competition with, 24n

Farms: abandonment in New England, 109n; differences in, 134; number of, 10; value of products, 10

Feed cutters, 249

Fencing, 118, 124

Fertilizers, types of, 63, 266-267

Fessenden, Thomas, 54

Fishlow, Albert, 4n, 13

Flail, persistence of, 226

Fleet, Samuel, 79, 80

Flint, Charles L., 155

Forage plants, 161-162

Foreign trade, 8, 11

Forwarding firms, 28

Franklin, Benjamin, 136

Freeborn, Gideon, 188

Freedley, Edwin T., 98

Gates, Paul W., 12n
Genesee Valley, 147
Gentlemen farmers, 52
Geological surveys, 63
Gould, James S., 70
Grading, grain, 44n
Graduation Act, 106
Grain: dealers, 33n; grading, 44n; ware-
   housing, 32
Grasses, domesticated, 162, 255
Green manure, 269n
Grinding mills, 249
Guano, 265-266
Gypsum, 256, 263

Hamilton, Alexander, 24
Harper & Brothers, 55
Harrow, 200-201
Harvest labor, shortages of, 248-249
Harvester: adoption of, 229, 237-249; costs
   of, 233, 247n; criticism of, 229, 231;
   inventions, 228-229; life of, 236n;
   manufacturers of, 235-236, 244; oppo-
   sition to, 229; requirements for appli-
   cation, 230-233, 237
Harvesting small grains and grass: by
   mechanical harvester, 247n; by scythe
   and cradle, 228
Hay: as cash crop, 219; importance of
   new implements, 161-162; problems in
   producing, 218; supplies of, 160
Hay baling presses, 250
Hay loaders, 218
Hay rake: acceptance of, 220; advantages
   of, 219, 227; revolver, 219; sulky, 220
Hay stacking equipment, 250
Hay tedders, 218
Headers, 243n
Hen fever, 64
Herefords, 172
Hessian fly, 157
Hired labor, 140, 141n
Hogs: American breeding of, 177-178;
   imports of, 177; razorback, 175-176;
   varieties of, 176-177
Home manufactures, 20-21
Homestead Act, 107
Horse-power: application to farm tasks,
   181; significance of, 279
Horse-powers: sweep or lever, 222; tread-
   mill or railway, 223, 227
Horses: breeds of, 178-179; use of, 142-144
Hussey, Obed, 228

Illinois: adoption of drill, 211, 213; of corn
   planter, 216; of improved plows, 194-
   198; of reaper, 243-244, 246-247; of

thresher, 225; crop rotations, 275;
   utilization of manures, 261-262
Implements required in farming, 97
Imports of new animals and plants, 157
Indiana: adoption of drill, 210; of improved plows, 197; of reaper, 247-248;
   of thresher, 225; crop rotations, 274;
   farm renting in, 93-94; settlement of, 20;
   urban growth, 8; utilization of manures,
   260
Innovation, farmer attitudes toward, 283-
   289
Interest rates, 86
Iowa: adoption of corn planter, 217; of
   drill, 211-212; of improved plows, 197;
   of reaper, 248; of thresher, 225; criticism of farming in, 136; crop rotations,
   276; farm mortgages, 83-84; farm
   renting in, 91
Italian rye grass, 172

Jacques, Samuel, 173, 283
Jefferson, Thomas, 24, 88

Ketchum, W. F., 232
Klein, Judith L. V., 1n

Labor utilization, 141
Land: capital requirements, 139; clearing
   costs, 15, 118; cultivated per man, 137,
   181; holdings criticized as excessive, 95,
   138-139, 252n; significance of abundance
   of, 1n; turnover in ownership of, 82;
   utilization of, 49-50; in New York, 256
Land grants, federal: to colleges, 290; to
   railroads, 106
Land policy of federal government, 104-
   107
Lane, John, 197
LeDuc, Thomas, 104n
Lee, Daniel, 69
Lespedeza, 162
Liebig, Justus, 54
Lime, 256, 264-265; necessary to establish
   clover, 162
Livestock: characteristics of native, 50,
   161, 164; diseases of, 68; feed problems
   in farm-making period, 160-161
Livestock breeders, role of, 163
Long Island, settlement of, 102n
Lorain, John, 158
Lumbering, 119
Lyell, Charles, 88

McCormick, Cyrus, 228, 231, 286
Mackay, John, 177
Madison, James, 65

Maine: adoption of drill, 208; of improved plows, 191; of mower, 242-243; agricultural societies, 61; guano and gypsum, 266; mortgages in, 82; urban growth, 8
Management. *See* Farm management
Manny, John H., 229
Manufactures, household, 18; abandonment of, 19-20
Manufacturing: farm interest in, 21*n*; growth of, 9; relation to agriculture, 2, 289
Manures: neglect of, 257-258; utilization in East, 258-259; in West, 259-262
Mapes, J. J., 202, 240
Market fairs, 41, 46-47
Market farming, 12
Marketing: by consignment, 46; by contract, 38, 40
Marketing of: butter, 39-40; cattle, 33-36; cheese, 40-41; hogs, 36-38; tobacco, 39; wheat, 31-33; wool, 39
Marketing system, criticism of, 44
Markets for agricultural products: city, 27; foreign, 12; frontier, 27; Southern, 12; significance of cash markets, 21
Marsh hay, 161
Maryland: adoption of reaper, 237, 238-239; crop rotations, 269; guano, 265; gypsum and lime, 264; urban growth, 8
Massachusetts: adoption of improved plows, 191; mower, 241; crop rotations, 270-271; farming prospects in, 112; gypsum and lime, 263
Massachusetts Agricultural Society cattle importations, 170
Merchants, functions of, 4, 29-30
Michigan: adoption of corn planter, 217; of drill, 210; of reaper, 247; of thresher, 225; crop rotations, 275; gypsum and lime, 263; markets of, 20-21; urban growth, 8; use of manures, 260
Middlemen, criticism of, 40*n*, 45-46
Mills, flour and grist, 31
Minnesota: adoption of improved plows, 197; of reaper, 248-249; of thresher, 226
Model farm plan, 114
Moore, Thomas, 53
Morrill Act, 72
Mortgages: average life in Iowa, 83-84; in Ohio, 82; frequency of use, 82; reasons for, 80-81
Motives: acceptance of profit, 22-23; changing, 17; self-improvement, 15-16; traditional, 17, 281
Mower: adoption of, 240-242; interchangeability with reaper, 231, 244;

Ketchum's, 239; preparations for use, 243. *See also* Harvester

New England: acreage per farm, 107; agriculture unprofitable in, 51, 113-114; cattle breeds in, 171; competition with the West, 15, 20*n*; corn cultivation in, 204, 215; crop rotations, 271-272; farm debt in, 79-80; home manufactures, 20; improved cattle in, 171; merchants, 29; population, 6-7; profitability of farming, 113. *See also* Connecticut; Maine; Massachusetts; New Hampshire; Rhode Island; Vermont
New Hampshire: farming in, 110; gypsum and lime, 263; sheep in, 166; urban growth, 8
New Jersey: adoption of drill, 210; of improved plows, 187; of reaper, 238; crop rotations, 270; farm renting in, 89; gypsum and lime, 264; settlement of southern, 102*n*
New York: adoption of drill, 208, 210; of harrow, 201; of hay rake, 219; of improved plow, 188, 190, 192; of mower, 240; of reaper, 238-239; of thresher, 224; agricultural societies, 61; crop rotations, 256, 272-274; farm renting, 90; farming advantages of, 108; guano, 266; gypsum, 262, 264; model farm, 114; mortgages, 82; soil utilization, 256; wheat varieties, 157
Newbold, Charles, 187
Newton, Isaac, 68
Nicholson, John, 70, 72
Norton, John P., 72
Nourse, Joel, 193

Oats, 155*n*, 272
Occupations, nonagricultural, 6
Ohio: adoption of drill, 210-211; of hay rake, 219-220; of improved plows, 194, 197; of reaper, 243-245; of thresher, 225; corn varieties, 159; crop rotations, 272; farm mortgages, 82; farm renting in, 91; farming advantages of, 108; farmmaking, 116-117; gypsum and lime, 263-264; sheep, 166; Shorthorns, 171; wheat varieties, 157
Ohio State Importing Company, 171
Oxen, 141, 143

Parker, William N., 1*n*
Patents: licensing of, 82, 188, 235; by Cyrus McCormick, 243, 245-246
Patterson, Robert, 169
Peacock, David, 182-183, 188